COMPUTER
BOOK SERIES
FROM IDG

# 1-2-3 For Windows® 5 For Dummies

Cheat Sheet

## The Function Keys

| Key | Action |
|---|---|
| F1 (HELP) | Displays on-line help that's usually relevant to what you're doing |
| F2 (EDIT) | Switches the program into Edit mode so that you can change the contents of the current cell |
| F3 (NAME) | Lists names of files, charts, ranges, query tables, drawn objects, versions, @functions, macro key names, and macro commands |
| F4 | In Edit, Point, or Value mode, cycles the cell references in formulas from absolute to mixed to relative; in Ready mode, anchors the cell pointer so that you can select a range of cells |
| F5 (GOTO) | Moves the cell pointer to a cell, named range, worksheet, chart, drawn object, query table, version, or active file |
| F6 (PANE) | Moves the cell pointer between panes in split windows and between worksheets displayed in perspective view |
| F7 (QUERY) | Updates the records in a query table (equivalent to the Query⇒Refresh Now command) |
| F8 (TABLE) | Repeats the last Range⇒Analyze⇒What-if Table command |
| F9 (CALC) | In Ready mode, recalculates all formulas; in Edit or Value mode, converts a formula to its current value |
| F10 (MENU) | Activates the menu bar to use the keyboard |

## Printing Options

| | |
|---|---|
| Print part of your worksheet | File⇒Print |
| Print specific pages | File⇒Print |
| Change the starting page number | File⇒Print |
| Number of copies to print | File⇒Print |
| Paper orientation | File⇒Page Setup |
| Change the margins | File⇒Page Setup |
| Headers or footers | File⇒Page Setup |
| Add page numbers | File⇒Page Setup |
| Print the date or time on each page | File⇒Page Setup |
| Print the filename on each page | File⇒Page Setup |
| Compress or expand the size | File⇒Page Setup |
| Don't print graphs or drawn objects | File⇒Page Setup |
| Print the worksheet frame | File⇒Page Setup |
| Print grid lines | File⇒Page Setup |
| Print rows/columns on every page | File⇒Page Setup |
| Change paper size | File⇒Printer Setup⇒Setup |
| Change print resolution | File⇒Printer Setup⇒Setup |

## Activating Sheets

| | |
|---|---|
| Ctrl+PgDn | Activates the preceding sheet, unless you're on the first sheet. (Then it has no effect.) |
| Ctrl+PgUp | Activates the next sheet, unless you're on the last sheet. (Then it has no effect.) |
| Home | Moves to the top of the file and moves cell pointer to the upper left cell. |
| Ctrl+Home | Activates the first sheet and moves the cell pointer to the upper left cell. |
| End, Ctrl+Home | Moves to the last cell that contains data on the last sheet that contains data. |

## Alt+Function Key Shortcuts

| | |
|---|---|
| Alt+F1 (COMPOSE) | Creates characters that you cannot enter directly from your keyboard |
| Alt+F2 (STEP) | Turns Step mode on or off |
| Alt+F3 (RUN) | Displays a list of the macros in the active files (equivalent to Tools⇒Macro⇒Run) |
| Alt+F6 (ZOOM PANE) | Enlarges the current horizontal, vertical, or perspective pane to the full size of the window or shrinks it to its original size |

IDG
BOOKS
WORLDWIDE

**. . . For Dummies: #1 Computer Book Series for Beginners**

# 1-2-3 For Windows® 5 For Dummies®

**COMPUTER BOOK SERIES FROM IDG**

For those times when you're even too busy to read *1-2-3 For Windows 5 For Dummies*, here is a quick reference of a few essential skills.

*Cheat Sheet*

## Basic Survival Skills

| | |
|---|---|
| Save your file | Ctrl+S |
| Quit 1-2-3 | Alt+F4 |
| Open a file | Ctrl+O |
| Undo last action | Ctrl+Z |
| Clear cell | Delete |
| Learn what a SmartIcon does | Right-click it |
| Get the Quick Menu to appear | Right-click in a selected cell or object |
| Move to different window in 1-2-3 | Alt+F6 |
| Move to another Windows application | Alt+Tab |

## Keyboard Combinations for Dialog Boxes

| | |
|---|---|
| Alt+ *hot key* | Selects the control of the hot key (underlined letter) that you press. |
| Tab | Moves forward and activates the next control. |
| Shift+Tab | Moves backward and activates the preceding control. |
| Spacebar | Checks or unchecks an option button or check box. |
| Alt+up arrow or Alt+down arrow | Opens and closes a drop-down listbox. |
| Arrow keys | Moves within a group of controls (such as option buttons). |
| End | Selects the last item in a drop-down listbox or listbox. |
| Home | Selects the first item in a drop-down listbox or listbox. |
| PgUp or PgDn | Moves to the top or bottom item in the list of items currently visible in a drop-down listbox or listbox and selects the item. |
| Enter | Completes the command and closes the dialog box (just like clicking the OK button). |
| Esc | Closes the dialog box without completing the command (just like clicking the Cancel button). |

## The Default SmartIcon Palette

| | |
|---|---|
| | Open existing file |
| | Save the current file |
| | Print current selection |
| | Preview the print selection |
| | Undo last command or action |
| | Cut to Clipboard |
| | Copy to the Clipboard |
| | Paste Clipboard contents |
| | Sum values |
| | Bold data |
| | Italicize data |
| | Underline data |
| | Left-align data |
| | Center data |
| | Right-align data |
| | Complete a sequence in selected range |
| | Select several objects |
| | Draw forward-pointing arrow |
| | Draw a rectangle or square |
| | Draw an ellipse or circle |
| | Draw a text block |
| | Draw a macro button |
| | Draw a chart |
| | Select the next SmartIcon palette |

## Formatting Shortcuts

| | |
|---|---|
| Ctrl+B | Adds or removes boldface |
| Ctrl+E | Centers cell contents |
| Ctrl+I | Adds or removes italics |
| Ctrl+L | Left-aligns cell contents |
| Ctrl+N | Removes bold, italics, and underlining from the current selection |
| Ctrl+R | Right-aligns cell contents |
| Ctrl+U | Adds or removes underlining |

*. . . For Dummies: #1 Computer Book Series for Beginners*

# COMPUTER BOOK SERIES FROM IDG

## *References for the Rest of Us!®*

Are you intimidated and confused by computers? Do you find that traditional manuals are overloaded with technical details you'll never use? Do your friends and family always call you to fix simple problems on their PCs? Then the *. . . For Dummies®* computer book series from IDG Books Worldwide is for you.

*. . . For Dummies* books are written for those frustrated computer users who know they aren't really dumb but find that PC hardware, software, and indeed the unique vocabulary of computing make them feel helpless. *. . . For Dummies* books use a lighthearted approach, a down-to-earth style, and even cartoons and humorous icons to diffuse computer novices' fears and build their confidence. Lighthearted but not lightweight, these books are a perfect survival guide for anyone forced to use a computer.

> *"I like my copy so much I told friends; now they bought copies."*
>
> **Irene C., Orwell, Ohio**

> *"Quick, concise, nontechnical, and humorous."*
>
> **Jay A., Elburn, Illinois**

> *"Thanks, I needed this book. Now I can sleep at night."*
>
> **Robin F., British Columbia, Canada**

Already, hundreds of thousands of satisfied readers agree. They have made *. . . For Dummies* books the #1 introductory level computer book series and have written asking for more. So, if you're looking for the most fun and easy way to learn about computers, look to *. . . For Dummies* books to give you a helping hand.

**IDG BOOKS WORLDWIDE**

# 1-2-3 FOR WINDOWS® 5

# FOR

# DUMMIES®

## 2ND EDITION

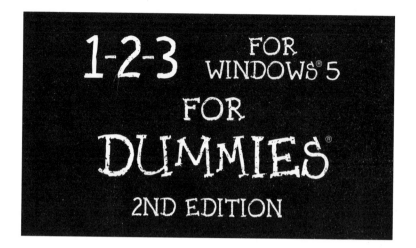

# 1-2-3 FOR WINDOWS® 5 FOR DUMMIES®
## 2ND EDITION

## by John Walkenbach

### Foreword by Richard Reily
Group Product Manager of Spreadsheets
at Lotus Development Corporation

IDG Books Worldwide, Inc.
An International Data Group Company

Foster City, CA ♦ Chicago, IL ♦ Indianapolis, IN ♦ Braintree, MA ♦ Dallas, TX

## 1-2-3 For Windows® 5 For Dummies, 2nd Edition

Published by
**IDG Books Worldwide, Inc.**
An International Data Group Company
919 E. Hillsdale Blvd.
Suite 400
Foster City, CA 94404

Library of Congress Catalog Card No.: 94-77752

ISBN: 1-56884-216-3

Printed in the United States of America

10 9 8 7 6 5

2B/QS/RR/ZV

Distributed in the United States by IDG Books Worldwide, Inc.

Distributed by Macmillan Canada for Canada; by Computer and Technical Books for the Caribbean Basin; by Contemporanea de Ediciones for Venezuela; by Distribuidora Cuspide for Argentina; by CITEC for Brazil; by Ediciones ZETA S.C.R. Ltda. for Peru; by Editorial Limusa SA for Mexico; by Transworld Publishers Limited in the United Kingdom and Europe; by Al-Maiman Publishers & Distributors for Saudi Arabia; by Simron Pty. Ltd. for South Africa; by IDG Communications (HK) Ltd. for Hong Kong; by Toppan Company Ltd. for Japan; by Addison Wesley Publishing Company for Korea; by Longman Singapore Publishers Ltd. for Singapore, Malaysia, Thailand and Indonesia; by Unalis Corporation for Taiwan; by WS Computer Publishing Company, Inc. for the Philippines; by WoodsLane Pty. Ltd. for Australia; by WoodsLane Enterprises Ltd. for New Zealand.

For general information on IDG Books Worldwide's books in the U.S., please call our Consumer Customer Service department at 800-762-2974. For reseller information, including discounts and premium sales, please call our Reseller Customer Service department at 800-434-3422.

For information on where to purchase IDG BooksWorldwide's books outside the U.S., contact IDG Books Worldwide at 415-655-3021 or fax 415-655-3295.

For information on translations, contact Marc Jeffrey Mikulich, Director, Foreign & Subsidiary Rights, at IDG Books Worldwide, 415-655-3018 or fax 415-655-3295.

For sales inquiries and special prices for bulk quantities, write to the address above or call IDG Books Worldwide at 415-655-3200.

For information on using IDG Books Worldwide's books in the classroom, or ordering examination copies, contact Jim Kelly at 800-434-2086.

For authorization to photocopy items for corporate, personal, or educational use, please contact Copyright Clearance Center, 222 Rosewood Drive, Danvers, MA 01923, or fax 508-750-4470.

 is a trademark under exclusive license to IDG Books Worldwide, Inc., from International Data Group, Inc.

# About the Author

John Walkenbach is a leading authority in the area of spreadsheets. He has written more than 250 articles and reviews, and his work appears frequently in magazines such as *PC World, Windows, PC/Computing,* and *InfoWorld.* He's the author of a dozen spreadsheet books, including *1-2-3 For Dummies Quick Reference* and *1-2-3 For Windows For Dummies Quick Reference.* In between books and articles, he does spreadsheet consulting work and develops shareware. He holds a Ph.D. in experimental psychology from the University of Montana. In his spare time, he's involved with music and spends as much time as he can playing around in his MIDI studio, trying to get his computer to help him compose decent music — but mostly just annoying his neighbors with weird synthesizer sounds.

# Behind the Scenes: The Making of 1-2-3 For Windows 5 For Dummies, 2nd Edition

Just in case you've ever wondered about the mechanics of writing a book like this, here's the inside scoop. I used Microsoft Word for Windows 2.0 to write this thing, based on an outline I developed in the same program. Each chapter was stored in a separate WinWord file. The Windows environment lets you switch instantly among different programs, so I usually had 1-2-3 for Windows running at the same time. That allowed me to jump easily back and forth between my writing and the spreadsheet to try things out and verify command names and procedures. I used HiJaak for Windows to capture the screen shots to .PCX files for the figures. I sent the chapter files and .PCX graphics files to IDG Books, where they were carefully scrutinized, checked for accuracy, and edited so they made sense. I then reviewed all these revisions and suggestions, made lots of changes, and sent the files back. This was all done electronically using CompuServe's e-mail (low-tech services such as the U.S. Post Office and Federal Express played only a minor role in getting this book done). The production people imported my WinWord and .PCX files into Pagemaker, a Macintosh desktop-publishing program that turns plain, ordinary text into something that looks like a book. What happens after that is all pretty much magic, and completely out of my control. But if all goes well, the next time I read this, it will be in the form of a real live book — complete with an ISBN number, a UPC code, and a suggested retail price.

— JW

Welcome to the world of IDG Books Worldwide.

IDG Books Worldwide, Inc., is a subsidiary of International Data Group, the world's largest publisher of computer-related information and the leading global provider of information services on information technology. IDG was founded more than 25 years ago and now employs more than 7,700 people worldwide. IDG publishes more than 250 computer publications in 67 countries (see listing below). More than 70 million people read one or more IDG publications each month.

Launched in 1990, IDG Books Worldwide is today the #1 publisher of best-selling computer books in the United States. We are proud to have received 8 awards from the Computer Press Association in recognition of editorial excellence and three from Computer Currents' First Annual Readers' Choice Awards, and our best-selling ...*For Dummies*® series has more than 19 million copies in print with translations in 28 languages. IDG Books Worldwide, through a joint venture with IDG's Hi-Tech Beijing, became the first U.S. publisher to publish a computer book in the People's Republic of China. In record time, IDG Books Worldwide has become the first choice for millions of readers around the world who want to learn how to better manage their businesses.

Our mission is simple: Every one of our books is designed to bring extra value and skill-building instructions to the reader. Our books are written by experts who understand and care about our readers. The knowledge base of our editorial staff comes from years of experience in publishing, education, and journalism — experience which we use to produce books for the '90s. In short, we care about books, so we attract the best people. We devote special attention to details such as audience, interior design, use of icons, and illustrations. And because we use an efficient process of authoring, editing, and desktop publishing our books electronically, we can spend more time ensuring superior content and spend less time on the technicalities of making books.

You can count on our commitment to deliver high-quality books at competitive prices on topics you want to read about. At IDG Books Worldwide, we continue in the IDG tradition of delivering quality for more than 25 years. You'll find no better book on a subject than one from IDG Books Worldwide.

*John J. Kilcullen*

John Kilcullen
President and CEO
IDG Books Worldwide, Inc.

IDG Books Worldwide, Inc., is a publication of International Data Group, the world's largest publisher of computer-related information and the leading global provider of information services on information technology. International Data Group publishes over 250 computer publications in 67 countries. Seventy million people read one or more International Data Group publications each month. International Data Group's publications include: **ARGENTINA:** Computerworld Argentina, GamePro, Infoworld, PC World Argentina; **AUSTRALIA:** Australian Macworld, PC TEST; **BELARUS:** PC World Belarus; **BELGIUM:** Data News; **BRAZIL:** Network World, PC World, Publishing Essentials, Reseller; **AUSTRIA:** Computerwelt, PC TEST; **BELARUS:** PC World Belarus; **BELGIUM:** Data News; **BRAZIL:** Annuário de Informática, Computerworld Brazil, Connections, Super Game Power, Macworld, PC World Brazil, Publish Brazil, SUPERGAME; **BULGARIA:** Computerworld Bulgaria, Networkworld/Bulgaria, PC & MacWorld Bulgaria; **CANADA:** CIO Canada, ComputerWorld Canada, InfoCanada, Network World Canada, Reseller World; **CHILE:** Computerworld Chile, GamePro, PC World Chile; **COLUMBIA:** Computerworld Colombia, GamePro, PC World Colombia; **COSTA RICA:** PC World Costa Rica/Nicaragua; **THE CZECH AND SLOVAK REPUBLICS:** Computerworld Czechoslovakia, Elektronika Czechoslovakia, PC World Czechoslovakia; **DENMARK:** Communications World, Computerworld Danmark, Macworld Danmark, PC World Danmark, PC World Danmark Supplements, TECH World; **DOMINICAN REPUBLIC:** PC World Republica Dominicana; **ECUADOR:** PC World Ecuador, GamePro; **EGYPT:** Computerworld Middle East, PC World Middle East; **EL SALVADOR:** PC World Centro America; **FINLAND:** MikroPC, Tietoverkko, Tietoviikko; **FRANCE:** Distributique, Golden, Info PC, Le Guide du Monde Informatique, Le Monde Informatique, Reseaux & Telecoms; **GERMANY:** Computer Business, Computerwoche, Computerwoche Extra, Computerwoche Focus, Electronic Entertainment, GamePro, I/M Information Management, Macwelt, PC Welt; **GREECE:** GamePro, Macworld & Publish; **GUATEMALA:** PC World Centro America; **HONDURAS:** PC World Centro America; **HONG KONG:** Computerworld Hong Kong, PCWorld Hong Kong, Publish in Asia; **HUNGARY:** ABCD CD-ROM, Computerworld Szamitastechnika, PC & Mac World Hungary, PC-X Magazine; **INDIA:** Computerworld India, PC World India, Publish in Asia; **INDONESIA:** InfoKomputer PC World, Komputek Computerworld, Publish in Asia; **IRELAND':** ComputerScope, PC Live!; **ISRAEL:** PC World 32 BIT, People & Computers; **ITALY:** Computerworld Italia, Computerworld Italia Special Editions, Lotus Italia, Macworld Italia, Networking Italia, PC Shopping, PC World Italia, PC World/Walt Disney; **JAPAN:** Macworld Japan, Nikkei Personal Computing, SunWorld Japan, Windows World Japan; **KENYA:** East African Computer News; **KOREA:** Hi-Tech Information/Computerworld, Macworld Korea, PC World Korea; **MACEDONIA:** PC World Macedonia; **MALAYSIA:** Computerworld Malaysia, PC World Malaysia, Publish in Asia; **MEXICO:** Computerworld Mexico, GamePro, Macworld, PC World Mexico; **MYANMAR:** PC World Myanmar; **NETHERLANDS:** Computable, Computer! Totaal, LAN Magazine, Macworld, Net Magazine; **NEW ZEALAND:** Computer Buyer, Computerworld New Zealand, MTB, Network World, PC World New Zealand; **NICARAGUA:** PC World Costa Rica/Nicaragua; **NIGERIA:** PC World Africa; **NORWAY:** Computerworld Norge, Computerworld Privat, CW Rapport Klient/Tjener, CW Rapport Nettverk & Telecom, CW Rapport Offentlig Sektor, IDG's KURSGUIDE, Macworld Norge, Multimedia World, PC World Ekspress, PC World Nettverk, PC World Norge, PC World's Produktguide, Windows Spesial; **PAKISTAN:** Computerworld Pakistan, PC World Pakistan; **PANAMA:** GamePro, PC World Panama; **PARAGUAY:** PC World Paraguay; **P. R. OF CHINA:** China Computerworld, China Infoworld, Computer & Communication, Electronic Product World, Electronics Today, Game Camp, PC World China, Popular Computer Week, Software World, Telecom Product World; **PERU:** Computerworld Peru, GamePro, PC World Profesional Peru, PC World Peru; **POLAND:** Computerworld Poland, Computerworld Special Report, Macworld, Networld, PC World Komputer; **PHILIPPINES:** Computerworld Philippines, PC Digest, Publish in Asia; **PORTUGAL:** Cerebro/PC World, Correio Informático/Computerworld, Mac•In/PC•In Portugal; **PUERTO RICO:** PC World Puerto Rico; **ROMANIA:** Computerworld Romania, PC World Romania, Telecom Romania; **RUSSIA:** Computerworld Rossiya, Network World Russia, PC World Russia; **SINGAPORE:** Computerworld Singapore, PC World Singapore, Publish in Asia; **SLOVENIA:** MONITOR; **SOUTH AFRICA:** Computing S.A., Network World S.A., Software World; **SPAIN:** Computerworld España, COMUNICACIONES WORLD, Dealer World, Macworld España, PC World España; **SWEDEN:** CAP&Design, Computer Sweden, Corporate Computing, MacWorld, Maxi Data, MikroDatorn, Nätverk & Kommunikation, PC/Aktiv, PCtip, Windows World; **SWITZERLAND:** Computerworld Schweiz, Macworld Schweiz, PCtip; **TAIWAN:** Computerworld Taiwan, Macworld Taiwan, PC World Taiwan, Publish Taiwan, Windows World; **THAILAND:** Thai Computerworld, Publish in Asia; **TURKEY:** Computerworld Monitör, MACWORLD Turkiye, PC WORLD Turkiye; **UKRAINE:** Computerworld Kiev, Computers & Software Magazine, PC World Ukraine, Telecom World; **UNITED KINGDOM:** Acorn User, Amiga Action, Amiga Computing, Amiga, Appletalk, CD Powerplay, CD-ROM Now, Computing, Connexion, GamePro, Lotus Magazine, Macaction, Macworld, Open Computing, Parents and Computers, PC Home, PC Works, The WEB; **UNITED STATES:** Cable in the Classroom, CD Review, CIO Magazine, Computerworld, Computerworld Client/Server Journal, Digital Video Magazine, DOS World, Electronic, InfoWorld, I-Way, Macworld, Maximize, MULTIMEDIA WORLD, Network World, PC World, PUBLISH, SWATPro Magazine, Video Event, WebMaster; **URUGUAY:** PC World Uruguay; **VENEZUELA:** Computerworld Venezuela, GamePro, PC World Venezuela; and **VIETNAM:** PC World Vietnam          10/3/95

# Acknowledgments

First of all, thanks to everyone around the world who purchased the first edition of *1-2-3 For Windows For Dummies*. It was gratifying to see the book appear on several best-seller lists — but even more gratifying to hear from readers who told me that the book helped them learn the product.

I've done several projects with IDG Books, and I continue to be impressed with the way this company is run. The success of this publisher is due, of course, to the many talented people who work there. Thanks again to Janna Custer, who selected me to write this book, and to Kezia Endsley who headed the editorial team that worked on the first edition. My thanks also go to Kristin Cocks, who helped make the second edition go so smoothly.

Finally, I wish to acknowledge VaRene, my best friend who never fails to provide encouragement, laughter, and many good times.

John Walkenbach
La Jolla, California

(The publisher would like to give special thanks to Patrick J. McGovern, without whom this book would not have been possible.)

# Credits

# Contents at a Glance

# Cartoons at a Glance
## By Rich Tennant

page 286

page 273

page 190

page 88

page 327

page 315

page 203

page 9

page 47

page xxvi

# Table of Contents

# Foreword

*I*f you're new to the world of 1-2-3, welcome aboard. If you're moving up from another version of our product, congratulations.

We at Lotus think 1-2-3 Release 5 for Windows is our best spreadsheet ever. We're proud to have developed a spreadsheet that's loaded with powerful features, yet very easy to use. We also realize that most people need some help when they're starting out with a new software product. And third-party books are a great way to get up to speed.

You couldn't have chosen a better beginner's guide. *1-2-3 For Windows 5 For Dummies,* 2nd Edition will tell you what you need to know about this software, without bogging you down with lots of technical details. You'll learn what you need to know to do meaningful work, and also build a foundation for learning even more.

In the following pages, John Walkenbach shares some of his hard-earned knowledge with you, in a manner that's entertaining and enlightening. John has been working with spreadsheets for more than a decade, and — as you'll see — he knows what he's talking about. But more important, he knows what's important to beginning users like yourself.

Thanks for wanting to learn more about 1-2-3 for Windows. Enjoy the book.

Richard Reily
Group Product Manager, Spreadsheets
Lotus Development Corporation
Cambridge, Massachusetts

# The 5th Wave

## By Rich Tennant

"WAIT A MINUTE! THE MONSTER SEEMS CONFUSED, DISORIENTED. I THINK
HE'S GONNA PASS OUT! GET THE NETS READY!!"

# Introduction

*"Big book, big bore."*

Callimachus (c. 300-240 BC)
from *The Greek Anthology*

• • • • • • • • • • • • • • • • • • • • • • • • • • • • • • • • • • • • • • • • • •

*O*K, let me guess your situation...

You need to learn 1-2-3 for Windows, but you don't want to get bogged down with all sorts of technical details. And I'll bet that you don't know much about computers, and you really have no aspirations of becoming a 1-2-3 for Windows guru. In other words, you're probably a bottom-line kind of person who likes to cut to the quick. And, unlike the stereotypical computer user, you also have a sense of humor. If that's true, you've come to the right place.

Welcome to *1-2-3 For Windows 5 For Dummies*, 2nd Edition — the best beginner's guide to one of the best spreadsheet programs available. Owning this book doesn't necessarily make you a dummy; that's a reputation you must earn on your own.

If you bought this book, thanks — now I can afford to feed my guppies this week. If you borrowed it from someone, please give it back and buy your own copy. If you're standing around in a bookstore trying to make up your mind about it, just buy it and be on your way (the clerk's getting suspicious).

Here's a sneak preview of what you'll find here:

- ✔ Down-to-earth information about the most useful parts of 1-2-3 for Windows that gets you up to speed in no time (well, actually it takes *some* time)

- ✔ Informative examples that demonstrate things that you may want to do (or things that someone *else* wants you to do)

- ✔ Very few extraneous details about things that you don't really care about anyway

- ✔ Lively, entertaining, and easy-to-read text, with subtle humor sprinkled liberally throughout its pages (I just love describing my own writing)

- ✔ A glossary of informative and hilarious terms about 1-2-3 for Windows, as well as general computer terms

- ✔ Cartoons by Rich Tennant that are guaranteed to be funnier than your average Sunday comic strip

✔ A high-brow quote from literature or famous people in history at the beginning of every chapter, pulled wildly out of context in an attempt to connect 1-2-3 for Windows with the reality of our world

Have no fear; this is not an advanced reference book. So if the office computer geek needs to look up all the gory details on macro command arguments, you won't find *this* book missing from your desk.

## What This Book Covers

This book is for people who are just starting out with Lotus 1-2-3 for Windows. This book is for you if you use either of the following versions:

✔ 1-2-3 Release 4 for Windows

✔ 1-2-3 Release 5 for Windows

If you use any other version of 1-2-3, this book won't do you much good. 1-2-3 Release 1 for Windows is very different from Release 4 and Release 5 — and practically nobody uses this version anymore. Lotus also has several non-Windows versions of 1-2-3. But these versions are so different from Release 4 and Release 5 that this book will be useless (except as kindling for a campfire).

By the way, I used Release 5 to create the figures in this book. If you're using Release 4, some of the figures may be slightly different. Don't be alarmed; things will still work the way I describe them.

Notice that the title of this book isn't *The Complete Guide to 1-2-3 For Windows For Dummies.* I don't cover everything about 1-2-3 for Windows — but then again you don't want to *know* everything about 1-2-3 for Windows, right?

## Why I Wrote This Book

I spend a lot of time helping others solve computer problems (especially spreadsheet problems). Somewhere along the line, I acquired a knack for explaining things in simple terms. I also discovered that there's an important difference between giving someone the solution to their problem and explaining things sufficiently so that they don't call me the next time a slight variation of the same problem crops up. The latter is the approach I tried to take in this book. I also happen to think that most spreadsheets books are very boring, so I jumped at the opportunity to have some fun with this one. Oh yeah, and I also got paid for doing this.

# Read the Whole Thing?

My intention is not that you read this book from cover to cover. Frankly, the plot stinks, the character development leaves much to be desired, and there aren't very many steamy sex scenes.

But if you do decide to read this book straight through, you'll find that the chapters *do* move along in a quasi-logical progression — but they also stand on their own. After you learn the basics of 1-2-3 for Windows, you can safely put the book aside until you need to move on to the next challenge. When that time comes, follow these simple steps:

1. **Refer to the table of contents for a general topic.**

   If you're in a real hurry, go straight for the index. If your problem is "How do I get rid of these stupid decimal points?," look under Decimal points, not Stupid.

2. **Based on what you discover in the table of contents or index, turn to the page that discusses the topic.**

3. **Read the informative and often jocund text that introduces the topic.**

4. **If that doesn't help, take a look at any examples provided and work your way through them.**

5. **If you still can't figure it out, panic. Then cry hysterically until someone in the office who might be able to help you notices.**

Unless the task you're trying to do is a fairly sophisticated or unusual one, this book will certainly shed some light on it. Even if an example for a topic doesn't seem to be related to what you're trying to do, you might find that working through it step-by-step provides some insights that let you figure it out on your own. But what I hope to get across more than anything is that you should feel free to play around in 1-2-3 for Windows and experiment with it. That's the best way to learn.

## Watch out for the nerdy stuff

The topics in this book usually start out with some introductory comments, and often include one or more examples and maybe even some step-by-step instructions. You can skim through the introductory text to see whether it's really what you want.

If you're just starting out, I recommend that you read some of the chapters in their entirety— or at least until the subject matter exceeds the level of complexity that you can stomach. For example, if you've never printed anything before, you'll find it helpful to start reading Chapter 10 from the beginning. Doing so gives you enough background so that you'll at least have a vague idea of what you're doing. At the very least, it steers you to the right menu or dialog box so that you can figure it out by yourself.

Some topics have additional information for those overachievers who want to know even more about what they're doing. Reading these sections will only increase the depth of your knowledge of 1-2-3 — and that's certainly not what this book is all about. So you may want to make a mental note: *See the Technical Stuff icon, skip the section.*

As long as you have your mental notepad out, here's another one for you: *See the Warning icon, read the section.* The Warning icon signals something that might eat your data, cause your computer to go into warp speed nine, suddenly turn your fingers green, or otherwise ruin your whole morning. More about icons later.

# How This Book Is Organized

Personally, I think that my editors and I are the only ones who really care how this book is organized. I started out with an outline — the part of the term paper you always hated writing, remember? (Actually, it was the part you hated the *most.* The whole thing was quite painful.) The outline eventually turned into the table of contents, which you can peruse if you're really into organizational issues. But you may prefer the following synopses of the book's major parts.

## Part I: First Things First

The three chapters in this section are for people who don't have a clue as to what a spreadsheet — much less 1-2-3 for Windows — is all about. Chapter 1 tells you lots of interesting things so that you can hold your own should you ever find yourself at a cocktail party populated with spreadsheet junkies (eww!). Chapter 2 tells you how to start and exit 1-2-3. If you want some quick and dirty experience, you can wade through Chapter 3. I'll walk you through a real-life 1-2-3 for Windows session, and you can pretend I'm standing over your shoulder helping you. If you make it through this chapter, you can honestly say, *"Yeah, I've used 1-2-3 for Windows."*

## Part II: Basic Stuff That You Must Know

Like it or not, you can't just jump into 1-2-3 for Windows and expect to start doing meaningful things immediately — you need some basic background information. Part II imparts this knowledge upon you in the form of nine short (usually) chapters. You'll learn about entering data, menus and dialog boxes, saving files, creating formulas, using built-in functions, printing, and lots of other things that you may or may not be interested in (but you should know about). You don't have to read everything in these chapters; you can always refer to them when the need arises.

# Part III: How to Impress the Easily Impressed

The five chapters in this section can be described as "gee whiz" stuff (with a bit of "jeepers" stuff thrown in for good measure). You can probably get by for quite a while by pretending these topics don't even exist. But sooner or later, you might need to expand your horizons. In the unlikely event that this actually occurs, you'll learn how to make your worksheets look great (or at least good), how to create and customize graphs, make nifty maps, and all kinds of short-cuts that can save you valuable minutes each day, giving you more time for more important things like goofing off.

# Part IV: Faking It

Aptly named, this is the section in which I tell you just enough about some of the more advanced topics so that you can get by. If you're so moved, you can learn about databases, steal some nifty formulas that I developed, and even learn how to use and create (horrors!) macros.

# Part V: The Part of Tens

For some reason, most of the books in the ... *For Dummies* series include short chapters with lists of 10 or so things in each. This book is no exception, and you'll find these chapters collected in Part V. You'll get concise lists of habits you should acquire, things you definitely must know, and even the 10 Com-mandments of 1-2-3 for Windows.

# Part VI: Appendixes

And what's a computer book without appendixes? Here, you'll find two of them: one on installing 1-2-3 for Windows and a glossary of weird terms you're likely to encounter in this book.

# Dumb (mie) Assumptions

People who write books usually have a target reader in mind. In the case of this book, my target reader is a conglomerate of dozens of beginning computer users that I've met over the years. The following points more or less describe this typical new user (and may even describe you):

- You have access to a PC at work, but working on the computer isn't the most interesting part of your job.
- Your computer has a hard drive, a printer, some version of the DOS operating system, and Microsoft Windows 3.1 installed on it. Although a mouse is not required, I do strongly suggest you buy one. Using Windows products without a mouse is like running a marathon without any shoes; it can be done, but who wants to do it?
- You have some experience with computers (word processing mostly), and have even gone so far as to copy a few files from the hard drive to a floppy.
- Someone just installed 1-2-3 Release 4 or 1-2-3 Release 5 for Windows on your computer, and you have to learn how to use the sucker.
- You've never used a spreadsheet before (but you may have used an old release of 1-2-3 at some time).
- You need to get some work done and have a low tolerance for boring computer books.

# Conventions — Typographical and Otherwise

As you work your way through the book, you may notice that it uses different type styles. This was done for two purposes: to show off the typographic skills of the production house, and to make it easy for you to distinguish various word meanings.

When I tell you to enter something into a cell, the "something" appears in a distinctive typeface (called *monospace*). If I want you to enter some words into a cell, they would appear as so:

```
Bills I Need to Pay This Month
```

This means that you should type exactly what you see. Most the time, you'll also have to press the Enter key to signal the end of what you're typing. If I want you to enter something that's short, I don't waste a whole line of valuable paper; I simply stick it in the text in **bold type**. Here's an example: "Enter **256** into cell A1." In this case, you simply type the three numbers and press the Enter key.

Occasionally, 1-2-3 for Windows displays some messages to you on its screen. When I talk about such messages, I use the monospace typeface, as so: READY.

Sometimes, you are asked to press a *key combination* — which means you hold down one key while you press another. For example, the Ctrl+Z key combination means that you should hold down the Ctrl key while you press Z once.

## Of mice and keyboards

You can use 1-2-3 for Windows with or without a mouse — although I strongly recommend a mouse for everyone; they are cheap and fun to use. But if you work in a high crime area and one day discover that someone has stolen your mouse, there's no reason to go home and hide under your bed until a new mouse is delivered. You can continue to be as quasi-productive as ever using only the keyboard. You can still access commands, make selections, and move the cell pointer all over the place. You just can't use the SmartIcons (and boy are they smart).

To issue a 1-2-3 for Windows command, mouse users simply click the menu and then click a command from the list that drops down. Without a mouse, you have to press Alt to access the menu, use the arrow keys to move to the selection you want, and then press Enter.

In this book, when I ask you to select a command, I *don't* waste time by giving directions for both keyboarders and mouseketeers. Rather than say something such as: "If you're using the keyboard, press **Alt+F** and then press **S** to save your file. Mouse users should click File and then click Save," I say, "Save your file by issuing the File⇨Save command". Then you can choose your method of payment. A lot simpler, no?

Chapter 3 is an exception to this rule. Because that chapter might be your first hands-on experience with 1-2-3 for Windows, I describe how to issue the commands in anagonizing detail.

By the way, notice that I underlined two letters when I mentioned the File⇨Save command. These represent the *hot keys* that keyboard users can press to issue the commands. Whenever I mention a command, the hot keys are underlined (just as they appear on-screen) for the convenience of our mouseless readers. Be careful, the hot keys aren't always the first letter of the command.

## I think icon, I think icon

Somewhere along the line, some market research company must have shown that computer books sell more copies if they have icons stuck inside their margins. Icons are those little pictures that are supposed to draw your attention to various features or help you decide whether something is worth reading.

Whether the research is valid remains to be proven, but I'm not taking any chances. So here are the icons you encounter in this book:

This icon signals material that no one in their right mind should care about. Read this only if you're interested in the nitty-gritty details — for the nerd in all of us.

Don't skip over these. They tell you about a shortcut that can save you lots of time and make you a hit at the next computer-geek party.

This icon tells you when you need to store information away in the deep recesses of your brain for later use.

Read these, otherwise you may lose your data, blow up your computer, cause a nuclear holocaust, or worse.

This icon alerts you to features found only in 1-2-3 Release 5 for Windows. If you're moving up from 1-2-3 Release 4 for Windows, these icons are for you.

This icon indicates text that you should pay attention to. It's not quite worthy of a Remember icon, and not as severe as a Warning icon.

## Now What?

If you've never used a spreadsheet, I strongly suggest that you read Chapters 1 and 2 before you do anything else. Chapter 1 tells you what a spreadsheet is and exactly what 1-2-3 for Windows can do. Chapter 2 tells you how to start the program (and how to get out of it when you've had enough).

But it's a free country (at least it was when I wrote this book), so I won't sic the Computer Book Police on you if you opt to thumb through randomly and read whatever strikes your fancy. If you have a particular task in mind — such as, "How do I sort all of these numbers?" — go to the index. Go directly to the index. Do not pass Go, do not collect $200.

Good luck and have fun.

# Part I
## First Things First

Bob's decision not to upgrade to Windows caused some suspicion on the part of those who did.

# In this part...

This part has only three chapters. If you've never used a spreadsheet before, or if you need a refresher course on the subject, you don't want to miss these chapters. In Chapter 1, you get some essential background information — as well as some not-so-essential background information. Chapter 2 tells you how to start 1-2-3 for Windows, put it aside temporarily, and (importantly) how to exit gracefully when your work is completed (or when you've simply had enough). You get the opportunity to acquire some hands-on experience with 1-2-3 for Windows in Chapter 3 — and if you follow my instructions, you have a real-live worksheet to show for your efforts.

# Chapter 1

# What Is This Thing Called 1-2-3 for Windows?

*"The question of common sense is always 'What is it good for?' — a question which would abolish the rose and be answered triumphantly by the cabbage."*

James Russell Lowell (1819–1891)
American poet, editor

- - - - - - - - - - - - - - - - - - - - - - - - - - - - - - - - - - - - - - - - - - - - - -

## In This Chapter

▶ What is 1-2-3 for Windows?

▶ What things can you do with this program?

▶ What things can't you do?

▶ What release of 1-2-3 for Windows do you have? Does it matter?

- - - - - - - - - - - - - - - - - - - - - - - - - - - - - - - - - - - - - - - - - - - - - -

*T*his chapter doesn't have any hands-on training stuff. In other words, it contains nothing that will help you learn 1-2-3 for Windows faster. If you're in a hurry to get started, or if you have little tolerance for background information and historical dribble, you can safely page ahead to Chapter 2. But if you want a good foundation for the rest of the book, you can find it right here — and you may even find it rather interesting.

This chapter paves the way for everything else that follows and gives you a feel for how spreadsheets fit into the overall scheme of the universe.

## OK, So What the Heck Is 1-2-3 for Windows?

Glad you asked. *1-2-3 for Windows is a software package that functions as an electronic spreadsheet.* Think of a large sheet of accountant's paper with grid lines drawn on it. Then try to envision an electronic version of this page that you can see on your computer monitor. The electronic version is huge — so big that you can see only a tiny portion at one time on your screen. But you can use the keyboard or mouse to move around in this worksheet so that you can see it all (but not all at one time).

In place of the grid lines, the electronic spreadsheet we call 1-2-3 for Windows has rows and columns. The place where each row and column intersects is called a *cell*. You can enter numbers and words into the cells, then print them out for the world to see. It's also easy to copy and move cells around. When it's quitting time, you can save all this good stuff in a file on your hard disk, and work on it later. Actually, a 1-2-3 for Windows file is more like a *pad* of accountant's paper, because you can store up to 256 pages of spreadsheets in a single file.

The real fun starts when you learn how to enter *formulas* into cells. These formulas perform calculations on other cells. For example, you might enter into a cell a formula that says, in effect, *Add up all the numbers in the first column, and then divide by the number of values in the column*. This formula displays the average of the numbers in its cell. But the neatest thing of all is that the formulas recalculate their results if you change the numbers in any of the cells they use. You may not appreciate this now, but you will later on (trust me).

## How much work can a worksheet work?

Imagine, for a minute, that you entered a number into every cell in a 1-2-3 for Windows worksheet. We're talking 256 sheets (or pages), each with 256 columns and 8,192 rows — which works out to be exactly 536,870,912 cells. Filling every cell is actually impossible, because your computer doesn't have near enough memory to hold all this information. But bear with me on this, OK?

If you entered the numbers manually into each cell, the task would take about 34 years (figuring a relatively rapid two seconds per cell, with no coffee breaks or time out for sleep). Hopefully, you save your work often while entering this amount of data, because it would be a shame to have to repeat five or six years of data entry due to a power failure.

You'd hate to lose all this work, so you'd better make a back-up of this 5.9 gigabyte file. Before you start, however, make sure you have about 4,765 blank floppy disks on hand (*Tip:* Use high-density floppies).

Using the default column width and row height, 1-2-3 for Windows can print 51 rows and eight columns (or 408 cells) on a sheet of 8½ × 11 paper. Therefore, printing the entire worksheet requires 1.32 million pages of paper. If you use cheap photocopier paper, this is a stack of pages about 407 feet tall — roughly the height of a four story building. If you splurge for better quality paper, your printout is about as tall as the St. Louis Gateway Arch.

Using a standard 4-page-per-minute laser printer, it would take about 530 days to print it all (not counting time spent changing paper and replacing toner cartridges). If you have a faster laser printer, you could easily print the entire job in less than a year.

If this worksheet has formulas in it, you have to take recalculation time into account. I have no way of estimating how long it would take to recalculate the formulas in such a worksheet, but it would probably be a good time to take that around-the-world cruise after pressing the F9 key.

But wait, there's more (he says in a late-night infomercial tone of voice). 1-2-3 for Windows also lets you apply slick formatting to the cells to make your worksheet look as if it were done by a graphic artist. And it also can make graphs that look as if they came from someone who actually knew what she/he was doing. 1-2-3 for Windows does lots of other things to ease your work (known in the trade as *features*) — you learn about these in due time.

# What Can This Puppy Do?

People use 1-2-3 for Windows for lots of things. Here's a brief sampling of what you have to look forward to.

## Crunch some numbers

People buy spreadsheet programs mainly to manipulate and calculate numbers. For example, if you need to create a budget (probably the most common thing people use spreadsheets for), you enter your budget category names and values for each month into cells. Then you stick in some formulas to add up the total for each month, and the annual total for each category — see Figure 1-1 to get an idea of what I'm talking about. Finally, you fiddle around with the numbers until the formulas come up with the results your boss wants. It's all pretty easy after you get the hang of it.

1-2-3 for Windows has hundreds of special built-in functions (called @*functions* and pronounced *at-funk-shuns*) that can do some outrageous calculations for you — and you don't even have to know what's going on behind the scenes. For example, most people have no idea where to start when needing to calculate the monthly payment for a car loan. But there's a built-in function that turns this process into child's play. 1-2-3 for Windows does the calculation work, giving you more time to go car shopping.

Here are a just a few examples of the types of worksheets you can develop in 1-2-3 for Windows:

- ✔ **Budgets:** Develop simple household budgets, corporate department budgets, budgets for a complete company, or even a budget for an entire country (maybe President Clinton's problems would be solved if he had 1-2-3 for Windows?).

- ✔ **Financial projections:** Figure out how much money you're going to make or lose this year, using formulas that rely on various assumptions that you (or your boss) makes.

✔ **Sales tracking:** Keep track of who's selling the most (and how much commission they receive) and who's falling down on the job (and when they should get their pink slips).

✔ **Loan amortization:** How much of that mortgage payment goes to interest (a lot), and how much to principal (not much)? A spreadsheet can tell you for every month of the loan's term.

✔ **Scientific things:** 1-2-3 for Windows has dozens of very specialized built-in functions that only white-coated laboratory inhabitants understand.

✔ **Statistical stuff:** Again, there are lots of built-in functions for people who think in terms of standard deviations.

**Figure 1-1:** 1-2-3 for Windows, hard at work crunching numbers.

| | A | B | C | D | E | F | G |
|---|---|---|---|---|---|---|---|
| 1 | 1994 Budget | | | | | | |
| 2 | | | Jan | Feb | Mar | Apr | May |
| 3 | Personnel | | | | | | |
| 4 | | Salaries | 425,980 | 425,980 | 450,000 | 450,000 | 450,000 |
| 5 | | Benefits | 132,054 | 132,054 | 139,500 | 139,500 | 139,500 |
| 6 | | Bonus | 21,200 | 0 | 0 | 0 | 0 |
| 7 | | Commissions | 15,000 | 5,000 | 5,000 | 15,000 | 5,000 |
| 8 | | Total Personnel | 594,234 | 563,034 | 594,500 | 604,500 | 594,500 |
| 9 | | | | | | | |
| 10 | Facility | | | | | | |
| 11 | | Rent/Lease | 19,125 | 19,125 | 19,125 | 25,000 | 25,000 |
| 12 | | Utilities | 4,315 | 4,315 | 4,315 | 5,400 | 5,400 |
| 13 | | Maintenance | 5,750 | 5,750 | 5,750 | 6,250 | 6,250 |
| 14 | | Other Facility Expenses | 13,150 | 13,150 | 13,150 | 22,000 | 15,000 |
| 15 | | Total Facility | 42,340 | 42,340 | 42,340 | 58,650 | 51,650 |
| 16 | | | | | | | |
| 17 | Supplies | | | | | | |

These examples just scratch the analytical surface. If you have a problem that involves numbers, chances are 1-2-3 for Windows is the ideal tool to use — especially if you can't find a baseball bat.

## *Make killer graphs (dude!)*

1-2-3 for Windows can take the numbers you put in a worksheet and transform them into a magnificent graph in just about any style you can imagine. And you won't believe how easy it is to do it. Here's what's great about spreadsheet graphs: If the numbers in your worksheet change, the graphs are updated automatically. And here's the best part: You can literally waste hours of your company's time playing around with the graphs to make them look just right.

Even if your numbers aren't worth diddly squat, you can still impress your boss (or your cat, depending on your proficiency level) with the quality of the graph. And that's what life is all about, right?

Figure 1-2 shows a modest example of a 1-2-3 for Windows graph.

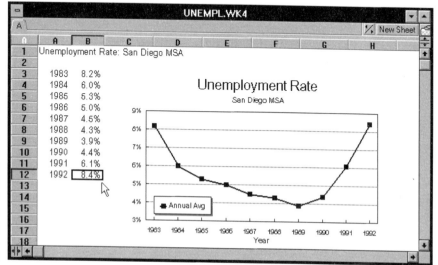

**Figure 1-2:**
1-2-3 for
Windows
lets you
transform
dull
numbers
into more
interesting
graphs.

## Show data on a map

If you deal with numbers that have a basis in geography — for example, if you track your company's sales by state — you'll groove on the new mapping feature (Release 5 only). Believe it or not, 1-2-3 for Windows can create an attractive map from a list of numbers with only a few mouse clicks on your part. Rand McNally, look out!

## Manage your lists

If numbers aren't your bag, you also can do some cool things with text. 1-2-3 for Windows has ready-made rows and columns, and you can make the columns as wide as you want — so it's a natural choice for keeping track of items of lists (even better than a mere word processor).

Here are some popular lists that you can store in a 1-2-3 for Windows worksheet:

  ✔ Things to do today

  ✔ Things to avoid doing today

> ✔ Any of David Letterman's top ten lists
>
> ✔ Logical flaws in "Gilligan's Island" (you may want to use a separate worksheet for each episode — otherwise, you quickly run out of room)

## The Magical Mystery Guided Tour

If you want to get an entertaining overview of what 1-2-3 for Windows can really do, check out the Guided Tour. One of your Windows Program Manager groups should contain an icon with a movie projector image called Guided Tour. Double-click this icon to start the guided tour, and then follow the instructions on-screen (the accompanying figure shows an example of this guided tour). You need a mouse to take the tour, and if you make it all the way through, it takes about a half hour of your time. It's actually rather entertaining. A little animated fellow in a tuxedo demonstrates various features. If you have some spare time, I recommend you go through it. At the very least, it gives you some practice with the mouse.

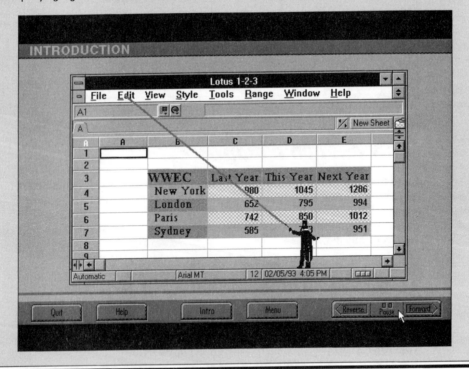

Lists can be either only words (like the preceding example) or a combination of words and numbers. If you use numbers in your lists, you can even make formulas to add them up or do other calculations. Here are some more lists that use numbers:

- ✔ Bills you can get by without paying this month

- ✔ How much the President of the United States spent on haircuts during his term of office

- ✔ Itemized costs for fixing up your wrecked car

- ✔ The amount of time the person in the next cubicle spends each day goofing off

Take a look at Figure 1-3 for an example of a simple list.

| | A | B | C | D | E | F |
|---|---|---|---|---|---|---|
| 2 | | | | | | |
| 3 | Resurface cabinets | 2,800 | | | | |
| 4 | New counter | 250 | | | | |
| 5 | New sink | 120 | | | | |
| 6 | New faucet | 69 | | | | |
| 7 | Flooring | 675 | | | | |
| 8 | Track lighting | 285 | | | | |
| 9 | Drywall repair | 225 | | | | |
| 10 | Paint & supplies | 55 | | | | |
| 11 | Curtains | 80 | | | | |
| 12 | Vertical blinds | 233 | | | | |
| 13 | Table & chairs | 645 | | | | |
| 14 | Light fixture | 75 | | | | |
| 15 | | | | | | |

**Figure 1-3:** 1-2-3 for Windows is great for keeping track of lists.

You discover also that you can do things with text that you may not think are possible. For example, if you have a list of people in firstname/lastname format, you can use 1-2-3 for Windows to convert them to lastname/firstname format so that you can sort them by last name. There are lots more things you can do with text, but you're just gonna have to wait for a later chapter.

## Manage that data (zzzz...)

If the term *database management* conjures up images of boring, obsessively neat people whose socks always match their pocket protector color, you're right on track. Actually, a database is nothing more than an *organized* list. If you have a lot of friends, you might keep track of them in a database, storing their names, addresses, phone numbers, and amount of money they owe you. By the way, with a bit of finagling, you can use such a list to print out labels for your Christmas cards directly from 1-2-3 for Windows.

Truth is, 1-2-3 for Windows is pretty good at helping you work with databases. You can sort the data, search for something in particular, display items that meet certain criteria, and lots of other things. And it's all pretty easy to do.

## Access other data (Bill's paycheck?)

If you have to deal with a huge database — such as your corporate accounting system that lives on a different computer — you won't be able to load the whole shebang into 1-2-3 for Windows because you'll run out of memory. Fortunately (or perhaps unfortunately), you can still access such *external* databases from 1-2-3 for Windows. If you learn how to do this stuff in 1-2-3 for Windows, you may not even have to buy a *real* database program.

Another thing you can do is transfer information across different programs using the Windows *Clipboard* (an area of memory that holds things that are copied so they can be pasted somewhere else). For example, if you want to put a table of numbers you created in 1-2-3 for Windows into a report that you're writing, you can copy the table and paste it right into your Windows word processor. And you can even set things up so that if the numbers change, the changes get transferred to your word-processing document automatically. Technology is indeed grand, eh?

## Automate actions with macros

For hard core spreadsheet junkies, 1-2-3 for Windows provides something called macros. A *macro* consists of a bunch of instructions that tell 1-2-3 for Windows what to do — kind of like a computer program. Macros can help you automate actions and take the drudgery out of repetitive spreadsheet tasks. If you want to take the time to learn, you can write macros for 1-2-3 for Windows, although the average user has no need for this sort of thing. You might, however, need to *execute* a macro that the office computer nerd named Melvin wrote. Those with inquiring minds (and for the nerd in all of us) can learn how to do this by going no further than this book.

## And into the great beyond

1-2-3 for Windows can do other things that I can't even think of. It's a very versatile piece of software, and if you stick with it long enough I guarantee that you'll figure out some use that no one else has thought of. If so, let me know so I can steal your idea and use it in the next edition.

# *What Can't It Do?*

Although 1-2-3 for Windows is sort of like a Swiss army knife, it's probably not the only software program you'll ever need. For example, it can work with small amounts of text and manipulate labels, but it's certainly no substitute for a real word-processing program. It has some great graph features, but if you're really into creating some cool computer graphics and images, there are many other products available that excel in that sort of thing. And although you can do some simple project management, there are better project management packages available. In other words, 1-2-3 for Windows is great, but owning it doesn't mean you can lasso the moon.

As I write this, the latest version of 1-2-3 for Windows is labeled Release 5.0. To find out which release you have, try to find the original box that it came in and find the release number on the box. If you've trashed the box, try to find the original diskettes and read the release number on the diskettes. If you've lost the original diskettes or acquired the product through illegal means (which I do not condone), you can tell what release you have by watching closely as it starts up. The opening screen tells you the release number.

Here's a quick rundown of some of the more popular releases of 1-2-3 for DOS and 1-2-3 for Windows, and how they differ:

- ✔ **1-2-3 Release 1A:** This was the original release for DOS, which surfaced in 1983, that pretty much made Lotus what it is today. People bought PCs just so they could run this program.

- ✔ **1-2-3 Release 2.x:** The follow-up to Release 1A, Release 2 (for DOS) first appeared in 1984. This release had lots of new features, including the capability to use add-in programs to extend the power of the basic spreadsheet. Release 2 had several sub-releases, and the current release is Release 2.4.

- ✔ **1-2-3 Release 3.x:** Even more powerful than Release 2, this DOS release featured 3-D files, file linking, improved database access and several other things. It, too, continues to be upgraded, and Release 3.4 is the current release.

- ✔ **1-2-3 Release 1.x for Windows:** This was the first Windows spreadsheet from Lotus. Many people, including myself, were rather disappointed with it because it left quite a bit to be desired when compared to other Windows spreadsheets. Still, lots of people bought it.

- ✔ **1-2-3 Release 4.0 for Windows:** This one came out in June, 1993. It has almost nothing in common with the preceding Windows version. By the way, Lotus skipped Release 2 and 3 for Windows, and went directly to Release 4 — probably to avoid confusion with the non-Windows versions (which are labeled Release 2 and 3).

- ✔ **1-2-3 Release 5.0 for Windows:** This version hit the streets in August, 1994. It's very similar to Release 4 but has lots of new features added in. (Look for the Release 5 icons in the margins of this book.)

## Why the weird name?

There aren't too many product names that consist only of numbers (Clorox's 409 and a bunch of car names are the only other ones that come to mind). What were they thinking when they came up with the name 1-2-3? Well, back in the old days of computing, software was typically very limited, and most programs did only one thing. But the people at *Lotus Development Corporation* who were developing a new spreadsheet wanted to give it powers far beyond those of mortal spread-sheets. Actually, their only real competitor at the time was VisiCalc, which was a rudimentary, yet very popular, spreadsheet. The Lotus people de-signed a product that had: 1) spreadsheet capa-bilities, 2) graphing powers, and 3) database fea-tures. Because Spreadsheet-Graphing-Database is a bit unwieldy for a product name, they settled on 1-2-3 instead. A side benefit of choosing this name was that marketing types could say things like, "It's as easy as 1-2-3" (even though it wasn't).

So what's the deal on all these versions, and does it matter? The answer is that Lotus is an amazing success story, and the original release of 1-2-3 played a major role in the popularity of personal computers in the office. Lotus is to spreadsheets what Anheiser Busch is to beer. 1-2-3 for Windows is a great product, and you're doing yourself a favor — and maybe even making a significant career move — by learning it. Feel good now?

But to learn how to use this program, you're gonna have to read the rest of the book first. So take my hand, walk slowly, and I'll take you on a journey through Lotus land.

## DOS, Windows, what's the difference?

As you may know, *DOS* (for *D*isk *O*perating *Sys*-tem) is the operating system software that makes your PC work. When you turn on your PC, the DOS software takes over and does its thing. Microsoft Windows is a complex program that runs *on top of* DOS and turns your PC into a graphical system, much like a Macintosh computer. You have to purchase DOS and Windows separately, although most computers that you buy nowadays include both of these packages for your convenience.

Today, PC-based programs fall into one of two categories: DOS programs or Windows programs. Most DOS programs look pretty dull and boring because all the letters look the same (although they usually use different colors to spiff things up a bit). Windows programs, on the other hand, show everything in full graphics splendor. You can see different type faces, different type sizes, all sorts of pictures, graphs, and so on. Therefore, Windows is often referred to as a *graphical user interface* (or *GUI*, pronounced *goo-eee*). Your work appears on your screen just as it will look on the printer. This is often referred to as *WYSIWYG*, which stands for *"what you see is what you get."*

So why doesn't everyone just run Windows and get on with it? The main reason is that Windows requires a faster and more powerful computer. Presumably, your PC is good enough to run Win-dows, but not everyone is so lucky. As older computers get replaced with faster models, Win-dows will become even more popular and many of the old DOS programs will go by the wayside.

# Chapter 2
# Jump Starting, Breaking, and Stopping

*"The real problem is not whether machines think, but whether men do."*

B. F. Skinner (1904 –1990)
*Contingencies of Reinforcement*

● ● ● ● ● ● ● ● ● ● ● ● ● ● ● ● ● ● ● ● ● ● ● ● ● ● ● ● ● ● ● ● ● ● ● ● ● ● ● ● ● ● ● ● ● ● ● ●

## In This Chapter

▶ What to do if 1-2-3 for Windows isn't on your computer

▶ How to start 1-2-3 for Windows

▶ How to temporarily leave 1-2-3 for Windows so you can do something else

▶ How to quit 1-2-3 for Windows (the right way and the wrong way)

▶ What to do if you get completely confused

● ● ● ● ● ● ● ● ● ● ● ● ● ● ● ● ● ● ● ● ● ● ● ● ● ● ● ● ● ● ● ● ● ● ● ● ● ● ● ● ● ● ● ● ● ● ● ●

*B*efore you can use 1-2-3 for Windows — or any software, for that matter — you must install it on your computer. When you install software, you're simply copying files from floppy disks to your hard disk in such a way that everything will work when you execute the program. Back in the old days, you could run software directly from floppy disks. But those days are pretty much over, and virtually every program you get now must be installed on your hard disk.

If 1-2-3 for Windows isn't already installed, refer to Appendix A for assistance. Better yet, bribe your office computer genius to do it for you (with a new pocket protector, perhaps?).

After 1-2-3 for Windows is installed, you can run the program, do all sorts of interesting things with it, and then exit the program when you're finished. To exit a program simply means to stop it from running. While a program is running, however, you can put it aside temporarily and do other things (such as run other programs, jump to another program that's already running, delete files, and so on). You'll learn about all this stuff right here in Chapter 2.

# Starting 1-2-3 for Windows

In order to benefit from having 1-2-3 for Windows, you need to run the program — otherwise, it just eats up space on your hard disk and you've wasted several hundreds of your company's dollars (or even worse, your dollars). There are a number of ways to start 1-2-3 for Windows, which I'll explain in the next few paragraphs.

## Starting 1-2-3 for Windows from the Windows Program Manager

Using the Program Manager is the best way, and by far the most common, of starting 1-2-3 for Windows. When 1-2-3 for Windows is installed, the installation program puts an icon in one of the Program Manager program groups, such as *Lotus Applications*. Depending on how your system is set up, this icon may always be visible, as it is in Figure 2-1. But in some cases, the Lotus Applications program group may be *minimized* (appearing as an icon), or the 1-2-3 for Windows may be in a program group with a different name.

If you can't find the 1-2-3 for Windows icon, try double-clicking some of the program group icons at the bottom of the Program Manager windows. When you double-click a program group icon, it opens up to display the program icons in that group.

After you locate the 1-2-3 for Windows icon, just double-click this icon with your mouse, and 1-2-3 for Windows starts up with a blank worksheet.

**Figure 2-1:**
In the program group called Lotus Applications, double-click the 1-2-3 for Windows icon to start the program.

The 1-2-3 for Windows icon          Program group name

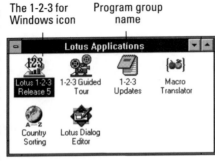

---

## What about those other icons?

Depending on how the product was installed, the Lotus Applications program group may have other icons in it. Some of the icons may be useful to you, but others definitely aren't. If you're curious, here's what these other icons do after you double-click them:

**1-2-3 Install** runs the installation program again, a useful function if you want to install some parts of 1-2-3 for Windows that weren't installed originally.

**1-2-3 Guided Tour** starts an interactive animated guided tour of 1-2-3. Try it.

**View Product Updates** shows you any late-breaking news that was not discovered in time to make it into the printed manuals.

**1-2-3 Macro Translator** translates macros that were developed in 1-2-3 Release 1 for Windows. You probably won't have much need for this one.

**Lotus Dialog Box Editor** lets you create your own dialog boxes. You need to have a pretty good understanding of macros to use this icon.

---

## Starting 1-2-3 for Windows from DOS

When you turn on your computer and the blank screen shows only the DOS prompt, you have to start Windows, then start 1-2-3 for Windows. The easiest way to do this is simply to type **WIN 123W** at the DOS prompt, then press Enter.

If that method doesn't seem to work, simply type **WIN** at the DOS prompt to start Windows. Then you have to find the 1-2-3 for Windows icon and double-click it, as described in the preceding section. Now you are running 1-2-3 for Windows!

If the WIN 123W command doesn't work properly, the directory that holds the 1-2-3 for Windows files isn't in your DOS path.

Ask a computer guru to edit the PATH line in your AUTOEXEC.BAT file (located in your C:\ root directory) to include the 1-2-3 for Windows directory. Don't try this yourself; you are liable to reconfigure your hard RAM semiconductor disk tube (yikes!).

## Get Me out of Here (at Least for a Moment)

When you start 1-2-3 for Windows, the Windows program is still running in the background. In fact, any other Windows programs that you may have started prior to 1-2-3 for Windows also continue to run. One of the real benefits of using

Windows is that you can run more than one software program at a time and switch among the programs whenever you like. You can even display multiple programs on the screen at one time, as demonstrated in Figure 2-2.

Why would you want to run more than one program at a time? Most busy people tend to work on more than one project at the same time. For example, you may be plugging away in your word processor (working on your resume) when your boss barges in and asks to see the latest sales figures. When you are working in Windows, you don't have to exit your word processing program before you fire up 1-2-3 for Windows to check the sales results (although you may want to minimize the window your word processing document is in if you're working on your resume).

Or suppose that you've been working all day on a spreadsheet that will revolutionize the way your company calculates sales commissions. You're burned out and need a break. Take a few minutes to jump into Program Manager and execute one of your favorite games. In Windows, you can leave 1-2-3 for Windows running so that you can return to it after you finish playing your game.

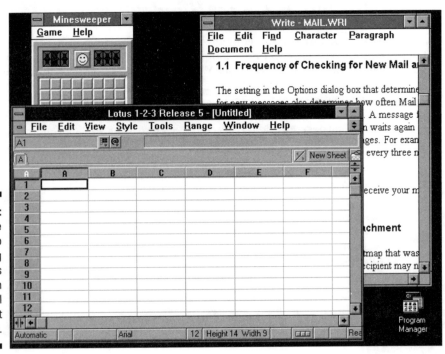

**Figure 2-2:**
One of the
benefits to
using
Windows is
that you can
run several
programs at
once.

Get into the habit of saving the file that you're currently working on before you jump to another program. You never know when another misbehaved program may cause everything to crash.

Use the following steps to activate other programs while you're in 1-2-3 for Windows:

1. **Press Ctrl+Esc to bring up the Windows Task List, which shows a list of all programs currently running, as illustrated in Figure 2-3.**

2. **If the program you want is on the list, select the program.**

   Click the <u>S</u>witch To button to activate the new program.

   If the program you want isn't running, it won't be listed.

3. **To run the program, select Program Manager from the list and then click <u>S</u>witch To.**

   In Program Manager, locate the icon for the program you want and double-click it.

4. **To return to 1-2-3 for Windows, press Ctrl+Esc again, select 1-2-3 for Windows, and click <u>S</u>witch To.**

To save yourself a step when switching out of 1-2-3 for Windows, just double-click the program name in the Task List and avoid the <u>S</u>witch To button altogether. You can also use Alt+Tab to cycle through all the active programs, including Program Manager. When you see the program you want, take your fingers off the Alt+Tab keys, and the program will be activated.

You won't learn all the ins and outs of Windows here, but picking up on some tips just may give your overall productivity a healthy kick in the pants.

While 1-2-3 for Windows is running, you can use other programs without exiting your spreadsheet. Use Ctrl+Esc to bring up the Windows Task List and then choose the program you want. If the program isn't currently running, switch to Program Manager and start it.

**Figure 2-3:**
When you press Ctrl+Esc, the Windows Task List appears, letting you jump to other programs that are running.

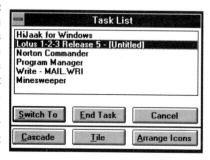

# Setting Yourself Free

Once you get 1-2-3 for Windows started, you'll be staring at a blank worksheet. You'll find out what you can do with this blank worksheet later on — in fact, that just happens to be the subject matter for the remainder of this book. But you need to know one more thing now: how to quit 1-2-3 for Windows — the right way and the wrong way.

## The right way

To exit 1-2-3 for Windows, use the menu and the following steps:

1. **Click the File menu.**

   Figure 2-4 shows the pull-down menu that appears. Then click Exit to get out of 1-2-3 for Windows. When you follow this procedure, you're actually executing the File⇨Exit command. You learn all about issuing commands later in the book.

2. **If you've saved your work, 1-2-3 for Windows unloads from memory, and you'll be back in the Windows Program Manager.** (Assuming that 1-2-3 for Windows is the only program running.)

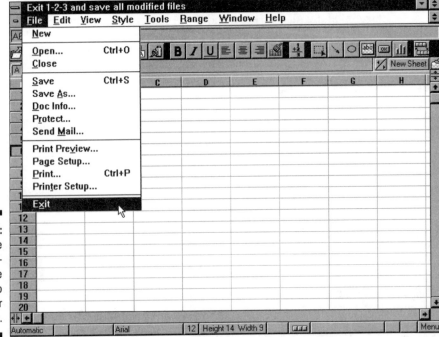

**Figure 2-4:**
Choose the
Exit com-
mand on the
File menu to
quit 1-2-3 for
Windows.

If you haven't saved your work, Windows prompts you to save it first. Unless the stuff you've been working on is totally bogus or simply for practice, you probably want to save it. I discuss all the ins and outs of saving files in Chapter 6.

For a shortcut that saves you two to four seconds (depending on how fast you can type), get into the habit of using Alt+F4 to exit 1-2-3 for Windows. In fact, the Alt+F4 shortcut works in just about all Windows programs. So if you learn the shortcut now, you'll have a head start on subsequent programs you may want to learn.

## *The wrong way*

One of the worst ways to exit a program is simply to turn off the computer. Even if you saved your file first, you should *never* use the power switch method to exit 1-2-3 for Windows. Why? Windows uses lots of other files that you don't even know about. If any of these files is not properly closed, you can potentially mess up your hard disk and scramble some information. Or you may end up with dozens of temporary files that merely take up space and do you no good.

So exit gracefully, as they say, by using the File⇨Exit command. Then you can turn off your computer and do what you normally do after you turn off your computer — such as head for the local pub, practice your couch-potato act in front of the TV, get some Zs, and so on.

---

# To power off or not: the ongoing debate

Over the past several years, I've read lots of articles debating the question of whether to turn off the computer at night or to leave it running all the time. (It seems computer people will argue about anything.) Those who vote for leaving the system on claim that the act of powering up potentially causes strain on the system components. To avoid this strain, leave the computer on at all times. (Most believers in this camp do recommend that you turn off the monitor when it's not in use.) If leaving an electronic unit on all the time sounds strange to you, think about your refrigerator.

Those who align themselves on the side of powering down after they've finished using the computer believe that they save money by reducing power consumption. These people don't buy the claim that switching components on and off causes any damage. (Some even say that the money you save on your electric bill can be used to replace any components damaged by on/off switching.)

So who do you believe? Beats me. I always turn my computers off when I'm not using them, but I don't feel bad about leaving them on for extended periods when I'm doing other things. I guess the jury is still out on this one, so you can do what you want.

# Chapter 3
# Jumping Right In

*"Fear is the main source of superstition, and one of the main sources of cruelty. To conquer fear is the beginning of wisdom."*

Bertrand Russell (1872 –1970)
*An Outline of Intellectual Rubbish*

· · · · · · · · · · · · · · · · · · · · · · · · · · · · · · · · · · · · · · · · · · ·

## In This Chapter

▶ Overcoming your irrational fears about working with a computer

▶ Getting a once-in-a-lifetime opportunity for some actual experience with 1-2-3 for Windows (and not having to know what you're doing)

▶ Creating a somewhat useful worksheet

▶ Learning about 1-2-3's SmartIcons — useful little clickable pictures that can save you time and energy

▶ Getting some experience with dialog boxes

· · · · · · · · · · · · · · · · · · · · · · · · · · · · · · · · · · · · · · · · · · ·

*1*t's no secret that many people are deathly afraid of computers (maybe even you). At the mere mention of a computer-related term, their hands sweat, their hearts race, and they exhibit other strange physiological phenomena. I've found that fear of computers seems to be related to age: the older you are, the more fear you're likely to have. I know a four year old who has absolutely no fear of jumping into a new program and clicking away to see what happens. I also know an 81 year old who never fails to ask me whether it's all right to click the Help menu.

The best way to overcome your fear of computers is to do things on a computer and to realize that you can't really cause too much damage. Well, you *can* cause some damage to a computer, but I'll tell you how to minimize this possibility. This chapter is designed to help you conquer your computerphobia by demonstrating that you (yes, even *you*) can do something reasonably productive — and that your computer will still be operable after you're finished.

Even if you're fearless when it comes to computers, if you take the time to work your way through this chapter, you may learn a few things. At the very least, you will have gotten your feet wet with 1-2-3 for Windows, and you can decide whether it's really something you want to learn.

# What You'll Be Doing

By the time you reach the end of this chapter, you will have created a 1-2-3 for Windows worksheet that can help you catalog your music collection. If you don't have a music collection, you can still use this chapter. (Just pretend that you have one.)

If this were a typical computer book, the example in this chapter would probably be a worksheet to calculate monthly payments on a mortgage, keep track of your business expenses, or do some equally boring exercise. My example, though certainly not the most exciting spreadsheet you'll encounter, is slightly more interesting than the run-of-the-mill financial examples.

## How to avoid data suicide

Avoid the following pitfalls if you're afraid that you'll screw things up while working on your computer. You may want to photocopy this page and nail it to your computer monitor (just kidding!). If you don't understand all the points, don't worry. You'll learn about this stuff later on in the book.

✔ Don't delete any files unless you know *exactly* what they do. The fact is, deleting one critical file can cause your computer to fail to start. If you have a doubt about a file, don't delete it (or ask Melvin, who knows about computer files).

✔ Don't turn off your computer until you exit all your programs properly. Exit 1-2-3 for Windows by selecting the File⇨Exit command. Also, avoid actions such as kicking the plug out, knocking your PC off of the desk, and dropping the computer from tall buildings or airplanes.

✔ If you plan to make major changes to a file that already works, start by saving the file with a different name by using the File⇨Save As command. That way, the original file remains intact, and all your changes (for better or for worse) go to another file. If your changes mess things up, you can get back to the file that worked.

✔ Make a floppy disk backup copy of every important file. The worst damage that can occur to your files may not even be your fault. Hard disks tend to crash on their own for no apparent reason. A crashed hard disk usually means that everything stored on it has entered the big bit bucket in the sky — never to return.

✔ Keep your floppy disk backups in a safe place — not next to your computer. If your office burns down during the night, your backups suffer the same fate as your computer — they become black biscuits.

✔ Be very careful when formatting floppy disks (formatting a disk is necessary before you can store data on it). First, make sure that the disk you format doesn't have anything good on it. Second, make sure that you're actually formatting a *floppy* disk — not your hard disk. When in doubt, call your computer guru over for help. (Don't forget to have a bribe handy — a bag of Cheetos usually works great.) Or you can just buy preformatted disks.

More specifically, the worksheet you develop does the following:

- Lets you keep track of CDs, cassettes, and even LPs (remember them?)
- Stores the artist, title, format, and total time of the recording in four columns
- Tells you the total number of recordings in the worksheet
- Calculates and displays the total time of the recordings

# First Steps

I'm assuming here that your system is all set up to run 1-2-3 for Windows and that you know how to start it.

Appendix A covers installation details, and Chapter 2 explains the various ways to start 1-2-3 for Windows.

You start out with a completely blank worksheet, the way 1-2-3 for Windows normally starts up. Usually, it's a good idea to spend a few seconds thinking about what you want to do before actually entering stuff into a worksheet. Because you're just starting out, I'll do the thinking for you.

When 1-2-3 Release 5 starts up, a dialog box that welcomes you to the program appears and asks if you want to create a new worksheet or work on an existing worksheet. Just click the OK button to dismiss this dialog box and create a new worksheet. Another dialog box appears with a list of SmartMasters. Again, just click OK, and you're on your way.

You're going to set up a worksheet that will hold information about the recordings in a music collection. Each recording occupies one row of the worksheet. For each recording, you'll keep track of the following four things:

- The recording artist's name
- The title of the recording
- The recording medium (CD, cassette, LP — and even 8-track tapes if you're living in a time warp)
- The total time of the recording in minutes

You'll use four worksheet columns to record the information. OK, that's enough time to think about the spreadsheet — now it's time to do it.

If you've never used a spreadsheet before, many of the things in this chapter will seem foreign to you. Don't worry if you don't understand everything that's going on. The point of this chapter is to give you an opportunity to do something, not to explain every detail. There's plenty of time for the details later.

## *Adding column headings*

Throughout this chapter I refer to cell addresses. A *cell address* consists of two parts: a *column letter* and a *row number*. For example, A1 is a cell address that refers to the upper left cell on the worksheet (column A, row 1).

You can start by entering labels for the four column headings that correspond to the information in each column. Follow the next steps carefully:

1. **Make sure that the cell pointer is in cell A1.**

   The second line of the display (directly under the menu bar) tells you which cell the cell pointer is in. Use the arrow keys or the mouse to move the cell pointer to cell A1 or press the Home key to take the express route there.

2. **Type** Artist **and then press the right-arrow key to move the cell pointer to cell B1.**

3. **Type** Title **into cell B1 and press the right-arrow key to get to cell C1.**

4. **Type** Format **into cell C1 and press the right-arrow key to get to cell D1.**

5. **Type** Time **in cell D1 and press Home to return to cell A1.**

Your screen should now look like Figure 3-1.

Tells you which cell
you have selected

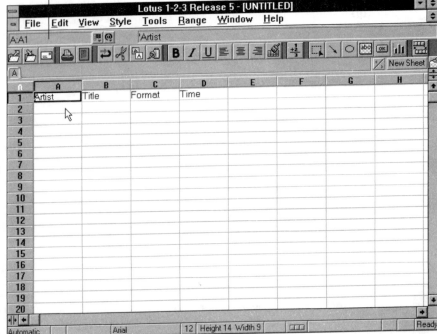

**Figure 3-1:**
Your
worksheet,
after
entering
labels into
the top row
to serve as
column
headings.

## *Making the headings bold*

Next, you're going to boldface the headings. This step isn't essential, but it will make the worksheet look a bit nicer. And boy, do those heads become coura-geous! Do the following steps to make the headings bold:

1. **Make sure the cell pointer is in cell A1 (the cell with the first column heading).**

   Use the arrow keys, the mouse, or press Home.

2. **Click the mouse and drag it right so that it highlights all the other cells that have labels (cells A1 through D1).**

   You've just selected a range of cells.

3. **Examine the row of little icons at the top of the screen and find the one that looks like Figure 3-2. Click it.**

   You've just used a SmartIcon to make the selected cells appear in bold type. You could have used a command from the menu to make them bold, but using the SmartIcon is much faster (and smarter).

**Figure 3-2:**
The bold
Smart Icon.

Your worksheet should now look like Figure 3-3.

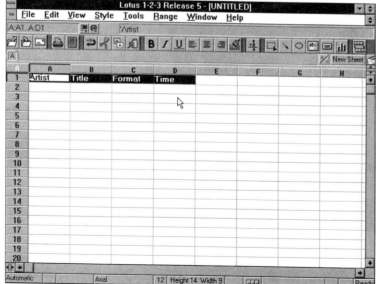

**Figure 3-3:**
Your
worksheet,
after
entering
headings
and making
them bold.

## *Adjusting the column widths*

Unless your music collection consists exclusively of one-word titles by artists with a single name, the column widths aren't going to be wide enough to display everything properly. You can make the column widths wider by doing the following:

1. **Move the mouse pointer to the right border of column A.**

   The mouse pointer changes shape and looks like two perpendicular arrows in a cross, as in Figure 3-4.

2. **Click and drag the column border to the right.**

   As you do so, you see the column width expand before your very eyes. Keep dragging until the column border is about three times its original size.

3. **Repeat this same procedure for column B.**

4. **Repeat the procedure for column D, but this time drag the border to the *left* to make the column a bit narrower.**

   Column C is OK as it is.

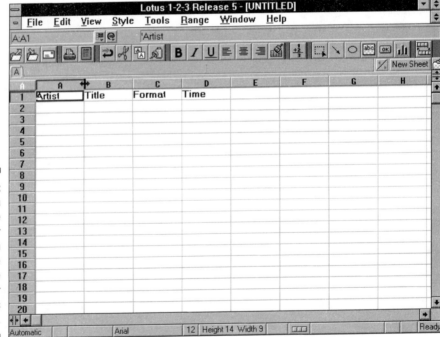

**Figure 3-4:**
When you
drag the
mouse over
a column
border, the
mouse
pointer
changes
shape.

You can change column widths at any time, so don't be too concerned about getting the exact widths at this point. In fact, there's a way to automatically adjust a column's width based on the longest entry in the column. But I'm getting ahead of myself.

# Entering the Data

Now, you're ready to put some entries into the worksheet. Remember, each recording goes in a separate row, and you'll use four columns in each row. Just follow these steps:

1. **Move the cell pointer to cell A2 (using the arrow keys or the mouse) and enter the name of a recording artist.**

    If you can't think of one, type **Eric Clapton**. Press the right-arrow key to move to the next cell.

2. **In cell B2, enter the title of the recording.**

    If you lack imagination, type **Unplugged.** Use the right-arrow key to move to the cell next door.

3. **Enter the format of the recording in cell C2.**

    If you're using my example, type **CD**. Press the right-arrow key again to go to cell D2.

4. **Enter the total time in minutes — a single number.**

    The example I'm using is 42 minutes long, so type **42**.

5. **Press Enter to end this entry.**

After you finish with this row, use the down-arrow key to move the cell pointer to the next row and then press the left-arrow key until you're in cell A3. Repeat the preceding procedure until you've entered your entire CD, cassette, and record collection. (Not really. You can stop after four or five or whenever it gets boring.)

Your worksheet should look something like Figure 3-5. If it looks *exactly* like this figure, congratulations — you either have excellent taste in music, or you have little imagination and simply copied my example.

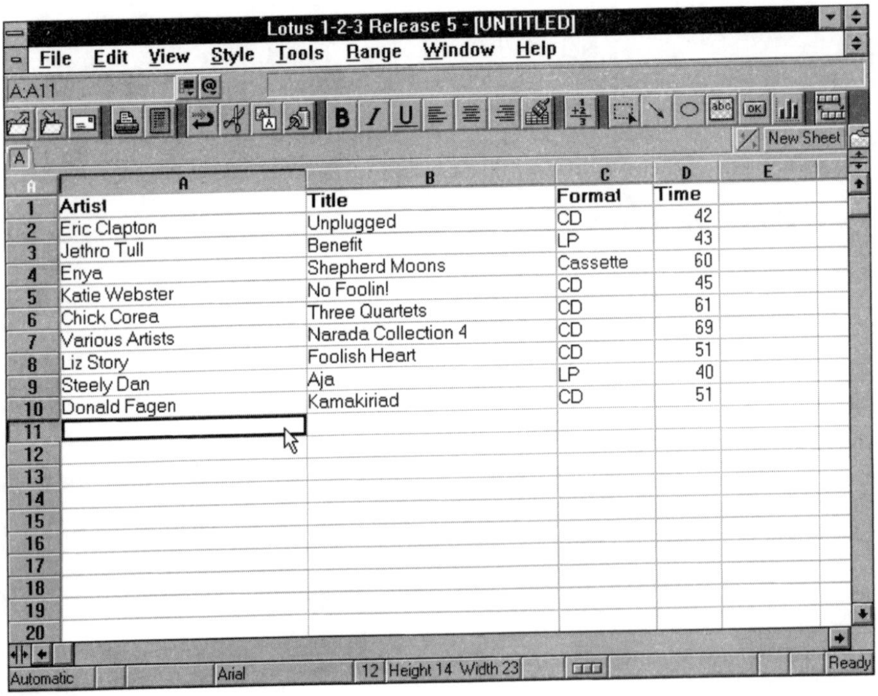

**Figure 3-5:**
Your work-
sheet, after
entering
some
recordings.

# And Now, a Formula

If you have only a few sample lines of data, you can tell at a glance how many recordings are in the list. But what if you have several hundred? Or several thousand? You would have to move down to the end of the list, make a note of what row number the last entry is in, and then mentally subtract one from the number of the last entry to account for the column headings row. Why do all these mental gymnastics when you can use a formula to do the counting?

A *formula,* as you learn in Chapter 7, is something that you put in a cell that uses information in other cells to display a result (usually a calculation of some kind). The formula you'll be using makes use of one of the built-in functions provided by 1-2-3 for Windows to count the number of nonblank cells in a range of cells.

A good place to put this formula is at the top of the worksheet. But because the top rows are occupado, you need to move the rows down by inserting new rows to make room for the formula.

## Inserting new rows

In this part of the exercise, you insert four new blank rows at the top of the worksheet. After you add the new rows, everything else gets pushed down (but you don't lose anything you've already done). To insert new rows at the top of the worksheet, do the following:

1. **Click the number on row 1 (the entire row is highlighted) and drag the mouse down three more rows to select a total of four rows (rows 1 - 4).**

   Your screen should look like Figure 3–6.

2. **Click the _right_ mouse button.**

   1-2-3 for Windows displays a small menu right where the mouse pointer is. Figure 3-7 shows what this shortcut menu looks like. If nothing happens, select the three rows again and make sure that you click the _right_ mouse button (not the left mouse button).

3. **Now use the left mouse button and click Insert in the shortcut menu.**

   1-2-3 for Windows goes to work and inserts four new rows for you (pushing everything else downward). Your screen should now look like Figure 3-8.

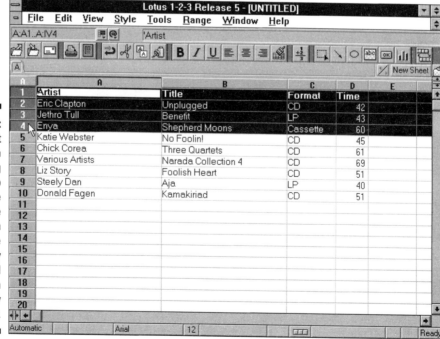

**Figure 3-6:** The first step in inserting rows is to select the rows where the insertion will take place by clicking and dragging on the row number.

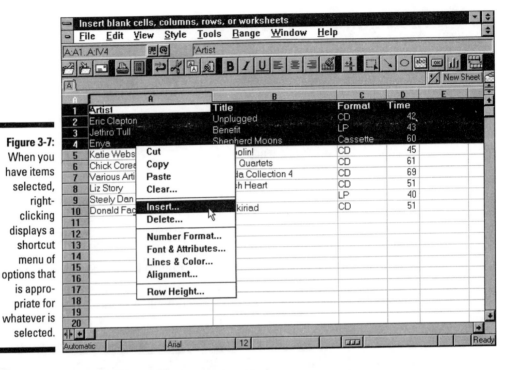

**Figure 3-7:**
When you
have items
selected,
right-
clicking
displays a
shortcut
menu of
options that
is appro-
priate for
whatever is
selected.

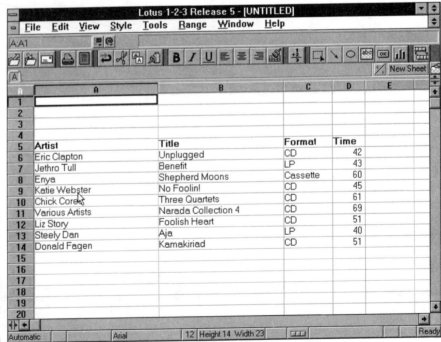

**Figure 3-8:**
Your
worksheet,
after
inserting
four rows at
the top.

# Sticking in the formula

Now that you have some extra room at the top of the worksheet, you can put in a formula to count the number of occupied cells. The formula can go in any unused cell, but cell B2 is a good place. To enter the formula, take the following steps:

1. **Move the cell pointer to cell B2.**

2. **Type the following formula into cell B2 and press Enter:**

```
@COUNT(A6..A8192)
```

After you press Enter, you don't see the formula in the cell; instead, you see the formula's result, which tells you how many recordings you've entered. When the cell pointer is on the cell, however, you can see the formula in the edit line at the top of the screen.

This formula uses a special function (@COUNT) that counts the number of nonblank entries in a range that is put in parentheses. In this case, the range is all the cells from A6 down to and including A8192, which is the last cell in column A.

3. **Move to cell C2 and type** Recordings, **a label that reminds you what the number in cell B2 refers to.**

Add another record or two and watch as the count is updated automatically. Are you in love with spreadsheets yet?

# Ready for another formula?

Now you can add another slightly more complex formula that calculates the total time of the recordings in hours. Follow these steps carefully:

1. **Move the cell pointer to cell B3.**

2. **Type the following formula and press Enter:**

```
@SUM(D6..D8192)/60
```

1-2-3 for Windows evaluates this formula by first calculating the sum of all the values in the cells from D6 up to and including D8192. Then the program divides this number by 60 (because the times entered are in minutes, and there are 60 minutes in an hour).

3. **Move to cell C3 and type** Total time in hours **for the new label.**

To see whether the formula works, add another record or two and watch as the total gets updated to include the new times. Now your worksheet should look something like Figure 3-9. The actual numbers in cells B2 and B3 depend, of course, on how many recordings you entered and how many minutes long they are.

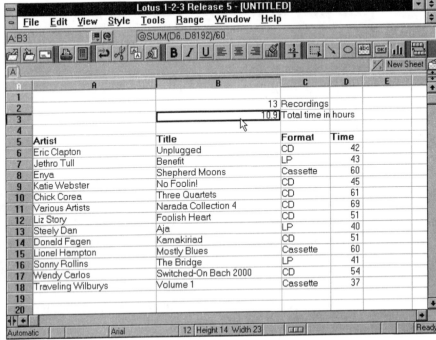

**Figure 3-9:**
Your
worksheet,
after
entering the
formula to
count the
recordings
and
compute the
total time.

# Adding a Title

Now you can add one last finishing touch — a title for your spreadsheet at the top — and you can make that a bit fancy, just for fun. To add a title to your spreadsheet, do the following:

1. **Move the cell pointer to cell A1.**

   The Home key gets you there in a jiff.

2. **Type** List of Recordings **and press Enter.**

3. **Click the right mouse button to get a shortcut menu for the current selection (cell A1).**

4. **With the left mouse button, click the Font & Attributes option on this menu.**

   A dialog box pops up, as shown in Figure 3-10.

5. **In the S̲ize box, click a larger number to change the size of the text in the selection.**

6. **In the Attributes box, click B̲old to make the text bold.**

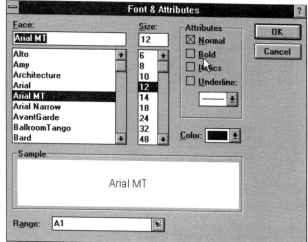

**Figure 3-10:**
The Font &
Attributes
dialog box
lets you
change the
way the cell
looks.

**7. Click the OK button to close the dialog box.**

Your worksheet now looks something like Figure 3-11.

**Figure 3-11:**
The work-
sheet, after
modifying
the attri-
butes of
cell A1.

| | A | B | C | D | E |
|---|---|---|---|---|---|
| 1 | **List of Recordings** | | | | |
| 2 | | 13 | Recordings | | |
| 3 | | 10.9 | Total time in hours | | |
| 4 | | | | | |
| 5 | Artist | Title | Format | Time | |
| 6 | Eric Clapton | Unplugged | CD | 42 | |
| 7 | Jethro Tull | Benefit | LP | 43 | |
| 8 | Enya | Shepherd Moons | Cassette | 60 | |
| 9 | Katie Webster | No Foolin! | CD | 45 | |
| 10 | Chick Corea | Three Quartets | CD | 61 | |
| 11 | Various Artists | Narada Collection 4 | CD | 69 | |
| 12 | Liz Story | Foolish Heart | CD | 51 | |
| 13 | Steely Dan | Aja | LP | 40 | |
| 14 | Donald Fagen | Kamakiriad | CD | 51 | |
| 15 | Lionel Hampton | Mostly Blues | Cassette | 60 | |
| 16 | Sonny Rollins | The Bridge | LP | 41 | |
| 17 | Wendy Carlos | Switched-On Bach 2000 | CD | 54 | |
| 18 | Traveling Wilburys | Volume 1 | Cassette | 37 | |
| 19 | | | | | |

Lotus 1-2-3 Release 5 - [UNTITLED]

File   Edit   View   Style   Tools   Range   Window   Help

A:B2    @COUNT(A6..A8192)

Automatic    Arial    12 Height 14 Width 23    Ready

# *Saving Your Masterpiece*

Everything you've done so far was done in your computer's memory. Your hard disk has been completely idle. If you (or some clod) should accidentally kick your PC's plug out of the wall socket, all this fine work would go down the proverbial tube. To prevent such a disaster, you need to save your file to disk with the following steps:

1. **Find the Save SmartIcon that looks like an arrow going into a folder (shown in Figure 3-12) and click it.**

**Figure 3-12:**
The Save
SmartIcon.

Because you haven't given your worksheet a filename yet, 1-2-3 for Windows pops up the dialog box shown in Figure 3-13 that lets you enter a name for the file. This dialog box also shows you a list of other worksheet files that may be in this directory.

2. **Type** MUSIC **(the name you'll use for this file) and press Enter.**

1-2-3 for Windows saves your work as MUSIC.WK4. This filename now shows up on the title bar of the worksheet window to remind you of what you're working on.

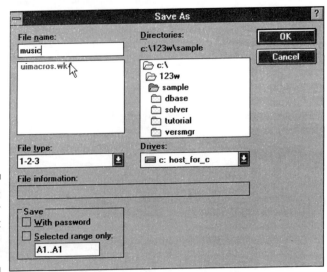

**Figure 3-13:**
Name your
worksheet
file in this
dialog box.

# Working with the File

This worksheet is in pretty good shape. Use the techniques you learned to add more recordings to the list. The formulas at the top always tell you exactly how many recordings you've entered and the total time in hours.

For practice, add some more recordings.

# Saving It Again, Sam

If you made any changes to the worksheet since you saved it, you need to save it again to keep from losing this additional work. Click the Save SmartIcon to save your file. Because the worksheet already has a name, 1-2-3 for Windows doesn't waste your time asking you for the name again — it simply saves the file. This process all happens so quickly that you may not even notice anything. However, if you watch your hard disk drive light, you see that it flashes on for a split second while the file is being saved.

## A personal anecdote

At one point in my college days, I had four roommates who also happened to be music lovers and computer buffs. Between the five of us, we had approximately 3,000 LPs. (This was long before CDs were available.) One of these guys was taking a computer class and needed a project.

Believe it or not, we actually keypunched all the titles, artists, and other information from these recordings onto IBM cards and created a data file on the campus mainframe. Using FORTRAN (an ancient computer language), we wrote a program to summarize and print the data. Then, when we were all sitting around in various states of consciousness and couldn't decide what to listen to, someone would call out a random number. We had a mutual agreement that we would play the record that corresponded to the number on the printout. Because our musical tastes were all pretty good, this usually resulted in an agreeable outcome, and we often heard an album that we would never think of playing otherwise. Occasionally, however, the scheme backfired, and we had to endure 45 minutes of the Carpenters or some group equally obnoxious.

The point of this story is that we all learned a great deal about programming because the project involved a topic that we were _interested_ in. The same goes for learning 1-2-3 for Windows or any other software for that matter. If you try to learn software by using stupid examples, you probably won't get too far. The best way to learn is by working on projects that are important to you.

# Quitting 1-2-3 for Windows

Now that you've set up this worksheet and saved it, you can call it quits. Press Alt+F4 (a shortcut way to exit 1-2-3 for Windows). If you've made any changes since the last time the file was saved, 1-2-3 for Windows prompts you and gives you a chance to save your file before exiting. Otherwise, the program ends and you're back at the Windows Program Manager screen.

# Retrieving Your Work

The next time you start 1-2-3 for Windows, you can work on this worksheet again by issuing the File⇨Open command. To open an existing file, follow these steps:

1. **Click the File option in the menu bar at the top of the screen or click the open file SmartIcon.**

2. **In the menu that is pulled down, click the Open command, which gives you the dialog box shown in Figure 3-14.**

   This dialog box looks remarkably like the one you get when you save a file.

3. **Type in the filename (or use the Open dialog box to locate the file) and choose OK.**

   The file opens and looks just like it did the last time you saved it.

 When you click the File command, the File menu drops down, nothing new. However, if you look at the menu, you'll notice that at the very bottom, after the Exit command, there are some files listed. These are the last five files you opened. If one of these files happens to be the one you want to open, simply clicking the filename opens that file. How convenient, huh?

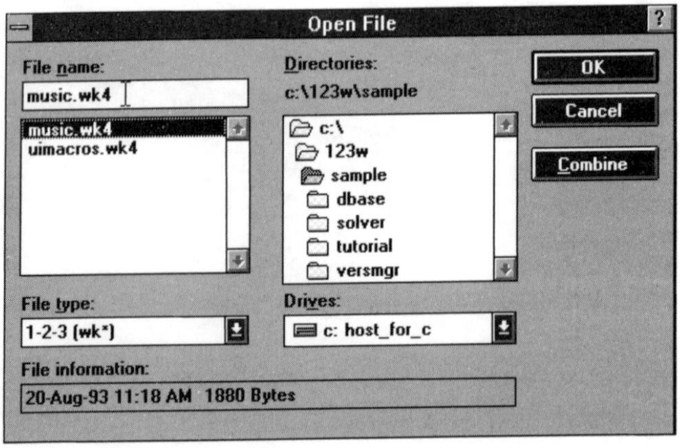

**Figure 3-14:** Use this dialog box to tell 1-2-3 for Windows what file you want to retrieve from disk.

Open File

File name:
music.wk4

music.wk4
uimacros.wk4

Directories:
c:\123w\sample

c:\
123w
sample
dbase
solver
tutorial
versmgr

OK
Cancel
Combine

File type:
1-2-3 (wk*)

Drives:
c: host_for_c

File information:
20-Aug-93 11:18 AM  1880 Bytes

# Still Afraid?

If you followed along with this exercise and had no problems, congratulations. If you found yourself getting lost and even more confused, don't despair. Try it again, starting with another blank worksheet. Take your time and follow the instructions carefully. I guarantee that you'll eventually get the program to work right. Your last vestiges of fear will begin to vanish as your confidence increases. If not, try some Valium.

# Other Stuff for Overachievers

Normal users can consider this chapter over and done with, and they can move on to other topics. But those who always turned in their science projects early will probably want to read more.

The worksheet you developed in this chapter is only a start. Imaginative users can do even more to it. Here's a list of some potential additions you can make to the spreadsheet:

- ✔ Add a formula to calculate the average recording length (*hint*: use the @AVG function).
- ✔ Add another column for the year the album was recorded.
- ✔ Add another column for your evaluation of the recording: excellent, good, poor, pure garbage, and so on. If you use numerical ratings, you can eventually sort the data by this column and instantly see your recordings from best to worst. Sorting is covered later.

You also can change the formatting. Changing the formatting simply means making the contents of the cell look different. Feel free to select some cells by dragging the mouse over them and then experimenting with the SmartIcons. Have some fun and be as outrageous as you want.

# Part II
# Basic Stuff That You Must Know

## In this part...

*T*he information in these nine chapters can best be described as fundamental. In other words, you won't get too far with 1-2-3 for Windows unless you know how to do these basic operations. If you're just starting out with 1-2-3 for Windows, this is *not* the section to skip.

# Chapter 4
# Entering Numbers, Words, and Other Things

*"Shall I, like a hermit, dwell on a rock or in a cell?*

Sir Walter Raleigh (1552 –1618)

. . . . . . . . . . . . . . . . . . . . . . . . . . . . . . . . . . . . . . . . . . . . . .

### In This Chapter

▶ Familiarizing yourself with the parts of the 1-2-3 for Windows screen

▶ Learning not to panic at a blank worksheet

▶ Moving from cell to cell (a common pastime among restless prisoners)

▶ Putting numbers and words into cells

▶ Removing the information in a cell

▶ Reviewing lots of marginally useful terminology that you can read once and then forget

. . . . . . . . . . . . . . . . . . . . . . . . . . . . . . . . . . . . . . . . . . . . . .

*I*f you took my sage advice and worked your way through Chapter 3 (as I looked over your shoulder), you now have some first-hand experience with 1-2-3 for Windows — and you even have a moderately useful worksheet to keep track of your music collection.

This chapter provides enough information to make you feel relatively safe in going off on your own to make something out of the vast wasteland we call a blank worksheet. There's a great deal of information crammed in here, so don't feel bad if you can't digest it all in one sitting.

# Sorry Folks, But You Just Gotta Know This

You already know that this book is designed to cut to the chase and protect you from lots of the gory details that get in the way of your becoming adequately proficient in 1-2-3 for Windows. Unfortunately, there are some things that you just can't overlook. Bear with me as I tell you about them.

## *The screen tour (it's the law)*

Federal Statute CB324.21.190 states that every computer book published in the U.S. must include a tour of the screen within its first 50 pages. I developed Figure 4-1 to satisfy this legal requirement. After you start 1-2-3 for Windows, the screen shows a blank worksheet just waiting to be used, abused, or misused.

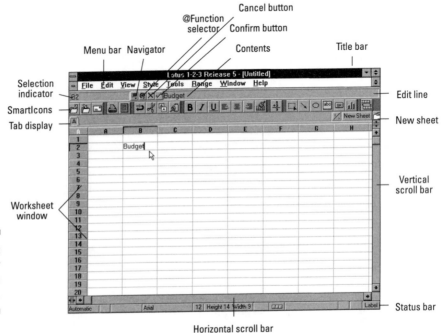

**Figure 4-1:** The 1-2-3 for Windows screen.

Your screen may look different, depending on what type of display driver you have installed for Windows. The screen in Figure 4-1 is in standard VGA mode, which shows 640 X 480 pixels. You may have a display driver installed that has a higher resolution. The other two common display resolutions are 800 X 600 and 1024 X 768. If you have an option, you're usually better off going with a higher resolution, because you can see more stuff on the screen. But make sure that your monitor can display high resolutions and that the text is not too small for you to read.

If your screen doesn't look anything like Figure 4-1 (and you're sure that you're actually using 1-2-3 for Windows), you probably have 1-2-3 Release 1 for Windows. The bad news: You're gonna have to buy the upgrade at least to 1-2-3 Release 4 for Windows if you want to get anything out of this book (the upgrade cost is inexpensive). The good news: Release 4 and Release 5 are light years better (and much easier to use) than Release 1. By the way, there is no 1-2-3 Release 2 or Release 3 for Windows. Jeez, you'd think that a company that makes spreadsheets would know how to count....

Like the human body, a spreadsheet is made up of various parts, some of which are definitely more interesting than others. Table 4-1 lists the parts that you eventually need to know. Don't be too concerned if you don't understand the terminology now. It'll become semicrystal clear as you go through this chapter.

| Table 4-1 | The More Popular 1-2-3 for Windows Body Parts |
|---|---|
| *Screen Part* | *Why It Exists* |
| Worksheet window | Designed to hold your work in its many cells, each worksheet has its own window. |
| Title bar | Displays the name of the program you're running as well as some messages from 1-2-3 for Windows. For example, after you click a menu item or right-click a SmartIcon, the title bar displays a brief description of the function. |
| Edit line | Shows the address of the active cell and also displays the contents of the current cell. |
| Cancel and Confirm buttons | When editing a cell, you click the cancel button to abandon changes, or the confirm button to accept them. |
| Selection indicator | Displays the cell address of the active cell or the range selected. |
| Navigator | Helps you move to specific worksheet locations or to insert range names into a formula. |
| @Function selector | Makes it easy to insert an @function into a formula. |
| Contents box | Displays the contents of the active cell. |
| Status bar | Tells you about the current selection and lets you change the number format, type size, and other things. The mode indicator tells you which mode 1-2-3 for Windows is in. The icon with three buttons lets you choose a different SmartIcon palette. |
| Menu bar | Displays the commands that you can choose to get 1-2-3 for Windows to work for you. |
| SmartIcons | Little pictures that, when clicked, perform shortcuts. |
| Vertical scroll bar | Click here to move up and down in a worksheet. |
| Horizontal scroll bar | Click here to move left or right in a worksheet. |
| Tab display | Provides quick access to the additional sheets in your file (if any). |
| New sheet | Adds an additional sheet to your file. |

I discuss body parts (of 1-2-3, I mean) in more detail as the need arises.

## Some useless terminology

What do you call the thing that you're working on in 1-2-3 for Windows? The official name is a *worksheet,* but lazy types often call it just a *sheet.* Some people call it a *spreadsheet,* and others simply call it a *file.* A few fools even call it a *document.* I call it several things throughout this book. All of this terminology gets even more confusing when you consider the fact that a 1-2-3 for Windows file can have more than one sheet in it — sort of like having extra pages. The bottom line? Don't worry about terminology. The important thing is to get your work done so you can move on to other things.

## Rows, columns, cells, and sheets

A worksheet is made up a bunch of cells. (I'll define the technical term *bunch* later.) Each cell is at the intersection of a row and a column. Rows are numbered 1, 2, 3, and so on up to 8,192. Columns are labeled A, B, C, and so on.

There are actually 256 columns in a worksheet, but because the English alphabet stops at the letter *Z,* a team of Lotus experts was formed to determine how to label spreadsheet columns after you run out of letters. The experts arrived at an ingenious solution: use two letters. After column Z comes column AA, which is followed by AB, AC, and so on. After AZ comes BA, BB, BC, and so on. If you follow this train of thought to its logical conclusion, you discover that column 256 is called IV.

Every file also can have more sheets stacked behind the first one, kind of like pages in a notebook. In fact, you can add as many as 255 more sheets behind the first one, each exactly the same size as the first one.

So how may cells are in a worksheet? If your math is rusty, I'll fire up 1-2-3 for Windows and do the calculation for you: 8,192 rows × 256 columns × 256 sheets comes to 536, 870,912 cells. If you need more cells than this, you're reading the wrong book.

One or two of you may be curious about why 1-2-3 for Windows uses such odd numbers. Why not 250 columns instead of 256? Why not an even 10,000 rows instead of 8,192? Why not 200 potential sheets? Good questions. Using these strange numbers is a by-product of the binary system rearing its ugly head. Computers rely heavily on the binary system (you know, the number system with only 0s and 1s in it). Here's where those odd numbers come from: 256 is 2 to the 8th power, and can be represented using exactly eight binary digits; 8,192 is 2 to the 13th power, and can be represented with 13 binary digits. Using these nice binary numbers actually optimizes the way things are stored within 1-2-3 for Windows.

## Gimme your address or your life

With a half billion cells in a worksheet, the normal person may have trouble keeping track of them. Actually, it's not all that hard, because each cell has its own address (but not its own ZIP code).

The address of a cell is made up of three things: its sheet letter (optional), its column letter, and its row number. The sheet letter has a colon after it, but the column letter and row number are stuck together with no space in between. Therefore, the upper left cell is known as cell A:A1. The last cell, way down at the bottom of the fifth sheet and in the last column, has an address of E:IV256.

If your worksheet consists of only a single sheet (which is how they all start out), you don't have to be concerned with sheet letters. In fact, cell addresses don't even use the sheet letter when you have only a single sheet. I discuss everything you need to know about working with multiple sheets in Chapter 11.

Cell addresses, by the way, are used in formulas, which are covered in the next chapter. As you may have already noticed, cell addresses can quickly turn into a bowl of alphabet soup. To combat this problem, 1-2-3 for Windows lets you give meaningful names to the sheets in a worksheet file. For example, you can name the first sheet *Income,* and the second sheet *Expenses.* Then, if you want to refer to the upper left cell on the second sheet, you can use a reference such as Expenses:A1. Much simpler, eh?

To change a sheet letter into a more meaningful name, just double-click the tab and then type in the new name. There are a few rules regarding sheet names, however. The main rule to remember is that you shouldn't include any spaces. Some people like to use the underline character to simulate a space. For example, rather than naming a sheet *First Quarter,* which has a space in it, you can name it *First_Quarter,* which looks almost the same but officially has no spaces in it.

You often can omit the sheet letter part of a cell address. If you don't include it, 1-2-3 for Windows simply uses the current sheet. For example, if you're working on the second sheet, you can refer to the upper left cell on that sheet as A1 rather than B:A1. But if you're on the second sheet and need to refer to the upper left cell on the first sheet, you have to use the full A:A1 reference (which makes sense).

## The cell pointer

Take a look at the worksheet in Figure 4-2. Notice that one of the cells has a darker outline than the others. This cell is the *active cell.* In this case, the active cell is cell C4. (I'm leaving off the sheet letter part of the cell address, because this file has only one sheet.) The active cell is where the cell pointer is. The edit line also tells you what cell is active. When you move the cell pointer around, the active cell changes. (Isn't technology grand?)

Current
address

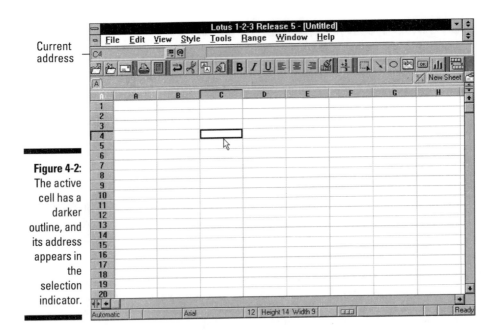

**Figure 4-2:**
The active
cell has a
darker
outline, and
its address
appears in
the
selection
indicator.

# *Move it along, doggies*

So how do you move the cell pointer? It's easy — with a mouse or your keyboard.

### *Moving around with a mouse*

When you move your mouse around, notice how the little mouse arrow (AKA the mouse pointer) moves on the screen. When the pointer is over one of the cells, click the left mouse button. The outline around the cell becomes thicker, and this cell magically becomes the active cell.

Mouse freaks can also use the scroll bars to move to other cells. There are two scroll bars, the vertical one and the horizontal one. To move down one full screen in a worksheet, click towards the bottom of the vertical scroll bar. To move up a screen, click towards the top of the vertical scroll bar. To move one screen to the right, click the right side of the horizontal scroll bar. To move one screen to the left, click the left side of the horizontal scroll bar. You also can drag the little button that appears on the scroll bar to scroll the worksheet either up or across. This scroll bar stuff is actually easier to do than it is to describe, so play around with clicking and dragging the scroll bars until you get the hang of it.

# Taming the wild rodent

If you've never used a mouse before, don't be alarmed if you find it all very awkward at first. Actually, I've found that a 4 year old can master a mouse faster than most adults (feel bad now?). One way to get in some practice with a mouse is to run the Windows Solitaire game (which should be located in your *Games* program group). A few hands of this will make you more comfortable.

You need to know some basic mouse techniques and terminology, which apply to all the other Windows programs you'll ever use. The following list of terms covers just about everything you need to know about using the mouse:

✔ **Click:** Move the mouse pointer over an object, press the left button, and release it right away.

✔ **Right-click:** Move the mouse pointer over an object, press the right button, and release it right away.

✔ **Double-click:** Move the mouse pointer over an object and press the left button twice in quick succession.

✔ **Drag:** Move the mouse pointer over an object, press the left button (but don't release it), and then move the mouse (drag it). You can move some items by releasing the mouse button, or you can select several items at one time by dragging over them.

If you run out of room to move the mouse on your desk top or mouse pad, just pick up the mouse and reposition it somewhere else. Picking up the mouse doesn't move the mouse pointer, but it does give you more room to move around. Some people have trouble with double-clicking an object after they pick up the mouse. Just remember that you need to keep the mouse pointer in the same location for both of the clicks in a double-click.

Using the scroll bars doesn't actually change the active cell — it just scrolls the worksheet. To change the active cell, you have to click a cell after you use the scroll bars.

You can activate another worksheet by clicking the appropriate tab at the top of the screen.

## Moving around with the keyboard

Because you have to remove your hand from the keyboard to use your mouse, you may find that using the keyboard is more efficient for moving around a worksheet. (I do, and I'm an expert.) Use the cursor movement keys, the keys with the arrows on them.

Many different styles of keyboards exist, with a common keyboard shown in Figure 4-3. This particular keyboard has two sets of cursor movement keys. Most keyboards have a separate numeric keypad at the right.

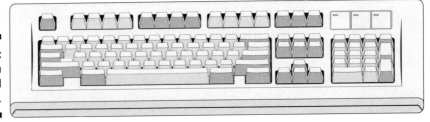

**Figure 4-3:**
A common
keyboard
layout.

The keys with the arrows move the cell pointer one cell at a time in the direction of the arrow. When you hold down one of these keys, the cell pointer zips along until you let go. A better way to move the cell pointer long distances is to use the keys labeled PgUp and PgDn. These keys move the cell pointer up or down one full screen. To move one screen to the right, use the Tab key (or Ctrl+right arrow). And to move quickly to the left, use Shift+Tab (or Ctrl+left arrow). Pressing Ctrl+PgUp moves you to the next sheet in the worksheet (if it has one), and pressing Ctrl+PgDn moves you to the preceding sheet (if it has one).

Moving by one screen gives you different results, depending on how large the worksheet window is. For example, if you make the worksheet window very small (say, five rows high), PgDn only moves you down five rows. If the worksheet windows is large and shows 20 rows, PgDn will move you down 20 rows.

At some point in your spreadsheeting life, you may find yourself lost deep in the bowels of a worksheet and trying to get back home (back to cell A:A1). To take the express route, just press Ctrl+Home and you'll find yourself safe and sound back in cell A1 of the first sheet. To quickly jump to cell A1 of the *current* sheet, just press Home.

### When the arrow keys don't work

If the arrow keys spit out numbers after your press them, just press the key labeled NumLock. Most keyboards have a little light that tells you the status of the NumLock key (either on or off). If your NumLock light is on, the numeric keypad produces numbers. If the NumLock light is off, the numeric keypad produces cursor movements. It's as easy as that.

### Really advanced secret stuff

If, for some unknown reason, you need to move the cell pointer to some off-the-wall cell address such as R:FE459, you can bang away on the cursor control keys all day and still not find your way there. Or you can use a shortcut: Press the F5 key on your keyboard (found either in a row along the top or in a separate section along the left side). 1-2-3 for Windows displays a Go To dialog box. Simply type **R:FE459** (or whatever obscure cell address you want to get to) and select OK. Voila! You're there. This shortcut is magic, and nobody else knows about it. Let's keep it our little secret, OK?

### Summary of movement options

After you first start out with 1-2-3 for Windows, you may have trouble remembering all the specific navigational options. Fortunately for you, I have put together a handy summary of keyboard movements in Table 4-2. You'll eventually discover the keyboard movements you enjoy using, or you may decide to use them all, depending on what you're doing.

| Table 4-2 | Navigational Options | |
|---|---|---|
| *Movement* | *Keyboard* | *Mouse* |
| One cell up | Up arrow | Click the cell |
| One cell down | Down arrow | Click the cell |
| One cell left | Left arrow | Click the cell |
| One cell right | Right arrow | Click the cell |
| One screen down | PgDn | Click bottom of vertical scroll bar |
| One screen up | PgUp | Click top of vertical scroll bar |
| One screen left | Shift+Tab or Ctrl+left arrow | Click left of horizontal scroll bar |
| One screen right | Tab or Ctrl+right arrow | Click right of horizontal scroll bar |
| Next sheet | Ctrl+PgUp | Click sheet tab |
| Preceding sheet | Ctrl+PgDn | Click sheet tab |
| Move a long distance | F5, then enter address | Drag scroll-bar button |

# What to Do with a Blank Worksheet

You've covered a great deal of ground so far: you're vaguely familiar with the parts of a worksheet, and you even know how to move the cell pointer to any cell in the worksheet. A lot of good that does on an empty worksheet, right? Your boss is going to want *information* in the cells of your worksheet. The next section details how the information goes into those cells.

## *Worksheet modes*

If you're really observant, you may have noticed the little word in the bottom right corner of your screen (in the status bar) that reads READY. This is the mode indicator: Until now, 1-2-3 for Windows has been in READY mode, which means that the program is ready for you to perform a task, such as move to another cell (which you already know how to do) or put information into a cell (which you're about to learn).

## *What goes in a cell?*

A worksheet cell can hold the following four types of information:

- ✓ **A number** (also known as a value). You won't have to stray any further than this chapter to learn how to enter numbers.

- ✓ **A label** (which you may recognize as normal words). You also learn how to enter labels in this chapter.

- ✓ **A formula** (which does miraculous things using the contents of other cells). You learn about formulas in Chapter 7.

- ✓ **Nothing** (zip, nada, zilch, nil). Cells can be completely empty, void of all content (like some of the chapters in this book).

A cell can hold only one of these four items at a time. But if it holds a formula, it will *look* like it has either a number or a label because a formula displays its answer, not the formula itself.

The preceding list of cell contents applies only to worksheet *cells*. As you learn later, a worksheet also can hold graphs, pictures, and drawings. But these items aren't *in* cells; they kind of "float" on top of cells and can be moved around and resized independently of the cells.

## *More about what goes in a cell*

So why the distinction between numbers and labels? When do you need numbers, and when do you need labels? And do you really need formulas? And does the refrigerator light really go out when you close the door?

You use numbers when you work with a subject that uses quantities or a values. If you make a worksheet to keep track of your gambling losses, for example, you might enter a number for the amount you lost on each bet. A nice fact about numbers is that you can refer to them in your formulas. For example, you can enter a formula that adds up a bunch of numbers and displays the total in a separate cell (but for your gambling loss worksheet, you may not *want* to know the total damage).

Labels, on the other hand, are more useful for describing what the numbers are and for adding titles to your work. In your gambling loss worksheet, you can put the following labels next to your numbers: Reno blackjack table, Santa Anita Racetrack, and so on. You also can use words just to make a simple list without getting any numbers involved.

Leave cells blank (or empty) when you don't have anything to put in them or when you want to have some space between cells that have information in them. By default, all cells are blank.

Figure 4-4 shows a worksheet with numbers, labels, formulas, and blank cells. Notice that you can't see the formulas, just the results of the formula. Actually, if the formula is in the active cell, the formula appears in the edit line at the top of the screen.

Words or labels

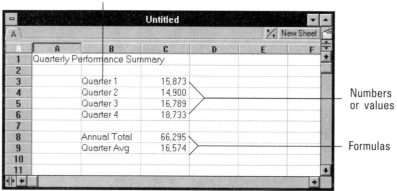

**Figure 4-4:**
A worksheet, showing examples of numbers, labels, formula results, and (yes) even blank cells.

Numbers or values

Formulas

# Typing in a number

Throughout the recent course of history, spreadsheets have acquired a reputation for being good to use with numbers. Therefore, it's only fitting that you get your feet wet by learning how to enter a number into a cell.

Before you put anything into a cell, make sure that you're in READY mode. If not, press Esc once or twice to get into this mode.

When you're ready to enter a number (and 1-2-3 for Windows is READY too), you have the following two choices for entering the numbers into the cells:

✔ You can use the number keys along the top of your keyboard (not the keys with Fs on them, but the keys with punctuation characters above the numbers).

✔ If your NumLock light is on, you can use the keys on the numeric keypad to input numbers.

Ready? Try entering some data into your spreadsheet by doing the following steps:

1. **Move to a cell — use cell B3 just for fun.**

2. **Type** 236 **or a number of your choice (but don't press Enter).**

   Notice that you're now in VALUE mode. After you type the first number, 1-2-3 for Windows reads your mind and realizes that you are entering a number (or value) into a cell.

3. **Press the Enter key to make the number stick in the cell.**

   Take a peek at the mode indicator — you're back in READY mode.

   When you press Enter after typing in a number, the cell pointer stays on the same cell.

4. **Use the down-arrow key to move to the cell below (cell B4) and type another number, such as** 314.

5. **Press Enter to record the number in the cell.**

   Repeat this procedure until you get the hang of it. Your numbers can have any number of digits (but 1-2-3 for Windows will display them oddly if they're too large). Remember, you can use any of the techniques you already know to move to any cell in the worksheet before entering a number into it.

You may not realize it, but you've come a long way. You now have enough knowledge to fill the entire worksheet with numbers. (But don't try it; it gets boring real fast.)

## Making numbers look right

After you start entering numbers into cells, you may not be happy with how the numbers look. If you have a real long number, 1-2-3 for Windows displays it using scientific notation. You might want other numbers to show up with commas in them. Or you might want all numbers to display with two digits to the right of the decimal point. And accountants usually like to see dollar signs tacked on to their numbers. And what if you work with percentages? The answer, my friend, is formatting.

### What is formatting?

Figure 4-5 shows some numbers. The numbers in the first column are plain old numbers, and the numbers in the second column are formatted. Which numbers do you like better?

| | Plain Numbers | Formatted Numbers | Numeric Format Used | | | |
|---|---|---|---|---|---|---|
| 1 | | | | | | |
| 2 | 123.45 | $123.45 | Currency | | | |
| 3 | 7873623 | 7,873,623 | Comma | | | |
| 4 | 0.128 | 12.80% | Percent | | | |
| 5 | 61287363123334 | 6.129E+13 | Scientific | | | |
| 6 | 34161 | 11-Jul-93 | Date | | | |
| 7 | 34161.58 | 01:55 PM | Time | | | |

**Figure 4-5:** The difference between plain and formatted numbers.

Formatting affects only how the numbers look; formatting does *not* change the actual number in any way. In Figure 4-5, the cells in each row hold exactly the same number. The only difference in the numbers is the way they look (one is formatted and the other is not).

### How to format numbers

Most of the time, you format numbers to make them look the way you want. You can format numbers by doing the following:

1. **First, move the cell pointer to the cell that has the number you want to format.**

   You also can select a range of cells by clicking and dragging.

2. **Select the Style⇨Number Format command.**

   1-2-3 for Windows displays the dialog box in Figure 4-6 that lists a bunch of names for numeric formats. You can also get to this dialog box by right-clicking after selecting the cell or range, and then selecting Number Format from the shortcut menu.

**Figure 4-6:** From the Number Format dialog box, you can select the numeric format you want.

**Number Format**

Format:
Times
Fixed
Scientific
, Comma
General
+/-
Percent

Decimal places: 2

OK
Cancel
Reset
Parens

☒ Show in status bar

Range: B3

Sample

3. **Scroll through this list until you find a format that looks appropriate**.

   Watch the Sample box to see what your number looks like. For most numeric formats, you also can indicate how many decimal places to use.

4. **Select OK, and the number's appearance changes.**

   After you format a number, you're not stuck with it. You can keep applying different numeric formats until you get the one you like.

You can even format empty cells. Then, if you ever decide to put a number in the cell, the number appears in the format that you gave it when the cell was empty.

You may find it easier to use the status bar to format numbers. The default numeric format is Automatic, which appears to the left on the status bar. Start by selecting a cell or range, and then click Automatic in the status bar. A list of numeric formats pops up, as in Figure 4-7. Click the name of the format you want. You can control the number of decimal places by clicking the button directly to the right of the numeric format button on the status bar. The only disadvantage to this method is that you don't see a sample, but it is a much faster way of formatting numbers.

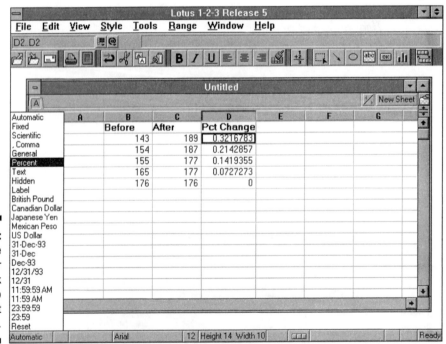

**Figure 4-7:** Using the status bar is a quick way to format numbers.

# Entering labels

Spreadsheets are boring enough as they are, but just think how much worse it could be if they held only numbers. As you already know, 1-2-3 for Windows can cope with words (known as labels) as well as with numbers. The steps for entering a label into a cell are similar to the steps for entering a number. To enter a word into a cell, do the following:

1. **Move to the cell you want and type a word or letters.**

   1-2-3 for Windows reads your mind and changes the mode indicator to LABEL.

2. **Press Enter.**

   A label can consist of more than one word, so you can use the spacebar as you normally would.

### More useless terminology

What do you call the non-numeric information that you enter into a cell? The 1-2-3 for Windows manual refers to non-numeric cell entries as *labels*. Some people call it *text*. Others call it *words*. You may catch me using the term *string*. The bottom line? It doesn't matter what you call it.

### What if the words don't fit?

Sometimes you want to put more than nine characters of text into a cell without adjusting the column width. The following procedure shows you what happens on-screen when you enter a long label:

1. **Move the cell pointer to any cell in a row that's completely empty.**

2. **Type the following:** Bills I Need to Pay This Month

   This text appears to spill over into the cells to the right of the active cell. Actually, the text is contained all in the one cell. Because the cells next door are empty, 1-2-3 for Windows simply borrows their space to display the spillover from the active cell.

3. **In cell B3, type a number, such as** 198.

4. **Move the cell pointer one column to the left (to cell A3) and type** Car Payment Amount **into this cell.**

   Because cell B3 is occupado, 1-2-3 for Windows can't borrow its space to display the spillover from cell A3. Therefore the program appears to shorten its display for this cell. Don't worry, all the text is still in there — it just doesn't show up on the screen.

When you start with a new worksheet, the columns are wide enough to display about nine characters (more or less, depending on the size of the font you use). The solution to the "failure to spill over problem" is to make the entire column A wider. (You can do this with the Style⇨Column width command.)

## Aligning labels and numbers

Normally, when you enter a label into a cell, 1-2-3 for Windows aligns it to the left in the cell. When you enter a number, the program aligns it to the right in the cell. You're not stuck with this alignment, however. You easily can change how numbers and labels are aligned within cells. Figure 4-8 illustrates several alignment choices you can make with labels and numbers by using 1-2-3 for Windows.

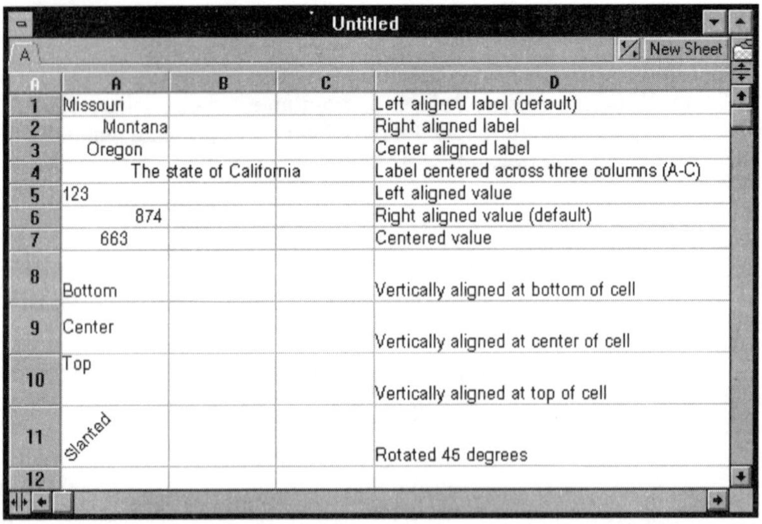

| | A | B | C | D |
|---|---|---|---|---|
| 1 | Missouri | | | Left aligned label (default) |
| 2 | Montana | | | Right aligned label |
| 3 | Oregon | | | Center aligned label |
| 4 | The state of California | | | Label centered across three columns (A-C) |
| 5 | 123 | | | Left aligned value |
| 6 | 874 | | | Right aligned value (default) |
| 7 | 663 | | | Centered value |
| 8 | Bottom | | | Vertically aligned at bottom of cell |
| 9 | Center | | | Vertically aligned at center of cell |
| 10 | Top | | | Vertically aligned at top of cell |
| 11 | Slanted | | | Rotated 45 degrees |
| 12 | | | | |

**Figure 4-8:** Different types of alignment for labels and numbers.

The easiest way to change the alignment is to use the SmartIcons designed expressly for this purpose. These icons are shown in Figure 4-9. Start by selecting the cells you want to align. Then click one of these icons.

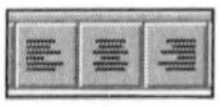

**Figure 4-9:** These SmartIcons change alignment.

After you enter a label, 1-2-3 for Windows adds a new character, which you can see only when you're in EDIT mode, to the beginning of the text. This initial character, called a *label prefix,* is a single quotation mark ', which automatically makes the contents of the cell left-aligned, the default. Actually, you can put your own label prefix at the beginning of a label to change how it's aligned. Table 4-3 is a list of the label prefixes that you can use. (By the way, you definitely can forget the term *label prefix* as soon as you finish with this chapter.)

| Table 4-3 | Label Prefixes and What They Do | |
|---|---|---|
| *Label Prefix* | *English Translation* | *How the Label Is Displayed* |
| ' | Single quote | Left aligned in the cell |
| " | Double quote | Right aligned in the cell |
| ^ | Caret | Centered in the cell |

## When Enter isn't good enough

Up until now, you've probably been using Enter to signal the end of your numbers and labels. Actually, you also can use any of the arrow keys in place of Enter. Using the arrow keys has a dual effect: the label or numbers stick in the cell, and the cell pointer moves in the direction of the arrow key. Over the past 10 years, this technique has saved me a cumulative total of 3 minutes and 18 seconds.

# Changing Things You've Done

The time will come when you realize that you have entered something incorrectly into a cell. (Although this has never happened to me personally, I have heard stories about people making such mistakes.)

Suppose that you have typed the following label into a cell: **An Analisys of 1994 Investments.** Your boss, a former grade school spelling bee runner-up, points out the misspelled word. To soothe any ruffled feathers, you have the following two choices (three, if you include taking spelling lessons from your boss):

 ✔ Move the cell pointer back to the offensive cell and re-enter the entire label.

 ✔ Edit the cell.

For all you major-league bad spellers out there, 1-2-3 for Windows has a built-in spelling checker, which you can invoke with the Tools⇨Spell Check command. But don't rely on this program too much. Like all computerized spelling checkers, it can't tell you whether a properly spelled word is used incorrectly in a sentence. For example, the spelling checker doesn't warn you if you enter **United Snakes of America** into a cell, because *snakes* is a legitimate word.

## Overwriting a cell

To replace the information that is already contained in a cell, do the following:

1. **Move the cell pointer to the cell that contains the information you want replaced.**

2. **Type in the new information.**

3. **Press Enter.**

   The old stuff is replaced by the new stuff. You can replace a number with a number, a label with a number, a number with a label, and so on.

## Editing a cell

If you need to make only a minor change to a cell, you can save a few seconds by *editing* the cell rather than reentering the information. Use the following steps:

1. **Move the cell pointer to the cell you want to change.**

2. **Press the F2 key.**

   The contents of the cell also appear up on the edit line, but the editing occurs within the cell itself. Notice that the mode indicator reads EDIT, a sure sign that you are, in fact, editing a cell.

3. **Type new characters, delete unwanted characters, or replace existing characters to make the cell correct. Use the editing keys (described below) to do this.**

   The flashing vertical bar thing-a-ma-jig that indicates where you are in the cell you're editing is known by the provocative term *insertion point.* (After you finish with this chapter, you can safely forget the official name for this item.)

4. **Press Enter.**

If you prefer, you can do your cell editing in the edit line. But you need a mouse to activate it. Start by pressing F2 to edit the cell (or double-click it with your mouse). Then move the mouse pointer up to the edit line and make your corrections. End with Enter (or click the Confirm button).

### The editing keys

While you're in Edit mode, a few keys come in mighty handy to speed up the editing process. If you're interested, check out Table 4-4. If not, you'll waste lots of time re-entering data.

| Table 4-4 | Handy Keys to Use while Editing a Cell |
|---|---|
| **Key** | **What It Does** |
| Backspace | Erases the character to the left of the insertion point |
| Left arrow | Moves the insertion point by one character to the left (and doesn't erase anything) |
| Right arrow | Moves the insertion point by one character to the right (and doesn't erase anything) |
| Delete | Erases the character to the right of the insertion point |
| Esc | Leaves the cell just as it was before you started this escapade (Press Esc if you screw up royally and want to start over) |

Use these keys to move around on the edit line, to erase unwanted characters, and to insert new characters. When the edit line looks right, just press Enter (or any of the arrow keys).

### Insert or overwrite?

When you edit a cell, inserting new characters causes the current contents to shift to the right. But you can change this process by pressing the INS key while you edit. The characters that you type now *overwrite* (or replace) those that get in the way. When you are in the overwrite mode, 1-2-3 for Windows substitutes the vertical bar insertion point for a solid color that fills the entire character to be overwritten.

Why would you ever want to be in overwrite mode? It is a minor time-saver, because it prevents you from having to erase a character and then type a new one. In overwrite mode, you can add a good character and get rid of a bad one with a single keystroke.

## Nuking a cell completely

You know how to change the contents of a cell, but what if you want to wipe it completely off the face of the earth and convert it to a blank cell? Easy! Move the cell pointer to the undesired cell, press Delete, and kiss it good-bye. Any formatting that you applied to the cell remains there — only the cell's contents go away.

Another way to delete a cell's contents is to use the Edit⇨Clear command. This method is a bit more versatile, because it gives you the option (by popping up a small dialog box) of clearing out only the cell's contents, only the cell's formatting (styles), or both of these. In other words, if you want to return a cell to its normal state, use Edit⇨Clear and select the Both option.

Never erase a cell by pressing the spacebar. Although this technique appears to get rid of the cell contents, it actually inserts an invisible space character (preceded by an apostrophe) into the cell. This invisible character can cause serious problems for the spreadsheet that are very difficult to diagnose. Take my word for it — pressing the spacebar to erase a cell is a no-no.

# If You Are Salivating for More

For all intents and purposes, you can consider this chapter over. But I did stay up late one night to write some additional bagatelle for those who just can't get enough. I hope you appreciate this sacrifice, because I missed the monster truck rally on ESPN for this.

## Changing the defaults

When you start a new worksheet, 1-2-3 for Windows makes some assumptions, known as *defaults,* about how you want the information to look. For example, it normally makes all columns 9 characters wide, makes labels left aligned, and uses "Automatic" formatting for numbers. You can change the defaults for a worksheet. For example, if you want all of your numbers to have dollar signs, you can change the default number format to "Currency." Then, whenever you enter a number it will show up with a dollar sign. You change the worksheet defaults by using the Style⇨Worksheet Defaults command. The resulting dialog box is shown in Figure 4-10.

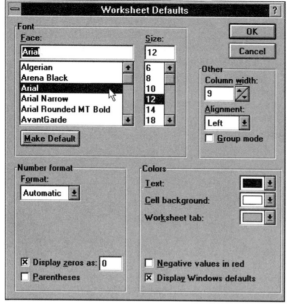

**Figure 4-10:**
The
Worksheet
Defaults
dialog box
lets you
change the
default
settings for
1-2-3 for
Windows.

Table 4-5 defines the default options that are available to you in 1-2-3 for Windows.

| Table 4-5 | The 1-2-3 for Windows Default Options |
|---|---|
| *Option* | *What It Means* |
| Face | The font that is used |
| Size | The size of the type |
| Number format | How numbers normally appear |
| Decimals | The number of decimal places for numbers |
| Display zeros as | How zeros look (can be displayed as blanks) |
| Parentheses | Whether to use parentheses for negative numbers |
| Column width | The normal column width (9) |
| Alignment | How labels are aligned |
| Group mode | Whether you are in group mode (a mode that lets you format all sheets at once) |
| Colors | Colors for text, cell background, and whether to display negative numbers in red |

The changes you make affect only the current file (not other files that you may be working with). However, any changes that you make to the formatting of *individual* cells and ranges remain intact in that particular cell or range. In other words, individual formatting that you do for cells or ranges always overrides the default settings for the entire worksheet.

# Chapter 5
# Let's Have a Look at the Menu and Have a Dialog

*"It is a fine thing to command, even if it be only a herd of cattle."*

Miguel de Cervantes (1547 – 1616)
Spanish novelist, dramatist, poet

. . . . . . . . . . . . . . . . . . . . . . . . . . . . . . . . . . . . . . . . . . . . . . . .

## In This Chapter

▶ Learning useful information about the 1-2-3 for Windows menu system

▶ Giving commands to make 1-2-3 for Windows do what you want

▶ Exploring what some of the more useful menu items do

▶ Learning about dialog boxes and how to use them efficiently

. . . . . . . . . . . . . . . . . . . . . . . . . . . . . . . . . . . . . . . . . . . . . . . .

Knowing how to put numbers and labels into cells is important, and you learned about that in the preceding chapter. But to do really useful tasks with 1-2-3 for Windows, you need to be familiar with its menu system. Using the menu system is one way to issue commands that tell the program what you want it to do. Most computer programs (and *all* Windows programs) have menus.

Unless you aspire to be a 1-2-3 for Windows instructor (or a spreadsheet book author), there's no reason to learn all the program's commands. But it is a good idea to know where to go to find an unfamiliar command, so a general under-standing of the menu system is definitely in your best interest. 1-2-3 for Win-dows — like most other Windows programs — displays dialog boxes when you issue some commands. Dialog boxes are what you use to give 1-2-3 for Windows more specific instructions about what you want it to do. This chapter explains everything you need to know about menus and dialog boxes.

After you learn how to use the menus and dialog boxes in 1-2-3 for Windows, you can apply most of this hard-earned knowledge to other Windows programs that you want to learn — they all work in much the same way.

# 1-2-3 for Windows: At Your Command

You can give orders to 1-2-3 for Windows by using any of the following methods:

✔ The menu system

✔ Dialog boxes that are displayed by some commands

✔ The seemingly endless supply of SmartIcons

✔ Shortcut-key combinations

✔ Function keys

✔ Inserting formulas into cells

✔ Running macros

In this chapter, you focus on menus and dialog boxes. SmartIcons, shortcut keys, and function keys are covered in Chapter 16. Working with formulas is the topic of Chapter 7, and I briefly cover macros in Chapter 20.

# Two Types of Menu Systems

1-2-3 for Windows has two menu systems: the *main menu* is always visible, and the *quick menu* is hidden but comes to life when you need it.

## The main menu

When you're running 1-2-3 for Windows, the main menu bar is always available at the top of the screen. The menu bar consists of a series of menu items. To refresh your memory, take a look at Figure 5-1.

As you may know, after you select a menu item, such as File, Edit, and so on, the menu drops down a list of commands.

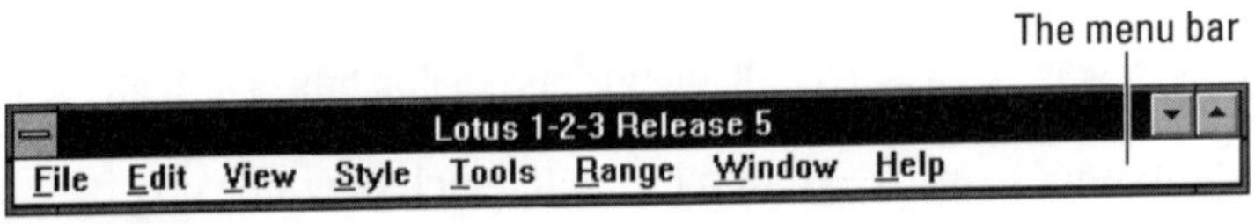

**Figure 5-1:**
The main menu bar is located directly under the application's title bar.

The menu bar

| Lotus 1-2-3 Release 5 | ▼ ▲ |

File   Edit   View   Style   Tools   Range   Window   Help

The actual menu items that are displayed at the top of your screen may vary slightly from what you see in Figure 5-1, depending on what type of information you have selected in your worksheet. For example, if you're working with a chart, the menu items are different from those that appear when you're doing normal spreadsheet work. (In this case, the Range menu item is replaced with the Chart menu item.) Just remember that 1-2-3 for Windows always displays a menu system that's appropriate for what you're doing at the time.

## Quick menus

The second type of menu, called a *quick menu,* isn't visible until you press the right mouse button after you've selected an item (such as a cell, a range, or a chart). A quick menu pops up wherever the mouse pointer is, making it very convenient to select a command from the list. The actual commands on the quick menu vary, depending on what you have clicked. The quick menu contains the most common commands that you can execute with the selection you have made. (It's almost as if 1-2-3 for Windows can read your mind — but it can't, so don't worry.)

Figure 5-2 shows a quick menu that appears when you right-click after selecting a range of cells.

The only way to access a quick menu is by right-clicking the mouse button. If you don't have a mouse, you have to live without quick menus.

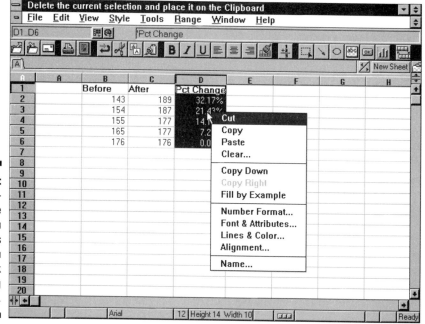

**Figure 5-2:** A context-sensitive quick menu appears when you right-click after making a selection.

# The 1-2-3 Classic menu

First there were classic cars; then there was Coke Classic; now you have the 1-2-3 Classic menu! This menu is for people who have learned an old DOS version of 1-2-3 and are moving up to the vastly improved Windows version. The Classic menu, as shown in the accompanying figure, appears after you press the slash key (/) in READY mode. An auxiliary 1-2-3 Classic menu (the WYSIWYG menu), used for formatting cells, appears after you press the colon key (:).

If you're moving up from an older version of 1-2-3, you might find the Classic menu useful if you can't

remember the actual 1-2-3 for Windows command. Use it if you must, but I strongly urge you not to get too dependent on it.

My advice? Forget that this menu exists. Compared to the normal 1-2-3 for Windows menu, the Classic menu is illogical, confusing, difficult to use, and it can't even deal with a mouse. I've discussed the Classic menu here, because if you accidentally hit the slash key and see the menu, you at least know what it is. You easily can get rid of it by pressing Esc.

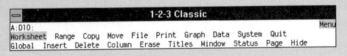

# *Using Menus*

In 1-2-3 for Windows, you first make a selection in the worksheet and then issue a menu command that adjusts the selection. The command often brings up a dialog box that enables you to define clearly what you want to do. (Dialog boxes are explained later in this chapter.)

A selection can include any of the following items:

- A single cell
- A range of cells
- A complete chart
- A part of a chart
- An object on a worksheet (a line, a rectangle, a text box, and so on)
- The results of a query on a database

Suppose that you want to change the size of the text in a range of cells. First select the cells by clicking and dragging the mouse over them. Then issue the Style⇨Font & Attributes command. This command brings up a dialog box so you can you adjust the components that you are interested in (in this case, the size of the text). After you close the dialog box (with the OK button), you see the changes made in the selected cells.

In most cases, you can use the quick menu to accomplish the task faster. For example, after you select a range of cells, right-click to bring up the quick menu, which also has the Font & Attributes command on it. Right-clicking is faster than moving the mouse up to the main menu and then clicking the Style menu.

## With a mouse

To access a menu item with your mouse, simply click it. The menu drops down to display its commands. Then click the command you need.

After you select an item, you can access the quick menu by right-clicking the mouse button to display a list of relevant commands. Not all commands show up on the quick menu, however. If the command you want isn't there, you have to use the normal menu system (or a SmartIcon, if one exists).

## With the keyboard

If you prefer, you also can access the main menu by using the keyboard (but quick menus require a mouse). The easiest way to select a menu item is to use a key combination that combines the Alt key with the underlined letter in the menu item (called a *hot key*).

For example, to access the View menu from the keyboard, press Alt+V (because the V in View is underlined, it is called the *hot key*). The View commands drop down, just as if you clicked View with the mouse. Then you simply press another letter that corresponds to the underlined letter of the command that you want (no need to keep holding down the Alt key, but it doesn't hurt). Notice that the hot key isn't always the *first* letter in the command.

Suppose that you want to change the alignment of a range of cells by using the Style⇨Alignment command. First select the cells you want to align and then press Alt+S, A. The Alignment dialog box appears. After you make your choices in the dialog box and close it, you can see the effect of the changes on your selected cells. As you see later, you can use the keyboard in dialog boxes, too.

Another way to access the menu with the keyboard is to press the Alt key by itself, which activates the menu bar but does not select a menu item. After the menu bar is activated, you can use the arrow keys to move among the menu items. After you get to the menu item you want, press Enter or down arrow. You then can use the arrow keys to move to the command you want and press Enter to execute the command.

## Another type of menu

As you work with Windows programs, you encounter yet another menu, the Control menu. Every Windows program (including 1-2-3 for Windows) has a Control menu that is used to control various applications of the program. You access the Control menu by clicking the control button in the upper left corner of an application's title bar. It's the square button that has a short horizontal line through it.

The Control menu, as shown in the accompanying figure, lets you do such things as minimize the window (make it an icon), maximize the window (make it fill the screen), close the application, or switch to another application that's already running.

The windows within an application usually have their own Control menus as well. Because every

1-2-3 for Windows worksheet is actually a separate window, each worksheet (window) has its own Control menu.

If you want to know more about this stuff (or more about the wonderful world of Microsoft Windows), I suggest getting a copy of *Windows For Dummies*.

# *More about Menus*

Before I discuss what you can do with menus, you need to know the following characteristics. Refer to Figure 5-3 to get your bearings.

- ✔ As you move through the menu selections and their commands, 1-2-3 for Windows displays a brief description of the items in the title bar. This description is a reminder to you.

- ✔ If you press F1 while working in a menu, 1-2-3 for Windows displays on-line help that tells you about the menu item or the command.

- ✔ When a command on a menu isn't appropriate for what you're doing, 1-2-3 for Windows *dims* the command (lightens the color). You can still see the command, but you cannot select it.

- ✔ Menu commands that are followed by three dots (an *ellipsis*) display a dialog box after you select the command.

- ✔ Menu commands that have a shortcut key display the shortcut key combination on the pull-down menu. For example, the Cut command on the Edit menu displays Ctrl+X on the right side of the menu; therefore, pressing Ctrl+X accomplishes the same thing as selecting the Edit⇨Cut command.

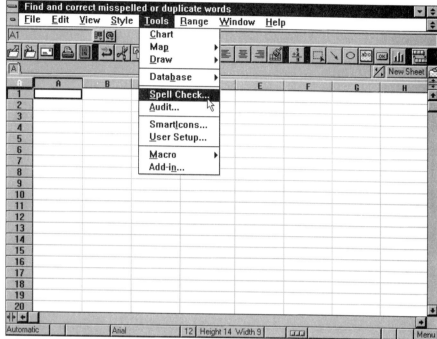

**Figure 5-3:**
A typical
menu, pulled
down to
show its
commands.

✔ Some commands are followed by a small right-pointing arrow. These commands, after being selected, display yet another list of commands. This secondary command list is known as a *cascading menu,* but you can call it a *whatchamadoojie* and it still has the same effect.

✔ The horizontal lines in the pull-down menus simply group the commands into logical groups; they have no great significance.

Now that you have a decent background in the 1-2-3 for Windows menus, it's time to see just what you can do with them.

# What the Menus Are Good For

The 1-2-3 for Windows menu system is very organized and complete. In fact, it's one of the best menus I've seen in *any* program (and I've see lots of them). Hopefully, you'll find the menus easy to work with. You'll learn the specifics of the menus in other parts of this book. But if you'd like a general overview of what you'll find under each menu item, you'll find it right here.

## The File menu

The File menu deals with (you guessed it) files. Here you find the commands that save your work to a disk file or load worksheet files from a disk. Odd as it may seem, the File menu also has the commands to print and preview your work.

Putting the print commands under the File menu is not a quirk of 1-2-3 for Windows. For some reason, this is standard practice for virtually all Windows programs. So when it comes time to put your work on paper, don't waste time looking for a print menu — head straight for the File menu. Think of the printing function as printing a file, not a worksheet.

One of the neat things about the File menu is that it displays a list of the files you've worked on recently. If you see the filename you want to open listed at the bottom of the File menu commands, you can just click it to open it. This is must faster than using the File⇨Open command.

## The Edit menu

If you want to rearrange your worksheet, chances are you'll find the commands you need in the Edit menu. The Edit menu has what you need to copy cells and ranges, move cells and ranges (using Cut and Paste), insert and delete rows and columns, and lots of other functions.

You can even search for text in your worksheet and automatically replace it with something else. The Edit menu also houses the all-important Undo command (which can reverse the effects of most anything you do in 1-2-3 for Windows).

## The View menu

True to its name, you can use the commands in the View menu to specify how you look at (or view) your worksheet. You find commands that let you zoom in for a close-up look or zoom out to get a bird's-eye view. You can split your worksheet window so that you can see two different parts at once, and you can drastically change how your screen looks. (For example, you can get rid of the grid lines.)

## The Style menu

The Style menu has what you need to add style and pizzazz to your work. When you want to make your work presentable, you certainly want to head for the Style menu. Because many of these commands also have SmartIcons, however, you may not spend too much time in this menu.

# The Tools menu

If TV's Tim (the Toolman) Taylor used 1-2-3 for Windows, he'd probably spend most of his time with this menu. The Tools menu has lots of commands on it, including such special tools as charting commands, mapping commands, drawing commands, database commands, spelling checker, SmartIcon management, and macros.

# The Range menu

The Range menu item doesn't appear if you have selected a chart or the results of a database query. It's available only when you select a cell or range in your worksheet.

The Range menu lets you work with ranges of cells. You do not copy or move the ranges in the Range menu. (That's the function of the Edit menu.) Instead, the Range menu lets you fill a range with data, sort a range, give meaningful names to a range, and do lots of advanced analytical stuff with the data in a range.

# The Chart menu

The Chart menu item appears only when you have a chart selected. The Chart menu replaces the normal Range menu at this time.

Use the Chart menu when you want to modify a chart that you've created. SmartIcons exist for many of these commands.

# The Query menu

The Query menu item appears only after you select the results of a database query. The Query menu then replaces the normal Range menu.

If you plan to use 1-2-3 for Windows to work with databases, you'll become very familiar with the Query menu. It lets you manipulate the fields and records in a database and pick out the data that meet your criteria.

# The Window menu

You won't have much use for the Window menu commands unless you work with more than one file at a time. These commands let you arrange the windows neatly on-screen or jump to a worksheet in another open file.

## The Help menu

Everyone needs a little help now and then when working with a computer program, and the Help menu is the place to go when you find yourself in that predicament. The Help commands let you access the 1-2-3 for Windows very comprehensive on-line help system. You also can find out which version of the program you're using (Help⇨About 1-2-3), and you even can start an interactive tutorial lesson to help you learn more about specific topics.

Pressing F1 also gives you on-line help. Most of the time, the help that appears is relevant to what you're currently doing (known in the trade as *context-sensitive help*). Try it; you'll like it.

# A Meaningful Dialog

Menu commands tell 1-2-3 for Windows what you want to do. But dialog boxes go a step further and let you tell the program exactly what you want to do. All menu commands that end with an ellipsis lead to a dialog box. A dialog box is, essentially, a convenient way for you to make your wishes known to the program.

To understand how a dialog box works, picture yourself in your favorite restaurant: after you arrive, you look at the menu and give your order to the waiter. The waiter looks down at you and asks you to choose between soup or salad, baked potatoes or French fries, and coffee or tea. Using a dialog box is like responding to the waiter's questions. In other words, you use a dialog box to clarify your order to 1-2-3 for Windows. And a benefit of using the dialog box is that you don't have to leave a tip for 1-2-3 for Windows.

Because dialog boxes appear in almost every Windows application, you need to understand these animals as best as you can. The dialog boxes you encounter in 1-2-3 for Windows have a similar look and feel. After you learn a few dialog box techniques, you'll feel fairly comfortable with just about any dialog box that the program throws your way. Figure 5-4 shows a typical dialog box, the one that appears after you select the File⇨Print Preview command.

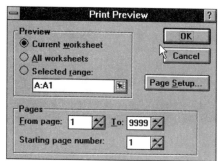

**Figure 5-4:**
A typical
dialog box.

# The anatomy of a dialog box

All dialog boxes in 1-2-3 for Windows have the following characteristics in common. Use Figure 5-4 to locate and visualize these characteristics:

✔ **A title bar at the top.** The title bar tells you the name of the dialog box (which is usually the command that you selected to get there).

✔ **A question mark in the upper right corner.** If you click the question mark, you get some on-line help that tells you how to use this particular dialog box.

✔ **A control button in the upper left corner.** The control button lets you move the dialog box around if you don't have a mouse (useful if the dialog box is hiding something that you want to see). To activate the Control menu, click it or press Alt+spacebar.

✔ **An OK button.** Click OK after you're finished using the dialog box and you want 1-2-3 for Windows to carry out your orders.

✔ **A Cancel button.** Click the Cancel button if you find yourself in a dialog box that you didn't want to get into. Even if you've made changes in the dialog box, clicking the Cancel button eliminates all the changes just as if you never opened the dialog box in the first place.

✔ **One or more controls.** You use dialog box controls to indicate your choices. I discuss these controls in the next section.

Occasionally, a dialog box pops up and covers up what you want to see on-screen. You can move the dialog box by clicking and dragging its title bar. If you don't have a mouse attached, press Alt+spacebar (to access the dialog box's Control menu) and select Move from the menu. Then use the arrow keys to move the dialog box out of the way. Press Enter after you're finished.

## *Dialog box controls*

Items that you manipulate in a dialog box are called *controls*. For example, a button (such as OK or Cancel) is a control. I discuss several other types of dialog box controls in this section. Learning to use these controls efficiently will make your life much easier, so pay attention. If this book had sound effects, this would be the point when bells would be ringing loudly.

### *Buttons*

Dialog box buttons have many functions. The most common dialog box buttons are the OK and Cancel buttons, which I discussed in the preceding list. If the text in the dialog box button is followed by an ellipsis (three dots), clicking this button leads to another dialog box.

Figure 5-5 shows an example of some buttons in a dialog box. Notice that two of the buttons produce another dialog box after you click them.

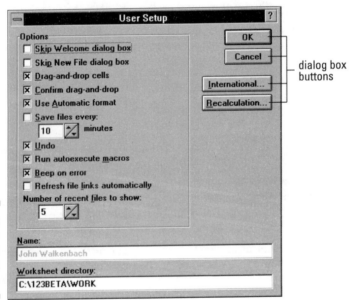

**Figure 5-5:**
An example
of some
dialog box
buttons.

### *Option buttons*

Option buttons are known also as *radio buttons,* because — like an old-fashioned car radio — clicking a button pops the current button out. Option buttons always come in groups from which you choose one (and only one) option from a list of options. After you click one of the options, the option that was previously selected is no longer selected.

Figure 5-6 shows an example of some option buttons in a dialog box.

**Figure 5-6:**
Dialog box option
option buttons
buttons.

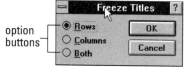

### Check boxes

A check box is either checked or not checked, which means that an option is either selected or not selected — as simple as that (or not). Unlike option buttons, clicking a check box does not affect any other check boxes. You can select more than one check box at a time.

Figure 5-7 shows an example of some check boxes in a dialog box. Notice how all the check boxes are selected — this is going to be one spiffy screen to look at!

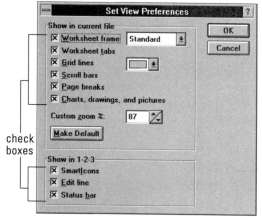

**Figure 5-7:**
An example check
of selected boxes
check
boxes.

## Learning about settings

After you make a selection in the worksheet and issue a command that uses a dialog box, 1-2-3 for Windows displays the current settings in the dialog box. For example, if you select a range of cells that is formatted in bold, the dialog box that pops up after you choose the Style⇨Font & Attributes command has the Bold check box checked. Being able to view the current settings of any selection is a pretty handy feature.

Sometimes the settings in your selected range are not the same for all of the cells in the range. For example, some of the cells in your selection may be bold while others are not. (Remember, you can format each cell separately.) In this case, 1-2-3 for Windows does not check the Bold check box, nor does the program leave it totally blank. Instead, 1-2-3 for Windows fills in the check box with gray shading, which indicates that the selection is mixed for this particular attribute.

### Listboxes

A *listbox* is just what its name suggests, a box with a list of items in it. You can choose only one of the items in each listbox. If the listbox contains a vertical *scroll bar,* the list contains more options than you can see at one time. To see the additional options, click the scroll bar.

Figure 5-8 shows an example of a listbox in a dialog box.

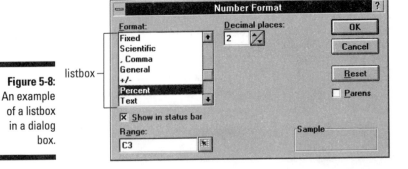

**Figure 5-8:**
An example
of a listbox
in a dialog
box.

A drop-down listbox normally displays only one item in the list. After you activate the control, however, the list drops down to show other items. You then can choose only one item from the list. A drop-down listbox is just a space-efficient way to put a long list into a dialog box.

Figure 5-9 shows an example of some drop-down listboxes in a dialog box.

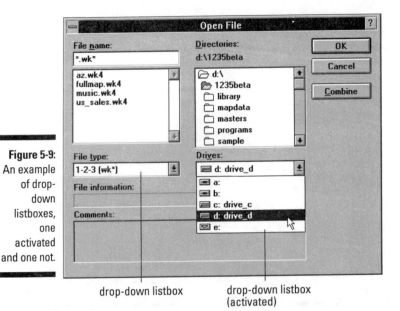

**Figure 5-9:**
An example
of drop-
down
listboxes,
one
activated
and one not.

drop-down listbox          drop-down listbox
                           (activated)

### Range selection boxes

Many of the dialog boxes used by 1-2-3 for Windows have *range selection boxes*. When you select a range before you issue a command, that range appears in the range selection box. You can change the range from the dialog box by clicking the diagonal arrow at the right of the range selection box. Clicking the arrow temporarily hides the dialog box and lets you select another range in the worksheet. If you need to make only a minor change, you also can manually edit the range specification.

Figure 5-10 shows an example of a range selection box.

**Figure 5-10:**
Some
selection
boxes.

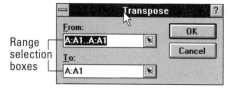

### Number selector boxes

I'm not sure whether number selector box is the official name for this control, but it is pretty descriptive. The *number selector box* lets you change a number by clicking one of the two arrows to advance or decrease the value of the number.

Figure 5-11 shows several examples of number selector boxes.

**Figure 5-11:**
Examples of
number
selector
boxes, a
control that
lets you
select a
number by
clicking an
arrow.

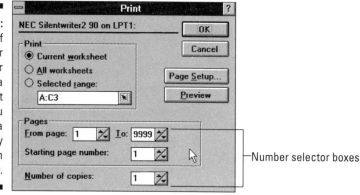

### Text box

The *text box* is simply a white box into which you enter some text. Figure 5-12 shows an example of some text boxes in a dialog box.

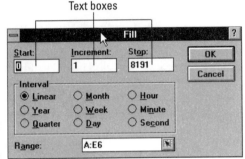

Text boxes

**Figure 5-12:**
An example
of some text
boxes.

### Sample box

The items in a *sample box* show you examples of what you get as you make changes to other controls. You cannot choose or select any items in a sample box — you only can look at the sample.

Figure 5-13 shows an example of a sample box in a dialog box.

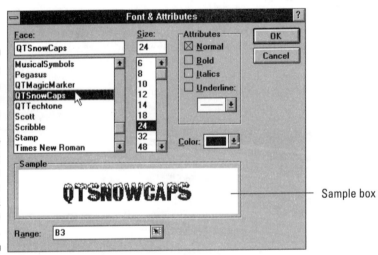

**Figure 5-13:**
An example
of a sample
box. This
one pre-
views how
the text will
look. The
contents are
only to look
at, not to
choose.

Sample box

## Mousing through dialog boxes

Dialog boxes were invented with mouse users in mind, so it's not surprising that most people prefer to use the mouse for most of their dialog box action.

Generally, you click the control that you want in order to activate it. After you have activated the control, you can make your selection — the exact technique varies with the specific control, but the controls do work pretty much as you expect them to work. In other words, the process is very intuitive. To check or uncheck a check box, click it. To select an option in an option button, click it. To select an option from a drop-down listbox, click the arrow and make your choice from the list by clicking. My best advice to you is to start clicking away and see what happens. You'll get the hang of it in no time. But save any work you have started before you go clicking away, just in case your mouse goes rabid!

## If you prefer the keyboard

Although most people like to use the mouse in a dialog box, other people find that the keyboard is actually faster, because they don't have to move their hands from the keyboard. The truth is, working with dialog boxes is more efficient after you get the hang of using the keyboard.

Table 5-1 lists some useful keys and key combinations that are active when you work with a dialog box from the keyboard.

| Table 5-1 | Keyboard Combinations to Use with Dialog Boxes |
|---|---|
| **Key Combination** | **What It Does** |
| Alt+ _hot key_ | Selects the control of the hot key (underlined letter) that you press. |
| Tab | Moves forward and activates the next control. |
| Shift+Tab | Moves backward and activates the preceding control. |
| Spacebar | Checks or unchecks an option button or check box. |
| Alt+up arrow or Alt+down arrow | Opens and closes a drop-down listbox. |
| Arrow keys | Moves within a group of controls (such as option buttons). |
| End | Selects the last item in a drop-down listbox or listbox. |
| Home | Selects the first item in a drop-down listbox or listbox. |
| PgUp or PgDn | Moves to the top or bottom item in the list of items currently visible in a drop-down listbox or listbox and selects the item. |
| Enter | Completes the command and closes the dialog box (just like clicking the OK button). |
| Esc | Closes the dialog box without completing the command (just like clicking the Cancel button). |

I've tried to get across to you in this chapter that understanding how to use menus and dialog boxes is pretty important in learning how to use 1-2-3 for Windows. You spend lots of time using menus and commands — especially dialog boxes. So the sooner you master these features, the better off you'll be. 'Nuff said.

The 5th Wave                    By Rich Tennant

IF BOB DYLAN HAD PURSUED A CAREER IN COMPUTERS.

"PUT HIM IN FRONT OF A TERMINAL AND HE'S A GENIUS, BUT OTHER-
WISE THE GUY IS SUCH A BROODING, GLOOMY GUS HE'LL NEVER
BREAK INTO MANAGEMENT."

# Chapter 6

# How to Keep from Losing Your Work

*"When they said some day you may lose them all, he replied 'Fish fiddle de-dee!'"*

Edward Lear (1812–1888)
*The Pobble Who Has No Toes* (1877)

## In This Chapter

▶ Why computer users lose their work, and how you can prevent such a tragedy from happening

▶ Why you should learn about files, disks, saving worksheets, and related topics

▶ Why you should save frequently and make backup copies of important files

▶ How to save 1-2-3 for Windows files so that other programs can use them

*I*f you work with computers, sooner or later you'll lose some work and be mighty upset. No denying it. Happens to everybody. When you've exhausted your supply of curse words, you simply have to bite the bullet and repeat things you've already done.

There are several things you can do to minimize the heartbreak of data loss. But if you like to live on the edge and don't mind wasting time redoing hours of work that disappeared down the toilet, feel free to skip this chapter.

 This chapter tells you about working with files — things that I think are very important for every computer user to understand. If you want to cut to the chase and simply learn how to do common file operations with 1-2-3 for Windows, skip ahead to the section called *Doing Things With a File — Step By Step*.

# *Protecting Your Work*

Use these two guidelines to avoid data loss when using 1-2-3 for Windows (or any computer program, for that matter):

1. **Save your work to a disk frequently.** I've seen far too many people spend the whole day working on a worksheet without saving it until they're done with it. Most the time, this practice doesn't get you into any trouble. But computers do crash occasionally, and power failures also have been known to occur. Both of these events cause you to lose everything that hasn't been saved, and you have to restart your system. It can ruin your whole day. 1-2-3 for Windows has a useful autosave feature, which I discuss later.

Saving a file takes a few seconds, but re-creating eight hours of lost work takes about eight hours. So, to avoid headache, panic, confusion, fatigue, and general hysteria, save your work often!!

2. **Make a backup copy of all your important files.** Most people who back up their work religiously do so because they've been burned in the past (and you can count me among these folks). Hard disks aren't perfect — one bad byte, if it's a critical byte, can make the entire disk unreadable. If a file has any value to you at all, you should make a copy of it on a floppy disk and keep the disk in a safe place. And don't leave the backup disk next to your computer — if the building burns down during the night, a melted floppy disk doesn't do you much good.

## Is it disk or is it Memorex?

One thing I've noticed over the years is that new computer users often get confused about memory and disks. This isn't surprising, because both of these objects are places you can store data. Here's the difference:

- **Memory:** This is a part of your computer that stores things you are currently working on. It also goes by the name of *RAM* (for *random-access memory*). Computer memory is very fleeting — a flick of the power switch and it's wiped out immediately.

- **Disks:** A disk stores information more or less permanently. Information stored on a disk is in files. If you turn off the power to your PC, the files that you've stored on-disk remain there. Disks come in a variety of sizes, which correspond to how much information they can hold. Your computer has a built-in hard disk (which holds a lot), and also can use removable *floppy disks* (which hold less, and which may or may not actually be floppy).

If you have a lot of programs and data files stored on your hard disk, you may at some time get a disk full message. This means that your hard disk is so full, it can't hold any more information (and this message has nothing to do with the amount of memory in your computer). You must erase files from your hard disk that you no longer need to free up some space. You can do this directly from DOS, or with the Windows File Manager program.

If you don't understand the preceding paragraphs, the remainder of this chapter provides enough information so that you will. And by the way, a lot of the information in this chapter is applicable to other programs as well.

# Using Files with 1-2-3 for Windows

When you start 1-2-3 for Windows, the program is loaded from your hard disk into your computer's memory. It stays on the hard disk and loads a *copy* of itself into memory. Actually, the complete program isn't loaded into memory — only the most important parts are. It leaves enough memory available so that there's room for you to work on your worksheets. As you use 1-2-3 for Windows, it may need other parts of the program. It loads these parts from the hard disk in the background, so you don't even notice what's going on unless you keep an eye on your hard disk light.

## A new worksheet

When you start working on a new worksheet, you're simply storing information in your computer's memory. Therefore, if you turn off your PC, your work is gone to the big PC in the sky. In order to keep your work from being an unpleasant memory, you need to save the worksheet to a file on your hard disk.

## Saving files

The first time you attempt to save a worksheet to disk, you have to tell 1-2-3 for Windows what filename to use. After that, it uses that same filename every time you save the file, unless you specify a new and different filename (using the File⇨Save As command). Every time you save the file, it replaces the file on-disk with the updated information from memory. It's a good idea to save your work at least every fifteen minutes or so. Otherwise, an unexpected power outage or an ungainly co-worker who kicks the plug out of the wall can destroy everything you did since the last time you saved.

There are some simple rules about filenames. First, they can be no longer than eight characters long, with no spaces. Second, they must start with either a letter or a number. And finally, you can't use these characters in a filename: period (.), quotation mark ("), slash (/), backslash (\), brackets ([ ]), colon (:), semicolon (;), vertical bar ( | ), equal sign (=), or comma (,). 1-2-3 for Windows attaches .WK4 as the file extension.

You may want to use the autosave feature in 1-2-3 for Windows. This means that your file will get saved automatically at a time interval that you specify. To turn on the autosave feature, select the Tools⇨User Setup command. In the dialog box that appears, turn on the Save files every option and specify a time interval in minutes. For example, if you choose 12, your file will be saved automatically every 12 minutes. Choose OK to close the dialog box. This is a handy feature for people who tend to get so caught up in their work they forget about important things like saving their work, eating lunch, going to the bathroom, and so on. (Unfortunately, 1-2-3 can't go to the bathroom for you or remind you to eat your lunch — maybe a later version.)

# A Visit to the File Menu

When you're working in 1-2-3 for Windows, everything you do with your files is controlled through the File menu item (somewhat intuitive, eh?). As with all menu items, when you select File from the menu (by clicking File or pressing Alt+F), 1-2-3 for Windows drops down a list that shows more commands, as seen in Figure 6-1. All these options can be somewhat intimidating at first, but they are all rather straightforward after you get used to them.

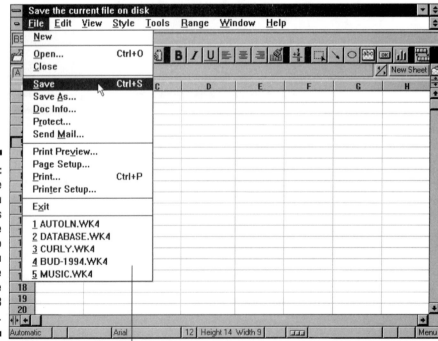

**Figure 6-1:**
The File menu commands become familiar to you as you gain more experience with 1-2-3 for Windows.

Last five files you worked on

## Files and windows

1-2-3 for Windows has a *multiple document interface*. In plain language, this means that you can work with more than one file at a time — something you can fully appreciate if you've ever used any of the old DOS versions of 1-2-3 Release 2.x. Working with more than one file at a time means you don't have to close one project to work on another one. If you tend to juggle a bunch of things at once (which is fairly common in the offices I've worked in), you'll enjoy this capability.

Every file that's open appears in its own window. You move the windows, resize them, compare their data, and lots of other things. Only one window can be active at a time. The others just lurk in the background waiting for their turn to be useful. Figure 6-2 shows several files, each in a separate window, arranged nicely on-screen. This way you can see what's in them and jump around among them.

But there's one more thing to remember. Every file can also have more than one sheet in it (like additional pages). Even if a file has extra sheets, the file is still contained in its own window. You use the tabs to move to different sheets within a file.

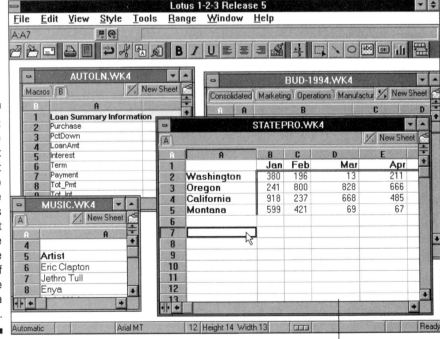

**Figure 6-2:** These worksheet windows plot how to balance the United States budget (not really). Notice that the title bar of the active window is a darker color.

Active window

Windows that hold files can be *maximized* to fill up the entire 1-2-3 for Windows workspace, or turned into a tiny icon (*minimized*). If a worksheet window is not maximized or minimized, you can move it around and resize it within the 1-2-3 for Windows workspace. Only one window at a time can be the *active window*. The active window is the one your cursor is currently in; it is on top of the stack of windows and has a different color title bar.

If you want to activate a different window, you can do so in any of three ways (take your pick):

- ✔ If any part of the window you want is showing, simply click it with your mouse and it miraculously appears at the top of the stack.

- ✔ You can press Ctrl+F6 repeatedly to cycle through all of the windows until the one you want appears.

- ✔ You can select the Window command. This command drops down a list of commands, and at the bottom of the list will be a list of all the windows you have open. Select the window you want to activate, and you're off to the races.

To minimize a worksheet window (AKA, iconize it), click the down arrow in the upper left corner of the worksheet window's title bar. Double-click the icon to restore it to its previous size. To maximize a window, click the up arrow. If a window is maximized, you can restore it to its former size by clicking the button with two arrows (one up, one down) that's directly below the 1-2-3 for Windows title bar.

If you have several worksheet windows open, the screen can become a bit cluttered, and some windows may even be hidden behind others. 1-2-3 for Windows provides two command to clean things up. The Window⇨Cascade command arranges all the windows in a tidy stack in such a way that you can see their title bars (see Figure 6-3). The Window⇨Tile command sizes and moves the windows so that each one is showing, with no overlaps (sort of like floor tiles).

If you have so many worksheet windows open that you have trouble locating the one you want, choose the Window menu item and select the window you want from the list that appears.

## The file-related File menu commands

OK, here comes the meaty stuff — a summary of the important File commands and their functions.

### File⇨New

When 1-2-3 for Windows starts up, you'll have a blank worksheet called *UN-TITLED*. You can use this worksheet to start a new project.

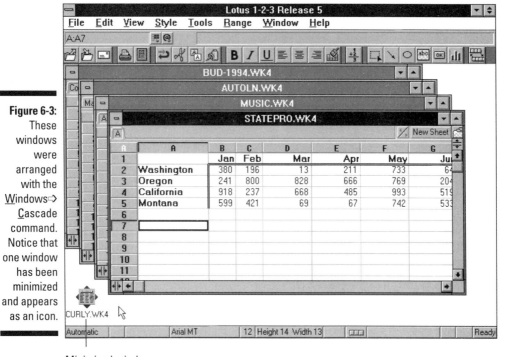

**Figure 6-3:**
These windows were arranged with the Windows⇨ Cascade command. Notice that one window has been minimized and appears as an icon.

Minimized window

If you need to start another new project, use the File⇨New command. This command creates a new blank worksheet on your screen, but doesn't save it to disk. If you're already working on a worksheet, this command starts a new one (and doesn't close the other one). Every new worksheet starts life with a generic name such as FILE0001.WK4. Create another one and it'll be named FILE0002.WK4.

When you start a new project and create a new worksheet, it's a good idea to save it immediately (even though it's empty). Saving it forces you to give it a name — hopefully more meaningful than FILE0001.WK4. Do this with the File⇨Save command (see the following section entitled "File⇨Save").

### File⇨Open

Use this command when you want to open a worksheet that already exists on your hard disk so that you can work on it some more. If you already have one or more worksheets open, this command brings yet another one on-screen (and doesn't close any of the others). The Open File dialog box is shown in Figure 6-4.

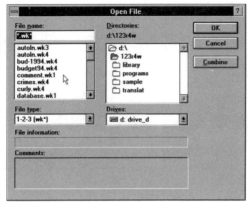

**Figure 6-4:**
Selecting the File⇨ Open command calls up this dialog box. You then specify which file you want.

Usually, the file you want is displayed in the listbox on the left. Just scroll through the list until you find it. Sometimes, you may have to select a different directory or drive. When you change the drive or directory, you'll see a new list of files. When you find your file, double-click it or highlight it with the arrow keys and press Enter.

If you need to open more than one file, you can hold down Ctrl while you click file names. Then click OK, and 1-2-3 for Windows opens all the files you selected.

1-2-3 for Windows remembers the names of the last five files you worked on and displays the filenames at the bottom of the File menu (check out Figure 6-1). To open one of these recent files, just click it once. This is *much* faster than trying to locate it in the Open dialog box.

### File⇨Save

This command saves your worksheet to a file on-disk. If you've already saved the file before, 1-2-3 uses the same name. If it's a new worksheet with a generic FILEXXX.WK4 name, 1-2-3 for Windows asks you for a name to use for the file. Just type a valid filename — the program supplies the .WK4 extension that identifies it as a 1-2-3 for Windows worksheet file. If you want to rename an existing file with a different name, use File⇨Save As (see the following section).

Filenames can be no longer than eight characters (with no spaces). Also, a few characters are verboten (\ (backslash), + (plus sign), : (colon), and a few others). If you try to use one of these characters, 1-2-3 for Windows complains (This filename is not valid) and makes you change the name.

### File⇨Save As

Use this command when you want to save your existing worksheet with a different name, or save it to a different directory or disk. This also is the command you use when you want to save a 1-2-3 for Windows file in a different file format so that other programs can read the data. See the sidebar, "Foreign files," for more information about saving files in different file formats. Figure 6-5 shows the dialog box that appears when you choose the File⇨Save As command.

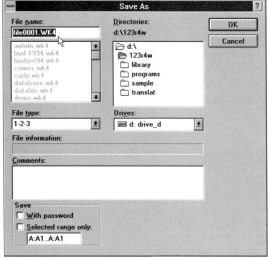

**Figure 6-5:**
Selecting
the File⇨
Save As
command
calls up the
Save As
dialog box.

When you save a file for the first time using the File⇨Save command, 1-2-3 for Windows is smart enough to know that your really meant to use the File⇨Save As command. Consequently, you receive the dialog box you normally get when you select the File⇨Save As command.

## Foreign files

If you have a VHS video cassette player, you probably know that you can't play old beta video cassettes in your machine. Besides being different physical sizes, the tapes are two different formats. Even if you took the tape out of a beta cartridge and spooled it onto a VHS cartridge, your VHS machine can't understand it. Similarly, if you save a file from 1-2-3 for Windows, you normally can't use that file in your word processor. This is because the two programs use different file formats. Similarly, if you tried to load a 1-2-3 for Windows worksheet file into dBASE, dBASE complains because it can't recognize the information — again, different file formats.

Actually, there *are* ways to save 1-2-3 for Windows files so that the information can be used in most other software programs. The trick is to save the file in a "foreign" file format — one that the other program can understand. You do this with the File⇨Save As command. You also have to specify the appropriate file extension so that 1-2-3 for Windows knows what to do.

1-2-3 for Windows can read worksheets produced by earlier versions of 1-2-3, and files produced by Microsoft's Excel spreadsheet (but not Excel 5.0 files). When you use the File⇨Open command, click the File type drop-down list in the dialog box and select the file type that you want. This displays only those types of files in the file list.

### File⇨Doc Info

Lets you enter some descriptive information about your worksheet. If you have trouble remembering what a worksheet is supposed to do, this command displays a dialog box that lets you enter lots of information about the worksheet. It also gives you lots of interesting (and not so interesting) details, such as the number of times it has been saved and the amount of time you've spent — or wasted — working on it.

### File⇨Close

Removes the current worksheet from memory. If the worksheet that you're trying to close hasn't been saved since you made any changes, 1-2-3 for Windows asks you whether you want to save it by displaying a dialog box like the one in Figure 6-6. To save it before closing it, select the Yes button. To abandon your changes and close it anyway, choose No. Select Cancel if you get cold feet and decide not to close the file after all.

**Figure 6-6:**
If you try to close a file that includes unsaved information, you receive this message.

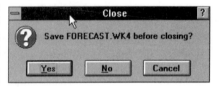

### File⇨Exit

Use this command when you are finished using 1-2-3 for Windows and are ready to call it quits. If you have any unsaved work, 1-2-3 for Windows lets you know about it and gives you the opportunity to save it to disk before quitting.

Alt+F4 is the standard Windows shortcut for File⇨Exit — it works also with 1-2-3 for Windows.

## Nonfile-related File menu commands

The File menu also has several other commands that really don't have anything to do with files on your disk. These other commands are the ones that you use to print or view your worksheet. Because these commands are irrelevant to the current topic, I put off discussing them until Chapter 10.

# *Doing Things with a File — Step by Step*

Now it's time to put all your file knowledge to work. You'll create a new worksheet file, put some information into it, save it, close it, and then open it again. These are the things you'll be doing every time you work with 1-2-3 for Windows.

Start by running 1-2-3 for Windows. What happens next depends on which version of 1-2-3 for Windows you're using.

If you're using Release 4, it gives you an empty worksheet window called UNTITLED.

When you start 1-2-3 Release 5 for Windows, the program first asks you if you want to create a new worksheet or work on an existing worksheet. If you reply that you want to create a new worksheet, it then displays another dialog box with a list of *SmartMasters* in it. SmartMasters are *templates* that you can use for various projects. For this exercise, just make sure the check box labeled Create a plain worksheet is checked, and then click OK. Doing so gives you a blank worksheet (named UNTITLED) to play with.

1. **Select the File⇨New command.**

   With Release 4, this command immediately creates a new workbook called FILE0001.WK4. With Release 5, you'll see the New File dialog box that lets you choose a SmartMaster. We don't need a SmartMaster, so just click OK and you'll get a new blank worksheet named FILE0001.WK4. This new worksheet exists only in your computer's memory and is not saved on disk.

2. **Enter some information in the worksheet. It doesn't matter what, just put in some numbers or labels.**

   Your screen should look something like Figure 6-7.

3. **Save this worksheet to a file by selecting the File⇨Save command.**

   Because this worksheet doesn't have a name (FILE0001.WK4 is not considered a real name), you'll be asked to supply one in the Save As dialog box.

4. **Type MYFILE in the dialog box (refer to Figure 6-8), and choose the OK button.**

   1-2-3 for Windows creates a new file on your hard disk called MYFILE.WK4.

5. **Close the file you're working on by selecting the File⇨Close command.**

   The file will be unloaded from memory. But that's OK, because it was saved to disk. If you hadn't save the file before closing it, 1-2-3 for Windows politely asks you whether you wanted to do so (it does all it can to save your rear).

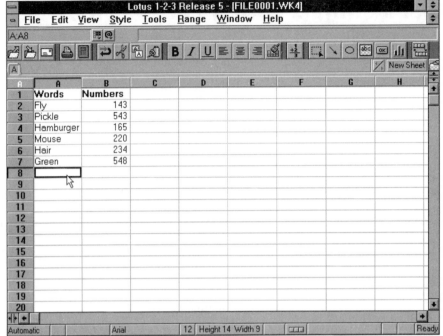

**Figure 6-7:**
Your new
worksheet
file after
putting
some
information
into it.

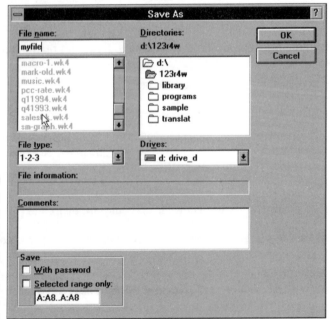

**Figure 6-8:**
The Save
As dialog
box is where
you give
your work-
sheet a
filename.

6. **Now you'll open the file again to work on it some more. Choose File⇨Open.**

   Figure 6-9 shows what the File menu looks like, and Figure 6-10 shows the Open File dialog box that it brings up.

7. **In the Open File dialog box, enter** MYFILE **into the File name box and press Enter (or choose OK).**

   If you can't remember the filename, you can look for it in the file list. You may have to use the scroll bar to display more filenames. When you find MYFILE.WK4, click it to select it, and then choose OK (or just double-click it and bypass the OK button).

   1-2-3 for Windows will open the worksheet file, and it will look just like it did when you last saved it.

1-2-3 for Windows displays the last five files you worked on when you choose the File menu. Rather than choose the Open command, you could have simply clicked on the 1. MYFILE.WK4 option — which would open that file without having to use the Open File dialog box.

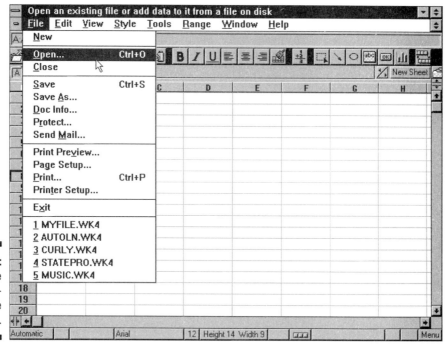

Figure 6-9:
The File menu displays these commands.

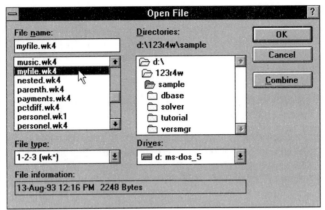

**Figure 6-10:**
The Open
File dialog
box lets you
type in the
filename you
want to
open, or
locate it in
the file list.

## Getting smart with SmartMasters

Beginning with Release 5, 1-2-3 for Windows includes a set of worksheet templates called SmartMasters. What's a template? Well, a template is a worksheet that's already set up to perform a common task. Say you're house hunting and you want to see what you can expect in the way of mortgage payments. You could spend several hours trying to put together a loan amortization worksheet in 1-2-3 for Windows — or you could use the loan amortization SmartMaster that's right on your hard disk.

When you choose the File⇨New command, 1-2-3 for Windows displays a list of all the SmartMasters on your hard disk. One of these just happens to be set up to amortize a mortgage loan.

If you choose this SmartMaster, 1-2-3 for Windows opens the template and virtually walks you through the steps you need. In this case, the template provides you with two buttons: one called Amortization, and the other called Information. If you click the Amortization button, you see the worksheet all ready to go. Just enter your loan details and the formulas do the rest. The Information button gives you instructions.

If you're about to embark on a new project, it won't hurt to see if there's a SmartMaster available. It'll save you lots of time — or at least give you some ideas as to how to proceed with your own worksheet.

# *Making Backups*

If there's one thing that almost all beginning computer users have trouble with, it's managing files on their hard drive and floppy disks. Most people don't take the time to learn the cryptic DOS commands normally used to copy files, rename files, move files, and other things. I don't blame you if you are one of these people — those commands are very confusing and much better ways exist. (Don't let the computer nerds tell you otherwise.)

Although this book isn't really the place for you to learn about the ins and outs of managing your files, I do want to tell you how to make a backup copy of a file — in fact, I tell you several different ways. That way, if you ever lose an important file, you can't blame me!

Making a backup of a file simply means placing a copy of the file in another location — usually a floppy disk. Some people make their backups to another hard drive on their system, to a network file server, or to magnetic tape. To keep things simple, I'm going to tell you three ways to get a 1-2-3 for Windows worksheet file on a floppy disk. They are

- ✔ Using 1-2-3 for Windows
- ✔ Using the Windows File Manager Program
- ✔ Using DOS

You (or the office nerd) may already have some procedures in place to make a complete backup copy of all the files on your hard disk. For example, you may own software that's designed specifically to back up all the files on your hard drive to a tape storage unit. I encourage you to make such backups regularly. But you need to realize that you still need to make separate backups of important files that you work on (what if someone's Haagen-Dazs melts all over the storage unit?). The procedures in this section tell you how to save your own files.

## Backing up from 1-2-3 for Windows

You can search the 1-2-3 for Windows menus all day and never find the File⇨Backup command (because there is no such animal). However, you can still save your worksheet to a floppy disk (if you haven't fallen asleep yet, you probably already have a pretty good idea of where this section is heading). The key is to use the File⇨Save As command and then specify drive A as the disk to save your file to.

Say you're ready to head for home after a long afternoon working on your department's budget. After embezzling all that money, you're tired and don't feel like thinking any more, but you know you have to save your info. Here's the easy way to save a copy of your file to a floppy disk:

1. **First, save your worksheet to your hard drive as you normally do.**

2. **Insert a formatted floppy disk into drive A.**

3. **Issue the File⇨Save As command.**

   In the Save As dialog box, click the arrow in the listbox labeled Drives. Select **a:** from the list and choose OK. 1-2-3 for Windows saves your current worksheet to the floppy disk in drive A.

4. **You can now use File⇒Exit to get out of 1-2-3 for Windows.**

   You should be rejoicing because you have two exact copies of your file: the one on your hard disk, and the one you just saved to the floppy disk.

5. **For good measure, stick that diskette in your shirt pocket and take it home with you.**

   (But watch out, someone might mistake you for a computer guru (*nerd*) and ask you questions about using upper memory locations.)

If you like, you can use drive B rather than drive A in all these procedures. It doesn't matter at all, as long as your diskette is in drive B rather than drive A. (Well, you might not be able to fit a 5 1/4-inch disk in your pocket, which might be a good thing, depending on your desired social status.)

When you come back to work the next day, use File⇒Open to open the file on your hard drive. If you make any changes to the file, repeat the floppy disk backup procedure after saving the file to your hard disk. Because the file already exists on your backup floppy, 1-2-3 for Windows makes you verify the fact that you want to overwrite this file with your newer version.

## *Backing up from the Windows File Manager program*

Microsoft Windows includes a program called *File Manager* that every Windows user should become familiar with. Figure 6-11 shows what File Manager looks like. Unless your hard drive is an exact clone of mine (hey!), your File Manager window will differ somewhat.

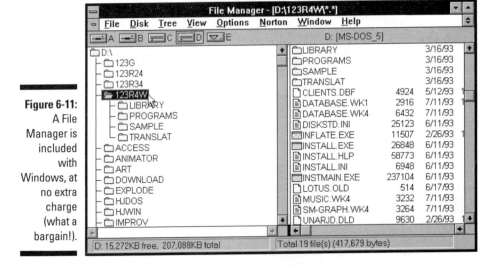

**Figure 6-11:** A File Manager is included with Windows, at no extra charge (what a bargain!).

This isn't the place to teach you all about using File Manager (*Windows For Dummies* explains this program pretty well). But I do want to give you step-by-step instructions for copying a file using File Manager:

1. **Save your worksheet as usual using the File⇨Save command. If you haven't named it yet, 1-2-3 for Windows asks for a name.**

2. **Press Ctrl+Esc to bring up the Windows Task List.** If File Manager is listed in the task list, double-click it. If File Manager is not listed in the list, select Program Manager to get to the Program Manager screen. Then, locate the File Manager icon in the Main program group (looks like a file cabinet with two drawers) and double-click it.

   When File Manager starts, its window is usually split into two vertical panes. Directories appear on the left, and the files in the selected directory appear on the right.

3. **In the pane on the left, locate the directory on your hard drive in which you save your worksheet files and click the directory name.** The pane on the right then displays the files in that directory.

4. **In the pane on the right, click the file that you were just working on to select it.**

5. **Issue the File⇨Copy command (or press F8). File Manager displays the dialog box shown in Figure 6-12.**

6. **In the To: text box, enter A: and choose OK. File Manager makes a copy of the file and puts it on drive A.**

7. **You can copy more files to the floppy disk using the same procedures. When you're finished copying, choose File⇨Exit to close File Manager.**

8. **If you're not back in 1-2-3 for Windows, press Ctrl+Esc and choose Lotus 1-2-3 from the task list.**

9. **Remove the floppy disk and put it in a safe place.**

10. **With your file safely backed up, you can now exit 1-2-3 for Windows, leave work, and get some elbow exercise at Joe's Place, if that is your desire.**

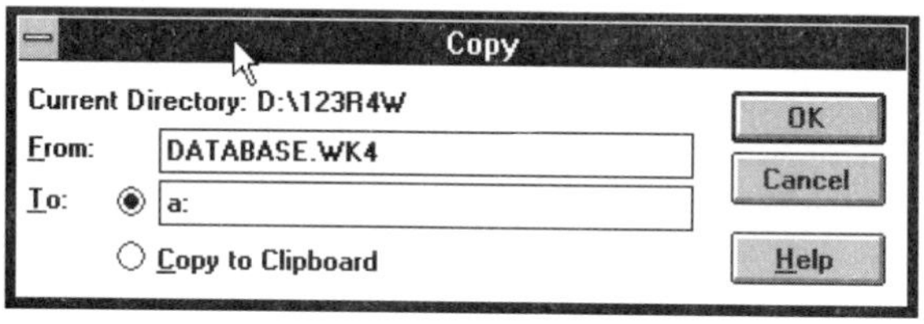

**Figure 6-12:**
Here's where
you tell File
Manager
where you
want to copy
your file to.

| Copy |
| --- |
| Current Directory: D:\123R4W |
| From: DATABASE.WK4 |
| To: ⦿ a: |
| ○ Copy to Clipboard |

OK

Cancel

Help

## *Backing up from DOS*

Another way to make a backup copy of a worksheet is to use the DOS COPY command. You can access DOS from Windows (using the MS-DOS icon), or you can exit Windows to return to DOS. In either case, you start this procedure at the DOS prompt (which is usually C:>):

1. **Insert a formatted diskette into drive A.**

2. **At the DOS prompt, type** CD C:\\*xxxx*, **where *xxxx* is the name of the directory that you want to store your worksheets in.**

   For example, if you keep your worksheets in the 123R5 directory, you enter **CD C:\123R5**. After you have correctly entered the command, press the Enter key.

3. **Next, type the following:**

```
COPY filename.wk4 a:
```

   where *filename.wk4* is the actual name of your file. When you press Enter, DOS copies the worksheet file to the floppy disk. (You'll see your floppy disk light come on if you have one.)

4. **Remove the floppy disk and store it in a safe place (that weird neighbor's bomb shelter, for example).**

## *Other ways to back up your work*

Your computer may have other file-management programs on it, such as Norton Desktop, PC Tools, XTree, Norton Commander, or any of several others. These programs can copy, organize, move, and rename files very easily. Consult the documentation that came with these programs (or buy a *...For Dummies* book!) to learn how to use them.

I spent a lot of pages telling you stuff that you won't fully appreciate until that fateful day comes when you realize that your only copy of an important file has bit the dust. Take some precautions and practice "safe spreadsheeting."

If you learn nothing else about saving your work in this chapter, remember to turn on the autosave feature. Select the Tools⇨User Setup command and set the Save files every option to 5 minutes. If all else fails, at least your machine is saving your work on a regular interval.

# Chapter 7
# The Secret of Formulas

*"I cannot give you the formula for success, but I can give you the formula for failure, which is: Try to please everybody."*

Herbert B. Swope (1882-1958)
American journalist

• • • • • • • • • • • • • • • • • • • • • • • • • • • • • • • • • • • • • • • • • • • • • • •

## In This Chapter

▶ Why spreadsheets are so popular and appealing

▶ What formulas are and why you need them

▶ How to enter a formula into a worksheet

▶ How to use the mathematical operators you thought you were finished with in high school (but maybe now you'll understand them)

▶ An look at what goes on when you enter a formula into a cell, with exclusive, behind-the-scenes photos

▶ A necessary discussion of absolute and relative cell references

• • • • • • • • • • • • • • • • • • • • • • • • • • • • • • • • • • • • • • • • • • • • • • •

*O*K, here's what you've been waiting for. The chapter that makes it all worthwhile. The chapter that finally makes your worksheets come to life. The chapter that gives you the skills necessary to actually do something useful. The chapter that teaches you about formulas.

If you're following this book in chapter number order, you now know just enough about moving around through a worksheet to be dangerous. You also can enter numbers and labels into cells with the best of them, and you even know the ins and outs of saving your work. Now you're ready for the next logical step in earning your bachelor's degree in 1-2-3.

# Formulas: The Definition

A worksheet without formulas is like the fake food you see displayed in the window of a Chinese restaurant — it looks pretty good on the surface, but it doesn't do a whole lot for you. In fact, without formulas you may as well be using a word processing program. Therefore, it's in your best interest to get turned on to formulas as soon as possible.

After you enter a number or a label into a cell, 1-2-3 for Windows simply displays that number or label in the cell. A formula, like a number or a label, is something that you enter into a cell. But the difference is that a formula does some type of calculation and displays the *answer* in the cell. However, you can still see the formula in the contents box in the edit line when you move the cell pointer to a cell that has a formula in it. Therefore, a cell that has a formula in it may display different things, depending on the current values of the cells it uses.

Simple formulas use only numbers and no cell addresses. For example, try entering the following formula into a cell (any cell will do):

```
+100+45
```

You'll find that 1-2-3 for Windows displays the answer (which is 145). Figure 7-1 proves that I'm not lying. Cell B2 has this simple formula in it, but the cell itself shows the result of the calculation that the formula performs. The actual formula appears in the contents box of the edit line.

The formula

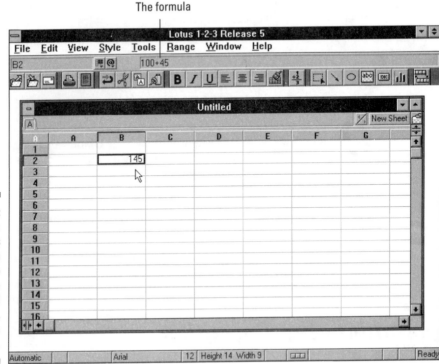

**Figure 7-1:**
A formula
displays its
results in
the cell. To
see the
actual
formula,
look in the
edit line.

But formulas are most interesting when you use cell addresses rather than actual values. Allow me to demonstrate. Take a look at Figure 7-2, which shows a worksheet with labels in column A, and numbers in column B. But cell B5 contains a formula. What you're seeing displayed in the worksheet is the formula's *answer* (or its result). Because the active cell happens to be cell B5, the contents of this cell (the *formula*) appears in the contents box of the edit line. Here it is again:

```
+B1+B2+B3+B4
```

What this formula is saying, in plain English, is this: *Hey 1-2-3 for Windows, take the number in cell B1 and add it to the number in B2. Then add the number in B3 to the total. And while you're at it, add the number in B4 to that total. Now, display the final answer in my cell. Thanks, dude.*

You may think that entering **+B1+B2+B3+B4** is a rather lengthy way to get the sum of these numbers. But you'll have to admit that it's sure easier than typing out the instructions in English.

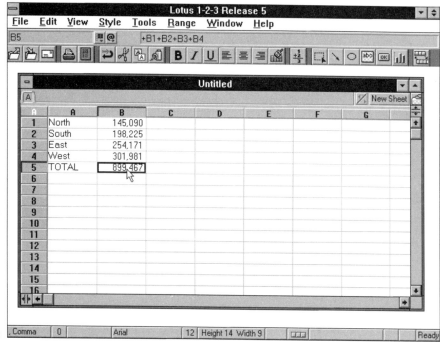

**Figure 7-2:**
A bunch of numbers? No way, José. Cell B5 has a formula in it.

Actually, there's a much easier way to get the sum of a bunch of cells, but that's the topic for another chapter. *Hint:* It involves @functions and a SmartIcon is available.

# Hello, Operator?

You've already seen how a formula can use the plus sign to add values. As you might expect, you can use other mathematical "operators" to perform even more amazing feats. For example, you can subtract values using the minus sign and multiply values using an asterisk (not an ×, as you might think). And, you can't overlook the ever-popular division operation that uses a slash. Finally, those with a penchant for large numbers might be interested in the exponential operator (^), which raises a number to a power.

Table 7-1 shows some examples of formulas using these operators.

| Table 7-1 Some Sample Formulas That Use Various Operators | |
| --- | --- |
| *Formula* | *What It Does* |
| +A1*23.5 | Multiplies the value in cell A1 by 23.5 |
| +A1-A3 | Subtracts the value in A3 from the value in A1 |
| +A4/A3 | Divides A4 by A3 |
| +A3^3 | Raises A3 to the third power (equivalent to +A3*A3*A3) |
| +(A1+A2)/A3 | Adds A1 to A2, and then divides the answer by A3 |

The cell references in the preceding table don't include a sheet letter because they are contained in a single worksheet file. Formulas, of course, can use sheet letters in formulas, such as this:

```
+B:A1*C:A1
```

This particular formula multiplies the upper left cell on sheet B by the upper left cell on sheet C.

## Using parentheses

OK, you caught me. The last entry in Table 7-1 introduced something new — parentheses. You can use parentheses to tell 1-2-3 for Windows in what order you want the calculations to occur. Why is this necessary? Here's how that example would look without any parentheses:

```
+A1+A2/A3
```

In this form, it's rather ambiguous. Do you want to add A1 to A2 and divide the result by A3? Or do you want to divide A2 by A3 and then add A1 to it? Does it matter? Yep. Read on to find out why.

### A formula with two answers

Just for the sake of argument, assume that you have three cells in column A, each with a value. The values are

```
A1:        4
A2:        10
A3:        2
```

Take another look at this now-familiar formula: +A1+A2/A3.

If you forget about cell addresses and use the real numbers, the formula would look like this:

```
4+10/2
```

Add 4 to 10 and you get 14. Divide 14 by 2 and you get 7. That's the answer, right? Well, you can look at it like this: Divide 10 by 2 and get 5. Add the 4 to this 5 and you get 9. Hmmmm. It turns out that this formula can produce an answer of either 7 or 9, depending on the order in which the operations are done. Computers, like some people, can't handle ambiguity well. Therefore, you need to be very specific at times. If you don't believe me, look at Figure 7-3 (figures don't lie).

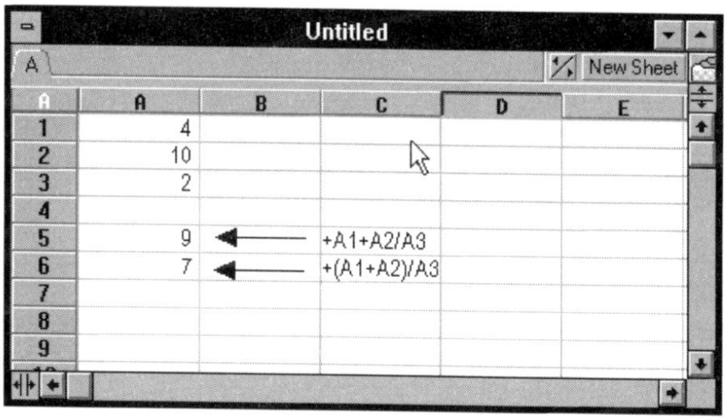

**Figure 7-3:**
Visual proof that a formula can produce different results by changing the order of the calculations.

The result of a formula may depend on the order in which the arithmetic operations are performed. You can control this order by using parentheses.

### How 1-2-3 for Windows copes with ambiguity

So what happens if you leave out the parentheses? Does 1-2-3 for Windows go into an endless loop trying to resolve the ambiguity? Not quite. The program has some rules built into it that determine how it handles ambiguities such as these. These rules are called *order of precedence* (a term that you can safely forget after you understand the concept).

For example, multiplication has higher precedence than addition, therefore **+2+3*4** produces an answer of 14, not 20. In other words, when it doesn't find any parentheses to guide it, 1-2-3 for Windows first does the multiplication (3*4) and then performs the addition.

Table 7-2 lists some of the world's most popular mathematical operators, and a number that indicates the precedence level. Operations with lower precedence numbers are performed first, and those with equal precedence are performed from left to right.

### Table 7-2    Some of the More Commonly Used Mathematical Operators and Their Precedence

| Operator | Description | Precedence |
|----------|-------------|------------|
| ^ | Exponentiation | 1 |
| * | Multiplication | 2 |
| / | Division | 2 |
| + | Addition | 3 |
| - | Subtraction | 3 |

If a formula doesn't have any overriding parentheses, 1-2-3 for Windows always performs the exponentiation (^) operator, then it performs multiplication and division, and finally it performs subtraction and addition.

### The thing about formulas

Here's the thing about formulas: They always look more complicated than they really are. That's because most people are used to seeing things that have some inherent meaning in them. A cell address such as +F13 is meaningless. Face it, things would be much less intimidating if you could write a formula such as this:

```
(current-previous)/previous
```

rather than this:

```
(C12-B12)/B12
```

Fact is, you *can* write formulas that use meaningful names. As you discover later in this book, you can give a name to a cell, to a range, and even to a complete worksheet.

Sometimes it's useful to include a note to yourself (or to others) that explains what's going on in a formula. That clever trickery you came up with last March may totally baffle you by July. You can add a note to a formula by sticking a semicolon at the end of the formula, and then typing in some descriptive text. 1-2-3 for Windows ignores everything appearing after the semicolon when calculating the formula. Your description then appears in the edit line when the cell pointer is on the cell, as shown in Figure 7-4. This is an *annotated* formula.

# *How to Enter Formulas*

One way to enter a formula is to simply type it into a cell. You can enter any of the formulas you've seen so far just by typing them exactly as they appear. This includes all the cell addresses, worksheet letters (if necessary), mathematical operators, parentheses, actual values, and whatever else is required.

But the best way to enter a formula is to *point* to the cells and let 1-2-3 for Windows help you build the formula. When you're entering a formula, 1-2-3 for Windows offers a slick alternative to typing the actual cell references. The typing method can be tedious as hell (not to mention very error-prone). This alternative method is called *pointing*. The best way to understand this method is to follow along with an example.

In this example, you build a formula that adds two cells and displays the results in another cell. And you do it without typing a single cell address. Figure 7-5 shows what my screen looked like when I was trying this.

Follow these steps to learn how to use the *pointing method:*

1. **Enter some numbers in cells A1, A2, and A3.** Any numbers will do.

2. **Move the cell pointer to cell A4.**

3. **Press + (the operator that means add) to tell 1-2-3 for Windows that a formula is on its way.**

4. **Use the Up arrow key to move the cell pointer to cell A1 (notice that the mode indicator now reads** POINT**).** Also notice that the formula is being created in the cell before your very eyes — and it's being created in the contents box of the edit line at the same time.

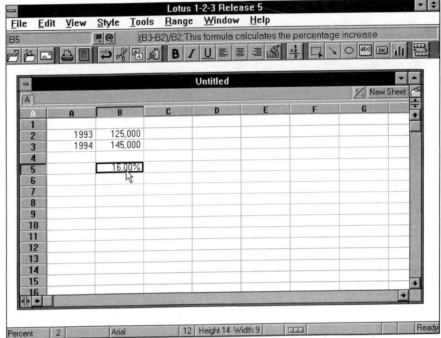

**Figure 7-4:**
A semicolon
in a formula
tells 1-2-3
for Windows
to ignore
everything
that follows.
You can
enter a
description
of your
formula so
you don't
forget its
purpose.

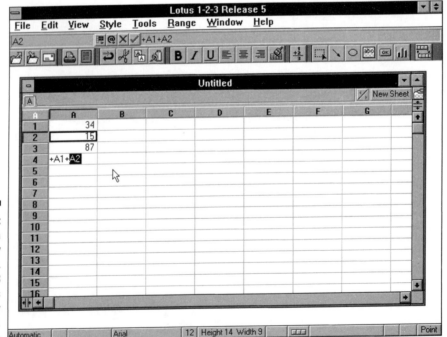

**Figure 7-5:**
Building a
formula by
pointing (or,
letting 1-2-3
for Windows
do the dirty
work).

5. **Press + again.** The cell pointer jumps back to cell A4, where the formula is being built.

6. **Use the up arrow key to move the cell pointer to cell A2.**

7. **Press + again.**

8. **Use the up arrow key to move the cell pointer to cell A3.** The contents box in the edit line should now read **+A1+A2+A3** (which is just what you want).

9. **Press Enter to stick the formula in cell A4.** The formula is evaluated, and the cell shows the formula's result, not the formula (but the edit line continues to show the actual formula).

Using this pointing technique means that you never have to be concerned with the actual cell address — just point to the cells you want and 1-2-3 for Windows takes care of the repulsive details. This technique also cuts down on errors. After all, it's easy to make a typing mistake when you enter a formula manually — or womanually — and you might not even discover the mistake until your boss asks you how 12+9 could possibly equal 197.

# The nesting instinct

Frankly, I've been using spreadsheets for more than a decade and I confess that I can never remember how this precedence business works (and I just don't trust it, for some reason). Therefore, I tend to use more parentheses than are necessary — which isn't bad, because it makes it very clear how the formula is calculated. However, it's easy to get confused when parentheses become *nested* several levels deep.

Examine the following formula:

```
(((A1+B1)*2)-((C1+D1)*2))/4
```

Notice that the number of left parentheses is exactly equal to the number of right parentheses.

If this isn't true, 1-2-3 for Windows does not accept the formula when you press Enter. When 1-2-3 for Windows evaluates a formula like this, it starts in the middle and works its way out. Whatever is enclosed by the most "deeply nested" parentheses gets first attention, and the result of that is used to evaluate the remaining parts of the formula.

This, of course, all happens in the blink of an eye (actually, a bit faster than that). The point I'm trying to make is that using more parentheses than you really need can actually help you make sense of gobbeldy-gook formulas such as this one.

## If your formula returns ERR

It's not unusual to enter a formula into a cell and be greeted with ERR, instead of a more friendly result. In a nutshell, this means that you made a boo-boo. This happens for a number of reasons:

✔ You made a mistake by typing a cell reference that doesn't exist (such as +ZA1). A formula with this nonexistent cell reference returns ERR.

✔ You're trying to do something impossible, such as calculate the square root of a negative number.

✔ You'll learn later that cells and ranges can be given meaningful names, and 1-2-3 for Windows lets you use such a name in a formula even if it doesn't exist. Formulas with nonexistent cell or range names always return ERR.

✔ Your formula is trying to use a cell that is returning ERR. If the formula uses a cell that is returning ERR, the formula also returns ERR. This is known as the *ripple effect*, because a single ERR can ripple through an entire worksheet.

Usually, if you examine the formula that's returning ERR, you can figure out the problem — look for unusual cell references or undefined range names. You can then edit the cell to correct the problem and the formula will return a better result.

When you're pointing to create a formula, you're not limited to pointing to cells on the current worksheet (assuming you have more than one sheet in your file). If you press Ctrl+PgUp while in POINT mode, you'll be transported to the next sheet. Pressing Ctrl+PgDn sends you to the preceding sheet. In either case, after you get to the new worksheet you can move the cell pointer to the cell you want to refer to in the formula. And it should go without saying that you can press Ctrl+PgUp and Ctrl+PgDn any number of times until you get to the right worksheet.

# Just How Complex Can They Be?

Like personalities, formulas can be simple or complex. All the formulas you've seen so far in this chapter fall into the "simple" category. Yes, even the formula that demonstrated nesting parentheses is pretty elementary in the whole scheme of things.

## I created a monster

Here's an example of an actual formula that I once developed in a moment of boredom (actually, it was quite a few moments):

```
@IF(B$25<>$A27,((@COUNT(@@(B$25))*@SUMPRODUCT(@@(B$25),@@($A27)))-
(@SUM(@@(B$25))*@SUM(@@($A27))))/
(@SQRT((@COUNT(@@(B$25))*@SUMPRODUCT(@@(B$25),@@(B$25)))-
@SUM(@@(B$25))^2)*@SQRT((@COUNT(@@(B$25))*@SUMPRODUCT(@@($A27),@@($A27)))-
(@SUM(@@($A27))^2))),"        —")
```

This formula is used to calculate correlation coefficients using indirect referencing. Believe it or not, some people actually have a use for this sort of thing. But the most amazing thing is that this monster actually works—although I no longer understand exactly *how* it works. By the way, 1-2-3 now has a built-in function that can simplify this formula significantly. This means I can replace this monster with something as simple as @CORREL(@@(B$25),@@($A27)).

The point of presenting this formula is not to impress you with my formula-building prowess (although you *should* be impressed), but to demonstrate that you really don't have to worry about creating formulas that 1-2-3 for Windows can't handle.

By the way, very lengthy formulas such as the preceding one are difficult to work with, because you can't see the whole formula while you're working on it (it scrolls to the left or right). It would be nice if 1-2-3 for Windows expanded the contents box of the edit line to show these long formulas on more than one line — but it doesn't. The best thing is to avoid long formulas, and use several different formulas to accomplish the same result.

# Behind the scenes

One or two of you may be curious about what goes on behind the scenes when you enter a formula into a cell. If you've ever wondered what a computer thinks about, you'll find out here.

When you start entering a formula into a cell, 1-2-3 for Windows goes through the following "thought" process:

1. **OK, this person is entering a formula.** It's not just a number or a label, so he must know *something* about 1-2-3 for Windows (little does the computer know, right?).

2. **Is she using POINT mode?** If so, I'll need to show her the cell addresses as she points to them and sticks them in the formula (sheesh, I have to do *all* the work).

3. **He just pressed Enter.** That means he is finished with the formula.

4. **I'll just check this formula to make sure it follows all my rules.** If it doesn't, I'll beep and make her feel foolish.

5. **Looks OK to me.** Now I'll calculate the results using the values in the cells he specified.

6. **Now I'll finish up by displaying the answer in the cell.**

Your computer continues thinking as you do your work. Every time you put a value into a cell or create a new formula, it checks every single formula on the worksheet to see whether it needs to be recalculated based on your new input. But this all happens so quickly that you usually don't even realize it.

# Relative and Absolute References

There's one additional topic that I just can't put off any longer: relative vs. absolute references. This can be rather confusing, but it's important stuff. So bear with me, OK?

## It's all relative

When you put a formula into a cell, you can copy that formula to other cells. In fact, copying formulas is one of the most common things that spreadsheet users do. You'll learn all about copying in Chapter 9. But for now, just understand that you can enter a formula once, and then copy it so the same formula works on another ranges. For example, if you have six columns of numbers, you can put a formula below the first column to add the preceding numbers. Then, you can copy that formula to the five cells to the right to add the other columns.

Up until now, all the cell references you've used in formulas have been *relative*. If you copy a formula that has relative references, the copies of the formula change. Here's an example. Assume the following formula is in cell A3:

```
+A1+A2
```

If you copy this formula to the cell next door (B3), the formula in cell B3 would read:

```
+B1+B2
```

In other words, copying the formula changed the cells in a *relative manner*. No matter where you copy the formula, it always computes the sum of the two cells directly above it. This is a good thing and most the time is exactly what you want to happen. This concept is demonstrated in Figure 7-6.

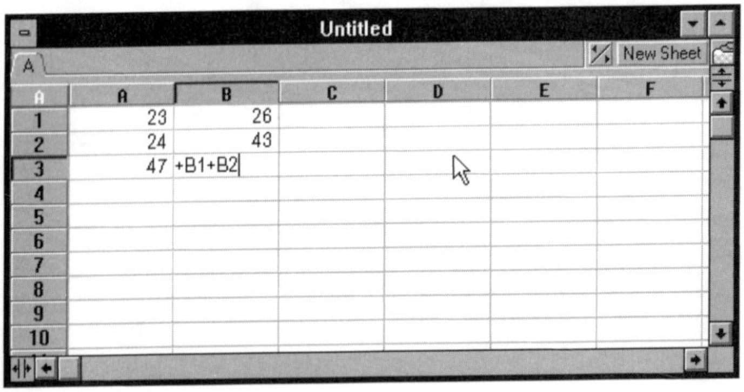

**Figure 7-6:**
This is what happens when you copy a formula. The cell addresses are changed automatically.

By default, all cell references are relative.

## Absolutely absolute

But what if you wanted the copy of the formula to return exactly the same result as the cell it was copied from? In this case, you need to specify *absolute* cell references. Here's a formula with absolute cell references:

```
+$B$1+$C$1
```

Thats all there is to it. Using a dollar sign before the column part and before the row part of a cell reference tells 1-2-3 for Windows that the cell reference is absolute — that it always refers to those specific cells, even if you copy the formula.

## Why use absolute references?

The best way to understand why to use absolute references is to go through an example. Figure 7-7 shows a worksheet designed to calculate the sales tax on several purchase prices. The sales tax rate is in cell B1. Column A has labels, column B has amounts, and column C has formulas that calculate the sales tax on the amount in column B.

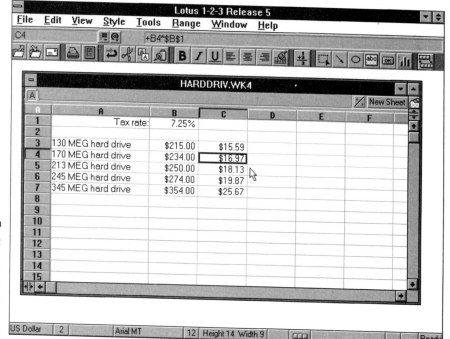

**Figure 7-7:** An example of when to use absolute references.

The formula in cell C4 is

```
+B4*$B$1
```

The first cell reference (B4) is a normal relative cell reference, but the second part of the formula ($B$1) is an absolute reference (because it always includes the tax rate). When you copy this formula down the column, the first part of the formula will change to reflect the price in the cell to the left of it, but the copied formula will *always* refer to cell B1 — which is just what you want. For example, the formula, when copied to cell C5 reads:

```
+C4*$B$1
```

If you used a relative reference (B1) rather than the absolute reference ($B$1), the copied formula would be:

```
+C4*B2
```

This formula would return the wrong answer, because the sales tax rate is not in cell B2. If this doesn't make sense read it again until it does. Believe me, this is important stuff.

By the way, copying formulas is covered in Chapter 9.

# Even More about Formulas

I'll wrap up this chapter with a few additional random thoughts. This section can be considered lagniappe.

## Controlling recalculation

As you know, a formula displays a different result if you change the values in any of the cells that the formula uses. Normally, 1-2-3 for Windows automatically performs this recalculation. Whenever you change anything in a worksheet, 1-2-3 quickly scans all the formulas to determine whether any of them need to be updated to show a new answer.

Some people, however, create very large worksheets that have hundreds or even thousands of formulas. In such a case, 1-2-3 for Windows continues to scan each formula every time you make a change in the worksheet and makes the appropriate recalculations. But because it takes a while — even for a computer — to scan thousands of formulas, you'll notice that you often have to wait for 1-2-3 for Windows to do its scanning. The net result is that your computer slows down, and it may even take some time for what you type to show up on the screen (a delayed reaction).

The solution to this is to tell 1-2-3 for Windows that *you* want to control when it does its recalculation. In other words, you want to turn off automatic recalculation and set it to manual recalculation. Here's how:

1. **In READY mode, issue the Tools⇒User Setup command.**

2. **In the dialog box that appears, select the Recalculation button, which brings up another dialog box, shown in Figure 7-8.**

3. **Click the Manual option button and then choose OK.**

To switch back to automatic recalculation, use the same steps, but select the Automatic option button.

But if you do choose to use manual recalculation, it's up to you to remember to recalculate. You do this by pressing the F9 key.

By the way, 1-2-3 for Windows reminds you when a recalculation is needed by displaying CALC in the status bar at the bottom of the screen. If the CALC indicator is showing, you know that you can't always trust that what's displayed on the screen (or on paper) is really accurate. After you press F9, the worksheet is recalculated and the CALC indicator disappears.

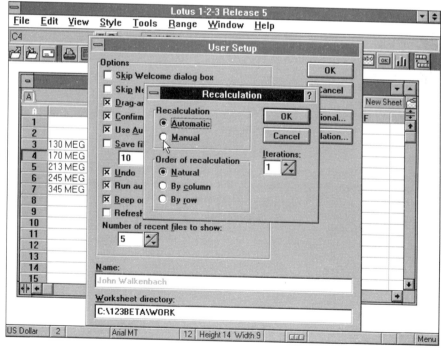

**Figure 7-8:**
Here's
where you
tell 1-2-3 for
Windows
that you
want to
control
when the
worksheet is
calculated.

If things start slowing down because you have lots of formulas, turn off auto-matic recalculation. But don't forget to press F9 periodically to recalculate manually!

## Using built-in functions

Formulas take on even more muscle when you use some of 1-2-3 for Windows built-in @functions (pronounced *at funk-shuns*). The reason for the unusual name is that they all begin with an *at sign*. For example, @functions exist that can calculate the sum of a range of cells (@SUM), compute the average (@AVG), do square roots (@SQRT), and lots of other more or less useful things.

I cover some of the more common @functions in Chapter 8, so you have a lot to look forward to.

## Other types of formulas

This chapter has focused exclusively on arithmetic formulas — formulas that deal with numbers and values. Two other types of formulas exist that you may run across:

- **Text formulas:** These formulas work with labels (AKA words) that you put in cells, and you can do some clever things. For example, you can create a formula such as this:

```
+"Hello"&" there"
```

  This formula uses the ampersand (&) operator to join two strings of text — sort of like adding them together. This formula, when evaluated by 1-2-3 for Windows, displays **Hello there** in the cell.

- **Logical formulas:** These formulas return either True or False. Most normal people don't have much of a need for logical formulas, so this book pretends that they don't exist.

If you want to learn more about formulas, and see some fairly useful ones, check out Chapter 19 of this very book.

# Chapter 8
# Making Formulas More Functional

*"Form ever follows function."*

Louis Henri Sullivan (1856 –1924)
American architect
*Lippincott's Magazine, (The tall office building artistically considered),* March, 1896

• • • • • • • • • • • • • • • • • • • • • • • • • • • • • • • • • • • • • • •

## In This Chapter

▶ Solutions for simple formulas that just can't cut the mustard

▶ An overview of @functions — what, why, when, and how

▶ Pointing skills that deal with ranges of cells

▶ @functions that just may come in handy some day

▶ An introduction to the delightful (and useful) concept of named ranges

• • • • • • • • • • • • • • • • • • • • • • • • • • • • • • • • • • • • • • •

*F*ormulas are great — as I tried to convince you in Chapter 7. But, as the saying goes, you ain't seen nothin' yet. This chapter tells you how to coax even more power from formulas by using some of the built-in functions that 1-2-3 for Windows provides for your analytical pleasure.

## Getting Functional

Sooner or later — probably later — you'll discover that your formulas need something more than the capability to refer to cell addresses and to use numbers, awesome as that is. There's gotta be more, right? You betcha.

The developers of 1-2-3 for Windows, realizing that number crunchers such as yourself may actually want to do something useful with their spreadsheets, included more than 200 @functions (232 to be exact) to help you out.

## So what's with the at sign (@)?

The at sign (@) is weird—I admit it. But the built-in functions in 1-2-3 for Windows are called @functions (pronounced *at funk shuns*). The at sign (@) is used to distinguish its functions from other information that you may type into a cell.

The reason for the name is mainly historical (and slightly hysterical). You see, the original version of 1-2-3 was developed a long time ago—before spreadsheet designers realized that they didn't really need to use such an arcane character to distinguish functions from other things. However, people got used to using the at signs, so Lotus keeps them in. Don't worry, it doesn't take long to get used to this weirdness. And besides, the at sign makes it very easy to spot an @function stuck in a long formula.

Most of the @functions aren't covered in this chapter, because they are beyond the scope of this book. Others are just plain worthless, frequently called *@dysfunctions*.

## OK, what is an @function?

Think of an *@function* as a shortcut for telling 1-2-3 for Windows to calculate some numbers. For example, there's an @function called @AVG, which computes the average of a range of numbers. This function saves you the trouble of adding up the numbers in the range and then dividing by the number of elements in the list. Another example is the @PMT function, which produces the monthly payment on a loan. ( You need only supply the loan amount, the interest rate, and the length of the loan.)

Using the @functions is like having your own personal calculator built into your own personal computer. The calculating capabilities of the @functions are well beyond those of you or me. As a matter of fact, many @functions enable you to perform some feat that simply can't be done in any other way. @SQRT, for example, returns the square root of a number. (Try to do that to 215 in your head!)

## A functional example

I start with an example so that you can see how to use @functions. Study the worksheet in Figure 8-1. The worksheet contains a range of numbers that you need to add up to get a total. Your knowledge level so far produces the following formula:

```
+B1+B2+B3+B4+B5+B6+B7+B8+B9+B10+B11+B12+B13+B14+B15
```

This formula certainly gets the job done, but a much easier and quicker way to create a formula is by using — you guessed it — an @function. In this case, the @SUM function does the trick just fine. Instead of typing the preceding unwieldy formula, simply type the following @function into any cell (cell B16 is a good place for it):

```
@SUM(B1..B15)
```

| A | A | B | C | D | E | F | G |
|---|---|---|---|---|---|---|---|
| 1 | 01-Jul | 192 | | | | | |
| 2 | 02-Jul | 133 | | | | | |
| 3 | 03-Jul | 154 | | | | | |
| 4 | 04-Jul | 34 | | | | | |
| 5 | 05-Jul | 19 | | | | | |
| 6 | 06-Jul | 168 | | | | | |
| 7 | 07-Jul | 155 | | | | | |
| 8 | 08-Jul | 144 | | | | | |
| 9 | 09-Jul | 189 | | | | | |
| 10 | 10-Jul | 54 | | | | | |
| 11 | 11-Jul | 33 | | | | | |
| 12 | 12-Jul | 189 | | | | | |
| 13 | 13-Jul | 173 | | | | | |
| 14 | 14-Jul | 155 | | | | | |
| 15 | 15-Jul | 131 | | | | | |
| 16 | Month-to-date | | | | | | |
| 17 | | | | | | | |

**Figure 8-1:** The @SUM enables you to determine the sum of all these numbers.

This formula consists of a single @function. The stuff in the parentheses is called the @function's *arguments* (more about the arguments later). In this case, there is just one argument, and it is a range of cells.

 You may have already discovered the SmartIcon in Figure 8-2 that automatically adds up cells. Clicking this icon specifies a range to total in the current cell by using the @SUM function. The icon examines your worksheet, figures out what you're trying to add, and does the work for you. Now, if only Lotus could come up with a SmartIcon that makes your coffee in the morning...

**Figure 8-2:** This SmartIcon activates the @SUM function.

## Cells and ranges

A cell is a cell, but a group of contiguous (consecutive) cells is a *range*. (For example, the cells A1 through A10 constitute a range.) You can specify a range of cells in a formula by using the following format:

```
FirstCell..LastCell
```

*FirstCell* and *LastCell* each represent a normal cell address. A *range reference* is simply two cell addresses separated by two periods (for example, A1..A12). The reason for using two periods goes back to the way the original 1-2-3 was set up. It's another strange practice that you'll just have to live with.

The following examples of range references give you an idea of how to interpret them:

- ✔ **A1..A12** 12 cells, beginning in cell A1 and extending to and including cell A12

- ✔ **A1..Z1**   26 cells, beginning in cell A1 and extending across to and including cell Z1

- ✔ **A1..B12** 24 cells, beginning in cell A1, going down to cell A12; and also including cell B1, going down to cell B12 (In other words, this range consists of 2 columns and 12 rows.)

1-2-3 for Windows also deals with a group of cells that is not contiguous. A group of noncontiguous cells is called a *collection*. You can refer to a collection by using a comma to separate the noncontiguous ranges or cell references that make up the collection. You can think of a collection as a range of cells that aren't contiguous. For example, to refer to cell A1 and the range C1..G1, the collection appears as follows:

```
A1,C1..G1
```

You normally use a collection when you select cells before you issue a command to act on the cells. Also, you can use a collection as an argument to an @function that's expecting a range of cells.

## Adding sheets to cell references

If the reference in your @function happens to extend across multiple sheets (or if you're referring to cells on a different sheet), you have to tack on a sheet reference so that 1-2-3 for Windows knows which sheets to use. You simply precede the range reference with a sheet letter and a colon, as illustrated in the following examples:

✔ **A:A1..A:A12** A range of 12 cells, all on sheet A, starting in cell A1 and going to cell A12 (In this case, use the sheet letters only if the @function is on a sheet other than sheet A.).

✔ **A:A1..C:A12** A three-dimensional range of 36 cells, beginning in cell A1 of sheet A and extending to cell A12 on sheet C.

# *Entering @Functions*

As you recall from Chapter 7, you can build a formula either by typing it directly into a cell or by pointing to the cells that you want to include in the formula. Use the same two processes for entering @functions into your cells.

## *The direct approach*

Entering an @function directly simply involves, well, entering an @function directly. In other words, if you want to add up the numbers in the range A1..C12 and have the answer appear in cell A13, put the following @function into cell A13:

```
@SUM(A1..C12)
```

By the way, you can type the @function in either uppercase, lowercase, or mixed case. The case doesn't matter at all, because 1-2-3 for Windows always converts the letters to uppercase.

## *The pointing method*

Sometimes, it may be faster to point out the cell or range (called an argument) rather than type it. To point out a range, using the example in the preceding section, do the following:

1. **Move the cell pointer to cell A13.**

2. **Type @SUM(**

3. **Use the arrow keys to move to cell A1, the first cell in the range.**

   Notice that the edit line displays the cell.

4. **Press the period key.**

   Pressing the period key makes the first cell "stick" so that you can point to the last cell in the range (this is known also as *anchoring* the cell).

**5. Use the arrow keys to move to the last cell in the range, cell C12.**

Notice that **@SUM(A1..C12** is now displayed in the edit line.

**6. Type a closing parenthesis.**

Actually, the closing parenthesis is optional. If you leave it off, 1-2-3 for Windows automatically puts it in for you — just another example of how this program is trying to be your friend.

**7. Press Enter to insert this formula into cell A13.**

Rather than go through all the preceding steps with your keyboard, you can simply click and drag the mouse over the range after you have typed **@SUM(** in cell A13. As you do so, 1-2-3 for Windows displays the selected range in the edit line. After you're finished, type the closing parenthesis in cell C12 (or just press Enter and let 1-2-3 for Windows do the work).

## Let's have an argument

The information that an @function uses to perform its calculations is called its arguments. Arguments are always enclosed in parentheses, directly following the @function name. You should remember the following information about @function arguments:

✔ Some @functions need more than one argument. In such cases, the arguments are separated with a comma.

✔ Some @functions need a single cell for an argument, and others need a range reference.

✔ Some formulas need numbers for arguments, and others need text (or labels).

✔ You usually can use a normal number or text in place of a cell reference.

✔ You also can use a range name as an argument for a range reference, or a cell name as an argument for a cell reference.

The following examples illustrate how the different arguments work in the @SUM function:

| | |
|---|---|
| **@SUM(A1..A12)** | Adds the numbers in the range A1..A12. |
| **@SUM(A1)** | Displays the number in cell A1. (Not a very useful formula, but it is valid.) |
| **@SUM(A1,A2,A3,A4)** | Adds the numbers in cells A1, A2, A3, and A4. This calculation can be done more efficiently by using @SUM(A1..A4). |

| | |
|---|---|
| @SUM(1,2,3,4) | Adds the numbers 1, 2, 3, and 4 and displays the result (which is 10). |
| @SUM(A1..A12)/2 | Adds the numbers in the range A1..A12 and then divides the result by 2. |
| @SUM(A:A1..C:A12) | Adds the numbers in the three-dimensional range, starting in cell A1 on sheet A and extending through cell A12 on the sheet C (the third sheet). |

## Editing @functions

It should come as no surprise that you can edit formulas that contain @functions. You edit @functions just like you edit any other cell — by pressing F2 (or clicking the edit line with your mouse or double-clicking the cell). Then you can use the normal editing keys (arrow keys, backspace, Delete) to change the formula. After you get the formula right, press Enter.

## Insert @function here, Insert @function here!

With more than 200 to choose from, how can you possibly remember the names and correct spelling of all the @functions? Well, chances are you'll only be using a small percentage of the @functions — but you can get a complete list when the need arises.

When you're entering a formula and need an @function, you can just click the @Function icon on the edit line. (Officially, this icon is known as the *@Function Selector.*) Clicking this icon drops down the list shown in Figure 8-3.

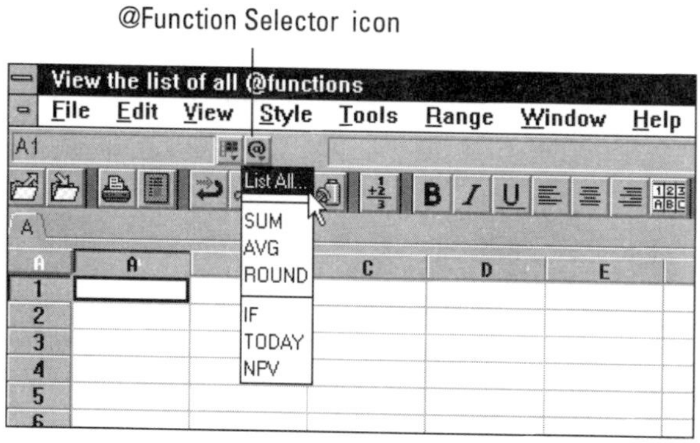

Figure 8-3: Clicking the @Function Selector icon drops down this list.

The first entry in the list in Figure 8-3 is List All. If you select List All, you get a drop-down listbox that contains the complete list of all the @functions, as shown in Figure 8-4. This list also shows some common @functions that you can select directly. (You can modify this list so that it shows the @functions that you use most often).

**Figure 8-4:**
A listing of all @functions, after you choose List All from the @Function Selector.

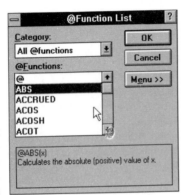

After you select an @function from the list (either from the drop-down listbox or the complete list), 1-2-3 for Windows inserts it into your formula — and even includes "dummy" arguments for you. After you insert an @function, notice that the first dummy argument is selected, or highlighted. This highlighting lets you type in the argument, point to the argument, or select a named cell or range from the Navigator icon (which is directly to the left of the @Function Selector icon).

If you use the @Function Selector to insert an @function, you have to substitute actual cell or range references for the dummy arguments. If you fail to replace the dummy arguments with real arguments, the formula returns an ERR message.

An easy way to change a dummy argument into a real argument is to double-click the dummy argument to select it and then enter the argument or point to it in the worksheet with the keyboard keys or your mouse. Your selection replaces the dummy argument.

If you don't know what function you need from this list, you can change the Category listbox in Figure 8-4 and search for the function by category. The next section discusses the various categories you can use.

# @Function Categories

1-2-3 for Windows divides its laundry list of @functions into ten categories. These ten categories make it easier to narrow your search when you need an @function but you don't know its name. The @function categories are shown in Table 8-1.

| Table 8-1 | @Function Categories |
|---|---|
| *Category* | *What It Does* |
| Calendar | Calculates values that deal with dates and times |
| Database | Performs queries and calculations in database tables |
| Engineering | Performs engineering calculations and other advanced mathematical operations |
| Financial | Deals with investments, annuities, securities, depreciation, cash flows, loans |
| Information | Returns information about cells, ranges, the operating system, and some 1-2-3 for Windows tools |
| Logical | Calculates the results of logical or conditional formulas |
| Lookup | Gets the contents of a cell in a table, based on some other information |
| Mathematical | Performs mathematical operations and trigonometric calculations |
| Statistical | Performs calculations on lists of values |
| Text | Provides information about text in cells and performs other operations on text |

Use the on-line help feature to figure out which @function is best for the job at hand. Press F1 to access the Help screen and then select the @Functions topic. In the next screen, choose the @Functions Categories topic. Select the category that best describes what you want to do and then keep navigating through the Help screens until you find what you're looking for. The @function on-line help in 1-2-3 for Windows is very good and contains lots of detailed information and examples for all the @functions.

# Some Useful Numerical @Functions

So far, you know about the @SUM function, and I also mentioned the every-popular @AVG function (which works just like @SUM, except it returns the average of the cells in its argument). Because you're probably yearning for more, I won't keep you in suspense any longer. Keep reading for details on some more useful @functions.

# @MAX

Suppose that you've started a worksheet with the monthly sales figures for all the sales people in your organization. The worksheet may look something such as Figure 8-5. You want to give an award to the top salesperson of the month. You can scan through the numbers and try to figure out which number is the highest — or you can use the @MAX function. Just type the following formula into the cell where you want to display the maximum sales figure:

@MAX(B2..B19)

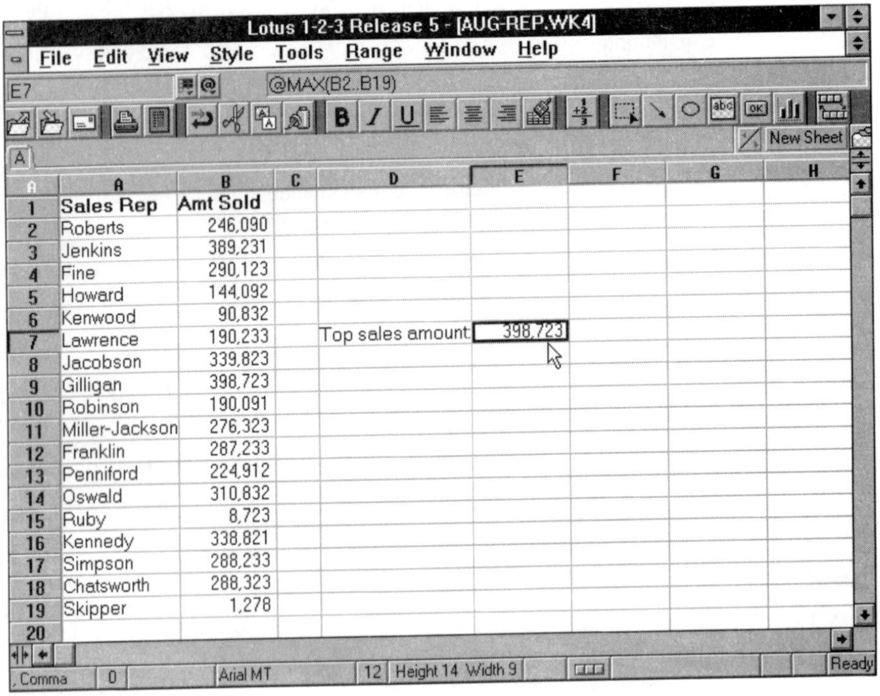

Figure 8-5:
The @MAX
function
tells you the
largest
sales figure.

| | A | B | C | D | E | F | G | H |
|---|---|---|---|---|---|---|---|---|
| 1 | Sales Rep | Amt Sold | | | | | | |
| 2 | Roberts | 246,090 | | | | | | |
| 3 | Jenkins | 389,231 | | | | | | |
| 4 | Fine | 290,123 | | | | | | |
| 5 | Howard | 144,092 | | | | | | |
| 6 | Kenwood | 90,832 | | | | | | |
| 7 | Lawrence | 190,233 | | Top sales amount: | 398,723 | | | |
| 8 | Jacobson | 339,823 | | | | | | |
| 9 | Gilligan | 398,723 | | | | | | |
| 10 | Robinson | 190,091 | | | | | | |
| 11 | Miller-Jackson | 276,323 | | | | | | |
| 12 | Franklin | 287,233 | | | | | | |
| 13 | Penniford | 224,912 | | | | | | |
| 14 | Oswald | 310,832 | | | | | | |
| 15 | Ruby | 8,723 | | | | | | |
| 16 | Kennedy | 338,821 | | | | | | |
| 17 | Simpson | 288,233 | | | | | | |
| 18 | Chatsworth | 288,323 | | | | | | |
| 19 | Skipper | 1,278 | | | | | | |
| 20 | | | | | | | | |

Lotus 1-2-3 Release 5 - [AUG-REP.WK4]

File   Edit   View   Style   Tools   Range   Window   Help

E7        @MAX(B2..B19)

# @MIN

If you need to locate the lowest sales volume in the list — to determine which underachiever gets your monthly motivational talk — you can use the following @MIN function, which works like the @MAX function but displays the lowest sales figure:

@MIN(B2..B19)

# @SQRT

The @SQRT function is a shortened version of the term *square root.* The square root of a number is the number that, when multiplied by itself, gives you the original number. For example, 4 is the square root of 16 because 4 x 4 = 16.

You can calculate the square root of the value in cell A1 by entering the following formula in any cell:

```
@SQRT(A1)
```

If cell A1 contained the value 225, the formula would return 15. @SQRT is an example of an @function that requires a single cell for its argument — perfectly logical, because it doesn't make sense to calculate the square root of an entire range.

# @ROUND

The @ROUND function rounds its argument and displays the result. If cell A1 contains 12.67, you can round it off to the nearest integer and display the result (13) in cell B1 by entering the following formula in cell B1:

```
@ROUND(A1,0)
```

Does this formula look different than you expected? To produce the correct results in your worksheet, this function needs two arguments. The first argument tells the program what cell you want to round off; the second argument tells 1-2-3 for Windows how many decimal places to round the number to. In this case, the second argument is 0, which tells the program to round off the number in cell A1 to no decimal places.

To round off the number to the first decimal place, 12.7, you change the formula to look like the following:

```
@ROUND(A1,1)
```

After you manipulate the value in a cell by using an @function, the actual value of the cell is affected. For example, after you change the value of 12.67 to 13 with the @ROUND function, the value of the cell becomes 13, and you lose the decimal value. Using the @functions to manipulate the value in a cell is very different than using numeric formatting, which only changes the way the number looks.

# @Functions for Dates and Times

The @functions that deal with dates and times get their information from your computer's internal clock. Make sure that your computer's clock is set properly, or these functions return the wrong dates and times. Procedures for setting computer clocks vary, so check your hardware manual.

If you want to enter dates in your worksheet, make sure that you read the sidebar. After you understand how 1-2-3 for Windows works with dates, you can do some interesting things with the date functions.

## @DATE

You can either enter a date into a cell with the formats you learned in the sidebar, or you can use the @DATE function. The @DATE function has three parts to its argument: a year, a month, and a day. To enter December 25, 1993, into a cell, use the following formula:

```
@DATE(93,12,25)
```

The program displays the number 34328, its special date number for the specific date that you entered. To make the date number show up as a date, use the Style⇨Number Format command and specify one of the date format options (or, use the numeric formatting button on the status bar).

---

### How about a date?

Adventurous types may have discovered that 1-2-3 for Windows doesn't always know what to do after you enter a date into a cell. Try entering the date *12-25-93* into a cell. The program responds with the number *-105* (definitely not Christmas), because it thinks that you are requesting a subtraction. The program does not recognize the format that you have used as a format for dates. Now try putting *12/25/93* into a cell. 1-2-3 for Windows recognizes the slash as an appropriate format for dates and automatically formats the cell to display it as a date.

Because 1-2-3 for Windows doesn't recognize all date formats, you must use one of the formats the program recognizes, such as 7/31/93 or 31-Jul-93. If you leave off the year (as in 31-Jul), 1-2-3 for Windows assumes the current year. If you leave off the day (as in Jul-93), the program assumes the first day of the month.

1-2-3 for Windows stores dates in a special date number system in which each number corresponds to a day. The date number system starts with January 1, 1900 (1) and goes up to December 31, 2099 (73,050) — almost 200 years of dates — enough for even the most aggressive budget projection.

## You got the time?

1-2-3 for Windows not only deals with dates but also handles time, by extending the date number concept to include decimal values. As you already know, the date number 34328 corresponds to December 25, 1993. By adding a decimal point to the number, you also can work with times during that day. For example, 34328.5 corresponds to 12:00 noon (half-way through Christmas day, 1993; 34328.1 corresponds to 2:24 a.m. (one-tenth of the way through the day).

Because there are 86,400 seconds in a day, one second works out to be .000011574074074 in this serial number format. One minute, on the other hand, equates to .0006944444. And one hour is .041666667. Therefore, to express 1:00 a.m. on December 25, 1993, you enter 33969.041666667 into a cell. If all these numbers have your head reeling, don't fret. Using the @TIME function makes it all relatively painless.

# @TODAY

This function doesn't need an argument. It simply returns the date number that corresponds to the current date stored in the computer's clock. For example, if you entered @TODAY into a cell on January 6, 1994, the function would return 34340 — the date number that corresponds to that date. If you save the file and load it again the next day, the function would then return 34341.

# @TIME

Like the @DATE function, the @TIME function also has three parts to its argument: an hour, a minute, and a second. To enter 5:30 p.m. into a cell, use the following formula:

```
@TIME(17,30,0)
```

Why the number 17? Remember that in 24-hour time, 5:00 p.m. is 5 hours past 12:00 noon, so that you add 12 + 5 to get 17 hours. The formula represents 17 hours, 30 minutes, and 0 seconds into the day, or 5:30 p.m. If you enter this @TIME function into a cell, 1-2-3 for Windows displays .7292824074. To see this number as readable time, use the Style⇨Number Format command and choose one of the time formats provided.

# Combined @Functions in Formulas

So far, the example formulas I've shown have consisted only of single @functions. You can, however, combine @functions in formulas. Take a look at the following formula, for example:

```
@SUM(A1..A10)+@SUM(C1..C10)
```

Here, the formula is simply taking the sum of the numbers in the range A1..A10 and adding the result to the sum of the numbers in range C1..C10. Another way of looking at the formula is that it's taking the sum of the range A1..C10, but skipping the range B1..B10. Therefore, the following formula produces the same result:

```
@SUM(A1..C10)-@SUM(B1..B10)
```

You also can work with dates and times in a formula. Suppose that you want to know the number of days between August 3, 1990, and July 16, 1993. Use the following formula to get the desired results:

```
@DATE(93,7,16)-@DATE(90,8,3)
```

In this case, it may be better to put the date formulas in separate cells (such as A1 and A2), and then use a simpler formula (such as +A2-A1) to do the subtraction. By putting the date formulas in separate cells, you easily can change the dates without having to mess with a more complex formula. In other words, you are making the spreadsheet more general, a good idea to keep in mind.

## The nesting instinct

The fact is, you can create some very complex formulas by using @functions. You can even use @functions as arguments for other @functions, a concept known as *nested @functions* (a topic that's for the birds).

Figure 8-6, for example, has values in column A, formulas in column B, and a nested @function in cell D13. The formula in cell B3 is @ROUND(A3,0), which rounds the value in cell A3 to zero decimal places. Rows 3–9 in column B each have similar formulas that round the values in their corresponding column A cells. The formula for the nested @function in cell D13 is as follows:

```
@ROUND(@SUM(A3..A9),0)
```

How can you interpret this complex formula? 1-2-3 for Windows tackles the formula as follows: First, the program evaluates the @SUM function and stores the answer in its memory. Then it uses this answer as the first argument for the @ROUND function and combines the answer with the second argument for the @ROUND function (which is 0). The program then displays the final answer in cell D13.

```
┌──────────────────────────────────────────────────────────────────────┐
│ ▭                         NESTED.WK4                          ▾ ▴       │
│ ┌A                                               ✎ New Sheet ◁          │
│   A        A        B            C            D              E      ▾   │
│   1                                                                ▲   │
│   2     Value    Rounded                                               │
│   3     12.4       12                                                   │
│   4     14.5       15                                                   │
│   5     18.7       19                                                   │
│   6     22.3       22                                                   │
│   7     11.2       11                                                   │
│   8     13.1       13                                                   │
│   9     13.4       13                                                   │
│  10                                                                    │
│  11              Sum of values:            105.6    @SUM(A3..A9)        │
│  12              Sum of rounded values:    105      @SUM(B3..B9)        │
│  13              Rounded sum:              106      @ROUND(@SUM(A3..A9),0)│
│  14                                           ▫                         │
│  15                                                               ▾    │
│ ◂▸ ◂                                                              ▸    │
└──────────────────────────────────────────────────────────────────────┘
```

**Figure 8-6:**
An example
of a nested
@function.

Rounding off the sum of the values does not produce the same result as summing the rounded off values. If you don't believe this, examine Figure 8-6 again and take a look at the formulas in cell D11 and cell D12.

## *Testing conditions*

One of the more useful @functions is the @IF function. This essentially allows your formulas to make decisions based on values in your worksheet. The @IF function requires the following three arguments:

- ✔ A condition to test
- ✔ What to display if the condition is true
- ✔ What to display if the condition is false

The following example is designed to test whether the number in cell A1 is positive or negative:

```
@IF(A1>0,"Positive","Negative or zero")
```

Notice that the three arguments are separated by commas. The first argument is the condition, which in this case is asking whether the number in cell A1 is greater than zero. If the number is greater than zero, the formula displays the word Positive; if the number is zero or less than zero, the formula displays the words Negative or zero.

Suppose that you want to know specifically whether the number in a cell is positive, negative, or zero (three responses — an added twist to the same concept). Now you need to use a nested @IF function to produce the desired results. Before you read the explanation, try to figure out the following formula on your own to see how it works:

```
@IF(A1>0,"Positive",@IF(A1<0,"Negative","Zero"))
```

1-2-3 for Windows first tests to see whether the number in cell A1 is greater than zero. If so, the program responds with the word Positive and is done with the formula. If the contents of cell A1 is not greater than zero, the program goes to the third part of the first @IF argument and discovers another @IF function there, which it proceeds to evaluate. This second (nested) @IF function checks to see whether the value of cell A1 is less than zero. If so, the program responds with the word Negative. If not, the program responds with the final choice of Zero.

If you understand how the nested @IF function works, congratulations! You're well on your way to being a more-than-adequate 1-2-3 for Windows user.

# Naming Cells and Ranges

Naming cells and ranges may not be absolutely necessary for your well-being, but you may find that it makes your spreadsheeting life easier. You can give a meaningful name to any cell or range ( you'll learn how to do this later). After doing so, you can use that name wherever you normally use a cell or range reference.

## An example

Suppose that you name cell F2 *num_employees,* because the value in this cell is the total number of employees. Using meaningful names makes your life even easier, but this is not a requirement. (1-2-3 for Windows doesn't mind whether you name the cell *kh82z1x7y,* but that name certainly doesn't help you to understand your spreadsheet any better.) Cell M12, named *total_salary,* has — you guessed it — the total salary of your employees. Now you want to determine the average salary of your employees. After you choose a cell in the worksheet, you can enter the following formula in the cell by using the name of the cell:

```
+total_salary/num_employees
```

You also can write the formula +M12/F2 to make the same calculations. However, the formula with the names is much easier to read, because anyone who looks at the formula has a pretty good idea of what it does.

# Another example

You also can give a name to an entire range. For example, if range G1..G12 is named *expenses,* you then can write the following formula that adds the expenses in the entire range, using the name of the range alone:

```
@SUM(expenses)
```

The formula @SUM(G1..G12) also requests the sum of the range but does not indicate what the formula is adding. Not only does using the name of the range simplify your formula, but it also makes the formula clear to anyone who sees it.

# Naming your cells and ranges

Naming a cell or range is easy. Just follow these steps:

1. **Move the cell pointer to the cell you want to name.**

    For this example, move the cell pointer to cell C9.

2. **Select the Range⇨Name command.**

    1-2-3 for Windows pops up the dialog box shown in Figure 8-7.

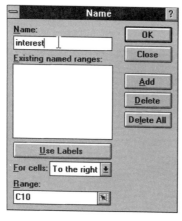

**Figure 8-7:** The Name dialog box, where you give a name to a cell or range.

3. **Type** interest **in the Name box and select OK.**

To give a name to a range, you either can begin by selecting the entire range you want to name, or you can select the range from the dialog box after you issue the Range⇨Name command.

Keep the following information in mind as you go about naming cells and ranges:

- ✔ Names can be up to 15 characters long, and you can't use math operators or spaces. Also, avoid creating names that look like cell addresses. For example, 1-2-3 might confuse a range named *ab1* with cell AB1.

- ✔ If you already have one or more names in your worksheet, 1-2-3 for Windows displays a list of these names in the Name dialog box. By choosing a name from this list, you can see the cell or range it refers to in the Range box.

- ✔ You can name a bunch of single cells that have labels next to them, and you can name them all with a single command. Use the Range⇨Name command and click the Use Labels button. In the listbox below the button, tell 1-2-3 for Windows where the labels are in relation to the cells that you want to name.

- ✔ You can quickly move the cell pointer to a named range by using the Range Selector icon in the edit line. Clicking the Range Selector icon displays a list of all named ranges, similar to the one in Figure 8-8. Select the range you want, and you're there in a flash.

Range Selector icon

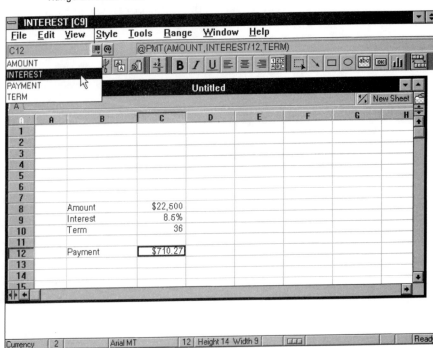

**Figure 8-8:** The Range Selector icon shows a list of all named cells and ranges.

# Chapter 9
# Cutting and Changing without Screaming and Crying

*"A living thing is distinguished from a dead thing by the multiplicity of the changes at any moment taking place in it."*

Herbert Spencer (1820 –1903)
English philosopher

• • • • • • • • • • • • • • • • • • • • • • • • • • • • • • • • • • • • • • • • • • • •

## In This Chapter

▶ Cutting and pasting (AKA moving) cells and ranges of cells

▶ Copying cells and ranges of cells (or, how to make many from one)

▶ Changing column widths to avoid the asterisks problem

▶ Making rows taller

▶ Inserting and deleting rows and columns

▶ Turning horizontal data into vertical data — and vice versa

▶ Using Find & Replace to make lots of changes with little effort

▶ Sorting a range of data — and all kinds of options you have

• • • • • • • • • • • • • • • • • • • • • • • • • • • • • • • • • • • • • • • • • • • •

*I*f you're like most people, you spend a large part of your spreadsheeting time changing things that you've already done. This is perfectly normal, and it's not a sign of an indecisive personality disorder. (I don't think so, anyway. On second thought, it might be. Well, then again, I'm not sure.)  Anyway, you'll soon discover that when you start making changes to a worksheet, it's far too easy to take something that used to work, and somehow mess it up so it doesn't work anymore.

Therefore, it's in your best interest to understand what goes on behind the scenes when you set out to change something in your worksheet. This especially applies to copying, cutting, and pasting cells and ranges — particularly when they contain formulas. That's why this chapter has more than its share of Warning icons.

# *Types of Changes You Can Make*

So what do I mean by making changes to a worksheet? Here are some examples:

- You spent five minutes creating a killer formula that does magic with a column of numbers. You have 20 more columns that need the same formula applied to them. What to do? Copy the formula so it works for the other ranges of cells.

- You have a nice table of numbers, but you fell asleep on the keyboard and put the table about 50 rows below where it should be. So, you need to move it up to a more reasonable location in the worksheet. This is known as cutting and pasting.

- You're just about ready to turn in your department budget when you realize that you forgot to enter a budget item (Pet Neutering) that should go right between the categories Outboard Motor Repair and Quilting Supplies (your department has many talented people). You need to insert a new row to make room for it.

- Your boss informs you that you can no longer budget for office mud baths. Eventually, regardless of the resentment you feel, you must zap the entire Mud Bath row in your budget worksheet.

- You've got a great worksheet, but the numbers are all crammed together and hard to read. You want to widen some of the columns.

- You've got a bunch of labels entered in a column — and you realize that you should have put them in a row. You need to transpose these labels, and you don't feel like typing them all again.

- Marketing just informed you that they changed the name of one of your company's products from Sugar Munchies to Health Munchies. Your worksheet has dozens of labels with this product name in it, and you need to change every occurrence of *Sugar* to *Health*. You can do it manually — or let 1-2-3 for Windows do it for you with its Edit⇨Find & Replace command.

- You just spent two hours entering all of your sales figures in alphabetical order by sales rep name. Then, your boss informs you that they need to be in descending order by sales amount. Unless you like to redo your work, you need to sort this range of cells.

The preceding list describes just some of the changes that people make to their worksheets. The rest of this chapter tells you how to do these types of changes — without destroying what you've already done and causing more work for yourself.

When you start making changes to a worksheet, remember that you can reverse the effects of most things that you do by selecting Edit➪Undo (or Ctrl+Z) immediately after you make the change. But you have to issue this command before you do *anything* else. Therefore, it's good to get into the habit of examining what you did before you move on to something else. It's also good to have a backup copy of your worksheet saved to a floppy disk. To make sure that Undo is enabled, select the Tools➪User Setup command. Make sure that the Undo option is checked; otherwise, Edit➪Undo will not work.

# Cutting and Pasting — Scissors and Glue Not Required

When you enter something into a cell, it's not stuck there for life. You can cut it and paste it anywhere else on the worksheet — or even paste it to a different worksheet. In other words, if you want to move something from one place to another, you cut it and then paste it.

## How cutting and pasting works

If you're going to use Windows, you've got to understand the concept of *cutting and pasting*. You cut something out of your worksheet, and then you paste it somewhere else. This cutting and pasting involves the infamous Windows Clipboard. (See "The Windows Clipboard" sidebar for additional information on this Clipboard business). When you tell 1-2-3 for Windows to cut, it takes whatever is selected at the time (a cell or a range), removes it from the work–sheet, and puts a copy of it on the Clipboard. Then, when you tell 1-2-3 for Windows to paste, it takes what's in the Clipboard and pastes it to your current selection (usually a different cell or a range). Once you understand this concept, you should have no problems with moving stuff.

When you paste a cell or range and the area that you're pasting to already contains something, 1-2-3 for Windows overwrites the cells with the pasted information — without warning. So if you have some important stuff on your worksheet, be careful when moving things around.

# The Windows Clipboard

As this chapter so eloquently describes, copying and moving within 1-2-3 for Windows uses something called the Windows Clipboard. Basically, this Clipboard is an area of your computer's memory that's sort of a temporary holding spot. So when you cut or copy a cell or a range, 1-2-3 for Windows puts the information on the Clipboard. When you paste something to a cell or range, 1-2-3 for Windows takes whatever happens to be in the Clipboard and pastes it wherever you want it to.

The Clipboard can hold only one thing at a time. So, if you copy a cell or range to the Clipboard, it replaces what's already there (if anything). The Clipboard is pretty versatile, and it can hold all sorts of information—the contents of a single cell, a range of cells, an entire graph, or part of a graph.

The neat thing about the Clipboard, though, is that all Windows programs have access to it. This means that you can copy a range of cells from 1-2-3 for Windows, and then paste them into your

Windows word processing program. The Clipboard works as the intermediary. Although not all types of information that can be stored on the Clipboard can be pasted into every application, you'll find that it's pretty versatile. Learning how the Clipboard works is useful in all of the Windows applications you run.

Microsoft Windows includes a program that simply displays what's currently on the Clipboard. This program is called Clipboard Viewer, and you can probably find it in the Windows Program Manager program group called Main. It's not necessary to run this program in order to use the Clipboard to cut, copy, and paste, but you may find it interesting. When you run this program, it simply displays whatever happens to be on the Clipboard. Just for fun, you might want to run the Clipboard program alongside of 1-2-3 for Windows. Then, when you copy something, you can see it show up immediately on the Clipboard.

When you're dealing with the Windows Clipboard, you can save yourself lots of time by getting into the habit of using shortcut keys or SmartIcons instead of menus. The shortcut keys and SmartIcons for cutting, copying, and pasting are

| Command | Shortcut Key | SmartIcon |
|---|---|---|
| Edit⇒Cut | Ctrl+X | ✂ |
| Edit⇒Copy | Ctrl+C | 🗐 |
| Edit⇒Paste | Ctrl+V | 📋 |

Throughout this chapter, I talk about the Edit⇒Cut, Edit⇒Paste, and Edit⇒Copy commands. A faster way to access these commands is by right-clicking after you make a selection. This brings up a shortcut menu, which enables you to choose Cut, Paste, or Copy.

## Why cut and paste?

Assume you entered a list of numbers into a worksheet column and then discovered that you forget to leave space for a heading. You *could* insert a new row and stick the heading in the new row. But if you have other information in the first row, inserting a new row would mess it up. Therefore, the easiest solution is to move the list of numbers down one row — cut it, and then paste it. Another reason to move things around in a worksheet is simply to better organize it. We all change our minds occasionally, right?

## Cutting and pasting a cell

Here's how to move the contents of a cell from one place to another: Assume that you're moving the number in cell A1 to its new home in cell B1. In other words, you're cutting the information from A1 and then pasting it into B1.

1. **Start by moving the cell pointer to the cell that you want to move (cell A1, in this case).**

2. **Select the Edit⇨Cut command (or press Ctrl+X).**

   1-2-3 for Windows removes the contents of the cell and places them on the Windows Clipboard.

3. **Next, move to the new location — which is cell B1 in this example.**

4. **Select Edit⇨Paste (or press Ctrl+V).**

1-2-3 for Windows puts the contents of the Clipboard in the selected cell.

It should be clear that using cut and paste on a single cell is no great time-saver — unless the cell contains a long label or a formula. If you just have a value or a short label, it may be faster just to delete it and retype it somewhere else.

## Cutting and pasting a range

The real value of cutting and pasting becomes apparent when you start dealing with ranges of cells. Moving a range of cells is very similar to moving one cell. Start by selecting the entire range you want to move, and select the Edit⇨Cut command (or press Ctrl+X) to remove the range and put in on the Clipboard. Next, move the cell pointer to the new location (you need to select only the upper left cell in the new range — not the entire range). Select Edit⇨Paste (or press Ctrl+V) and 1-2-3 for Windows will retrieve the information from the Clipboard and put it in the new location you specified.

You can relocate dozens, hundreds, or even thousands of cells using cut and paste.

## Cutting and pasting formulas

You can move cells that contain formulas just like you move other cells. So if you cut and paste a cell that has a formula such as +A1+A2, the formula continues to refer to those same cells no matter where you move it (this is almost always what you want to happen).

Moving cells that contain formulas does not change the cell references in the formulas.

## The E-Z way to move things

Now that you know how to use the Clipboard to cut and paste information, you might be interested in learning another, easier way to move cells or ranges — but you'll need a mouse to do it. This method's really easy: simply select the cell or range that you want to move, drag it to where you want to put it, and then drop it in place.

The only thing you have to remember is that the mouse pointer has to look like a hand before you can drag a cell or range. To get the mouse pointer to turn into a hand, just move it to one of the edges of the selection. When it turns into a hand, click and hold down the left mouse button. The hand will close, and the cell or range will have a dashed outline around it. You can then drag your selection to its new location. When you release the mouse button, the cell or range will appear in its new location, and you're done. Figure 9-1 shows what this hand looks like before you click (open hand) and after you click (closed hand).

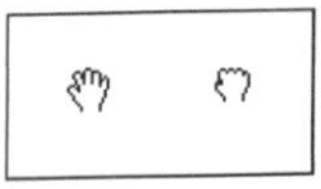

**Figure 9-1:**
The mouse pointer as an opened and closed hand.

Figure 9-2 shows a live-action shot of drag-and-drop operation in progress. Note that you don't drag the actual selection. Rather, you just drag a dashed outline of the selection.

If drag-and-drop moving isn't working, it's probably because this feature is disabled. To enable drag-and-drop, select the Tools⇨User Setup command, and make sure the Drag-and-drop cells option is checked.

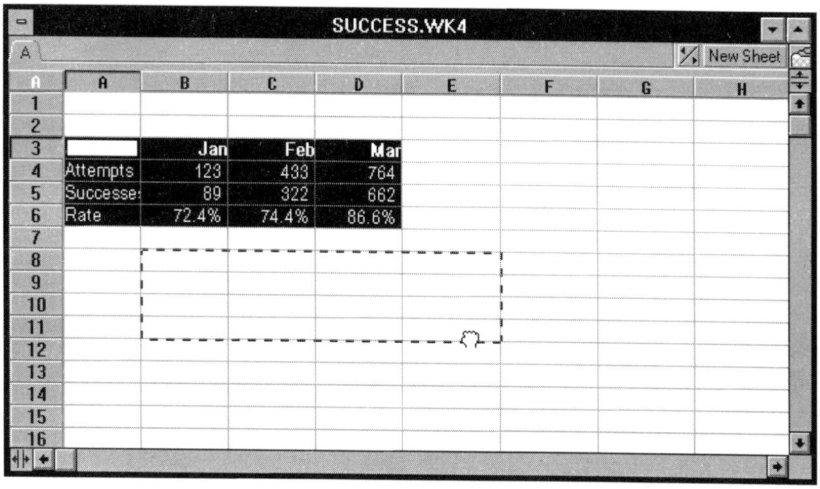

| | A | B | C | D | E | F | G | H |
|---|---|---|---|---|---|---|---|---|
| 3 | | Jan | Feb | Mar | | | | |
| 4 | Attempts | 123 | 433 | 764 | | | | |
| 5 | Successe: | 89 | 322 | 662 | | | | |
| 6 | Rate | 72.4% | 74.4% | 86.6% | | | | |

SUCCESS.WK4

**Figure 9-2:**
Moving a
range of
cells by
dragging.

With Release 5, you can even use these drag-and-drop procedures to move information from one worksheet to another. Just make sure both worksheets are visible on-screen (you may have to rearrange the windows a bit). Then use the techniques described previously to move it.

# Copying Things Things Things

One of the most common spreadsheet operations is copying. Here are your three options when it comes to copying:

- ✔ Copy a single cell to another cell
- ✔ Copy a single cell to a range of cells
- ✔ Copy a whole range of cells to another area

## How copying works

As you might expect, copying is rather similar to moving — and both operations use the Clipboard. The difference, however, is that 1-2-3 for Windows leaves the copied cell or range contents intact when it puts them on the Clipboard. When you make a copy of a cell or range, the original cell or range remains the same — you're simply making a replica of it and sticking it somewhere else.

This is the same warning I gave earlier about cutting and pasting. When you copy something and the area that you're copying to already contains some-thing, 1-2-3 for Windows overwrites the cells with the new copied information — without warning you about it. So if you have some important stuff on your worksheet, be careful when copying.

## Why copy?

The most obvious reason to copy a cell or a range of cells is so you don't have to type it in again. Copying is also useful for duplicating a formula so that the formula works on other ranges. When you copy a formula, 1-2-3 for Windows does some interesting things, as I'll explain in the next section.

## Copying a cell to a cell

Here's how to copy the contents of cell A1 to B1.

1. **Move the cell pointer to A1.**

2. **Issue the Edit⇨Copy command.**

   1-2-3 for Windows makes a copy of the cell contents and stores it in the Windows Clipboard. The contents of cell A1 remains intact.

3. **Next, move the cell pointer to cell B1 and select the Edit⇨Paste command.**

   1-2-3 for Windows will retrieve the contents of the Clipboard and insert them into cell B1. Mission accomplished.

Cell B1 will now contain the same information as cell A1.

Figure 9-3 shows this operation just prior to pasting the Clipboard contents into cell B1.

## Copying a cell to a range

Copying a single cell to a range of cells works exactly the same as copying to a single cell. You start by selecting the cell you want to copy, and then issue the Edit⇨Copy command (or press Ctrl+C). The only difference is that you will select a *range* of cells before you issue the Edit⇨Paste command (or press Ctrl+V). After you do so, the single cell you originally copied to the Clipboard will be duplicated in every cell in the range you selected.

Figure 9-4 shows what happens when you copy a single cell to a range of cells.

## Copying a range to a range

Copying a range of cells to another range is very similar to the other copy operations I described. Select the range to be copied and issue the Edit⇨Copy command. Then, move the cell pointer to the new location and select Edit⇨Paste. You need only select the upper left cell before you do the Edit⇨Paste command (you don't have to select the entire range).

Figure 9-5 shows a range of cells that has been copied to another range.

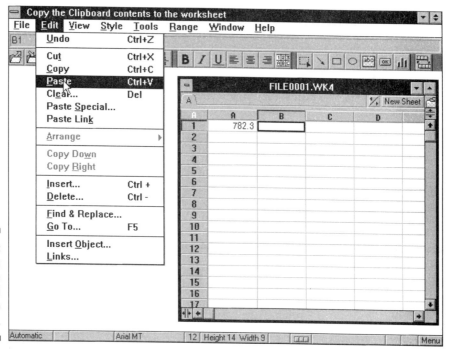

**Figure 9-3:**
Preparing
to paste the
Clipboard
contents to
cell B1.

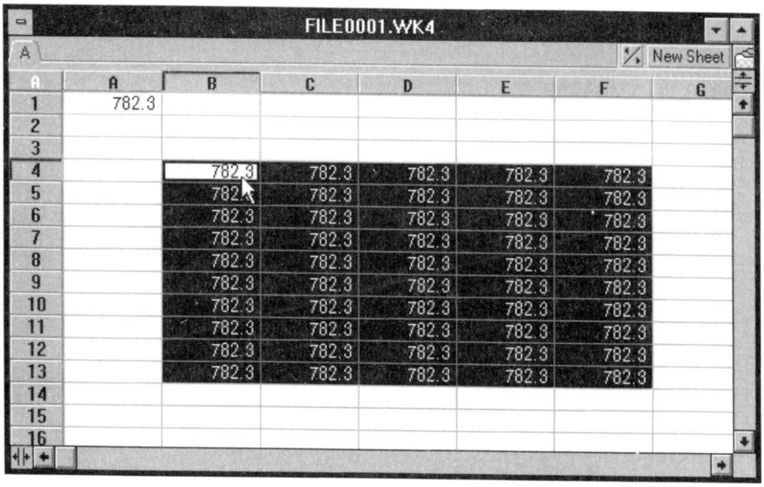

**Figure 9-4:**
Copying a
single cell to
a range puts
the contents
of the cell
into every
cell in the
range.

| SUCCESS.WK4 | | | | | | | | |
|---|---|---|---|---|---|---|---|---|
| | **A** | **B** | **C** | **D** | **E** | **F** | **G** | **H** |
| **1** | | | | | | | | |
| **2** | Northern Region | | | | | | | |
| **3** | | Jan | Feb | Mar | | | | |
| **4** | Attempts | 123 | 433 | 764 | | | | |
| **5** | Successe: | 89 | 322 | 662 | | | | |
| **6** | Rate | 72.4% | 74.4% | 86.6% | | | | |
| **7** | | | | | | | | |
| **8** | | | | | | | | |
| **9** | Southern Region | | | | | | | |
| **10** | | Jan | Feb | Mar | | | | |
| **11** | Attempt | 123 | 433 | 764 | | | | |
| **12** | Successe: | 89 | 322 | 662 | | | | |
| **13** | Rate | 72.4% | 74.4% | 86.6% | | | | |
| **14** | | | | | | | | |
| **15** | | | | | | | | |
| **16** | | | | | | | | |

**Figure 9-5:**
Copying an entire range duplicates that range somewhere else.

## Copying formulas

Copying formulas works exactly like copying anything else. In other words, you can copy a single formula to another cell, copy a single formula to a range of cells, or copy a range of formulas to another range of cells.

When you copy a formula, something special happens: all of the cell references in the formula are adjusted. Assume for a minute that cell A3 has the formula +A1+A2. When you copy this formula to cell B3, the formula will read +B1+B2. In other words, the cell references change to refer to the same relative cells in their new position.

This might seem contrary to your expectation. If you make a copy of a formula, the copy should be exact, right? Copying a cell that contains +A1+A2 should produce +A1+A2 in the cell that it gets copied to. Well, if you think about it, you usually never want to make an exact copy of a formula. Rather, you want the copied formula to refer to a different set of cells. And that's exactly what 1-2-3 for Windows does — automatically.

Figure 9-6 shows what happens when you copy a formula.

An exception to this is an absolute cell reference, which I discussed in Chapter 7. As you may recall, an absolute cell reference uses dollar signs (for example, +$C$9) to specify that you don't want the cell reference to change when it's copied.

When you copy a formula, the cell references are adjusted automatically — unless you use absolute cell references.

**Figure 9-6:**
When you
copy a
formula,
1-2-3 for
Windows
automatically
adjusts
the cell's
references
so that the
copied
formula
works as it
should in its
new home.

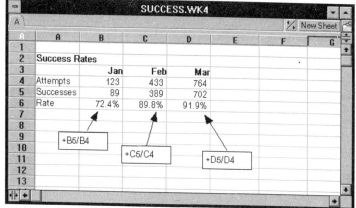

# Drag-and-drop copying

If you read the previous section that covered moving cells or ranges by copying and pasting, you know that you can also move things using a simple drag-and-drop procedure. 1-2-3 for Windows extends this and lets you *copy* cells or ranges using drag-and-drop. Again, you'll need a mouse to do this.

This procedure has a minor limitation. You can copy a single cell to another location, or copy a range of cells to another location — but you *cannot* copy a single cell to a range. You have to use the normal copy and paste procedure to do that.

To copy using drag-and-drop, start by selecting the cell or range to be copied. Then, move the mouse pointer to an edge of the selection until the mouse pointer turns into a hand. *Hold down the Ctrl key while you press the left mouse button.* The hand will close, and it will also have a plus sign (+) on it (see Figure 9-7). Drag the selection to where you want to copy it and release the mouse button. 1-2-3 for Windows will place a copy of your original selection in the new location.

If drag-and-drop copying isn't working, it's probably because this feature is disabled. To enable drag-and-drop, select the Tools⇨User Setup command, and make sure the Drag-and-drop cells option is checked.

Release 5 owners can use this drag-and-drop procedure to copy a range from one worksheet to another. Just make sure both worksheets are visible on-screen (a bit of window rearrangement may be in order). Then use the techniques described previously to copy it.

**Figure 9-7:**
If you hold
down Ctrl
when you
click, the
hand pointer
closes and
has a plus
sign on it.
This lets you
copy the
selection by
dragging it.

| | A | B | C | D | E | F |
|---|---|---|---|---|---|---|
| | | Jan | Feb | Mar | | |
| 1 | | | | | | |
| 2 | Phone calls | 1455 | 1398 | 1277 | | |
| 3 | Letters | 434 | 366 | 322 | | |
| 4 | Faxes | 487 | 550 | 569 | | |
| 5 | E-mail messages | 611 | 790 | 812 | | |
| 6 | Total | 2987 | 3104 | | | |
| 7 | | | | | | |
| 8 | | | | | | |
| 9 | | | | | | |
| 10 | | | | | | |
| 11 | | | | | | |
| 12 | | | | | | |
| 13 | | | | | | |

COMM.WK4 — New Sheet

# *Adjusting Column Widths*

When you start a new worksheet, all of the 256 columns are the same width:
nine characters. You can make any or all of these columns wider or narrower to
accommodate the information you put in them. It should be obvious that when
you change a column width, the entire column changes. In other words, you
can't adjust the width of individual cells.

The preceding paragraph stated that a standard column is nine characters
wide. Actually, this is a rather arbitrary number, because the number of
characters that will display in a "9-character" cell depends on the actual
characters used, the type size, the font, and whether they're bold. In other
words, it's best to adjust column widths based on what you see on-screen, not
the number of characters in the cells.

## *Why widen columns?*

I can think of three reasons to adjust column widths:

- ✔ To make long numbers display properly. Numbers that are too wide to fit
  in a column show up as a series of asterisks, like this: *********.

- ✔ To make the worksheet look better by spacing things out or moving them
  closer together.

- ✔ To make long labels display properly. Labels that are too wide have a
  truncated display if the cell adjacent to the right is occupied.

Figure 9-8 shows a worksheet that has several different columns widths to
accommodate various entries.

**Figure 9-8:** You can adjust the widths of columns to handle practically anything you can put in a cell.

| | A | B | C | D |
|---|---|---|---|---|
| 1 | Sales Person | Date Hired | Code | Comments |
| 2 | Shirley Peterson | 12/02/56 | 145 | Shirly finally made quota. Give her a bonus. |
| 3 | Richard P. Wilson | 04/05/92 | 154 | Dick couldn't sell his way out of a paper bag. |
| 4 | Kelly Richards | 06/03/67 | 121 | Why is this guy still around? Fire him! |
| 5 | Mike Ubangi | 08/03/93 | 154 | Mike is doing OK. Let's promote him. |
| 6 | Jill Ferguson | 08/04/92 | 143 | Jill is doing very well, considering she's only 11 years old. |
| 7 | Glen Jenkins | 02/04/89 | 123 | No comment on this one! |
| 8 | | | | |
| 9 | | | | |
| 10 | | | | |
| 11 | | | | |

COMMENTS.WK4

# Adjusting column widths using the menu

Here's how to change the width of one or more columns.

1. **Select any cell in the column or columns you want to adjust.**

   To select non-adjacent columns, hold down Ctrl while you click cells.

2. **Select the Style⇨Column Width command.**

   1-2-3 for Windows displays the dialog box shown in Figure 9-9.

**Figure 9-9:** This dialog box lets you adjust column widths.

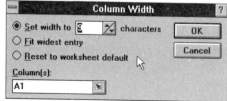

3. **Change the setting to the desired number of characters.**

   If you click the Fit widest entry option, each column in the selection will be made just wide enough to handle the widest entry in the column. Choose the Reset to worksheet default option to return the columns to their standard width.

4. **Choose OK to close the dialog box.**

   The columns will be adjusted per your specs.

## Global column widths

By default, every column in a 1-2-3 for Windows worksheet is nine characters wide. If you ever find yourself wanting narrower or wider columns on an entire worksheet, you don't have to go through the normal steps to set the column widths — just change the default. Use the Style➪Worksheet Defaults command, and set the global column width in the dialog box that

appears. Changing the global column width will *not* change the widths of any columns that you already changed. For example, if you make column A 24 characters wide and then change the global column width to 15, column A's width will stay at 24 characters, and all of the other column widths will change.

## E-Z ways to adjust column widths

The preceding section showed you how to use the Style➪Column Width command to change column widths. That method was pretty easy, but there are even easier ways to do this.

### What a drag

Probably the best way to change a column's width is to drag the column border (you need a mouse for this). You have to grab the right column border, directly to the right of the column's letter. When you move the mouse pointer to the column border, the mouse pointer will change shape to let you know that you can drag. Drag the border to the right to make the column wider, or to the left to make it narrower. You can also watch the cell address box to see the column width numbers change as you drag the mouse. Figure 9-10 shows what dragging a column border looks like.

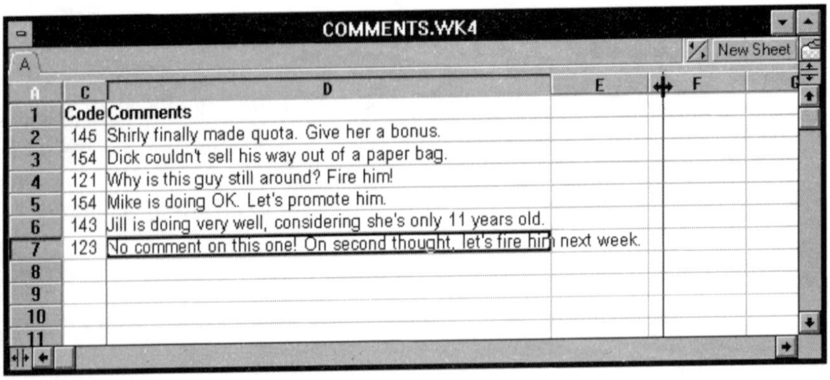

**Figure 9-10:** Dragging a column border is the easiest way to change a column's width.

| | C | D | E | F | G |
|---|---|---|---|---|---|
| 1 | Code | Comments | | | |
| 2 | 145 | Shirly finally made quota. Give her a bonus. | | | |
| 3 | 154 | Dick couldn't sell his way out of a paper bag. | | | |
| 4 | 121 | Why is this guy still around? Fire him! | | | |
| 5 | 154 | Mike is doing OK. Let's promote him. | | | |
| 6 | 143 | Jill is doing very well, considering she's only 11 years old. | | | |
| 7 | 123 | No comment on this one! On second thought, let's fire him next week. | | | |
| 8 | | | | | |
| 9 | | | | | |
| 10 | | | | | |
| 11 | | | | | |

COMMENTS.WK4

To change the widths of several columns by dragging, first select the complete columns that you want to change. Do this by clicking and dragging across the column letters. Then drag the border of any of the selected columns to change the widths of all of them.

### Double-clicking

If you want to make a column just wide enough to display the widest cell entry, simply double click the right border of the column (in the column letter area). Again, you can pre-select multiple columns to auto-adjust more than one column with one double-click.

There's a SmartIcon that automatically adjusts column widths (Figure 9-11 shows what this looks like). To use this, you have to select the entire column or columns first.

**Figure 9-11:**
This
SmartIcon
automatically
adjusts
column
widths.

# Changing Row Heights

You can also change the height of rows. Most of the time, you'll be satisfied with the fact that 1-2-3 for Windows handles this automatically. For example, if you make a cell's font larger, 1-2-3 for Windows will automatically increase the row height to handle the bigger font. But you can also increase the row heights yourself to adjust spacing.

If you want to "double space" your work, increasing row heights is a better approach than skipping rows.

Figure 9-12 shows a worksheet with several different row heights.

To change the height of a row, select the entire row and then choose the Style⇨Row Height command. You'll get the dialog box shown in Figure 9-13. Adjust the row height as you like and select OK.

An easier way to change row heights is to drag the row border with your mouse — just like you do when adjusting a column width. Click the bottom border and drag it down to make the row taller, or drag it up to make it shorter.

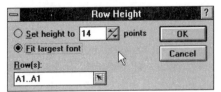

**Figure 9-12:**
You can
adjust the
height of
individual
rows to
space things
out vertically.

| A | A | B | C | D | E |
|---|---|---|---|---|---|
| 1 | California | 984 | | | |
| 2 | Oregon | 143 | | | |
| 3 | Washington | 443 | | | |
| 4 | Total West Coast | 1570 | | | |
| 5 | | | | | |
| | Missouri | 322 | | | |
| 6 | Illinois | 543 | | | |
| 7 | Kansas | 124 | | | |
| 8 | Total Midwest | 989 | | | |
| 9 | New York | 665 | | | |
| 10 | New Jersey | 589 | | | |
| 11 | Massachusetts | 498 | | | |
| 12 | Rhode Island | 143 | | | |
| 13 | Total East Coast | 1895 | | | |
| 14 | | | | | |

**Figure 9-13:**
You adjust
the height of
rows with
this dialog
box.

**Row Height**

- ○ Set height to [14] points [OK]
- ● Fit largest font [Cancel]

Row(s):
[A1..A1]

# Erasing Cells and Ranges

Getting rid of the contents of a cell — or a whole range of cells — is easy. This is known as erasing, deleting, wiping out, nuking, killing, annihilating, zapping, and all sorts of other terms that aren't suitable for all family members. Regardless of what you call it, after you do it, the information is gone.

The alert reader will know that the Edit⇨Cut command will get rid of the contents of cells and ranges. Another way to erase a cell or a range is to use the Edit⇨Clear command. Start by selecting the offending cell or range and then issue the command. Or, to save some time, simply press the Del key and avoid the menu altogether.

Why two commands to do the same thing? The difference is that Edit⇨Clear (or Del) doesn't put the erased information on the Clipboard. So, if you have something on the Clipboard that you want to remain there (so you can paste it later), you can use Edit⇨Clear to erase cells without affecting the Clipboard.

# Adding New Rows and Columns

You can insert new rows and columns into your worksheet. Actually, the number of rows and columns always remains the same (8,192 rows and 256 columns). Inserting a new row simply scoots everything down, and the last row in the worksheet disappears.

Inserting a new column scoots everything over to the right, and the last column in the worksheet disappears. If the last column has something in it, you can't insert a new column. The same goes for rows. If the last row in your worksheet is not empty, you can't insert a new row.

## Why do it?

It's not uncommon to discover that you need to insert something between two other cells. You might have a list of products and prices and discover that you left one out. One approach is to move part of the range down one row to make room for the new entry. A faster method is to simply insert a new row. This pushes everything down and makes room for your forgotten stuff.

If you insert a new row or column, you have to be careful that it doesn't mess up other areas of your worksheet. See "A word of caution" for more information about this.

By the way, if you performed the "hands-on" exercise in Chapter 3, you already have experience inserting new rows.

## A word of caution

It may sound like a pretty dumb warning, but you need to remember that deleting a row or column does just that — it deletes an entire row or column. Lots of users tend to focus on just one part of their spreadsheet, and forget that there are other parts out of view. They go about inserting and deleting rows and columns, and are then surprised to discover that another area of their worksheet is all messed up. So let that be a warning. Actually, if your worksheet has a bunch of separate parts, you might be better off using separate sheets for the various parts (use the New Sheet button to add new sheets). That way, things you do on one worksheet won't affect the other worksheets in the file. See Chapter 11 for more details on using these 3-D multisheet files.

## Adding new rows

Here's how to add a new row to your worksheet.

1. **Select the complete row that's just below the row that you want to insert.**

   To do this, click the row number.

2. **Issue the Edit⇨Insert command.**

1-2-3 for Windows will push all of the rows down and give you a new blank row.

If you want to add more than one row, simply start by selecting more than one row. For example, to add 5 rows below row 10, select rows 10 through 15 before you issue the Edit⇨Insert command. In other words, the row or rows that you select before issuing the Edit⇨Insert command will be blank rows after you execute the command.

You can also use Ctrl++ as a shortcut for Edit⇨Insert — but you have to use the + on the numeric keypad (not the one above the equal sign). And, of course, right-clicking also gives you access to the Insert command.

## Adding new columns

Adding one or more columns works just like adding rows. The only difference is that you start by selecting one or more columns. Then, issue Edit⇨Insert, and 1-2-3 for Windows will give you the new columns. Ctrl++ also works for column inserts.

# Getting Rid of Rows and Columns

Because you can add rows and columns, you ought to be able to take them away, right? 1-2-3 for Windows lets you remove as many rows and columns as you like. However, the total number of rows and columns always remains the same. If you remove a row, for example, all of the other rows move up one slot and 1-2-3 for Windows inserts another row at the bottom. The comparable thing happens when you remove a column.

Be careful when removing rows and columns. If they contain cells that are used in any of your formulas, the formulas are useless; they will no longer return the correct answer.

## Why do it?

If you discover that the information in a row or column is not needed, you can get rid of it quickly by deleting the entire row or column. This is a much faster alternative to deleting the range and then moving everything else around to fill up the gap.

## Eliminating rows

To get rid of a row, select the entire row and then issue the Edit⇨Delete command. To delete more than one row, simply extend the row selection before you issue the command.

## Deleting columns

Getting rid of entire columns works the same way as deleting rows — except that you start out by selecting the column or columns that you want to zap. Then, select the Edit⇨Delete command to do the deed.

You can also use Ctrl+– as a shortcut for Edit⇨Delete — but you have to use the minus sign on the numeric keypad (not the one to the left of the equal sign). Right-clicking gives you access to the Delete command also.

---

# Hiding things

1-2-3 for Windows lets you hide individual cells, ranges, or complete columns (but not rows). When something is hidden, it's still in the worksheet and can be referred to in formulas — it just doesn't appear on-screen. Hiding is often handy when you are printing, and you don't want particular information to be printed. Simply hide the unwanted cells or columns and commence printing.

To hide a cell or range, select it and issue the Style⇨Number Format command. Choose Hidden from the list of formats (this works with labels as well as values). To unhide hidden cells, use the same command and select the Reset button.

Hiding cells isn't really intended to be used for security purposes, because the contents of a hidden cell still appears in the edit line when the cell pointer is on the cell. To make it so hidden cells don't appear in the edit line, you need to protect the cells (with the Style⇨Protection command), and seal the file (with the File⇨Protect command).

To hide entire columns in the worksheet, select the columns to be hidden and then issue the Style⇨Hide command. To display hidden columns, use the same command and choose the Show button.

Although you can't officially hide rows, setting them to a height of 1 with the Style⇨Row Height comes pretty close.

# Transposing Rows and Columns

Transposing a range means changing its orientation. If you have numbers in a single column, you can transpose them so they appear in a single row — and vice versa.

## Why do it?

You transpose rows and columns if you discover that information in the worksheet is in the wrong orientation: vertical when it should be horizontal, or horizontal when it should be vertical. Figure 9-14 shows a range of cells before and after being re-oriented.

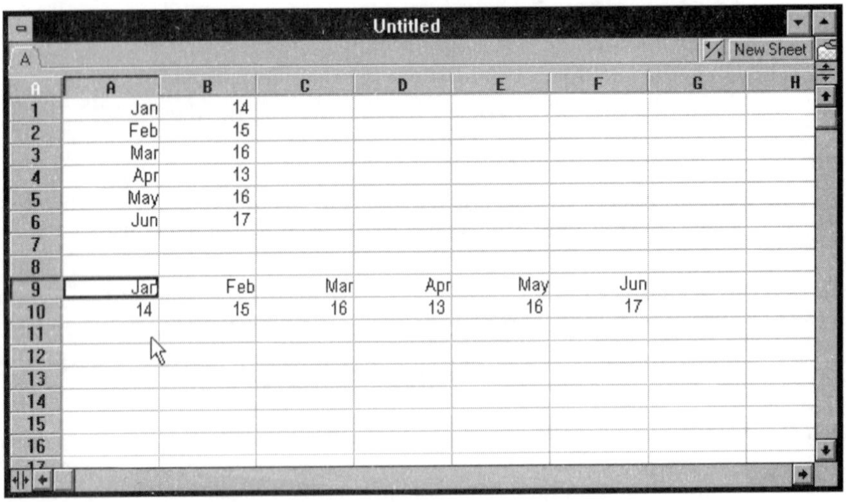

**Figure 9-14:** Transposing a range changes its orientation.

## How to do it

You start by selecting the range to be transposed, and then choose the Range⇨Transpose command. 1-2-3 for Windows displays the dialog box shown in Figure 9-15.

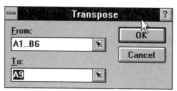

**Figure 9-15:**
The
Transpose
dialog box.

The From box will display the range you selected. In the To box, you need to specify the upper left cell of the range that you want to transpose it to. After you do this, choose OK to close the dialog box. 1-2-3 for Windows will copy the original range to the new area — but transposed.

If the area you specify to hold the transposed data already contains information, 1-2-3 for Windows — in its typical presumptuous fashion — will overwrite the information without telling you about it. So be careful out there.

# *Finding and Replacing — Wherefore Art Thou, Text String?*

Every word processor I've ever seen has a pretty sophisticated find and replace feature. You can instruct your software to find a particular text pattern (or *string*) and replace it with something else. You can do this automatically, or have it stop and ask you each time it finds the string. 1-2-3 for Windows isn't a word processor, but it also has this feature — which is great for making large-scale changes to a worksheet.

You can find and replace only text strings. The command doesn't work with values.

Fortunately, using this powerful tool is very straightforward. Start by selecting the Edit⇨Find & Replace command. You'll get the dialog box shown in Figure 9-16.

Enter the text you're looking for in the Search for box. Select the Replace with option, and enter the text you want to replace it with in the text box. If you want to limit your operation to a specific range, you can specify the range in the Search through box. You also have the option of replacing text in labels, formulas, or both.

Choose OK, and 1-2-3 for Windows goes to work looking for the string. If it finds it, you'll be asked if you want to replace it — or you can specify that you want to replace all occurrences of the string automatically.

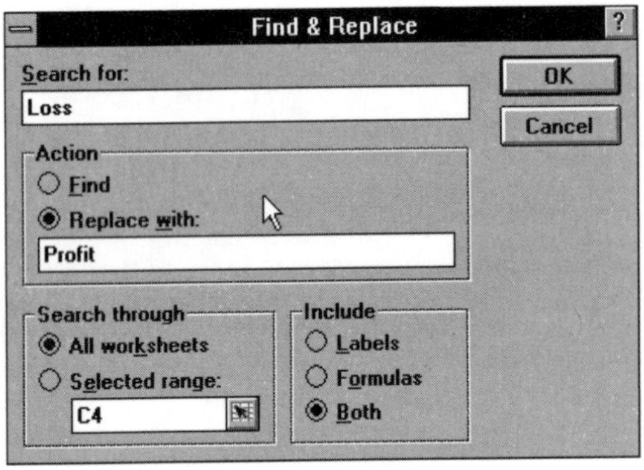

---

**Find & Replace**                                          ?

Search for:
| Loss |

─ Action ─
○ Find
● Replace with:
| Profit |

OK

Cancel

**Figure 9-16:**
The Find &
Replace
dialog box.

─ Search through ─           ─ Include ─
● All worksheets             ○ Labels
○ Selected range:            ○ Formulas
| C4 |                       ● Both

---

# Sorting Ranges of Cells — Head 'Em Up and Move 'Em Out

When you rearrange a range of cells such that the order of the rows gets changed, this is called *sorting*. This is a very common operation among the group known as "spreadsheet people."

## Why do it?

There are many reasons why you would want to sort a range of data. You may have entered data haphazardly, and need to print it out in some order. Or, you may want to sort your data to make it easier to find. Or, you want to see how a group of numbers looks in terms of rank orders. Or, you may want to change the order before charting the numbers. And so on, and so on.

I've found that mistakes made when sorting are one of the primary causes of "messed up spreadsheets" problems. Be on the safe side and save your worksheet before you sort any data. That way, if you mess up (and Edit⇨Undo can't come to the rescue), you can always go back to the old file and start again.

## How to do it

To demonstrate how to sort a range of data, I'll run through an example. Figure 9-17 shows a range of unsorted data. The goal of this exercise is to sort the range by state. And when more than one row has the same state, you sort by city within the state. In other words, you use two sort keys.

# What to watch out for when sorting

One of the most common mistakes people make with spreadsheets is to screw up when sorting. They do this because they don't select the entire range as the sort range. For example, suppose you have a range that consists of three columns: Name, age, and salary. If you want to sort the range in alphabetical order using Name as the sort key, it's critically important that you select *all* three columns when you specify the sort range. If you only select the column with the names, only the names will be sorted. This means that everyone will have a different age and salary. In other words, the data is royally messed up, all the work you put into entering this information will be for naught, you'll lose your job, the house goes on the auction block, and your dog will hate you.

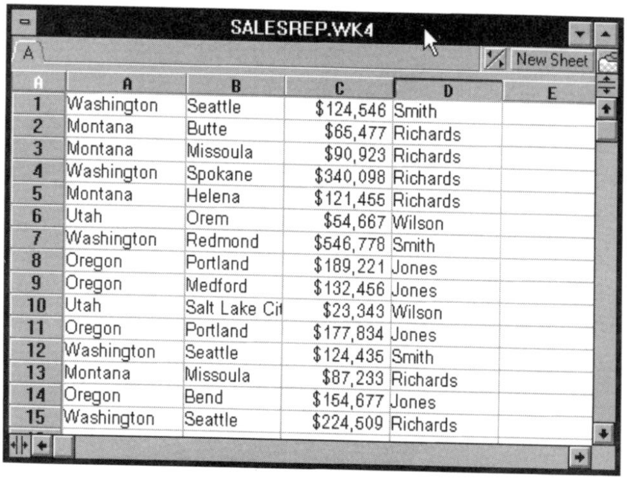

**Figure 9-17:** Unsorted data.

1. **Select the entire range to be sorted.**

   In this case, it's A1..D15.

2. **Select the Range⇨Sort command.**

   1-2-3 for Windows displays the Sort dialog box, shown in Figure 9-18.

3. **Specify which column to sort on.**

   Because states are in column A, you can click in *any cell* in the range A1..A15. This tells 1-2-3 for Windows which column to sort on.

4. **Select OK to do the sorting.**

   1-2-3 for Windows goes to work, and your data will now be sorted per your instructions (see Figure 9-19).

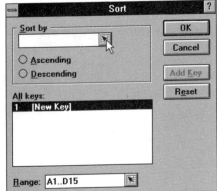

**Figure 9-18:**
The Sort
dialog box.

**Figure 9-19:**
The sorted
data.

| | A | B | C | D | E |
|---|---|---|---|---|---|
| 1 | Montana | Butte | $65,477 | Richards | |
| 2 | Montana | Helena | $121,455 | Richards | |
| 3 | Montana | Missoula | $90,923 | Richards | |
| 4 | Montana | Missoula | $87,233 | Richards | |
| 5 | Oregon | Bend | $154,677 | Jones | |
| 6 | Oregon | Medford | $132,456 | Jones | |
| 7 | Oregon | Portland | $189,221 | Jones | |
| 8 | Oregon | Portland | $177,834 | Jones | |
| 9 | Utah | Orem | $54,667 | Wilson | |
| 10 | Utah | Salt Lake Cit | $23,343 | Wilson | |
| 11 | Washington | Redmond | $546,778 | Smith | |
| 12 | Washington | Seattle | $124,646 | Smith | |
| 13 | Washington | Seattle | $124,435 | Smith | |
| 14 | Washington | Seattle | $224,509 | Richards | |
| 15 | Washington | Spokane | $340,098 | Richards | |

When you do a sort, 1-2-3 for Windows remembers the settings you give it. The next time you issue the Range⇨Sort command, it will attempt to use exactly the same range and sort keys that you specified earlier. To make 1-2-3 for Windows forget your previous sort specs, select the Reset button in the Sort dialog box.

Normally, 1-2-3 for Windows considers letters to be "greater than" numbers when it sorts. In other words, if the entries in your sort key column contain both values and labels, it will put the values before the labels. If you want to change this rule so sorting places labels before numbers, you have to run the 1-2-3 for Windows Install program.

# Chapter 10
# Getting It on Paper

*"Some said, 'John, print it'; others said, 'Not so.'*
*Some said, 'It might do good'; others said, 'No.'"*

John Bunyan (1628 – 1688)
*The Pilgrim's Progress*

· · · · · · · · · · · · · · · · · · · · · · · · · · · · · · · · · · · · · · · · · · · · ·

## In This Chapter

▶ Why printing can be a pain in the drain

▶ How to print what you've done

▶ How to get more control over printing in worksheets

▶ What a crash course on printer types can do for you: the pros and cons of each

· · · · · · · · · · · · · · · · · · · · · · · · · · · · · · · · · · · · · · · · · · · · ·

Most of the time, you'll want to get a hard copy of the results of your spreadsheeting efforts. You basically have two choices: to use a Polaroid camera to photograph your computer monitor or to send the worksheet to your printer. Most people choose the latter option, because Polaroid prints are too small and are difficult to staple together into reports.

# The Seedy Side of Printing

Both beginning and advanced users agree that dealing with printers can be one of the most frustrating parts of working with computers. But it's worth it when you finally have something you can hold in your hand to show for the long hours you spent sweating over your keyboard.

Here are few observations about printers (maybe you recognize some of them):

> ✔ Your printer is never good enough for what you want it to do. And, of course, the day after you buy a new printer, the manufacturer comes out with a better model that's several hundred dollars cheaper than what you have just plunked down.

- ✔ The paper always jams at the most inopportune times.

  Never start printing a 30-page job and then go to lunch. Printers know when you leave the office and purposefully pick that time to jam.

- ✔ Printers have minds of their own. When you want to print in Helvetica typeface, sometimes the document comes out in Courier for no apparent reason. (It must have something to do with the phase of the moon.)

- ✔ The ribbon dries up, the ink cartridge clogs up, and the toner cartridge bites the dust just as your boss is yelling, "I need that report NOW!"

- ✔ Nobody really knows what all those little buttons and lights are for. And the 700-page printer manual is printed in Japanese.

That Polaroid print option is looking better and better, isn't it?

# Printing 101

To print a document in a perfect world, you simply issue your software's Print command, and everything instantly appears on paper just as you expect it to. Although the world is far from perfect, printing from 1-2-3 for Windows comes fairly close to perfection (except for the "instantly" part).

If you want to print the entire worksheet you're working on, be sure that you do the following steps in *exactly* the order I have laid out for you here: (If you stray from this order, you are liable to do *very bad things* to your boot disk auto exec file archive system!)

**1. Click the Print SmartIcon shown in Figure 10-1 and press Enter.**

That's it! One-step printing (well, actually two steps if you count pressing Enter). Clicking this SmartIcon displays the Print dialog box. Pressing Enter closes the dialog box and prints with the current settings. By default, 1-2-3 for Windows prints the current worksheet.

**Figure 10-1:**
The Print
SmartIcon.

The Print SmartIcon sends your worksheet off to the printer with the current printer settings. In the vast majority of cases, the current settings work just fine. But using computers can't be this simple, right? As you may expect, *tons* of options (no exaggeration) are available so you can change the way your work gets printed and let you do *tons* (do you believe me yet?) of other nifty things. That's why the rest of this chapter exists.

# Getting a Sneak Preview

Before you get bogged down with all the print options available to you, you should know about a handy option available to you: print preview. As you know, printing is not instant. In fact, it's often downright s-l-o-w. You can waste a lot of time waiting for something to print — only to find that it came out all wrong. Fortunately, 1-2-3 for Windows offers a handy print preview feature that lets you take a peek at your printed page in the privacy of your computer screen.

To preview your printout, just click the Preview SmartIcon (or choose the File⇨Print Preview command). You get the same Print dialog box that appears when you click the Print SmartIcon. Just hit Enter and your screen transforms to a full-screen view of your printout.

You can use the SmartIcons in the preview window to zoom in or out and move back and forth between pages. If all looks OK, click the Print SmartIcon and off it goes to the printer. If it doesn't look OK, click the Close SmartIcon to return to your worksheet, where you can fix it.

If you're using Release 5, you have additional SmartIcons that let you see more than one page at a time — great for getting a bird's-eye view of your multi-page report.

---

## Windows makes printing easy

Before the dawn of Microsoft Windows, every software program that you bought had to be configured for your particular printer. If you used eight different software products, for example, you had to go through the tedious printer configuration routine eight times.

The Windows programs (including 1-2-3 for Windows) have changed this process, because they aren't concerned with the mechanics of printing. All the printing is done by Windows, not by the individual programs.

In other words, you only have to configure Windows for your printer. You don't have to go into every Windows program and set it up again so that it works with your new printer. If you're new to computing, you probably don't appreciate how nice this shortcut is. But we old-timers think that it's the cat's pajamas. And when you go running to MIS to install your printer for you, they will be happy too.

---

# Printing 202

As you learned in a previous section, one click of a SmartIcon is all it takes to print or preview your worksheet with the current print settings. There may be times, however, that you want to make some changes in how your worksheets are printed. The following list contains examples of the printing adjustments you can make in the wonderful world of 1-2-3 for Windows:

- The range to be printed (when you don't want to print everything)
- Print orientation (tall or wide)
- Paper size
- The margins on the paper
- Headers or footers that appear on every printed page
- Page numbers
- The date or time printed
- The cell grid lines (printed or not)
- The row and column borders (printed or not)
- Certain worksheet rows or columns that print on each page
- Compressed print, so that it fits on one page
- The number of copies to print

The rest of this chapter tells you how to change some of the more common print options.

## Printing part of your worksheet

If you don't want to print your entire worksheet, you have to tell 1-2-3 for Windows what parts you do want to print. (After all, it can't read your mind.) After you select the File⇨Print command (or the Ctrl+P shortcut), 1-2-3 for Windows displays the dialog box shown in Figure 10-2. Notice that the dialog box also has buttons to guide you to the Page Setup dialog box or preview your work on-screen with the Preview button.

Normally, 1-2-3 for Windows prints everything on the current worksheet. To change the current settings, select one of the options. You can print all the sheets in a multisheet worksheet file by selecting the All worksheets option. If you want to print just a part of your current worksheet, choose the Selected range option and then specify the range.

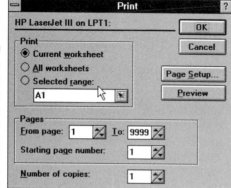

**Figure 10-2:**
The Print
dialog box
lets you
specify
some of
your print
options.

If you select the range you want to print before you issue the File⇨Print command, that range appears in the Selected range box. Then you simply click OK, and you're off to the races. As you probably know, you select a range by dragging the mouse over it.

## Printing specific pages

The Print dialog box also enables you to specify a range of pages to print using the From page text box and the To text box. Printing more than one page is relevant, of course, only if your worksheet is large enough to use more than one page when it is printed. If you have a large worksheet that normally has ten pages, you can print pages 9–10 by specifying these numbers in the appropriate boxes in the Print dialog box.

If you use page numbers on your printout, you can change the starting page number. For example, you can specify that page 9 actually prints out as page 1, so that when you give the printout to your boss, it doesn't look like you forgot the first eight pages.

## Printing multiple copies

If you want to print more than one copy, specify the number of copies in the Number of copies box. You can enter a number up to 9,999 (gee whiz, only 9,999!). Actually, if you need more than a dozen or so copies, you may want to check out the wonderful world of photocopiers.

## Changing the print orientation

You normally print a page in *portrait orientation,* where the printed page is taller than it is wide. Printing sideways on the page is called *landscape.* These terms may seem strange to you — and I have no idea where they come from either — but everybody uses them, so get with the program, OK?

You can change lots of printing options, including the orientation of your paper, in the Page Setup dialog box, shown in Figure 10-3. To get to this dialog box, select the File⇨Page Setup command. Changing the orientation of your paper, then, is as simple as selecting either the Portrait or the Landscape option.

Everything you do in the Page Setup dialog box is saved along with the worksheet. So the next time you load the worksheet, all these settings are still with the worksheet, and clicking the Print SmartIcon prints the worksheet with these settings.

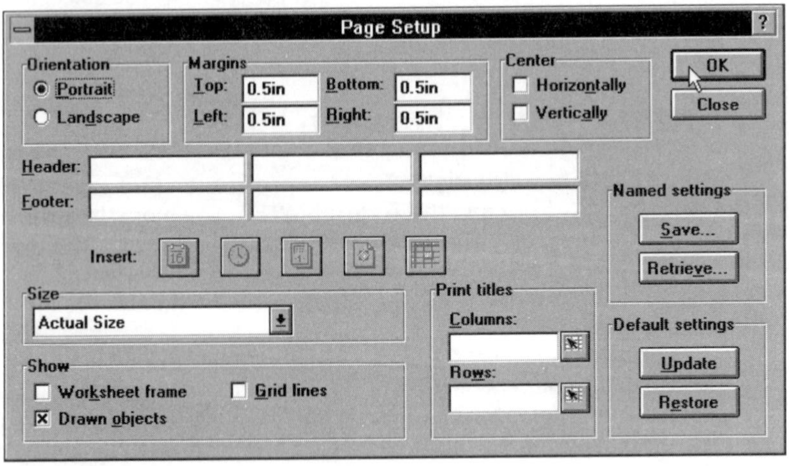

**Figure 10-3:**
The Page
Setup dialog
box has
many
printing
options.

| | Page Setup | ? |
| --- | --- | --- |

Orientation
⦿ Portrait
◯ Landscape

Margins
Top: 0.5in   Bottom: 0.5in
Left: 0.5in   Right: 0.5in

Center
☐ Horizontally
☐ Vertically

OK
Close

Header:
Footer:
Insert:

Named settings
Save...
Retrieve...

Size
Actual Size

Print titles
Columns:
Rows:

Default settings
Update
Restore

Show
☐ Worksheet frame   ☐ Grid lines
☒ Drawn objects

## Adjusting paper sizes

Most of the time, you'll probably use normal-size paper, which is 8 ½ × 11 inches, for printing. However, if you need to print something that's very tall or wide, you may opt for legal size paper (8 ½ × 14 inches). Or you may have some oddball-size paper that you want to use for one reason or another. The 1-2-3 for Windows program lets you specify different paper sizes, assuming that your printer is capable of handling these different sizes. To specify the paper size, use the File⇨Printer Setup command. Choose the printer you're using from the list that appears and then choose the Setup button. Select the paper size you want from the drop-down listbox.

Figure 10-4 shows an example of the dialog box that appears with the HP LaserJet III printer. The actual dialog box that appears on your screen depends on which printer you're using.

The paper size you specify in 1-2-3 for Windows may affect some of your other Windows applications (programs vary in how they deal with this problem). So if you change the paper size to 8½ × 14 in 1-2-3 for Windows and then switch over to your word processor, check to make sure that you have the correct page size for your work in the new program.

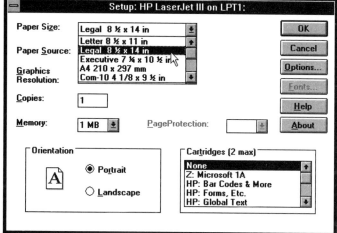

**Figure 10-4:** The Printer Setup dialog box produces a drop-down listbox to select paper size.

## Adjusting margins

The margins on a page refer to the white space along the edges. As you may suspect, 1-2-3 for Windows lets you change the margins to whatever you like. For example, if your company has a policy that all reports must have 1-inch margins on all sides, you easily can set these margins. Or you may want to make the margins even narrower so that everything fits on one page.

The Page Setup dialog box lets you change any or all of the four margins on the page. The default margins are ½ inch on all sides.

## Adding headers and footers

If you want information to appear at the top or bottom of every page you print, you need to know about headers and footers. *Headers* appear at the top of the page, and *footers* appear at the bottom. If you have trouble keeping this straight, think of an upright human body. The head is at the top, and the foot is at the bottom.

Why use headers or footers? Well, some people like to identify what the printout is about. For example, your third quarter report about tardiness can have a header that reads *3rd Quarter Tardiness Report.* Headers and footers each have three parts (all of which are optional): information printed flush left, information centered, and information printed flush right. When you check out the Page Setup dialog box, you see six text boxes. You can put whatever you want into any or all of the six Header and Footer boxes.

After you activate any of these text boxes, the five Insert icons directly below the text boxes become available, as they appear in Figure 10-5. Clicking the appropriate icon puts special codes into the header or footer for the date, time, page number, filename, or contents of a particular cell. If you want the contents of a particular cell to appear in a header or footer, click the contents icon. 1-2-3 for Windows inserts a slash, and you simply enter the cell address (for example, A1).

**Figure 10-5:**
These icons print special information in your headers or footers.

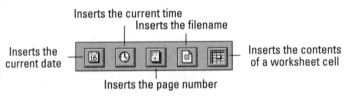

Inserts the current time
Inserts the filename
Inserts the current date
Inserts the contents of a worksheet cell
Inserts the page number

For lengthy reports, it's a good idea to add page numbers to the header or footer of your printout. Then, if someone opens the door on a windy day and the report blows all over the office, you won't have as much trouble putting the report back together.

You also can use an @function that updates the date or time in a cell. Go to any cell and type **@NOW**, then format the cell so that it appears as a date, a time, or both. Whenever the worksheet is recalculated, the cell's date or time is updated.

## *Sizing your printout*

1-2-3 has some pretty spiffy options that shrink a print selection so that printed data is smaller and more data fits on a printed page. Or, you can have the program automatically expand a print selection so that the printed data is larger and less data fits on a printed page.

You can adjust the size of the printed data with the Size pull-down listbox in the Page Setup dialog box. Adjusting the information to fit on one page is handy for those situations in which your printout doesn't quite fit on a single page (it may have one row or one column printed all by itself on the second page). Choose the Fit all to page option to solve this problem.

## Suppressing and printing certain elements

The Show box in the Page Setup dialog box gives you the following options as to what you can print or ignore in your printout:

**Wor<u>k</u>sheet frame:** Some people like to see row and column borders on their printouts because they then can tell the exact address of a cell. To have the borders appear on your printout, select this option.

**Drawn <u>o</u>bjects:** If you don't need to see charts or other drawn objects on paper, turn off this option. Printing is much faster.

**<u>G</u>rid lines:** Normally, 1-2-3 for Windows doesn't print the grid lines that appear on-screen around each cell. If you like to see grid lines on your printout, however, just turn on this option.

## Printing title rows or columns on every page

If you have a lengthy multipage printout, you may want the top row or two (the title rows or the rows that contain the field names) or even the entire left column to print on every page, a technique especially useful for databases. By specifying that these rows or columns appear on every page of your printout, your report is easier to read, because you get the name fields printed on each page, not just the first one.

To get a row or column to appear on every page, go to the Print titles box in the Page Setup dialog box. Simply specify (or point to) the row(s) or column(s) that you want to print on each page.

When you use the Print titles technique, you must first set the print range separately by using the <u>F</u>ile⇨<u>P</u>rint command. (You can't simply print the entire worksheet.) Do not include the title rows or columns in the print range you specify. If you do include them, they print twice on the first page. Everybody makes this mistake at least once, so don't feel bad if it happens to you. Again, you simply can't print the entire worksheet.

# Quick Reference for Printing

Unless you're a genius, you may be a bit overwhelmed by all of these printing options. Even worse, you have to go to several different dialog boxes to change things. Wouldn't it be nice if someone put together a handy table of these options that told you exactly where to go to do what? You're prayers are answered; Table 10-1 does just that.

| Table 10-1 | Printing Options and Uses |
|---|---|
| *Printing Option* | *Command to Issue* |
| Print part of your worksheet | File➪Print |
| Print specific pages | File➪Print |
| Change the starting page number | File➪Print |
| Number of copies to print | File➪Print |
| Paper orientation | File➪Page Setup |
| Change the margins | File➪Page Setup |
| Headers or footers | File➪Page Setup |
| Add page numbers | File➪Page Setup |
| Print the date or time on each page | File➪Page Setup |
| Print the filename on each page | File➪Page Setup |
| Compress or expand the size | File➪Page Setup |
| Don't print graphs or drawn objects | File➪Page Setup |
| Print the worksheet frame | File➪Page Setup |
| Print grid lines | File➪Page Setup |
| Print rows/columns on every page | File➪Page Setup |
| Change paper size | File➪Printer Setup➪Setup |
| Change print resolution | File➪Printer Setup➪Setup |

# Printing Charts, Drawings, and Other Neat Stuff

Printing charts and other graphic objects is no big deal. If charts or drawn objects are inserted on your worksheet, they simply are printed along with everything else on the worksheet.

If your charts don't print, select File➪Page Setup and make sure that the Drawn objects check box is checked.

# Printers du Jour

You should know what type of printer you have so that you can order supplies for it. If you didn't purchase the printer and are not sure what kind you are using, check the printer: most printers have a name printed somewhere on them. And if you have been around the different types of printers that are currently available, you usually can tell what type of printer you have by the quality of the output, called *resolution*.

*Resolution* refers to the number of dots per inch on the paper. If you look closely at something printed on a laser printer, you notice that the image is actually made up of lots of tiny dots. If you can't see the dots, try using a magnifying glass (or just take my word for it). The more dots there are per inch, the higher the resolution is of your printer. For more information on resolution, read the sidebar, "You say you want a resolution," later in this section.

This section gives you a quick rundown of the pros and cons of each of the four general types of printers you may encounter.

## Laser printers

No, you can't shoot anyone with them. But laser printers are the best printers because they are fast, quiet, easy to work with, and do great graphics. The street price of laser printers ranges from about $400 up to several thousands of dollars. Laser printers differ in print speed, amount of memory, and maximum print resolution. A maximum resolution of 300 dots per inch is most common, but you also see printers that can print at 600 dots per inch. Laser printers are now considered the standard for office use, but many home computer users also choose laser printers.

Instead of using old-fashioned pin-feed paper, laser printers use normal single-sheet paper (and you even can use photocopier paper). Using regular paper makes laser printers much easier to work with, because you don't have to worry about aligning the top of the page, tearing the pages apart, or ripping off the perforations along the side of the paper. However, the main disadvantage of a laser printer is that you can't print multipart forms with it. Keep this in mind when you purchase a printer.

Laser printers work by composing the image in their memory, which is separate from the computer's memory. When the image is fully composed, it is sent to the paper. Usually this system of printing works very well; however, your laser printer may occasionally spit out the page without completing it (ahhhchooo!). If your printer is sneezing out incomplete pages, you can do one of the following two tasks to correct the problem:

  ✔ Add more memory to your printer. (See your printer's manual for details — all printers handle this task differently.)

  ✔ Print at a lower resolution. (See the accompanying sidebar, "You say you want a resolution," for more information.)

The changes that you make to the printer settings with the File⇨Printer Setup command are in effect for all your Windows printing. So if you need higher resolution for another program that you use, you need to change the printer settings back.

## Inkjet printers

Inkjet printers do their thing by spraying a very thin stream of ink on a page. They can handle both text and graphics, and some models even print in color. Because there is no physical contact with the paper, these printers are very quiet. An inkjet printer uses either tractor-feed paper or a single-sheet paper feeder.

# You say you want a resolution!

The quality of your laser printer output is a function of the resolution at which you're printing. As you read earlier, *resolution* refers to the number of dots per inch on the paper.

Printing at higher resolutions means that the printer needs more memory to compose the image before it puts the dots on the paper. Therefore, if your output is very complex (which means lots of graphics), your printer may not have enough memory to print the page at its maximum resolution. You can buy more memory for your printer, or you can change the resolution that your printer uses. Many laser printers offer a choice of 300, 150, or 75 dots per inch (dpi).

To adjust your printer's resolution setting directly from 1-2-3 for Windows, do the following:

1. **Choose the File⇨Printer Setup command.**

   You get a small dialog box that lists all the printers installed for Windows. (There can be more than one.)

2. **Select the printer that you want to adjust and choose the Setup button.**

   You get another dialog box, which looks different for each printer. The Setup dialog

box for an HP III laser printer is represented in the accompanying figure.

3. **Choose the Graphics Resolution drop-down listbox and select a lower resolution.**

4. **Choose OK to close the dialog box and then choose OK again to close the first dialog box.**

Now, try printing your job again. You should be able to print the entire page (although it may not look as good as it does at a higher resolution).

The output from inkjet printers is very good — nearly as good as from a laser printer (and they're usually cheaper, too). Because there is no physical contact with the paper, however, you can't use an inkjet printer to print multipart forms.

## Dot-matrix printers

Dot-matrix printers come in a variety of styles and have price tags that range from very cheap to very expensive. Their output quality matches their price range — from very bad to pretty good, and most of them do a reasonably good job with graphics. The main advantage in having a dot-matrix printer these days is that it can print multipart forms (which lasers and inkjets can't handle). However, these printers can be very noisy and some are dreadfully slow.

## Daisywheel printers

You rarely see daisywheel printers anymore, except at garage sales. Because these printers don't even work with Windows, I won't bother discussing these dinosaurs. They do make superb doorstops, though.

# Chapter 11
# In Another Dimension

*"Something hidden. Go and find it. Go and look behind the Ranges."*

Rudyard Kipling, (1865 – 1936)
*The Explorer*

· · · · · · · · · · · · · · · · · · · · · · · · · · · · · · · · · · · · · · · · ·

## In This Chapter

▶ Making the most of those 255 extra sheets available in every 1-2-3 for Windows file

▶ Understanding the basic 3-D worksheet operations: adding and removing sheets, naming the sheets, printing them, and seeing more than one at a time

▶ Navigating and selecting across multiple sheets

▶ Formatting a bunch of sheets at once in Group mode

· · · · · · · · · · · · · · · · · · · · · · · · · · · · · · · · · · · · · · · · ·

*Y*ou may already know that 1-2-3 for Windows, like all other Windows spreadsheets, enables you to store as many as 256 sheets in a single worksheet file. Each of these sheets has 8,192 rows and 256 columns. If you do your arithmetic, you see that the total works out to more than a half billion cells at your disposal. This chapter explains how to use this powerful feature for fun and profit (well, at least for profit — maybe).

# First, Some Terminology

Before you get too far into this chapter, you need to understand some terminology. For example, you may be tempted to call each separate sheet in a worksheet file a page — after all, it's easy to picture a 3-D worksheet as a huge notebook with lots of pages in it. For the record, here is a list of the standard terminology for 1-2-3 for Windows:

✔ **Worksheet file:** a 1-2-3 for Windows file that can have between 1 and 256 sheets.

✔ **3-D worksheet:** a worksheet file that has more than one sheet, also known as a *multiple worksheet file* or a *multisheet file.*

✔ **Sheet or Worksheet:** one page of a worksheet file with 256 columns and 8,192 rows.

But if you want to substitute the term pages for sheets, be my guest. I call them pages, too, when I'm not writing books about them.

# Why Use 3-D Worksheets?

Jeepers, a half billion cells! Don't get too excited, however, because you can never use all these cells. (You'd run out of memory long before you even got close.) The benefit of a 3-D worksheet is *not* in the number of cells you can access. The benefit, rather, is in the great way you can organize your work and break it up into more manageable units.

Many spreadsheet projects can be broken down into distinct chunks. For example, you may have a chunk that holds your assumptions, several different chunks that hold tables of values, a chunk to store data for graphs, and so on. Before the days of 3-D worksheets, one of the most difficult aspects of dealing with large spreadsheets was figuring out where to put all the various chunks. With a 3-D worksheet, however, it's simple: put each chunk on a separate sheet.

Figure 11-1 shows an example of several sheets in a 3-D worksheet. Notice that the name of each department appears on the tab; therefore, you can jump to a department's budget just by clicking the tab.

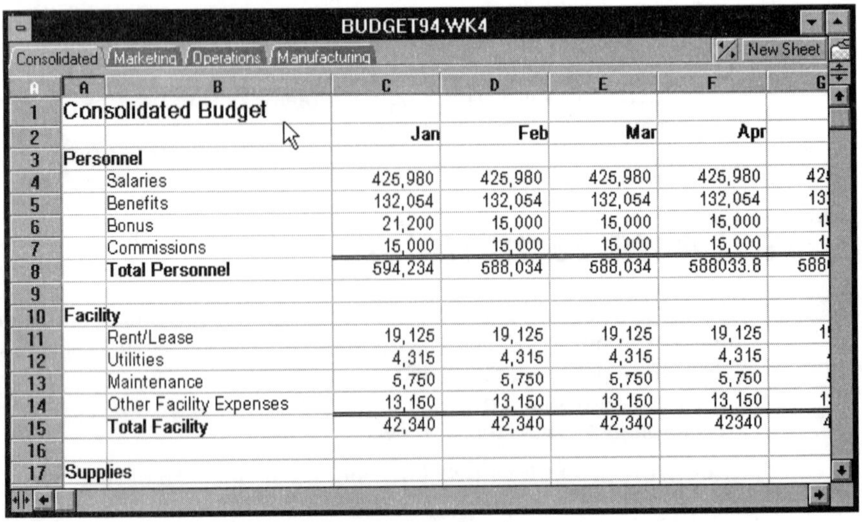

**Figure 11-1:** Using separate sheets is ideal for budget applications.

| | A | B | C | D | E | F | G |
|---|---|---|---|---|---|---|---|
| 1 | Consolidated Budget | | | | | | |
| 2 | | | Jan | Feb | Mar | Apr | |
| 3 | Personnel | | | | | | |
| 4 | | Salaries | 425,980 | 425,980 | 425,980 | 425,980 | 42! |
| 5 | | Benefits | 132,054 | 132,054 | 132,054 | 132,054 | 13: |
| 6 | | Bonus | 21,200 | 15,000 | 15,000 | 15,000 | 1! |
| 7 | | Commissions | 15,000 | 15,000 | 15,000 | 15,000 | 1! |
| 8 | | Total Personnel | 594,234 | 588,034 | 588,034 | 588033.8 | 588! |
| 9 | | | | | | | |
| 10 | Facility | | | | | | |
| 11 | | Rent/Lease | 19,125 | 19,125 | 19,125 | 19,125 | 1! |
| 12 | | Utilities | 4,315 | 4,315 | 4,315 | 4,315 | |
| 13 | | Maintenance | 5,750 | 5,750 | 5,750 | 5,750 | !|
| 14 | | Other Facility Expenses | 13,150 | 13,150 | 13,150 | 13,150 | 1! |
| 15 | | Total Facility | 42,340 | 42,340 | 42,340 | 42340 | 4 |
| 16 | | | | | | | |
| 17 | Supplies | | | | | | |

BUDGET94.WK4

Consolidated / Marketing / Operations / Manufacturing — New Sheet

# Ideas for Using 3-D Worksheets, No Weird Glasses Needed

Before you get into the meat of 3-D worksheets, let me whet your appetite with a few ideas on how to put this 3-D worksheet business to use. You may be able to use some of these ideas, or — better yet — maybe you can come up with some new ideas on your own. (If so, let me know. I'm always looking for good ideas for future books!)

- ✔ **Store results for different time periods.** If you track such information in a spreadsheet as sales, orders, or new customers, you may want to organize your work by time periods. For example, you can have a separate sheet for each month or each quarter, enabling you quickly to locate what you want and still use formulas to get grand totals and summaries.

- ✔ **Document your work.** If you're working on a fairly complex worksheet, you may want to use a separate sheet to make notes to yourself to remind you of what you did, why you did it, and how you did it. And if you're really industrious, you even can keep an historical log that describes the changes you made to the worksheet over time.

- ✔ **Use a 3-D worksheet in place of separate files.** If you're working on a project that uses five different single-sheet worksheets, for example, you may find it more practical to keep them all in one 3-D worksheet file (each on a separate sheet). In that way, when you're ready to work on the project, you simply load the one worksheet file, and everything you need is handy.

- ✔ **Store different scenarios.** Many people use a spreadsheet to do "what-if" analysis, and 3-D worksheets make this process easier. For example, you can copy an entire sheet of a 3-D worksheet to other sheets. Then you just make some experimental changes in the assumptions for each copy and give the sheets such names such *BestCase, WorstCase, LikelyCase, JoesScenario*, and so on.

If managing different scenarios is your bag, a better approach is to use the Version Manager feature in 1-2-3 for Windows.

Those extra worksheets have a great deal of other uses, too, but first you need to learn a few basic concepts.

# *Things You Should Know about 3-D Worksheets (That Your Mother Never Told You)*

Keep in mind the following concepts when you're working with more than one sheet in a 1-2-3 for Windows worksheet file:

- ✔ The extra sheets in a worksheet file don't appear automatically. Every file starts out with one sheet, and you have to insert the other sheets yourself.

- ✔ The sheets are normally labeled with letters, starting with sheet A and continuing through sheet IV (the 256th sheet in a file). This labeling method is the same as the one used for columns.

- ✔ Each tab displayed at the top of the screen represents a sheet. If you have lots of extra sheets, you may not be able to see all the tabs at once, but you can scroll the tabs horizontally to get to the one you need.

- ✔ You can change the sheet letters to names that are more meaningful to you and that reflect the contents of the sheet.

- ✔ You can change the color of the sheet tabs to make it easier to identify certain sheets.

- ✔ When you refer to cells or ranges on another sheet, you must precede the cell reference with the sheet letter (or sheet name, if it has one). For example C:A1 refers to the upper left cell on the third sheet (sheet C).

- ✔ Formulas that use range references can use ranges that cut across sheets. For example, @SUM(A:A1..C:C3) adds up a $3 \times 3 \times 3$ cube of cells starting with the upper left cell on the first sheet and extending through to the cell in the third row and third column of the third sheet (27 cells in all).

- ✔ You can format all the sheets in one fell swoop with Group mode — a real time-saver when you want all your sheets to look the same.

# *Fundamental Stuff*

This section explains how to do some basic operations involving 3-D worksheets, including adding, removing, and naming sheets, displaying three sheets at once, and other basic concepts.

# Adding sheets

When you create a new 1-2-3 for Windows worksheet, it has only one sheet (sheet A). If you want to use additional sheets, you have to insert them yourself. Inserting additional sheets is actually pretty easy to do. If you have a mouse, simply click the New Sheet button at the upper right of the worksheet window, as you can see in Figure 11-2. The 1-2-3 for Windows program sticks a new sheet directly after the one you're currently working on and makes the new sheet the *active* one. (The *active sheet* is the one that you're working on and contains the cell pointer.)

**Figure 11-2:**
Clicking the
New Sheet
button adds
a new sheet
directly after
the current
sheet.

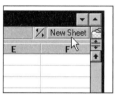

Our rodentially challenged friends need to use the menu to add a new sheet. The Edit⇨Insert command does the trick and displays the dialog box shown in Figure 11-3. You select the Sheet option, specify whether you want the sheet(s) inserted before or after the current sheet, and then select the number of sheets you want to add.

**Figure 11-3:**
The Insert dialog
box, where you
tell 1-2-3 for
Windows to
insert one or
more new sheets.

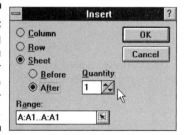

# Removing sheets

If you want to get rid of an entire sheet (including everything that's on it, of course), activate the sheet that you want to zap and then select the Edit⇨Delete command. The dialog box in Figure 11-4 appears. Select the Sheet option and then choose OK.

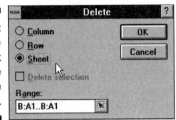

**Figure 11-4:**
The Delete
dialog box
can eliminate
an entire
sheet.

By the way, if you try to delete the only sheet in a worksheet, 1-2-3 for Windows objects and displays a message telling you that you can't delete all sheets.

A quicker way to delete the current sheet is to right-click the sheet's tab to display a shortcut menu. After you choose Delete from the menu, the current sheet disappears in a flash.

Deleting an entire sheet is a pretty drastic measure, because everything on the sheet is gone in an instant. If any of your formulas refer to cells on a deleted sheet, they'll return ERR (for error). So before you nuke a sheet, make sure that's what you really want to do.

## Naming sheets

You should give a meaningful name to every sheet that you use. By naming the sheets, you make it easy for you (or anybody else who may inherit the file) to identify what's on each sheet. After all, it's easier to remember that your boss's sales projections are on a sheet named *BOSS* than on a sheet named *R*. You also can use sheet names in formulas, which can make the formulas more understandable. Calculating a ratio with a formula such as +BOSS:A1/BOSS:A2 makes more sense than using +R:A1/R:A2, no?

Naming a sheet requires a mouse. Oddly enough, 1-2-3 for Windows does not have a menu command to perform this operation. So if you're working on a new file on a mouseless laptop (for example), you have to live without named sheets for a while. Sorry.

To give a sheet a name, just double-click the sheet's tab and then type in a name. Sheet names can be up to 15 characters long (1-2-3 for Windows does not distinguish between upper- and lowercase letters in names). Avoid using spaces, commas, semicolons, periods, or any other nonletter or nonnumber characters. And finally, don't create sheet names that look like cell addresses (such as AB12); 1-2-3 for Windows may get confused.

You can continue to use the original sheet letter, even if you give the sheet a name. For example, if you name the first sheet *IntroScreen*, you can enter either a formula such as @SUM(INTROSCREEN:A1..A6) or a formula such as @SUM(A:A1..A6). The program recognizes both formulas as the same request for information, one using the sheet name and the other using the sheet letter. However, 1-2-3 for Windows always replaces a sheet letter reference that you enter with its name (if it has one).

If you want to change a sheet name, just double-click the tab. The program highlights the current name. Just type in a new name to replace the old one. Any formulas that have references to the old name are changed automatically to the new name.

## Color-coding your tabs

There's no need to settle for drab tabs. You can make your sheet tabs any color you like. Besides adding some pizzazz to your screen, using different colors for your sheet tabs makes it easier to identify the sheets. Here's how to do it. Just right-click a sheet tab and choose Worksheet Defaults from the shortcut menu. A rather imposing dialog box appears. Check out the bottom-right part of the dialog box and look for the pull-down list labeled Worksheet tab. Click the list and you can choose from 255 glorious colors.

## Displaying three sheets at once

Normally, you can see only one sheet at a time. But if you want to see or work with three consecutive sheets from a 3-D worksheet, you can get a perspective view, as shown in Figure 11-5.

To get into the perspective view, select the View⇨Split command and then select the Perspective option in the dialog box that appears. To get back into the normal viewing mode, choose the View⇨Clear Split command. You'll learn how to navigate through these sheets later in the chapter.

## Printing multiple sheets

If you read Chapter 10, you already know how to print a worksheet. But what about printing a worksheet that has more than one sheet? Easy. Issue the File⇨Print command and then select the All worksheets option. That's all there is to printing more than one sheet.

| | | | BUDGET94.WK4 | | | | | |
|---|---|---|---|---|---|---|---|---|
| | **C** | **A** | **B** | **C** | **D** | **E** | **F** | **G** |
| | **1** | Operations | | | | | | |
| | **2** | | | Jan | Feb | Mar | Apr | May |
| | **3** | Personnel | | | | | | |
| | **4** | | Salaries | 89,000 | 89,000 | 89,000 | 89,000 | 89,000 |
| | **5** | | Benefits | 27,590 | 27,590 | 27,590 | 27,590 | 27,590 |
| | **6** | | Bonus | 15,000 | 15,000 | 15,000 | 15,000 | 15,000 |

| | **B** | **A** | **B** | **C** | **D** | **E** | **F** | **G** |
|---|---|---|---|---|---|---|---|---|
| | **1** | Marketing | | | | | | |
| | **2** | | | Jan | Feb | Mar | Apr | May |
| | **3** | Personnel | | | | | | |
| | **4** | | Salaries | 125,980 | 125,980 | 125,980 | 125,980 | 125,980 |
| | **5** | | Benefits | 39,054 | 39,054 | 39,054 | 39,054 | 39,054 |
| | **6** | | Bonus | 5,000 | 0 | 0 | 0 | 0 |

| | **A** | **A** | **B** | **C** | **D** | **E** | **F** | **G** | **H** |
|---|---|---|---|---|---|---|---|---|---|
| | **1** | Consolidated Budget | | | | | | | |
| | **2** | | | Jan | Feb | Mar | Apr | May | |
| | **3** | Personnel | | | | | | | |
| | **4** | | Salaries | 425,980 | 425,980 | 425,980 | 425,980 | 425,980 | |
| | **5** | | Benefits | 132,054 | 132,054 | 132,054 | 132,054 | 132,054 | |
| | **6** | | Bonus | 21,200 | 15,000 | 15,000 | 15,000 | 15,000 | |
| | **7** | | Commissions | 15,000 | 15,000 | 15,000 | 15,000 | 15,000 | |

**Figure 11-5:**
A perspective view of three consecutive sheets.

If you want each sheet to start on a new piece of paper, insert manual page breaks at the top of each sheet. To insert manual page breaks, move the cell pointer to the upper left cell in the second sheet. Select the Style⇨Page Break command and then select the Row option. The program inserts a page break before it prints that sheet. Repeat this process for each sheet in the worksheet.

# Navigating in the Third Dimension (without the Help of Captain Picard)

You already know how to navigate through a 2-D worksheet by using the arrow keys, mouse, scroll bars, and so on. Moving around in a 3-D worksheet requires a bit more effort, however, because you have another dimension to be concerned about. But again, learning to move around a 3-D worksheet is fairly logical once you get the hang of it. It's kind of like driving on the Los Angeles freeway, only infinitely safer (and with much less gridlock).

## Activating other sheets

Before you can scroll around on a sheet, you must activate, or display, it on-screen. The easiest way to activate a specific sheet in a 3-D worksheet is to click the tab with your mouse. If you have lots of sheets or sheets with long names, the tab you want may not appear. You can click the little arrows to the left of the New Sheet button, as shown in Figure 11-6, to scroll the tabs to the left or right until the one you want appears.

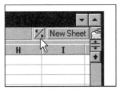

**Figure 11-6:**
Click these
arrows to
scroll the
tab display
left or right.

If you're in perspective view (with three sheets showing), you simply can click any of the visible sheets to activate one.

Sometimes, using the keyboard to activate a different sheet may be more efficient. Table 11-1 lists the keyboard combinations necessary to activate a sheet.

| Table 11-1 | Keyboard Combinations to Activate Sheets |
|---|---|
| *Key Combination* | *What It Does* |
| Ctrl+PgDn | Activates the preceding sheet, unless you're on the first sheet. (Then it has no effect.) |
| Ctrl+PgUp | Activates the next sheet, unless you're on the last sheet. (Then it has no effect.) |
| Ctrl+Home | Activates the first sheet and moves the cell pointer to the upper left cell. |
| End, Ctrl+Home | Moves to the last cell that contains data on the last sheet that contains data. |

A fast way to activate a far-off sheet is to press F5, the Goto key. 1-2-3 for Windows asks you what address you want to go to. Enter a sheet letter followed by a colon, and you're there in a jif. For example, if you want to activate sheet M, press F5, type **M:**, and then press Enter. If the sheet has a name, you can enter the name followed by a colon. Wouldn't life be wonderful if we had Goto buttons on our cars?

## *Selecting 3-D ranges*

When you're building a formula that references information on more than one sheet, you can either enter the cell references manually, or you can use pointing techniques similar to those used in a single sheet.

For example, assume that you are building a formula in cell A:A1 that adds up the figures in range B:A1 through F:A1, a common formula to consolidate the numbers in six sheets. You can either type **@SUM(B:A1..F:A1)**, or you can point to the argument and let 1-2-3 for Windows create the range reference for you. Do so by performing the following steps:

1. **Move to cell A:A1 and type @SUM( to start the formula.**

2. **Press Ctrl+PgUp to move to the next sheet and then move the cell pointer to cell B:A1, if it's not already there.**

   Watch the formula being built in the edit line.

3. **Press the period to anchor the first cell in the selection.**

4. **Press Ctrl+PgUp four more times until you get to sheet F and move the cell pointer to cell F:A1, if it's not already there.**

5. **Type ) and press Enter to finish the formula.**

   1-2-3 for Windows brings you back to the cell that holds the formula.

Rather than press Ctrl+PgUp to activate other sheets while pointing, you can hold down the Shift key and click a sheet tab.

## Preselecting 3-D ranges

When you're formatting ranges that extend across different sheets, you may prefer to select the range before you issue the formatting commands. (But as you'll see later, Group mode can simplify formatting all the sheets.)

When you're dealing with a single sheet, you simply drag the mouse across the range to select it (or you can press Shift+arrow keys to preselect the range). Preselecting across several sheets is very similar: just hold down the Shift key while you activate another sheet either by clicking a tab or by pressing Ctrl+PgUp or Ctrl+PgDn.

## Group Mode

Before putting this chapter to bed, I want to discuss one more topic that's relevant and actually pretty useful at times — Group mode. Group mode enables you to format all the sheets in a 3-D worksheet file at once. After you're in Group mode, any changes you make on one sheet using the Style menu (or its equivalent SmartIcons) affect all other sheets in the file. For example, if you're in Group mode and you change the font in cell A1 on sheet A, the program also changes the font in cell A1 on all the sheets in the file.

To get into Group mode, do the following:

1. **Choose the <u>S</u>tyle⇨<u>W</u>orksheet Defaults command, which brings up the dialog box shown in Figure 11-7.**

2. **To enter Group mode, turn on the <u>G</u>roup mode check box and choose OK.**

   As a reminder that your formatting applies to all sheets in the file, 1-2-3 for Windows displays the word Group in the status bar at the bottom of the screen.

3. **To get out of Group mode, use the same command but uncheck the <u>G</u>roup mode check box.**

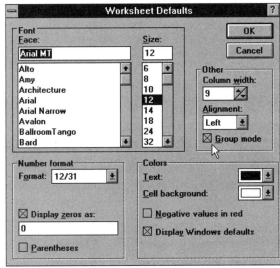

**Figure 11-7:**
The
Worksheet
Defaults
dialog box,
where you
select Group
mode.

Group mode can be very handy if you want all the sheets in your file to look the same. For example, after you change column widths or the formatting of cells in one sheet in a group, the other sheets all follow suit. Obviously, using Group mode can be a real time-saver — and it also makes your work look more consistent.

# *A Final Note*

If you find that dealing with the third dimension is rather confusing, don't despair. It's all very logical, and you'll get the hang of it after you start playing around with 3-D worksheets. Once you master it, you'll wonder how you ever got along without out it. If you find yourself getting really frustrated, however, just stick with single-sheet worksheets. After all, people have been using only one sheet for more than a decade — and they got along just fine.

# Chapter 12
# Making 1-2-3 Work Like Your Indentured Servant

*"The important thing is not to know more than all men, but to know more at each moment than any particular man."*

Johann Wolfgang von Goethe (1749–1832)

● ● ● ● ● ● ● ● ● ● ● ● ● ● ● ● ● ● ● ● ● ● ● ● ● ● ● ● ● ● ● ● ● ● ● ● ● ● ● ● ● ● ● ● ● ● ●

## In This Chapter

▶ Adjusting how the screen looks by zooming in and out and removing things you don't want to see

▶ Splitting a worksheet window into panes

▶ Freezing rows or columns so that they always appear on-screen

▶ Changing the default settings for a worksheet

▶ Setting the Autosave feature so your work is saved automatically

▶ Avoiding embarrassing misspellings in your worksheet

● ● ● ● ● ● ● ● ● ● ● ● ● ● ● ● ● ● ● ● ● ● ● ● ● ● ● ● ● ● ● ● ● ● ● ● ● ● ● ● ● ● ● ● ● ● ●

*I*f you're reading this book in a sequential fashion, you already have a great deal of nitty-gritty 1-2-3 for Windows knowledge — more than enough to do some meaningful work. But as you probably realize, you can do lots of creative tasks with 1-2-3 for Windows, too. This chapter is like the proverbial icing on the cake: you don't really have to know how to do the tasks explained here, but they can make your life easier — and they're sort of fun, too. Several of these topics show you how to make 1-2-3 for Windows work or look differently than it normally does.

You may not be interested in everything I discuss in this chapter, but at the very least, I suggest that you glance through the pictures to see whether anything here strikes your fancy.

I don't go into a lot of detail in this chapter, because this stuff is all fairly straightforward. If you're interested in more information, play around with the software or check the documentation (aarrrrgggh!!).

# *Having It Your Way*

Burger King used to use the slogan, "Have it your way." When it comes to the appearance of 1-2-3 for Windows on-screen, you also can have it your way (as long as you don't want onions).

As you know, the 1-2-3 for Windows screen is made up of many different parts, but there may be times when you don't want to see all its parts at once. For example, when you want to see as much information on-screen as possible, you may want to remove the scroll bars and even the worksheet frame from the screen.

Fortunately, you have lots of freedom to put exactly what you want on-screen at any particular time, and you can drastically change the way your 1-2-3 for Windows screen looks. The secret is in the View⇨Set View Preferences command. After you select this command, you get the dialog box shown in Figure 12-1.

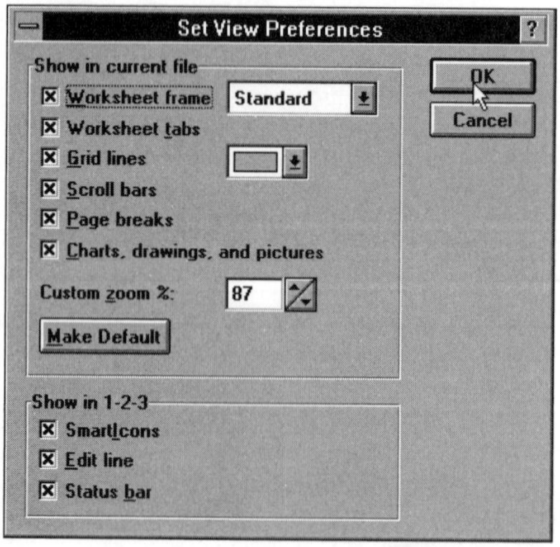

**Figure 12-1:**
The Set View Preferences dialog box, where you can change the on-screen appearance of 1-2-3 for Windows.

The Set View Preferences dialog box is divided into two parts. The choices in the top part of the dialog box apply to the current worksheet file. Here you choose whether to display the worksheet frame, the worksheet tabs, the grid lines that delineate the cells, the scroll bars, the dashed-line page-break display, or charts and other graphical objects.

The choices in the bottom part of the Set View Preferences dialog box enable you to turn off the following three parts of 1-2-3 for Windows: SmartIcons, the edit line, and the status bar.

Figure 12-2 shows the result of turning off *all* these elements. As you can see, you are left with pretty much of a blank slate, with only the menu bar remaining. Also, notice that after you turn off the edit line display, you have no idea where the cell pointer is at any given time, unless it's on-screen. And without scroll bars you can't use the mouse to navigate around. You probably don't want your screen to be *this* naked, but turning off a few of these elements may do you some good in the right circumstances (if you get a thrill from a naked worksheet).

If you're a prankster at heart, here's a suggestion. Next time weird Harold leaves his desk, sneak over and remove all of the parts from his 1-2-3 for Windows screen. He'll return to his desk, freak out, and yell for help. Then you can casually walk over and fix it up. He'll think you're a genius.

| Lotus 1-2-3 Release 5 - [SALESREP.WK4] | | |
|---|---|---|
| File Edit View Style Tools Range Window Help | | |
| Washington | Redmond | $546,778 Smith |
| Oregon | Portland | $189,221 Jones |
| Oregon | Medford | $132,456 Jones |
| Utah | Salt Lake City | $56,122 Wilson |
| Oregon | Portland | $177,834 Jones |
| Washington | Seattle | $124,435 Smith |
| Montana | Missoula | $87,233 Richards |
| Oregon | Bend | $154,677 Jones |
| Oregon | Medford | $87,233 Jones |
| Utah | Salt Lake City | $23,343 Wilson |
| Oregon | Portland | $290,822 Jones |
| Oregon | Medford | $132,456 Jones |
| Utah | Salt Lake City | $23,343 Wilson |
| Oregon | Portland | $177,834 Jones |
| Washington | Seattle | $143,566 Smith |
| Montana | Missoula | $87,233 Richards |
| Oregon | Bend | $154,677 Jones |
| Oregon | Medford | $132,456 Jones |
| Utah | Salt Lake City | $23,343 Wilson |
| Oregon | Portland | $177,834 Jones |
| Washington | Seattle | $233,091 Smith |
| Montana | Missoula | $87,233 Richards |
| Oregon | Bend | $154,677 Jones |
| Washington | Seattle | $224,509 Richards |

**Figure 12-2:** 1-2-3 for Windows with all its optional display elements removed — pretty minimalist, eh?

If you like to zoom your worksheet to 50 percent of its normal size, use the Set View Preferences dialog box to set the custom worksheet zoom amount that appears in the View menu. Simply choose 50 as the Custom zoom percent, and the View menu changes to reflect this percentage (more on zooming later in this chapter).

Normally, 1-2-3 for Windows displays only row numbers and column letters in its frame, but you can request the program to display other things as well by making choices in the Set View Preferences dialog box. Next to the Worksheet frame check box is a drop-down listbox that produces the choices you see in Figure 12-3. Go ahead and experiment with these choices.

Arguably, the most useful is the Inches choice. After you select Inches, the program displays the worksheet frame in inches rather than in row numbers and column letters. Having the inches displayed in the frame can be very useful if you're trying to line up a worksheet so that it prints on a preprinted form.

**Figure 12-3:**
Here, you can change the way the worksheet frame looks.

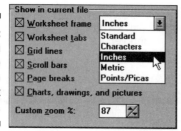

# It's Not Default of the Worksheet

1-2-3 for Windows enables you to change many default settings while you're working. After you select a cell or a range, for example, you can then change the font, size, numeric format, column width, alignment, color of the text and background, and so on.

While you enter data into a cell, keep in mind that 1-2-3 for Windows is using its *default* settings. For example, your information is entered in a default font with a default numeric format in default background color, and so on. If you don't like these defaults, you easily can change them. Head for the Style⇨Worksheet Defaults command to make the changes. The command produces the dialog box shown in Figure 12-4.

If you want to make all the type on your worksheet larger, it's easier to change the default type size than to format all the cells.

Changing any of the defaults in the Worksheet Defaults dialog box affects only the current worksheet. Also, if you've already made any modifications to individual cells or ranges, these modifications are not affected by the changes in the default settings. For example, if you have selected a different font for a particular range, changing the default font does not affect that range.

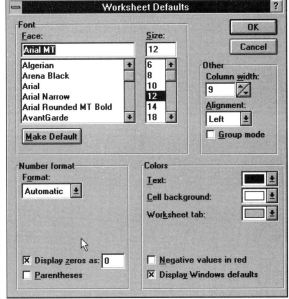

**Figure 12-4:**
The
Worksheet
Defaults
dialog box,
where you
change the
default
settings for
1-2-3 for
Windows.

# User Setup (Including Autosave)

You also can change the way 1-2-3 for Windows operates by using the Tools⇨User Setup command. After you select this command, it produces the User Setup dialog box shown in Figure 12-5.

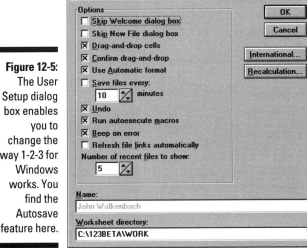

**Figure 12-5:**
The User
Setup dialog
box enables
you to
change the
way 1-2-3 for
Windows
works. You
find the
Autosave
feature here.

Most people are satisfied with the normal settings here; however, you may want to experiment with these setting just for fun. One important setting in the dialog box is the automatic file save feature. You should definitely activate this feature by clicking the box and entering the number of minutes you want. Then, 1-2-3 for Windows automatically saves your work to disk at a time interval that you specify.

# Splitting Windows (Not with Your Baseball)

If you have a great deal of information in a worksheet, scrolling through the worksheet can get tedious when you're examining it. The split windows option can help you out, however. This feature displays the same sheet in both "panes" or different sheets from the same 3-D worksheet file. If you have a very large worksheet, this feature is handy because it enables you to refer to one part while you're working on another part that may be far away. The split windows option is useful also for copying cells and ranges across long distances, because you can quickly jump back and forth between the panes.

Figure 12-6 shows an example of a "panefull" worksheet window that has been split vertically. The left pane displays sheet A, and the right pane displays sheet C.

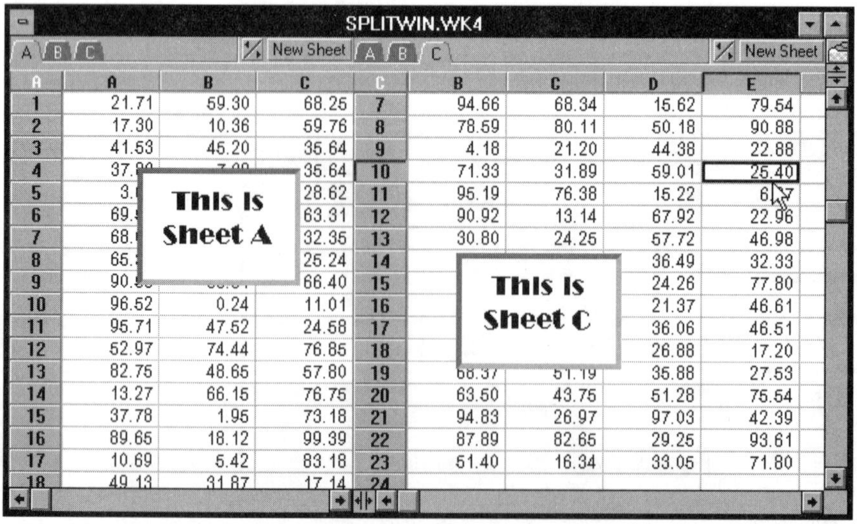

**Figure 12-6:**
This window has been split into two independently scrolling panes.

As you know, every worksheet is displayed in its own window. You can split this window into two panes so that you can see two different parts of a worksheet at the same time.

One way to split a window is to use the <u>V</u>iew⇨Split command. This command gives you the choice of splitting the window vertically or horizontally. The window splits wherever the cell pointer is when you issue the command.

An easier way to split windows is to use the mouse to drag the windows splitter icon to the place where you want to split the screen. Actually, two windows splitter icons exist— one for vertical splitting and one for horizontal splitting. Figure 12-7 shows where these icons are located.

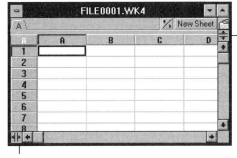

Click and drag here to split
window horizontally

**Figure 12-7:**
These icons
split your
window into
two panes.

Click and drag here to
split window vertically

Use F6 to jump quickly between the panes in a split window.

# Freezing Rows and Columns (Even in the Dead of Summer)

Lots of worksheets have row and column labels that describe the cells. A standard budget is a good example. Typically, the top row has month names and the left column has budget categories. However, after you start scrolling around through the worksheet, the first row and first column often are no longer visible, so it's easy to lose track of what a particular cell is. If you have difficulty remembering your cell labels, then you need to learn how to freeze rows and columns.

The View⇨Freeze Titles command comes in handy and is worth your while to learn. To freeze a row or column means that you arrange it so one or more rows and/or columns always display on-screen, regardless of where the cell pointer is. Suppose that you want the first row and the first column in your worksheet to always appear on-screen. To freeze them, do the following:

1. **Move the cell pointer to cell B2 and choose the** View⇨Freeze Titles **command.**

   You see the dialog box shown in Figure 12-8.

2. **Because you want to freeze both a row and a column, you choose the** Both **option.**

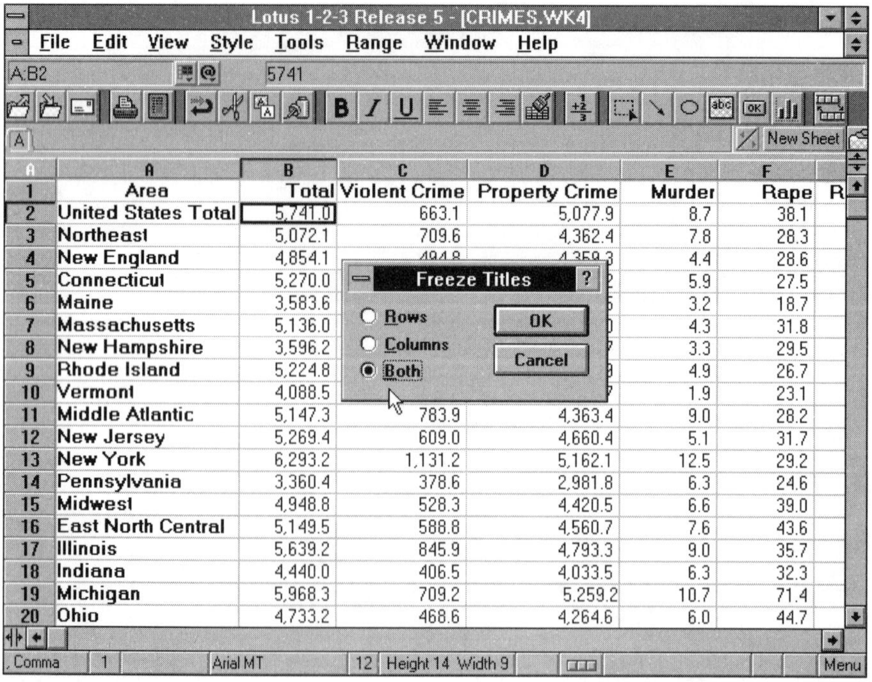

**Figure 12-8:**
The Freeze Titles dialog box enables you to tell 1-2-3 for Windows what to freeze.

3. **Click OK.**

   After you close the dialog box, everything looks the same — until you start scrolling the window. You then discover that 1-2-3 for Windows always displays row 1 and column A.

Figure 12-9 shows a worksheet with the first row and first column frozen. Notice that row 1 and column A are displayed at the same time that the cell pointer is far away from the upper left corner.

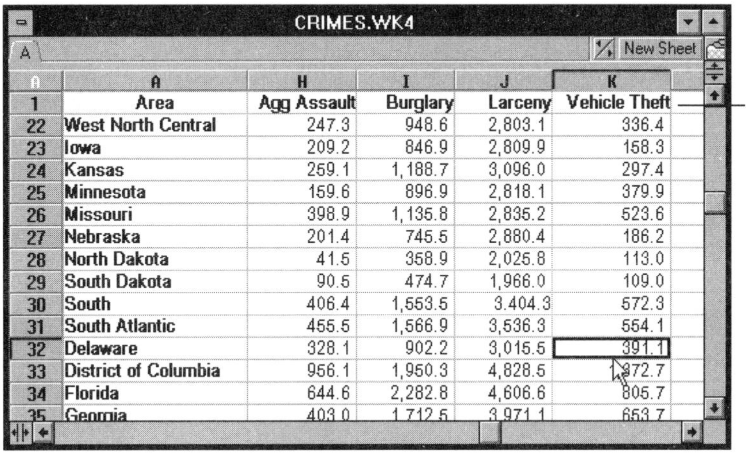

| | A | H | I | J | K | |
|---|---|---|---|---|---|---|
| | Area | Agg Assault | Burglary | Larceny | Vehicle Theft | |
| 22 | West North Central | 247.3 | 948.6 | 2,803.1 | 336.4 | |
| 23 | Iowa | 209.2 | 846.9 | 2,809.9 | 158.3 | |
| 24 | Kansas | 259.1 | 1,188.7 | 3,096.0 | 297.4 | |
| 25 | Minnesota | 159.6 | 896.9 | 2,818.1 | 379.9 | |
| 26 | Missouri | 398.9 | 1,135.8 | 2,835.2 | 523.6 | |
| 27 | Nebraska | 201.4 | 745.5 | 2,880.4 | 186.2 | |
| 28 | North Dakota | 41.5 | 358.9 | 2,025.8 | 113.0 | |
| 29 | South Dakota | 90.5 | 474.7 | 1,966.0 | 109.0 | |
| 30 | South | 406.4 | 1,553.5 | 3.404.3 | 572.3 | |
| 31 | South Atlantic | 455.5 | 1,566.9 | 3,536.3 | 554.1 | |
| 32 | Delaware | 328.1 | 902.2 | 3,015.5 | 391.1 | |
| 33 | District of Columbia | 956.1 | 1,950.3 | 4,828.5 | 372.7 | |
| 34 | Florida | 644.6 | 2,282.8 | 4,606.6 | 805.7 | |
| 35 | Georgia | 403.0 | 1,712.5 | 3,971.1 | 653.7 | |

CRIMES.WK4

Frozen column

**Figure 12-9:**
An example
of a frozen
row and
column.

To unfreeze (thaw out) the frozen rows or columns, choose the View⇨Clear
Titles command.

# Zooming Windows

If you have a video camera, it probably has a zoom lens. This lens enables you
to zoom in on your subject for a closer look (handy at your local nude beach),
or zoom out to record the big picture (to fit all those "large" relatives in the
scene). 1-2-3 for Windows isn't a video camera, but it does have a zooming
feature. The View menu has a Zoom In command and a Zoom Out command.
These commands enable you to change the amount of magnification of the on-
screen display (and have nothing to do with how the worksheet looks when it's
printed).

Figure 12-10 shows two worksheet windows. The one on the left is zoomed in to
show close detail, and the other is zoomed out to give a bird's-eye view.

Why might you want to zoom in or out? Many reasons exist. If you're working
on a chart (Chapter 14) or using some of the drawing tools (Chapter 16),
zooming in gives you more control over the details. And if you have a large
worksheet, you can zoom out to get a better idea of how the worksheet is laid
out. Zooming out also makes it easier to select large ranges with a mouse.

After you select the View⇨Zoom In or View⇨Zoom Out command, 1-2-3 for
Windows changes the display of cells by 10 percent. The View⇨Custom command
zooms the worksheet to a percentage that you specify by using the View⇨Set
View Preferences command. (Normally, the custom zoom factor is 87 percent.)

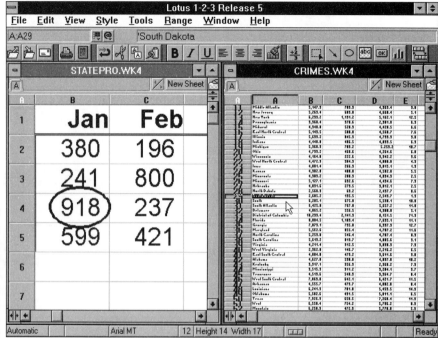

**Figure 12-10:** Zooming can show the details up close or give you the big picture.

# Chekking Your Speling

If you use a word processor, you are probably on friendly terms with its built-in spelling checker. 1-2-3 for Windows isn't a word processor, but it does have a spelling checker, which can save you a great deal of embarrassment (but good spelers lyke me don't knede sutch thingz).

You access this feature by selecting the Tools⇨Spell Check command. 1-2-3 for Windows then displays the dialog box shown in Figure 12-11.

**Figure 12-11:** Running spell check is a good idea before you print important spreadsheets.

You can run the spell check on the entire worksheet file, the current sheet only, or just a range that you specify. Click the Options button to specify some additional spell checking options. After 1-2-3 for Windows finds a word it doesn't recognize, up pops the dialog box shown in Figure 12-12. You can enter the correct spelling in the Replace with text box, or you can select one of the alternatives and click the Replace button.

**Figure 12-12:**
The Spell Check dialog box appears after finding a word it doesn't recognize.

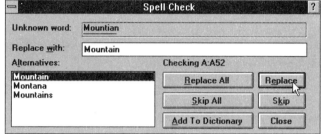

The spelling checker isn't a substitute for a careful review of your worksheet. The checker can't identify words that are spelled correctly but used incorrectly in a sentence. In the following example, all the italicized words are used incorrectly but are in the spelling checker as being correct (so the text passes the spelling checker with flying colors): I like *two* go to *sea* the *see inn* May *sew* that *eye* can drink *tee* at the golf *tea* while I try *too* get the little ball in the *whole.* Whew! This golfer needs my editor for sure.

# Part III
# How to Impress the Easily Impressed

## In this part...

The five chapters in this section can be described as "gee whiz" stuff (with a bit of "jeepers" stuff thrown in for good measure). You can probably get by for quite a while by pretending these topics don't even exist. But sooner or later, you might want to expand your horizons. In the unlikely event that this actually occurs, you'll learn how to make your worksheets look great (or at least good), how to create and customize graphs, and all kinds of shortcuts that can save you valuable minutes each day, giving you more time for more important things like daydreaming and gossiping.

# Chapter 13
# Fancy Formatting Footwork

*"It is better to be beautiful than to be good. But it is better to be good than to be ugly."*

Oscar Wilde (1854–1900)

● ● ● ● ● ● ● ● ● ● ● ● ● ● ● ● ● ● ● ● ● ● ● ● ● ● ● ● ● ● ● ● ● ● ● ● ● ● ● ● ● ● ● ● ● ● ● ●

## In This Chapter

▶ How to make your worksheets look great

▶ The ins and outs of dealing with fonts — or, making sure WYS is really WYG

▶ All sorts of other formatting options, including drawing borders, changing cell colors, and messing with cell alignment

▶ Some suggestions to keep you from going hog wild

● ● ● ● ● ● ● ● ● ● ● ● ● ● ● ● ● ● ● ● ● ● ● ● ● ● ● ● ● ● ● ● ● ● ● ● ● ● ● ● ● ● ● ● ● ● ● ●

*W*hen it comes to type fonts, sizes, and colors, many people are quite content to accept all of 1-2-3 for Windows' default settings. Using these defaults produces a perfectly acceptable — but rather boring — worksheet. Not too many years ago, spreadsheet users didn't even have a choice in these matters. Everything that spewed forth from the printer looked pretty much the same: all in one font and no accouterments, such as borders and shading. Nowadays, even regular people like yourself can produce worksheets that look like they were prepared for a software ad.

If you want to add some pizzazz to your work (and give your creative juices a chance to flow — or trickle), this chapter tells you all about the stylistic formatting options at your disposal.

## What Is Stylistic Formatting?

This chapter is mainly about aesthetics. In other words, you'll learn how to use the formatting commands that make your work look good and stand out in a crowd. By formatting, I'm not talking about the *numeric* formatting you do with the Style▷Number Format command. Rather, I'm taking about the following types of formatting (sometimes referred to as *stylistic formatting*):

   ✔ Changing the type font

   ✔ Changing the point size of the type

   ✔ Changing the type attributes (bold, italic, underlined)

   ✔ Adding borders, lines, and frames

   ✔ Changing the colors (or shading) of the text and the background

   ✔ Adjusting the alignment of cell contents

# Why Bother?

How something is presented can often have a major influence on how it's accepted. Consider this scenario: Both you and your counterpart at a competing company submit a proposal to a potential client. One proposal uses plain old Courier type (like a typewriter), and the other is nicely formatted with different type sizes, attractive borders, and even some shading. Which one do you think the potential client will read first?

An attractive presentation demands more attention, is easier to read, and makes the reader think that you really care about your work. Figure 13-1 shows an example of an unformatted report. Figure 13-2 shows that same report after applying some formatting. Which one do *you* prefer?

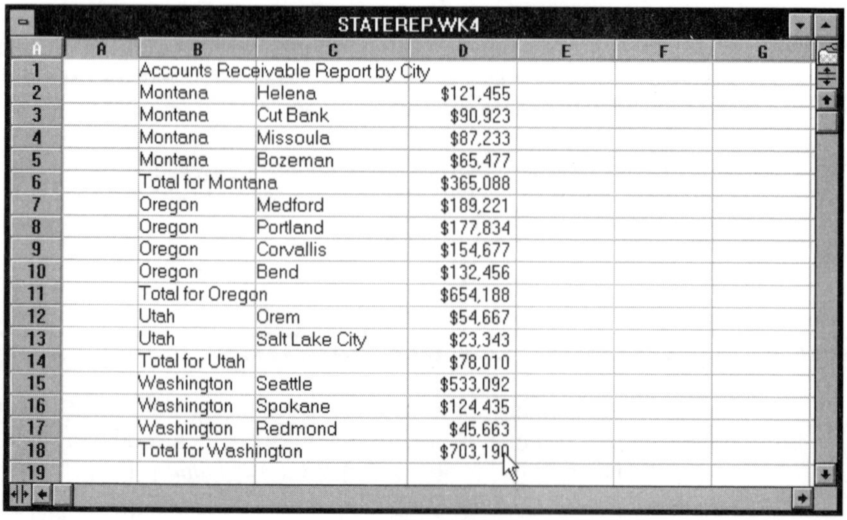

| | A | B | C | D | E | F | G |
|---|---|---|---|---|---|---|---|
| 1 | | Accounts Receivable Report by City | | | | | |
| 2 | | Montana | Helena | $121,455 | | | |
| 3 | | Montana | Cut Bank | $90,923 | | | |
| 4 | | Montana | Missoula | $87,233 | | | |
| 5 | | Montana | Bozeman | $65,477 | | | |
| 6 | | Total for Montana | | $365,088 | | | |
| 7 | | Oregon | Medford | $189,221 | | | |
| 8 | | Oregon | Portland | $177,834 | | | |
| 9 | | Oregon | Corvallis | $154,677 | | | |
| 10 | | Oregon | Bend | $132,456 | | | |
| 11 | | Total for Oregon | | $654,188 | | | |
| 12 | | Utah | Orem | $54,667 | | | |
| 13 | | Utah | Salt Lake City | $23,343 | | | |
| 14 | | Total for Utah | | $78,010 | | | |
| 15 | | Washington | Seattle | $533,092 | | | |
| 16 | | Washington | Spokane | $124,435 | | | |
| 17 | | Washington | Redmond | $45,663 | | | |
| 18 | | Total for Washington | | $703,190 | | | |
| 19 | | | | | | | |

STATEREP.WK4

**Figure 13-1:** An unformatted report. Boring, huh?

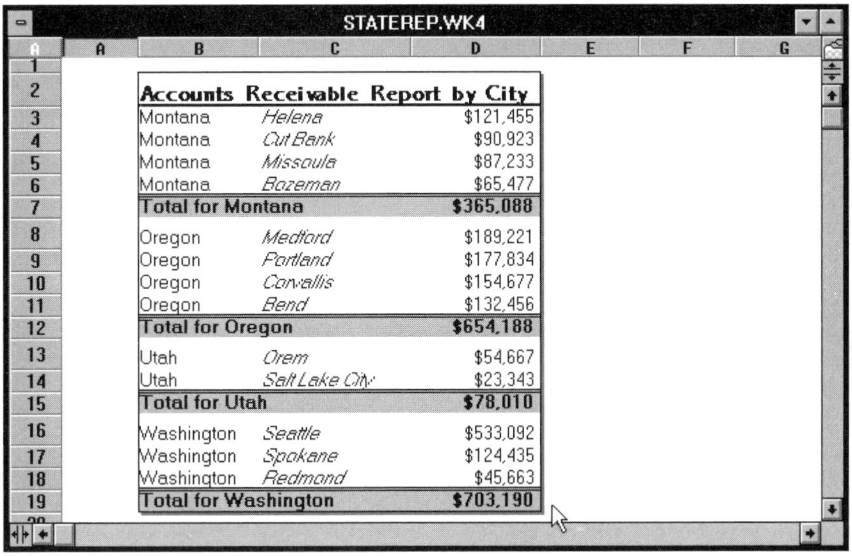

| Accounts Receivable Report by City | | |
|---|---|---|
| Montana | *Helena* | $121,455 |
| Montana | *Cut Bank* | $90,923 |
| Montana | *Missoula* | $87,233 |
| Montana | *Bozeman* | $65,477 |
| **Total for Montana** | | **$365,088** |
| Oregon | *Medford* | $189,221 |
| Oregon | *Portland* | $177,834 |
| Oregon | *Corvallis* | $154,677 |
| Oregon | *Bend* | $132,456 |
| **Total for Oregon** | | **$654,188** |
| Utah | *Orem* | $54,667 |
| Utah | *Salt Lake City* | $23,343 |
| **Total for Utah** | | **$78,010** |
| Washington | *Seattle* | $533,092 |
| Washington | *Spokane* | $124,435 |
| Washington | *Redmond* | $45,663 |
| **Total for Washington** | | **$703,190** |

**Figure 13-2:**
A report with some simple formatting. What a difference!

The preceding is not meant to imply that a nicely formatted worksheet report can compensate for a lousy analysis. In most cases, you must have the content before you add the flair. But if you take the time to do some stylistic formatting, at least you won't have a lousy analysis *and* a lousy-looking report.

But there's one more reason to make time to format your work nicely: It's fun. In fact, you'll probably find that formatting your work is a great deal more interesting than building formulas and copying ranges (I do).

# General Principles of Formatting

Before we get too far into these principles, I'll offer a few general words of wisdom on this topic. Take it as gospel, or with a grain of salt.

## Screen or printer?

One thing to remember is WYSIWYG — *what you see is what you get.* When you format your worksheet, the printed image looks very much like the image you see on-screen. Change the font on-screen, and the worksheet prints with that new font. Add a border around a table of numbers, and the border appears in the printout. And so on and so on.

An important difference between printed and on-screen appearance is color. Because most people don't have color printers, your printer translates the on-screen colors into shades of gray when you print your work. It's important to keep this fact in mind, because some color combinations look great on-screen, but they look terrible when they're printed. If you need to have something that looks good on paper *and* looks good on-screen, the best approach is to experiment with various colors.

## General formatting how-tos

When it comes to stylistic formatting, 1-2-3 for Windows makes it pretty easy on you. In general, you select the range of cells that you want to format, and then issue a formatting command. You'll generally get a dialog box in which you specify the formatting you want. When you close the dialog box, the range of cells that you selected stays selected, so you can continue to do other formatting with that same range, if necessary.

You have a great deal of choices when it comes to accessing the formatting commands:

- ✔ Use the main Style menu
- ✔ Use the shortcut menu (right-click your selection)
- ✔ Use the SmartIcons for some formatting operations
- ✔ Use the status bar at the bottom of the screen for some formatting operations
- ✔ Use automatic styles (discussed later)
- ✔ Copy existing formats to other cells

You'll learn all this fun stuff in this chapter, so don't go away.

# Dealing with Fonts

One thing that can drastically change the look of your work is the font or fonts that you use. A *font* refers to the typeface that's used for text and numbers. The actual fonts that you can use depend on what fonts are installed on your computer system. There are a great deal of different fonts, and they come in many different sizes. Some are designed for ordinary work, and others can best be described as "decorative."

## Types of fonts

You can use only the fonts that are installed for your system. Actually, the fonts come in files and are installed in Windows, not in the individual programs you run. In essence, this means you have no control over the fonts on your system, unless you are willing to learn much more about installing fonts. Don't fret though, because Windows usually provides an impressive array of fonts for you.

Fonts come in two different flavors:

- **Fixed size fonts.** These fonts come only in fixed point sizes. For example, your machine happens to have the Helvetica font in 12-point and 10-point. Therefore, you can use either 10-point or 12-point, but you _can't_ use 11-point Helvetica.

- **Scalable fonts.** These fonts are the most versatile. A scalable font can appear in virtually any size you want. If you have a scalable Helvetica font installed, you can use it any size. You can have a 6-point Helvetica footnote and a 20-point Helvetica title.

Chances are, you already have access to some scalable fonts known as _TrueType fonts._ A few of these fonts are included with Windows. They have names like Arial, Times New Roman, and Courier New. TrueType fonts appear on-screen exactly as they will on the printout.

When you install 1-2-3 for Windows, you have the option of installing some different types of scalable fonts, called _ATM_ (Adobe Type Manager) _fonts._ In general, you don't have to install these if you use the TrueType fonts that came with Windows.

You install new fonts through the Windows Control Panel. After running Control Panel, click the Fonts icon, and then click the Add button. You'll need to tell the program where the new fonts are located (usually, on a floppy disk). Consult your Windows manual if you need help. When you install new TrueType fonts, these fonts are available automatically in all your Windows programs.

## Changing fonts

One way to change the font of your selection is to choose the Style⇨Font & Attributes command (you also can right-click the selection to get a shortcut menu with this command on it). You'll get the dialog box shown in Figure 13-3. Select the font you want from the list. In this dialog box, you also can change the font size (font size is measured in points: the larger the number, the larger the font size), make the text bold, italic, or underlined, and select which group of cells you want these changes to affect. You also can adjust the text _color_ here — but that topic is covered later.

## Got a case of font envy?

You may have seen some printed output from a colleague that used some great looking fonts. Chances are, this person acquired some new TrueType fonts from one of many sources. The accompanying figure shows a sampling of some TrueType fonts that I have installed. As you can see in the following figure, there's a good variety — although not all of them are appropriate for a board report.

So where do you get these new fonts? Sometimes, when you install a new software program, the program adds some new fonts. You also can buy separate font collections and install them in Windows. And if you know where to look, you can get many new fonts for free. For example, you can download fonts from computer bulletin boards or on-line services such as America Online or CompuServe. Or, you can get collections of shareware or public domain fonts by mail order or in your local computer store (very cheaply, I might add).

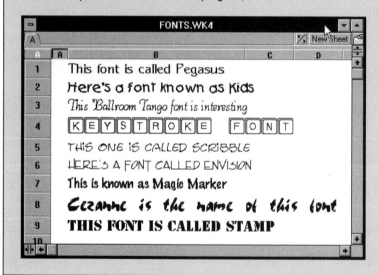

 When you select a font from a list in the Font & Attributes dialog box, a sample appears in the sample box. As you scroll through the list of fonts, notice that the TrueType fonts have a distinct *TT* logo to their left. This logo indicates that this font is a TrueType scalable font.

Another way to change the font of your selected cells is to use the status bar. The status bar shows the font name for the cell or range you have selected, and you can just click this font name to display a list of available fonts and select a new one. See Figure 13-4 for an example of what this popup font list looks like (remember, the fonts you have might vary).

Fonts   Point size   Other attributes

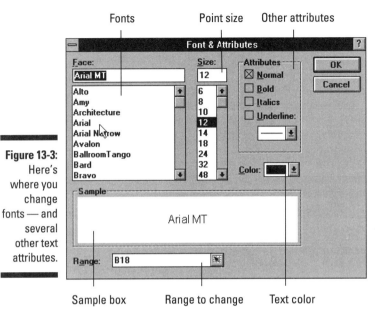

**Figure 13-3:**
Here's
where you
change
fonts — and
several
other text
attributes.

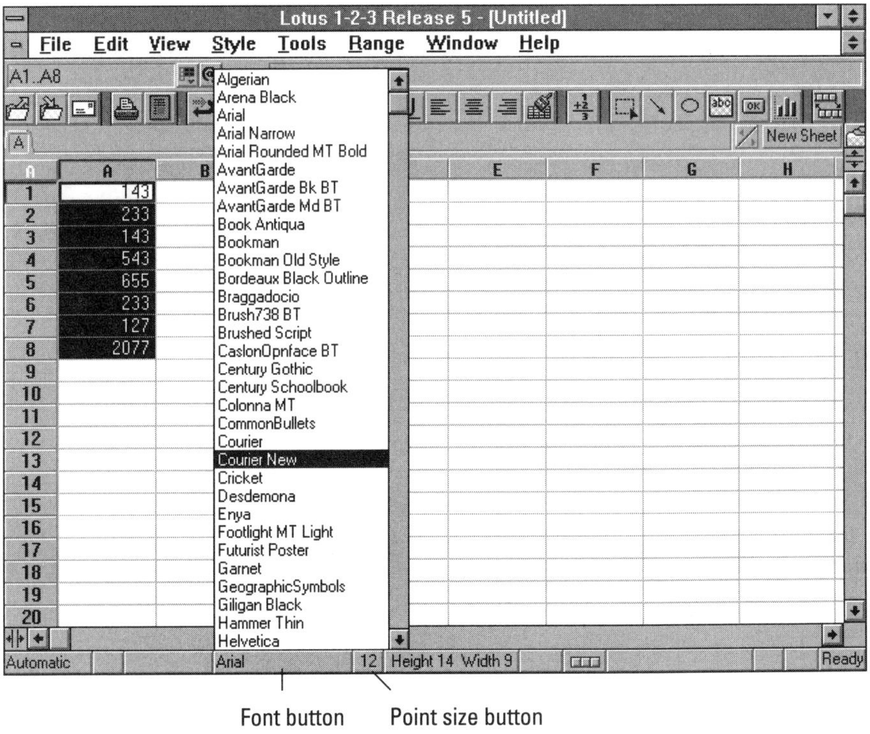

Sample box    Range to change    Text color

**Figure 13-4:**
Clicking the
font button
on the
status bar
displays a
list of fonts.

Font button    Point size button

Directly to the right of the font name button in the status bar is the point size button. Clicking this button is a quick way to change the size of the font in your selection.

If the font or font size is not shown in the status bar, the range you have selected contains two or more different fonts or two or more different font sizes. You can still use the status bar to select a font or size for your entire selection.

If your worksheet text is hard to read on-screen, you don't necessarily have to use a larger font to make it readable. You can always change the zoom factor to enlarge the screen image. Choose the <u>V</u>iew⇨<u>Z</u>oom In command to do this. Zooming like this has no effect on the printed output.

# Borders, Lines, and Frames

The grid lines that normally appear on your screen make it easy for you to see where the cells are. Normally, you don't print the grid lines (although you can, if you want). But 1-2-3 for Windows enables you to add all sorts of lines to your worksheet — and you have plenty of control over how they look. Adding lines or borders can greatly enhance your worksheet, as you can see in Figure 13-5 This figure shows an example of a range before and after adding some lines and borders.

**Figure 13-5:**
Adding borders can make a table look more organized.

| | A | B | C | D | E | F | G | H |
|---|---|---|---|---|---|---|---|---|
| 1 | | | | | | | | |
| 2 | | Goal | Actual | | | | Goal | Actual |
| 3 | Philips | 175 | 199 | | Philips | | 175 | 199 |
| 4 | Jergens | 175 | 187 | | Jergens | | 175 | 187 |
| 5 | Richardson | 175 | 173 | | Richardson | | 175 | 173 |
| 6 | Omar | 175 | 168 | | Omar | | 175 | 168 |
| 7 | Quincy | 150 | 144 | | Quincy | | 150 | 144 |
| 8 | Charles | 150 | 132 | | Charles | | 150 | 132 |
| 9 | Tinker | 125 | 111 | | Tinker | | 125 | 111 |
| 10 | Elders | 125 | 94 | | Elders | | 125 | 94 |
| 11 | Average | 156.25 | 151 | | Average | | 156.25 | 151 |
| 12 | | | | | | | | |
| 13 | | | | | | | | |
| 14 | | | | | | | | |

BORDERS.WK4

If you add lines and borders to your worksheet, it's a good idea to turn off the cell grid display. Doing so makes it easier to see the lines that you add. To get rid of the cell grid display, select the View⇨Set View Preferences command, and uncheck the box labeled Grid lines.

## Adding lines or borders

The Style⇨Lines & Color command is where it's happening when it's time to add some lines or borders. As always, make sure you select the cell or range you want to format before you choose this command. Figure 13-6 shows the dialog box that this command brings up. For the time being, you can ignore the top part that's labeled Interior — that's where you change colors.

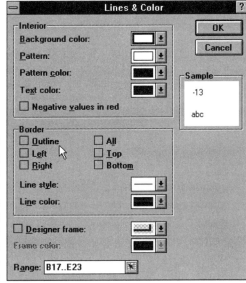

**Figure 13-6:** You have many options when it comes to adding lines and borders.

This dialog box also shows a sample of what you'll get as you change various attributes. Keep your eye on the sample box to avoid surprises when you exit the dialog box.

When you work with this dialog box, remember that the lines you specify apply to the entire range selected. You can turn on a particular line by clicking the box. For example, to put an outline around the entire selected range, click the Outline box. 1-2-3 for Windows then shows you what line type is used. You can change the line by using the Line style drop-down list.

Outlining a range is different than adding a line around every cell in a range. To put an outline around a range of cells, use the Outline box. If you want to create a grid with lines around each cell, click the All box.

You can add lines to as many parts of the selection as you like, and each line part can be a different line style. In other words, you can go crazy with line drawing options. When you're satisfied (or too crazy to continue), select OK.

To remove all lines from a selection, just make sure that all the line options are not checked.

If the check boxes in the Lines & Color dialog boxes are *grayed,* the selected range of cells contains mixed lines. In other words, the lines in the selection aren't consistent.

## Adding designer frames

The Lines & Color dialog box has another option at the bottom, called *Designer frame.* With this feature, you can put one of 16 "designer frames" around your selection. Figure 13-7 shows your designer frame options. You also can change the color of the designer frame, if you like (watch the sample box to see what you'll get). These can give you some pretty slick effects — just don't overdo it.

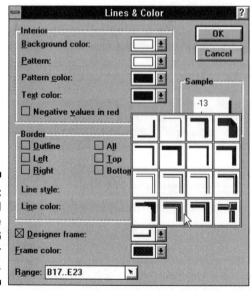

**Figure 13-7:** For special FX, choose one of the 16 designer frames.

# Color, Color, Everywhere

When I first started out in computing, a color monitor was considered a luxury item. And the color monitors that were available were pretty wimpy by today's standards. Nowadays, practically every system is equipped with a color monitor (except laptops and portables — but that's also rapidly changing). Color is great. It lets you make certain text stand out from the crowd, and coloring the background of a range makes it easy to remember that those cells belong together (not to mention the fact that it's easier on the eyes).

1-2-3 for Windows lets you change the color of the text in the cells, as well as the background of the cells. I can't really demonstrate with a screen shot, because this book is strictly black and white. But suffice it to say that you can get some nice looking worksheets — as well as some very gaudy worksheets — by changing the color of the text and background.

You change colors by using the Style⇨Lines & Color commands. I showed you a picture of the resulting dialog box in the previous section, so you might want to turn back to refresh your memory.

Here's what you can change in your current selection:

- ✔ **Background color:** The background of cells can use two colors, combined in a pattern. Use this option to choose the background color (if desired). You can choose from 255 colors.

- ✔ **Pattern:** You have 64 choices for the background pattern. The choices here show up using the background color and pattern color currently chosen.

- ✔ **Pattern color:** You have 255 colors to choose from for the second background color. This feature has no effect if you choose either the solid or transparent (T) pattern choices.

- ✔ **Text color:** Although it looks like you have 255 colors to choose from for your text color, you'll find that some of these colors are translated into solid colors.

When you print your worksheet on a black and white printer, different colors appear as shades of gray. Some combinations of text colors and background colors that look great on-screen look terrible when they are printed. And to make things even more unpredictable, the results you get depend on the printer you're using. All I can say here is to experiment and see what you get.

# Alignment and Misalignment

You probably already know about the common ways of aligning stuff in cells (check out Chapter 4 if you forget). You can either make the contents of a cell flush left, flush right, or centered. And the SmartIcons make this process a breeze. But there are some other alignment options that you might find interesting in your stylistic pursuits. These choices are made in the Alignment dialog box (Figure 13-8) — which you get when you choose the Style⇨Alignment command.

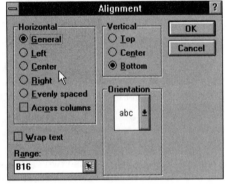

**Figure 13-8:**
With the Alignment dialog box, you can drastically change the way cells appear.

## Word wrap

One of my favorite features in 1-2-3 for Windows is its Wrap text option. This option makes each formatted cell work like a tiny word processor. In other words, when you type a long label into the cell, the words wrap around and the row height increases to accommodate the extra lines. Figure 13-9 shows an example of this process. As you can see, it's great for the headings in tables.

**Figure 13-9:**
Using the Wrap text alignment option makes long labels wrap around within a cell.

| | A | B | C | D | E | F |
|---|---|---|---|---|---|---|
| 1 | | | | | | |
| 2 | | Amount Budgeted for 1992 | Amount Actually Spent in 1992 | Difference (Budget vs Actual) 1992 | 1993 Budgeted Amount | |
| 3 | Personnel | 784,000 | 754,988 | 29,012 | 825,000 | |
| 4 | Equipment | 65,000 | 82,500 | (17,500) | 85,000 | |
| 5 | Outside Services | 145,000 | 175,000 | (30,000) | 200,000 | |
| 6 | Other | 90,000 | 15,670 | 74,330 | 20,000 | |
| 7 | Total | 1,084,000 | 1,028,158 | 55,842 | 1,130,000 | |
| 8 | | | | | | |
| 9 | | | | | | |
| 10 | | | | | | |

BUD-SMRY.WK4

# Centering across cells

Another handy feature lets you center a label across a group of cells. Figure 13-10 shows a label that's actually in cell B2, but it's centered across the range B2..F2. This option is a good way to put titles across a multicolumn table of numbers. Back in the dark ages (1989), people used to add spaces to their labels (by trial and error) to get this effect.

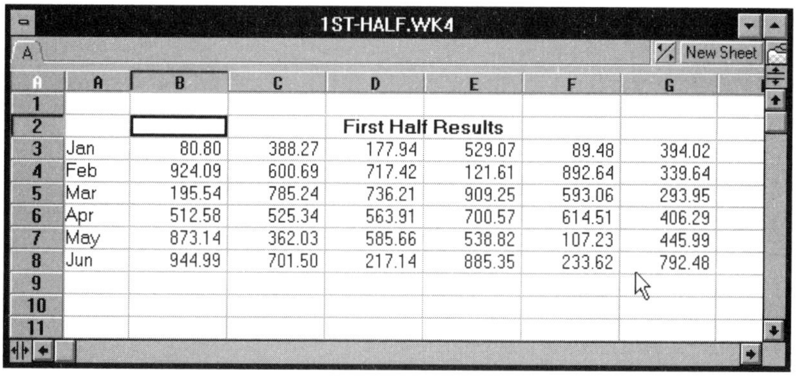

**Figure 13-10:**
The label is actually in cell B2 — but it's centered across a bunch of columns.

| | A | B | C | D | E | F | G |
|---|---|---|---|---|---|---|---|
| 1 | | | | | | | |
| 2 | | | | First Half Results | | | |
| 3 | Jan | 80.80 | 388.27 | 177.94 | 529.07 | 89.48 | 394.02 |
| 4 | Feb | 924.09 | 600.69 | 717.42 | 121.61 | 892.64 | 339.64 |
| 5 | Mar | 195.54 | 785.24 | 736.21 | 909.25 | 593.06 | 293.95 |
| 6 | Apr | 512.58 | 525.34 | 563.91 | 700.57 | 614.51 | 406.29 |
| 7 | May | 873.14 | 362.03 | 585.66 | 538.82 | 107.23 | 445.99 |
| 8 | Jun | 944.99 | 701.50 | 217.14 | 885.35 | 233.62 | 792.48 |
| 9 | | | | | | | |
| 10 | | | | | | | |
| 11 | | | | | | | |

1ST-HALF.WK4

To center a label across a group of columns, first enter the label in the left-most cell of the range you want the label in. Then, select that cell and the cells to the right — enough to cover the entire area that you're centering across. Choose Style⇒Alignment, select the Center option, and check the Across columns check box. Choose OK and you'll see your label centered across the entire selection.

# Spacing

Yet another option, *Evenly spaced,* lets you space out the letters in a label to fill an entire cell or an entire horizontal range. Figure 13-11 shows a few examples of this. To do it, select the Evenly spaced option. If you want to space a label out across a bunch of cells, also check the Across columns check box. This option is a special effect, so don't feel compelled to use this alignment option on your next budget summary report.

Normally, stuff you enter in a cell sits at the bottom of the cell. Even if you make the row height high, the cell contents still remain at the bottom of the cell. You can change this default using the vertical alignment options in the Alignment dialog box. Figure 13-11 shows some examples.

Vertical alignment option          Evenly spaced option

**Figure 13-11:**
Alignment
options
enable you
to change
the vertical
or horizontal
alignment of
the cell's
contents.

| | A | B | C | D | E | F |
|---|---|---|---|---|---|---|
| 1 | | | | | | |
| 2 | | | | | | |
| 3 | | This has vertical alignment of Center | | | | |
| 4 | | | | | | |
| 5 | | | | | | |
| 6 | Normal –> | This is a sentence | | | | |
| 7 | Even spacing –> | T h i s | i s | a | s e n t e n c e | |
| 8 | | | | | | |
| 9 | | | | | | |

SPACE.WK4 — New Sheet

## *Changing orientation*

Another interesting feature lets you change how the text is oriented in a cell. You have five choices, which you can select by choosing the Orientation pull-down menu in the Alignment dialog box. If you choose the diagonal option, you can even adjust the angle. Figure 13-12 shows several examples of text with various sorts of orientations.

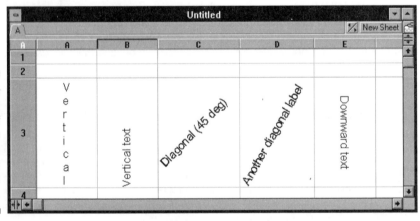

**Figure 13-12:**
You have a
great deal of
choices as
to the
orientation
of the text in
your cells.

# *And Now, the E-Z Way to Format Stuff*

If you made it through the preceding sections of this chapter, you should have a pretty good handle on formatting your worksheets. And now you can fully appreciate a pretty cool time-saver known as *style templates*.

Assume you have a table of numbers in your worksheet. You can use any or all of the techniques I discussed previously to turn this into a pretty spiffy looking table. Doing so might take you a good 15 minutes or more. Or, you can take the express route and have 1-2-3 for Windows do the work for you — in about two seconds.

To format a table of numbers automatically, first select the entire table. Then, choose the Style⇨Gallery command. 1-2-3 for Windows displays the dialog box shown in Figure 13-13. From this dialog box, you can select from a list of 14 templates. The dialog box shows you an example as you scroll through the template list.

**Figure 13-13:**
Here, you
can select
one of 14
canned
styling
templates.

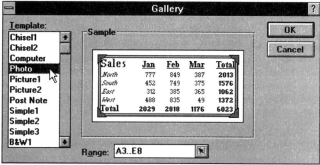

| Sales | Jan | Feb | Mar | Total |
|---|---|---|---|---|
| *North* | 777 | 849 | 387 | 2013 |
| *South* | 452 | 749 | 375 | 1576 |
| *East* | 312 | 385 | 365 | 1062 |
| *West* | 488 | 835 | 49 | 1372 |
| Total | 2029 | 2818 | 1176 | 6023 |

Range: A3..E8

Applying one of these templates to a selected range can cause some drastic changes in the look of your worksheet. For example, the column widths may change, the fonts and attributes may change, and you may see many new colors. If you don't like the looks of things after you close the dialog box, select Edit⇨Undo immediately to reverse the effects (or save your original file before applying a template). As an alternative to scrapping the whole formatting job, you can simply reformat the part of the table that you don't like.

# Some Final Words

I've found that it's really easy to get carried away with formatting. Once you learn what you can do (and you can do a great deal), it's very tempting to waste too much time trying to get everything just perfect. You have to weigh the value of what you're doing against the value of your time. In other words, don't spend three hours formatting a report that took you 15 minutes to develop — especially if no one reads it anyway.

Bad formatting is worse than no formatting. So don't go overboard with colors and lines. As a rule of thumb, you should not use more than two different fonts in a document. If you want variety, it's often better to change the size of some of the text, or make it italic or bold.

And finally, remember that *substance* is what really counts. It's better to spend your time making sure your analysis is correct than making it look good. 'Nuff said.

# Chapter 14

# Impressing Your Boss with Championship Charts

*"And the first rude sketch that the world had seen was joy to his mighty heart. Till the Devil whispered behind the leaves 'It's pretty, but is it art?'"*

Rudyard Kipling (1865–1936)

## In This Chapter

▶ How to turn a range of common, everyday numbers into an attention-grabbing chart

▶ How to change some of the chart's parts

▶ An overview of some of the more interesting chart types you can create in 1-2-3 for Windows

Because people tend to be visual by nature (which is a polite way of saying we can't read), we often can grasp a concept better if it's in the form of a picture or a diagram. Take a look at Figure 14-1. It shows a range of numbers on the left, and the same numbers expressed as a chart on the right. Which tells the story better?

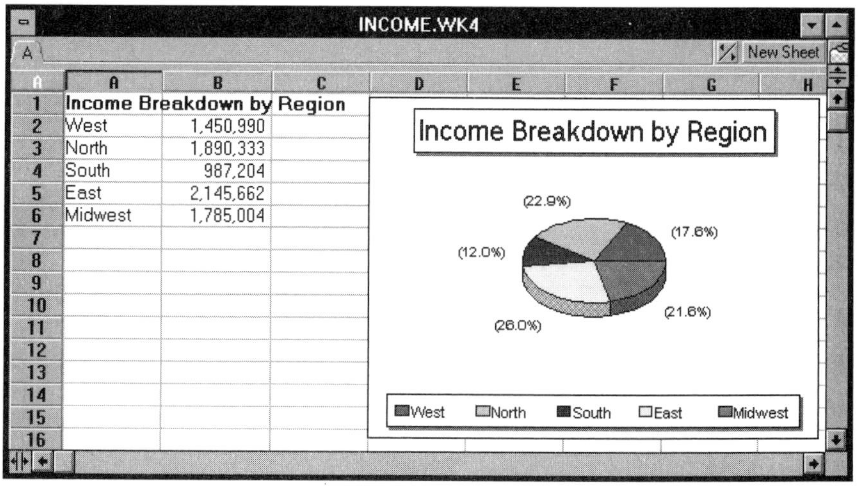

**Figure 14-1:** Boring old numbers, or a titillating chart? Take your pick.

1-2-3 for Windows has some great charting capabilities, and with them, you can create some awesome looking charts. It's easy to make simple charts, and if you spend some time playing around, it won't take long to discover how to customize them to your liking and make them even better.

In earlier versions of 1-2-3, Lotus called these graphics *graphs.* Now they call them *charts.* Call them what you will, but I refer to them throughout this chapter as *charts.* But in real life (which Lotus once referred to as *reality*), I call them graphs.

If you created graphs in earlier versions of 1-2-3, you're in for a pleasant surprise. Release 4 and Release 5 do charts very differently, taking almost all the drudgery out of this task, and even making it sort of fun. So forget everything you learned about 1-2-3 charts, and discover the better way to do it.

## The Chart's Parts

Figure 14-2 shows a chart I created in 1-2-3 for Windows, with all the major parts labeled. Many of these parts are optional, and you can get rid of them if you don't want to see them. For example, when you're plotting only a single series of data you probably don't want a legend. I refer to various parts of a chart throughout this chapter, so you may want to familiarize yourself with these terms.

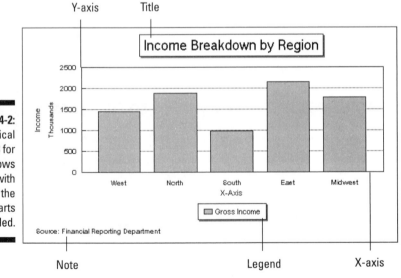

**Figure 14-2:**
A typical
1-2-3 for
Windows
chart, with
some of the
major parts
labeled.

Charts typically display one or more series of numbers graphically. A series of numbers is stored as a range in your worksheet. The series can be displayed as lines, bars (or columns), pie slices, and several other options. In the example shown, it displays a company's income in each region, depicted as bars. There are many types of charts and lots of variations on each type. You learn much more about these issues throughout the chapter.

# Charts Is Charts

Before you charge into this challenging chart chapter, take a few minutes to digest the following factoids:

✔ To create a chart, 1-2-3 for Windows needs to use numbers that are stored in a worksheet. The numbers can be values or the results of formulas.

✔ When you change any of the numbers used by a chart, the chart automatically changes to reflect the new numbers.

✔ A 1-2-3 for Windows chart can show as many as 23 different series of numbers in a single chart — but don't go overboard.

✔ You can choose from a long list of chart types: bar charts, line charts, pie charts, and more (sorry, no eye charts). And a single chart can have both lines and bars, for example.

✔ You don't have to have a legend if you don't want one. A *legend* (like on a map — not the King Arthur type) explains what each color or line stands for.

✔ You have almost complete control over the colors used, the "hatch patterns," line widths, line markers, fonts used for titles and labels, and so on.

✔ Charts live right on your worksheet. Because of this fact, you can print a chart along with the data it uses — and you also can move a chart and change its size.

✔ A worksheet can have any number of charts stored in it.

# How to Create a Chart

Okay, I've wasted enough pages with this preliminary chart chitchat. Now it's time to get down to the nitty gritty.

Despite what your cousin the whiner might have told you, creating a chart is easy. Very easy. Figure 14-3 shows a range of data that's practically begging to be turned into a chart. Here's how to make a chart out of these numbers. If you want to follow along at home, take a minute to re-create this worksheet first.

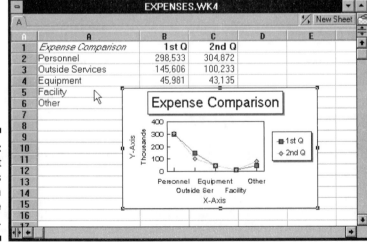

**Figure 14-3:**
This
information
is begging to
be a chart.

| A | B | C | D |
|---|---|---|---|
| 1 | *Expense Comparison* | **1st Q** | **2nd Q** | |
| 2 | Personnel | 298,533 | 304,872 | |
| 3 | Outside Services | 145,606 | 100,233 | |
| 4 | Equipment | 45,981 | 43,135 | |
| 5 | Facility | 11,500 | 11,500 | |
| 6 | Other | 45,646 | 75,903 | |
| 7 | | | | |
| 8 | | | | |

EXPENSES.WK4 — New Sheet

1. **Select the data that will make up your chart.**

   This includes cells that will hold labels and legends. For this example, select A1..C6.

2. **Click the Chart SmartIcon (the one you see in the margin).**

   You'll notice the following message up in the title bar: *Click and drag where you want to display the chart.* Also, the mouse pointer turns into a small chart.

3. **Click and drag the chart mouse pointer in your worksheet.**

   The exact size or location isn't important. Make it approximately four cells wide by 10 cells high. When you release the mouse button, 1-2-3 for Windows displays the chart in the area you outlined (see Figure 14-4).

That's all there is to it. After selecting the data, all it takes is a click of a SmartIcon and a bit of dragging in your worksheet — and you've got yourself a chart.

**Figure 14-4:**
The chart
appears
with only a
few mouse
clicks.

EXPENSES.WK4 — New Sheet

Expense Comparison

The chart that 1-2-3 for Windows created may not be exactly what you want, but it's probably very close. Notice the following characteristics of this chart:

✔ It got the title from the upper left cell in the range.

✔ It realized that the first column had labels, and used these for the x-axis.

✔ It also figured out the text for the legends.

✔ It created a line chart — which is its default chart type.

✔ It examined the values, and decided how large to make the y-axis values (it also scaled the y-axis values and inserted a label that tells you that these values are in thousands).

✔ It inserted *dummy* labels for the x-axis label and the y-axis label.

If you want to learn how to change some of these features, don't stop now. Keep reading.

# *Making a Chart Be Your Eternal Slave*

After 1-2-3 for Windows draws a chart on your worksheet, you have lots of control over it. You can change its chart type, move the chart around, change its size, print it, and even wipe it off the face of the planet if you don't like it. This section tells you how to do it all.

Before you can do anything to a chart, you must select it. You do this by clicking it. 1-2-3 for Windows informs you that a chart is selected by displaying the chart name in the edit line. Actually, you can select several different parts of a chart. When you select the entire chart, eight small *handles* appear on its borders. Clicking a chart outside of the actual plot area selects the entire chart. If you click inside the plot area, the plot area is selected. See Figure 14-5 for a peek at what these *handles* (tiny squares) look like.

When you select a chart, you'll notice that the SmartIcon palette changes to show some SmartIcons that are relevant to charts. Figure 14-6 shows the SmartIcon palette as it appears when you have a chart selected. With these icons, you can quickly change a chart type — but (as you'll see) you're not limited to the chart types depicted in the SmartIcons.

**Figure 14-5:**
When you
select a
chart, 1-2-3
for Windows
displays
eight handles
on the
chart's
borders.

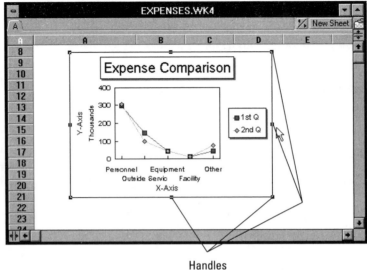

Handles

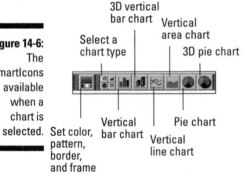

**Figure 14-6:**
The
SmartIcons
available
when a
chart is
selected.

3D vertical
bar chart   Vertical
            area chart
Select a        3D pie chart
chart type

Set color,   Vertical   Pie chart
pattern,    bar chart   Vertical
border,                 line chart
and frame

## *Changing the chart type*

You can choose from 12 chart types from the basic food groups. You can
customize each of these quite a bit, so you really have more flexibility than
you'll probably ever need. How do you know what type of chart to create? Don't
ask me. There are no hard and fast rules on choosing chart types, but I do have
some advice: use the chart type that gets your message across in the simplest
way possible. To display quantities over time, a line, bar, or area chart is a good
choice. To show percents of a total, use a pie chart.

To change the chart type, first select the chart (click it) and then choose the Chart⇨Type command. You see the dialog box shown in Figure 14-7. Select the desired chart type, and choose either Vertical or Horizontal orientation. *Orientation* refers to where the x-axis appears. Normally, charts use a vertical orientation, placing the x-axis on the bottom of the chart. If you opt for horizontal orientation, the x-axis appears on the left. The orientation you choose is mostly a matter of personal preference.

If your x-axis labels are long, try using a horizontal orientation. This usually looks better because the labels aren't all crammed together.

You also can select a specific format for the type of chart you pick. For example, in Figure 14-7, the six large buttons to the right of the list of types show various formats for a line graph. Select the specific format you want, click OK, and the chart appears as a new chart type.

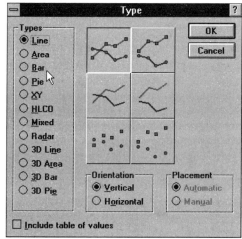

**Figure 14-7:**
The Type dialog box enables you to change the chart type.

A faster way to change the chart type is to click the appropriate SmartIcon. However, not all chart types appear on the SmartIcon palette. If you want a chart type that's not in the SmartIcon palette, you have to use the Chart⇨Type command.

## Moving and resizing a chart

To move a chart, click and drag it. The mouse pointer turns into a hand when you can drag it. You also can use the Windows Clipboard to move graphs to places where you can't drag them. For example, it you want to move a graph from one sheet to another, you can cut it with the Edit⇨Cut command, and then paste it in another sheet with the Edit⇨Paste command.

To resize a chart, first select it and then grab any of the eight handles and drag it. You can make a chart as large or as small as you like.

## Chart annihilation techniques

To remove a chart from your worksheet (and from the universe), select it and issue the Edit⇨Clear command (or simply press Delete).

## Printing charts

Charts look best on-screen, because they show up in living color (assuming you have a color monitor, of course). But most of the time, you have to print a chart on paper so you can share it with someone who likes (or, unfortunately, demands) to see such creations.

When a chart is inserted on your worksheet, you simply include it in your print range and it prints. That's all there is to it.

If your charts don't print, select File⇨Page Setup and make sure that the Drawn objects check box is checked.

When using a laser printer, it's not uncommon to try to print several charts on one page and discover that the entire page is not printed. This means that your printer doesn't have enough memory to print the entire page. You have three choices: Rearrange your worksheet to print fewer graphs on one page, add more memory to your printer (usually an expensive proposition), or use the File⇨Printer Setup⇨Setup command to change the print resolution to a lower number. For more information on printing and resolution, see Chapter 10.

# Rearranging Your Chart's Furniture

Like practically everything else you do in 1-2-3 for Windows, you can change objects in the charts you generate. The easiest way to change something in a chart is to right-click the part that you want to change. 1-2-3 for Windows pops up a shortcut menu where you select what you want to do.

## Changing chart titles and labels

Charts can have lots of text in them: two lines for the title, two lines for notes, and axis labels. To change any of the chart's text, just double-click the text. The dialog box you get depends on which text you click. In any case, you can change the text that's displayed, and also adjust other features having to do with the text.

Figure 14-8 shows the dialog box that appears when you double-click the title in a chart. You can enter up to two lines of text for the title, plus two more lines that appear as a note at the bottom of the chart. Chart-shaping dialog boxes like this have lots of other options that you can easily explore on your own.

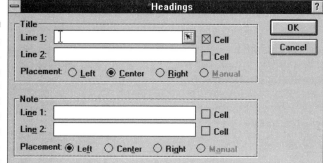

**Figure 14-8:** Double-clicking the chart's title gives you the Headings dialog box.

## Changing chart colors

To change the color or patterns used in any part of a chart, just right-click it and choose Lines & Color from the shortcut menu. Figure 14-9 shows the dialog box that enables you to adjust the colors in a bar chart. This should be very familiar, because it's much like the dialog box that enables you to change background colors in a worksheet range.

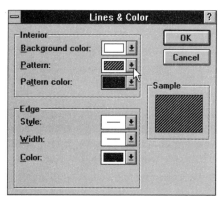

**Figure 14-9:** With the Lines & Color dialog box, you can adjust the color used in a chart part.

## Hungry for more chart power?

There's lot more you can do with charts. Here's some advice: You learn much more by simply digging in and playing around than you do by reading instructions. So just go for it, eh?

When you want to change something in a chart, just remember these three rules:

1. **First, look for a SmartIcon that does what you want to do.**

2. **If you can't find a SmartIcon, try double-clicking the part that you want to change.**

3. **If you can't change it from the dialog box that results from Rule #2, right-click the part that you want to change, and use the shortcut menu to get to the right dialog box.**

Ninety-nine percent of the time, you'll be able to do what you want to do by using these three rules.

# Charming Chart Choices

I'll close this chapter by filling the pages chock-full of choice charts that you can check out and choose from (cheap). These examples demonstrate some of the fun you can have with charts, and maybe give you some ideas that you can adapt to your own situation.

## A 3-D bar chart

This chart in Figure 14-10 shows a different slant on bar charts. This consists of two series of data. The chart type is called 3D Bar, and is useful when you want to add some extra visual appeal to a normal bar chart.

## A horizontal bar chart

Bar charts don't always have to start from the ground and work their way up. The chart in Figure 14-11 shows a bar chart — but with the Horizontal orientation option chosen. This chart type is particularly useful when the x-axis labels are long.

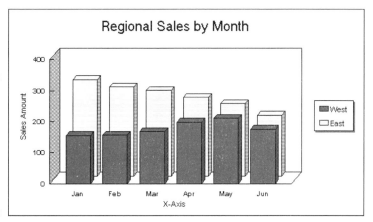

**Figure 14-10:**
Three-dimensional charts can add some pizzazz to an otherwise boring topic.

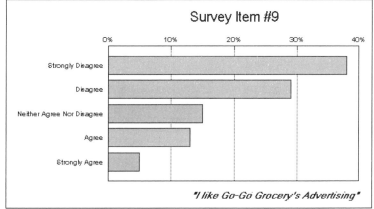

**Figure 14-11:**
A horizontal bar chart.

## A chart that knows how to accessorize

This chart, shown in Figure 14-12, has some stuff added to it by using the drawing tools (you learn about this in the next chapter). I used two text boxes and two arrows to annotate this chart. This is a good way to make a chart say more than mere numbers can.

## A mixed chart

When is a bar chart not a bar chart? When it also includes lines. The chart in Figure 14-13 is usually called a mixed chart. Notice that this chart has two different scales. The bars belong with the left y-axis, and show the monthly sales. The line goes with the right y-axis and shows the percent of sales goal reached. If I used the left scale for both series, the line would not have even shown up, because all the values are less than 1.2 (120%).

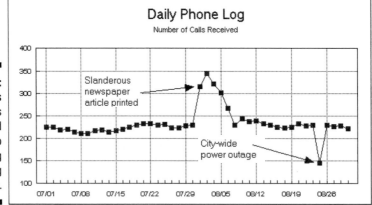

**Figure 14-12:**
It's sometimes useful to add comments to a chart using drawing tools.

This chart began life as an ordinary bar chart. Then I changed the second series to be shown as a line. To do this, click on the chart series and then choose the Chart⇨Ranges command. Change the type for the series using the Mixed type drop-down box. To use the second y-axis for series, check the box labeled Plot on 2nd y-axis.

**Figure 14-13:**
This mixed chart has bars and a line (hence the name).

## Stacked bars

Originally, I wanted to create two pie charts next to each other to compare expenses across two years. Because you can't have two pie charts within a single chart in 1-2-3 for Windows, I used a stacked bar chart to get a similar effect (shown in Figure 14-14). Both of the data series had values that added to 100 percent.

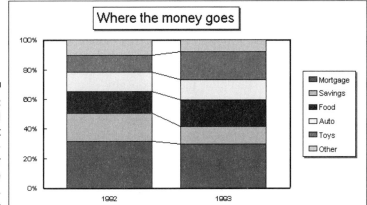

## An XY chart

The chart in Figure 14-15 is an XY chart (sometimes known as a *scattergram*). Each dot represents one person and shows his or her height and weight. As you can see, there's an upwards linear trend: taller people generally weigh more than shorter folks. I also used the drawing tools (a text box and an arrow) to make a tasteless comment about the person who belongs to one of the dots.

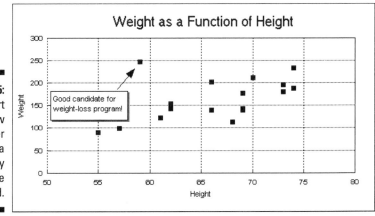

## A stock market chart

Stock market analysts love this sort of chart. The chart in Figure 14-16 shows stock performance over a period of time. For each day, the chart shows the daily high, the daily low, and the closing price. There's also another option (not shown in the example) that plots the daily opening price.

**Figure 14-16:** This chart shows the month's performance of this stock at a glance.

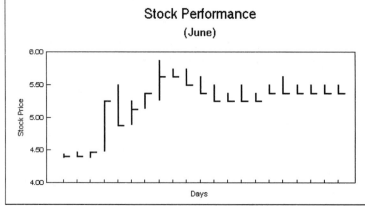

## A 3-D line chart

Figure 14-17 shows another twist on 3-D charts — this one's called 3D Line (although a ribbon chart might be a more appropriate name).

**Figure 14-17:** A 3-D line chart is another 3-D variation offered by 1-2-3 for Windows (and it shows that Jill seems to crush Bob fairly regularly).

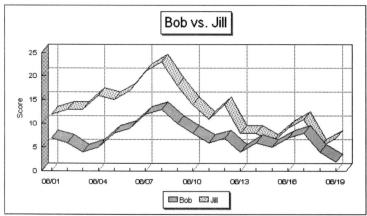

## Another XY chart

Figure 14-18 shows that you can have some fun (in an academic sort of way) with charts. This XY chart plots data generated with formulas that use trigonometric functions (namely, the @SIN and @COS functions).

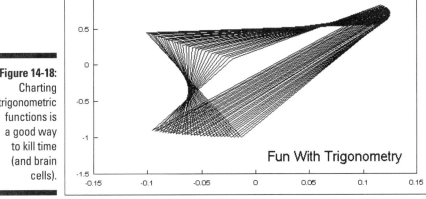

**Figure 14-18:**
Charting trigonometric functions is a good way to kill time (and brain cells).

# Chapter 15
# Mapmaker, Mapmaker, Make Me a Map

*"Journey over all the universe in a map, without the expense and fatigue of traveling, without suffering the inconveniences of heat, cold, hunger, and thirst."*

Miguel de Cervantes (1547-1616)
From *Don Quixote de la Mancha*

. . . . . . . . . . . . . . . . . . . . . . . . . . . . . . . . . . . . . . . . . . .

## In This Chapter

▶ Learning about the new mapping feature in 1-2-3 for Windows

▶ Creating a map with only a few mouse clicks

▶ Using techniques to help make your map look the way you want it

. . . . . . . . . . . . . . . . . . . . . . . . . . . . . . . . . . . . . . . . . . .

**M**apping is a brand-new feature, introduced in Release 5. If you're still using Release 4, you'll have to do your maps the old-fashioned way: with messy marking pens that always seem to run out of ink at the wrong time.

# Why a Map?

As you saw in the preceding chapter, 1-2-3 for Windows can create a bewildering variety of charts to help you display your data graphically. But not all data benefits from a chart. Take a look at the chart in Figure 15-1, which shows a company's sales broken down by state. This was the best I could do to try to show this data in a chart. Doesn't really tell you much, eh?

1-2-3 for Windows gives you a better option: maps. A map is simply another method to present your data graphically. People use maps for lots of purposes. Maps are suitable for data that has a basis in geography. If you classify something by state, province, or country, chances are you can make a map out of the data. A common example is to display sales figures on a map. If your company sells its products all over the U.S., it may be useful to show the annual sales by state. Take a look at Figure 15-2 for an example. This map shows the same data as Figure 15-1, but it's much easier on the eye.

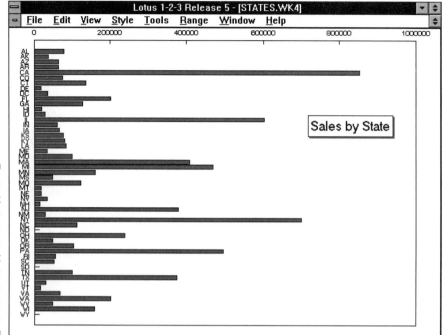

**Figure 15-1:**
This chart
shows sales
for each
state and is
almost
worse than
looking at a
huge table
of numbers.

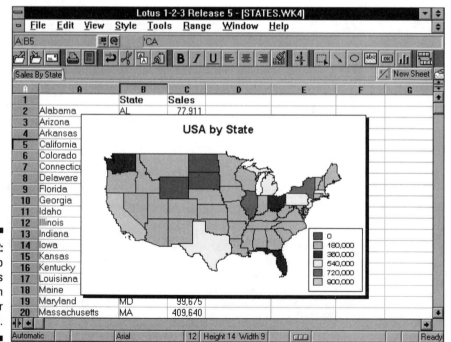

**Figure 15-2:**
This map
shows sales
for each
state, color
coded.

The map view of the data tells you quite a bit. For example, you can see at a glance exactly where this company's biggest sales are (California and New York, with Texas and Florida not too far behind). And a big cluster of states in the Northwest have no sales. If you looked at the data in a standard chart, it would be difficult to notice the big sales gap in these states.

# Types of Maps Available

The U.S. map (by state) is just one of many maps built into 1-2-3 for Windows. Other maps you can use follow:

✔ Alaska

✔ Australia

✔ Canada

✔ Countries of the world (Planet Earth, that is)

✔ Europe

✔ Hawaii

✔ Japan

✔ Mexico

✔ Taiwan

Don't ask me why Alaska and Hawaii aren't included in the U.S. map by state. Last time I checked, they were still part of the United States.

And if this map selection isn't good enough for you, you can purchase more from Strategic Mapping, Inc. For example, you might want a map for your state, divided by zip code. It's available. Call Strategic Mapping at 408-970-9600 — or see your 1-2-3 for Windows documentation for complete details.

# Map-Making Overview

Making a map is easy — just as easy as making a chart. You start out with your data, identified by map region. If you're creating a map of the U.S., your regions are states. If you're making a map of Canada, your regions are provinces. And so on.

Map-making in 1-2-3 for Windows is a four-step process (the fourth step is optional):

1. **Enter your region names in a column.**

2. **Enter the data for each region in the column directly to the right of the region names.**

3. **Issue the Tools⇨Map⇨Insert Map Object command and click the location in the worksheet where you want the map to go.**

   The map is then created before your very eyes.

4. **Modify the colors and "bins," if desired.**

# Creating a Map

In this section you learn how to prepare your data for mapping and create a map.

## Setting up a map

The important thing to remember is that your regions must be identified using words that 1-2-3 for Windows can interpret. You can use either the official region name or an abbreviated map code.

For example, the official region name for the state that I live in is *California*, and the abbreviated map code is *CA* (U.S. state map codes just happen to correspond to the official post office abbreviations). If I try to use an unrecognized region name or map code (such as *Calif* or *Cal* ), it won't work. Before the map is generated, 1-2-3 for Windows scans each region name and tells you if it doesn't recognize the name; you'll have an opportunity to select from a list of all regions for the particular map — but more about this later.

You don't have to include each region for your map. If you only do business in the western part of the U.S., for example, you can simply omit all the regions (states) for which you don't have data. 1-2-3 for Windows won't mind.

To find out the region names that 1-2-3 for Windows can deal with, use the on-line help system. You may not need to resort to this for states in the U.S., but for unfamiliar regions you'll want to consult the on-line help system. For example, off the top of your head, can you name the map code for Azerbaijan? Time's up. It's *AZ*. The astute reader will have deduced that a particular map code has different meaning depending on which map you use. (For a U.S. map, AZ is the map code for Arizona.)

For the eternally curious, Figure 15-3 pinpoints the exact location of Azerbaijan. With 1-2-3 for Windows on your computer, you have a new tool to help you prepare for your next appearance on "Jeopardy".

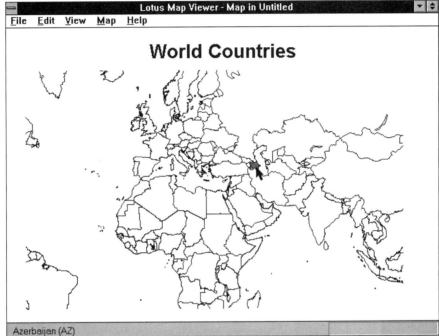

**Figure 15-3:**
Yes,
Virginia,
there really
is an
Azerbaijan.

## Creating your mapsterpiece

After you have your regions and data set up in your worksheet, move the cell pointer anywhere within the range that has your data. (You don't even have to select the entire range.) Then click the Tools⇨Map⇨Insert Map Object command. The mouse pointer changes shape to look like a miniature globe. Click the area of the worksheet where you want the map to be. (One click will do, and dragging to define the size has no effect — unlike creating a chart.) The upper left corner of the map will be located in the cell that you click.

1-2-3 for Windows analyzes the region names and/or map codes and chooses the appropriate map. In a few moments, you'll have a map suitable for framing. It's as easy as that.

If the cell pointer is not in the map data range when you issue the Tools⇨Map⇨Insert Map Object command, 1-2-3 for Windows displays a dialog box that asks you to select the range that has the data for your map.

## *More about mapping*

Here are some additional things to keep in mind — all explained later on, for those who just can't get enough of this map-making business:

✔ You can change the size and location of the map.

✔ If you have data for more than six regions, 1-2-3 for Windows will create six "bins" and color-code the regions based on the bins (not based on the actual values).

✔ You can change the bin ranges, the colors, and the text that appears in the map legend.

✔ You can change the title and adjust the font of the title and legend.

✔ If you change the data for any of the regions, the map updates automatically (just like a chart does).

✔ You can zoom a map to show more detail — perfect if you don't have data for all map regions (for only the Western U.S., for example).

✔ You can use patterns in your map to further identify characteristics of a region. For example, you can identify sales territories by different patterns.

✔ You can add "pin characters" to a map. This is similar in concept to inserting pins on a wall map to mark locations.

# *Modifying a Map*

In many cases, the default map that 1-2-3 for Windows spits out will be just fine. In other cases, however, you may want to customize the map. Here's where you learn how to do it.

## *Moving and resizing a map*

Maps, like charts, aren't fixed in size or position. You can move a map anywhere you want by clicking and dragging it. And, as you may expect, you can also change its size. Just click the map once to select it and then drag any of its eight "handles" to make it the size you want. Be careful, however, because resizing a map can change its proportions and cause it to be distorted.

To restore a map to its default size and proportions, double-click the map to open a separate map window. Then choose the View⇨Reset command, followed by the File⇨Exit and Return command.

## Changing the title

One of the most frequent changes to a map is changing the title. 1-2-3 for Windows sticks in a title that merely describes the map — for example, "USA by State." You'll probably want to change the title to describe what you're mapping. For example, "Number of Nasty Letters Received by State."

To change the title of a map, click the map and then choose the Tools⇨Map⇨Ranges and Title command. You'll see the dialog box shown in Figure 15-4. Select the text box labeled Title and enter your new title. Click OK and the map is updated with a more meaningful title.

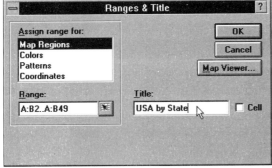

**Figure 15-4:**
This dialog box lets you change the map's title (among other things).

## Changing the bins, colors, and legend text

Customizing your map by changing the bins, legend text, and map colors is easy. It's all done in one dialog box, which appears when you choose the Tools⇨Map⇨Color Settings command (see Figure 15-5).

This dialog box has three columns: Values, Legend Labels, and Colors. Notice that, by default, each of these is set to Automatic.

### Changing the bins

If your map has six or fewer regions, each region's exact value appears in the map legend. But a map's legend is limited to six items, so if you have more than six regions, 1-2-3 for Windows automatically creates "bins" for the data values. It will then create a legend using these bins. A bin represents a range of values. If the data for a region falls within the range for a particular bin, it will be mapped with that bin's color.

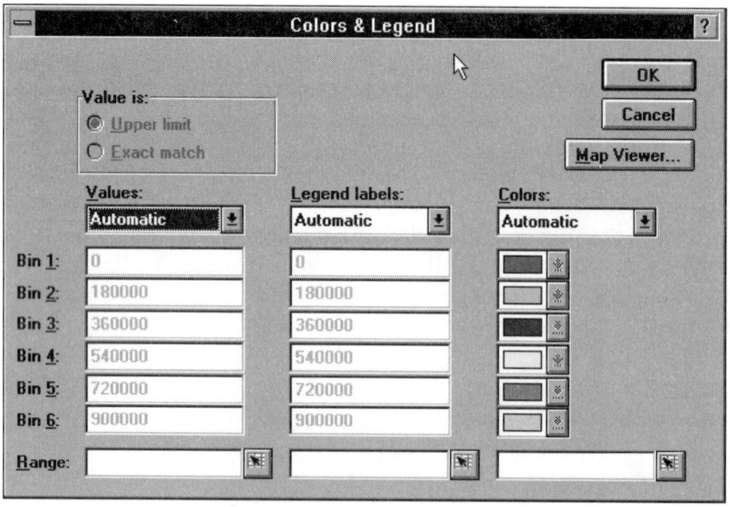

**Figure 15-5:**
This dialog
box lets you
override the
automatic
bins,
change the
legend text,
and pick
your favorite
colors.

When 1-2-3 for Windows creates bins, it makes each one the same size (for example: 1-10, 11-20, 21-30, and so on). The number shown in the legend is the *upper* value for the bin. In many cases, the automatically created bins are just fine. But you may want to adjust the bins manually. It's not difficult.

To change the bin values, click the pull-down menu labeled Values and select Manual. This allows you to put your own bin values in the Value column. The value you put in for bins can be either of the following:

✔ *Upper Limit.* The region's data value must be less than or equal to the bin value but greater than the previous bin.

✔ *Exact Match.* The region's data value must be exactly equal to the bin value.

You control how this works by clicking the appropriate option button at the top of the Values column. In the vast majority of cases, you'll want to use Upper Limit.

Then it's simply a matter of typing in the new bin values. If your first bin value is 100, regions that have a data value less than or equal to 100 are colored the color for the first bin. If your second bin value is 200, regions that have a bin value greater than 100 but less than or equal to 200 are colored the color for the second bin — and so on.

### Changing the legend labels

The text in the legend is normally Automatic — which means that it corresponds to the values in the bins column. If you want to change the legend text, click the pull-down list labeled Legend Labels and select Manual. This allows you to put your own bin values in the Value column.

Why would you ever want to change the legend labels, you might ask. One reason is to make the labels easier to read. If your data consists of large numbers — like millions, the legend labels will be rather difficult to read. Compare the legend in Figure 15-6 to the legend labels in Figure 15-5. I changed the legend in Figure 15-6 so it's easier to read.

**Figure 15-6:**
Changing
the legend
labels can
make your
map easier
to read.

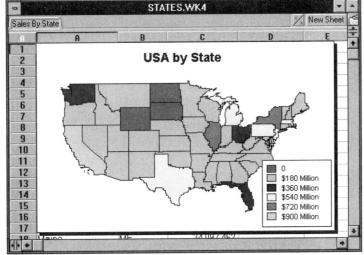

You can also add other text that has nothing to do with the numbers. For example, if you're mapping sales, you may have legend labels that read "Above Quota," "At Quota," "Below Quota," and "Way the Heck Below Quota."

### Changing the map colors

If you don't like the default colors used in your map, change 'em! Changing the colors on a map works the same way as changing the bins or legend labels. Use the third column of the Color Settings dialog box; start by clicking the drop-down list and select Manual. Then, for each bin, click the color drop-down list and choose the color you want. Piece of cake, no?

## Zooming your map

Sometimes you may not want to show the entire map. If so, you can zoom the map to get rid of extraneous regions and enlarge the region of interest. You do this by double-clicking the map to open up a separate map window — as shown in Figure 15-7.

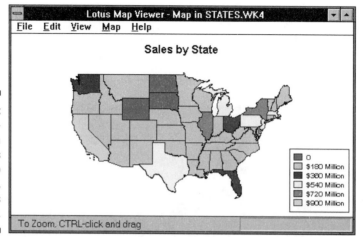

**Figure 15-7:**
Double-
clicking a
map opens
up a map
window,
which is
zoomable.

After you're in the map window, just click and drag the mouse over the area
that you want to zoom in on. Then close the map window by selecting the
File⇨Exit and Return command. The map in your worksheet then shows just
the area you zoomed in on. Figure 15-8 shows a U.S. map that has been zoomed
in to show only a few states.

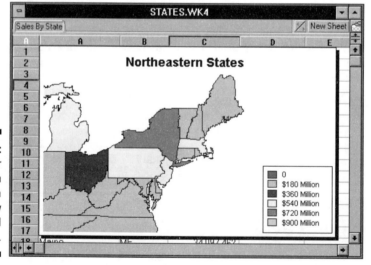

**Figure 15-8:**
A map, after
zooming in
to show a
few
selected
states.

# Advanced Mapping

If you've made it this far into the chapter, you're either really into maps or you're extremely bored. (Hopefully not the latter.) I'll conclude this section with a few more words about the mapping feature in 1-2-3 for Windows.

Up until now, the data you wanted to map occupied only two columns: one for the region names or codes and the other for the data. Actually, a map range can consist of up to seven columns, as seen in Figure 15-9.

**Figure 15-9:**
This data
will all be
represented
in a map.

| | A | B | C | D | E | F | G |
|---|---|---|---|---|---|---|---|
| | Map Code | Color Values | Pattern Labels | Pin | Latitude | Longitude | Pin Color |
| 1 | | | | | | | |
| 2 | CA | 55 | South | S | 32.814899 | -117.135696 | 255 |
| 3 | AZ | 32 | South | | | | |
| 4 | WA | 43 | North | N | 47.621799 | -122.350304 | 255 |
| 5 | OR | 22 | North | | | | |
| 6 | MT | 10 | North | | | | |
| 7 | UT | 15 | South | | | | |
| 8 | WY | 8 | North | | | | |
| 9 | NV | 32 | South | | | | |
| 10 | ID | 10 | North | | | | |
| 11 | | | | | | | |
| 12 | | | | | | | |
| 13 | | | | | | | |

FULLMAP.WK4 — New Sheet

You can use a third column to hold labels that will be represented as a pattern. The fourth column can be used to hold text (or a symbol) that appears at a specific latitude and longitude in the map. The latitude and longitude go in columns five and six, respectively. The seventh column can hold a value (from 0-255) that represents the color of the text in Column 4.

Figure 15-10 shows the map that results from the data shown in Figure 15-9.

Notice that each state's sales region is represented by a pattern. I also used text (the letters *N* and *S*) to show the locations of the regional sales offices. Notice that you must supply the latitudes and longitudes to pinpoint where this text should be displayed. In this example, the sales offices are located in Seattle and San Diego.

I got the latitudes and longitudes from a file stored in your SAMPLES\MAPS directory. This directory has several worksheet files with tons of useful (?) data. If you're a data maven, check it out!

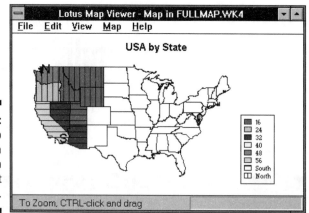

**Figure 15-10:**
This map
uses data
from seven
worksheet
columns.

# Chapter 16
# A Very Expensive Doodle Pad

*"Life is painting a picture, not doing a sum."*

Oliver Wendell Holmes (1841–1935)
From *Speeches* (1913)

• • • • • • • • • • • • • • • • • • • • • • • • • • • • • • • • • • • • • • • • • •

## In This Chapter

▶ Adding lines, arrows, circles, squares, polygons, diagrams, and even freehand drawings to your worksheet, and why you'd want to do so

▶ Learning about clip art and how to paste it into your worksheet

▶ Discovering serious uses for the drawing tools to justify the fun you have playing with the drawing tools

• • • • • • • • • • • • • • • • • • • • • • • • • • • • • • • • • • • • • • • • • •

*1*-2-3 for Windows is known primarily as a spreadsheet. As you've been finding out, the cells come in pretty handy for holding numbers and formulas. But did you know that you can use this program to draw geometric shapes, too? Every 1-2-3 for Windows worksheet includes an invisible draw layer that sits right on top of the cells. You can add all sorts of art (lines, arrows, and other shapes) to this draw layer to augment your work. This chapter explains what you need to know about the draw layer and gives you some ideas on how to put it to use (some serious, some not).

You can do many things with the 1-2-3 for Windows drawing tools (limited only by your imagination, as they say). And in many cases, you may find that this program includes all the drawing software you need — so you can save yourself or your company some big bucks by not having to buy special drawing software.

Your computer must be equipped with a mouse in order to do the exciting things in this chapter.

# The Draw Layer — Like Your Guardian Angel

Every sheet of every worksheet file has a *draw layer.* You can't see the draw layer, but it's always there (just like your guardian angel). If you've created a chart in 1-2-3 for Windows, you've already used the draw layer. Charts reside on the draw layer, and they can be moved around freely, independent of and above the cells in the worksheet.

Besides charts, you can add geometric shapes, boxes that hold text, and pictures from graphics files, and you even can draw freehand, if you're so inclined. As in charts, all these objects can be moved and resized as much as you want. You also can combine several elements into one. Figure 16-1 shows some examples of what you can do on the draw layer.

**Figure 16-1:** The draw layer enables you to add all sorts of cool art to your worksheet.

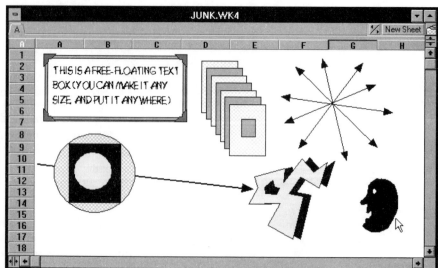

# The Drawing Tools

You may have noticed that some of the SmartIcons have geometric shapes on them. These SmartIcons, pictured in Figure 16-2, are used to draw objects on a worksheet.

Select several objects
Select all objects
Double-headed arrow
Forward-pointing arrow
Line
Draw freehand
Segmented line

**Figure 16-2:**
The
drawing-
tool
SmartIcons.

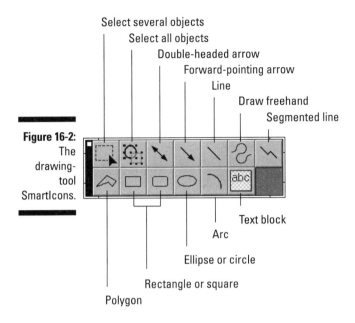

Text block
Arc
Ellipse or circle
Rectangle or square
Polygon

Not all the drawing SmartIcons appear on the default SmartIcons palette. If you want to make more of the drawing SmartIcons available, you have to customize a SmartIcon palette (a topic that's covered in Chapter 17). But even if you don't customize a SmartIcon palette, you still can access all the drawing tools by using the Tools⇨Draw command. Figure 16-3 shows what this cascading menu looks like.

# Tooling with the Drawing Tools

The drawing tools are easy to use; they work just as you expect. As I mentioned in the preceding note, you can access the drawing tools either by clicking a SmartIcon or by using the Tools⇨Draw command. In either case, using the drawing tools is just a matter of clicking and dragging, much easier to do than to describe. I suggest that you jump right in and play around. I guarantee you'll get the hang of using the drawing tools in no time.

Here's an example of how to draw a rectangle:

**1. Click the rectangle SmartIcon.**

Notice the instructions in the title bar: `Click and drag; for a square hold down SHIFT as you drag.` Also, the mouse pointer changes shape.

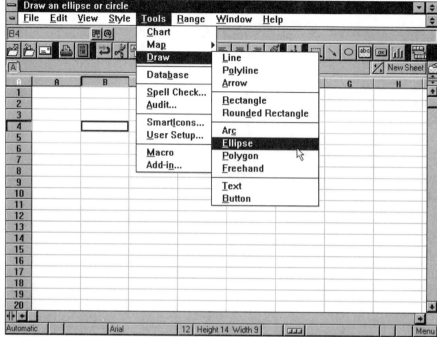

**Figure 16-3:**
The
Tools⇨Draw
command
gives you
access to all
the drawing
tools.

**2. Click in the worksheet, and drag. You'll see the rectangle being created.**

**3. When the rectangle is the size you want, release the mouse button.**

> After you draw the object, it is selected (you can tell by the *handles* around it — to see a handle, check out Figure 16-5).

When you're creating an object, don't be too concerned about placing and sizing it exactly. You always can select an object and then change its size and position at any time.

## Moooving objects

To move an object on the draw layer, click the object to select it and then drag it to its new position. Just make sure that you don't click one of its handles (if you do, a handle appears as a tiny dark square on the object).

You also can use the Windows Clipboard to cut, copy, and paste these objects. Select the object(s) you want to manipulate and then use the Edit menu to copy, cut, or paste. If you want to move an object to a different sheet or different file, for example, using the Clipboard is your only alternative, because you can't drag the object across sheets or worksheet windows.

## Resizing objects

To change the size of an object on the draw layer, click the object to select it and then drag one of its handles to change its size. You drag toward the center of the object to reduce its size and drag away from the object to increase the size.

## Redecorating your picture (so it looks maavelous)

When you put an object on the draw layer, you have control over color, line width, pattern, and so on. The easiest way to change these specifications is to double-click the object to bring up its Lines & Color dialog box. Figure 16-4 shows an example of a Lines & Color dialog box for a rectangular object (the dialog box varies with the object). You can adjust the controls in this dialog box just as in any other dialog box.

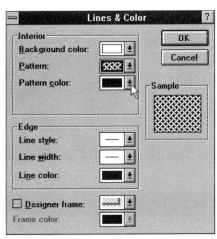

**Figure 16-4:** The Lines & Color dialog box enables you to change the specifications for the selected object.

## *Restacking objects*

You can add any number of objects to the draw layer. The objects even can overlap each other; in fact, the objects are actually stacked on top of each other. You can manipulate this stack of objects by selecting one of the objects and then sending it to the top or bottom of the stack. To restack the objects, do the following:

1. **Select the object.**

2. **Issue the Edit⇨Arrange command.**

   This command produces the cascading menu shown in Figure 16-5.

3. **Choose Bring to Front to move the selected object to the top of the stack.**

4. **Choose Send to Back to move the selected object to the bottom of the stack.**

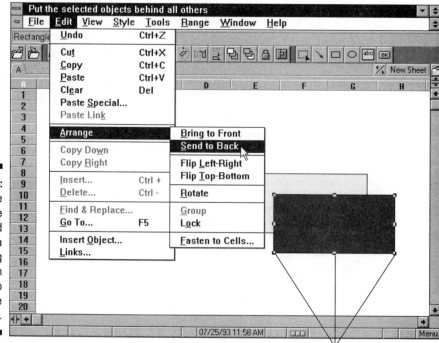

**Figure 16-5:** The Edit⇨Arrange command produces a cascading menu with options to restack the objects.

Handles

## Combining objects — you're the match maker

If you create a diagram by using several different objects, you may find it advantageous to combine them into a single object so that you can manipulate the diagram (move it or resize it) as a single object. For example, you might create a simple flow chart that uses several rectangles and arrows. After you get the flow chart drawn, you can combine the elements into one object. To combine several objects into one object, follow these steps:

1. **Select all the objects that you want to combine.**

   Use the Select Several Objects SmartIcon or hold down Shift while you click each object that you want to add to the group.

2. **Choose the Edit⇨Arrange⇨Group command to join the objects in holy matrimony.**

   Now, this group of objects has only one set of handles. You can move or resize it just like any other object.

   You can always divorce (ungroup) them by selecting the object and choosing the Edit⇨Arrange⇨Ungroup command (it's too easy nowadays, isn't it?).

When working with drawn objects, the right mouse button is quite handy. After selecting one or more objects, right-click to display a shortcut menu. In most cases, this menu contains the command you want to use.

# Adding Your Van Gogh as Clip Art

The drawing layer also can hold clip art images that are stored in files. *Clip art* is the computer's way of storing a variety of images that you can use in your programs. Clip art files range from simple line drawings to detailed photographic quality color images.

## Importing clip art

Although 1-2-3 for Windows doesn't include any clip art files, you easily can import them from other sources. Other software that you have (especially graphics packages) may include some clip art files, and thousands of files are available on computer bulletin boards. (Ask your local computer guru about bulletin boards — they are a great way to get free software legally!)

Clip art comes in a variety of file formats and you usually can identify the file's format by its file extension. The most common clip art file types are .BMP, .PCX, .GIF, .CGM, and .WMF. These file types fall into two main categories: *bitmapped* and *picture.*

If you've upgraded from 1-2-3 for DOS, you may have some .CGM clip art files. 1-2-3 for DOS includes several dozen .CGM files, all of which you can use in 1-2-3 for Windows.

Bitmapped graphics files, such as .BMP, .PCX, and .GIF, are composed of individual dots. They usually look best at their original size, and if you make them larger or smaller, they tend to get distorted. Picture graphics files, on the other hand, are composed of lines that are described mathematically. These types of files usually can be shrunk or enlarged and still look very good. The most common picture file formats are .CGM and .WMF.

You can get clip art into your worksheet in the following two ways:

✔ Read the file directly with the File⇨Open command (applies only to .CGM files).

✔ Use the Windows Clipboard to copy the file from another application and then paste it into your worksheet.

## *Reading .CGM files*

The only clip art file format that 1-2-3 for Windows can read directly is .CGM. To add a .CGM file to your worksheet, do the following:

1. **Select the File⇨Open command.**

2. **From the File type listbox, select Ansi Metafile (cgm) from the list.**

   This will cause 1-2-3 for Windows to display only filenames with a .CGM extension.

3. **Specify the directory that has the .CGM files and choose a file from the list.**

4. **Because the OK button isn't available, select the Combine button to read the file into your current worksheet.**

   The image appears at the current cell pointer position, but you can move it and resize it just like any other object.

Figure 16-6 shows a worksheet with an added .CGM file.

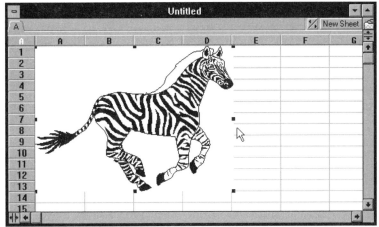

**Figure 16-6:**
This .CGM image was read into the worksheet by using the File⇨Open command.

# Using the Clipboard for clip art

If your clip art images are stored in any file format other than .CGM, the only way to get the clip art into your worksheet is by copying and pasting from the Clipboard. Follow these steps when your clip art is in another file format:

1. **Display the image in some other software.**

   For example, the Windows Paintbrush program can read .BMP and .PCX files — or you can create your own art in Paintbrush and copy it to 1-2-3 for Windows. If you don't understand this process, stand up at your cubicle, grab your hair by the roots, look up at the sky, and yell "Oh, Lord, Help Meeeee!!" You are sure to find someone willing to help.

2. **Select the image. (This procedure varies with the program you're using.)**

3. **Choose the graphic program's Edit⇨Copy command.**

The image is copied into the Clipboard at this time.

4. **Activate 1-2-3 for Windows and select its Edit⇨Paste command to copy the image from the Clipboard.**

The accompanying figure shows an image I created in Paintbrush, and how it looks after I copied it to a 1-2-3 for Windows worksheet.

# Serious Uses for the Draw Layer

OK, now you know about the draw layer, the drawing tools, and clip art. What good is this knowledge? Well, besides being fun to play with (and great for doodling when you're on the phone), you can use these tools to make some useful enhancements to your work.

## Calling attention to cells

If you want to draw attention to a particular cell (when the information in it is particularly good or bad), you can use a number of approaches. For example, you can change the font or attributes — make the information bold or italic — to make the cell stand out from the others. But if you want to make the cell even more attention grabbing, consider using the draw layer.

Figure 16-7 shows an example of how you can use the draw layer to emphasize a cell. In the figure, I drew an oval around a cell and used a text box and arrow to really make the cell stand out.

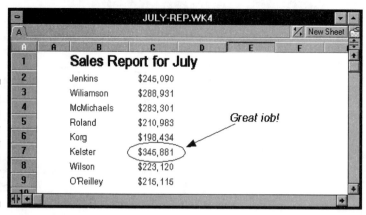

**Figure 16-7:**
Using the draw layer to draw attention to a particular cell.

## Improving your charts

Any art work you add to your regular worksheets can be added to charts, as well. You can stack objects on top of each other, and you can enhance a chart by adding all sorts of interesting objects and images to it. Figure 16-8 shows an example of a plain chart and one that has been beefed up with some annotations.

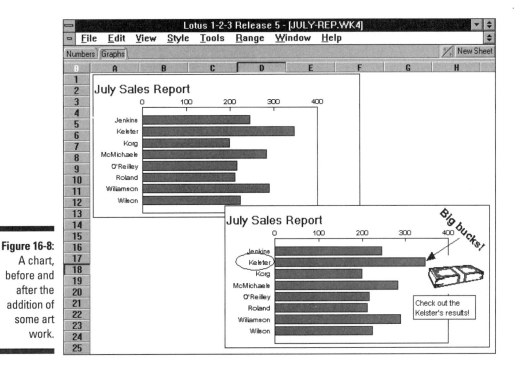

**Figure 16-8:**
A chart,
before and
after the
addition of
some art
work.

## Creating diagrams

You can use the drawing tools to create flow diagrams, like the one in
Figure 16-9. This diagram uses text boxes and arrows.

## Brown nosing your boss

Yet another use for drawing tools is to add pizzazz to your printed reports (and
impress your boss at the same time). For example, you may want to add your
company's logo to the reports, as in the example in Figure 16-10.

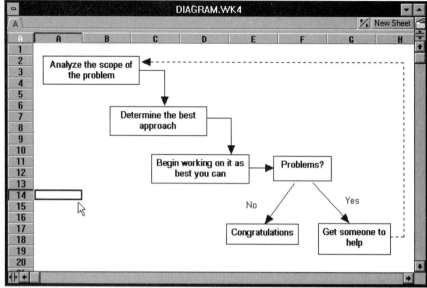

**Figure 16-9:**
Text boxes
and arrows
used to
create a
diagram.

**Figure 16-10:**
Impress
your boss
with the
company
logo on your
next report.

# Chapter 17
# Showing Off with Shortcuts and SmartIcons

*"Wickedness is always easier than virtue; for it takes the short cut to everything."*

Samuel Johnson (1709–1784)
From *Boswell, Journal of a Tour to the Hebrides* [1785]. September 17, 1773

## In This Chapter

▶ Making the most of those weird little pictures at the top of your screen

▶ Finding out what a SmartIcon does

▶ Getting the right SmartIcon palette to appear

▶ Putting SmartIcons somewhere else (or making them disappear temporarily)

▶ Creating your own SmartIcon palette

▶ Learning other keyboard shortcuts

*N*ew 1-2-3 for Windows users usually wonder about those cryptic little pictures at the top of their screen. What do they mean? Are they some form of computer hieroglyphics? Secret messages from Elvis? As you may or may not have figured out by now, those pictures are called *SmartIcons*. They can save you a great deal of time and trouble if you learn what they're all about and how to take advantage of them for all they're worth.

In addition to SmartIcons, 1-2-3 for Windows hides lots of other time-saving tricks up its sleeves. The following pages give you enough shortcuts to more than make up for the time you spend reading this chapter.

 You need a mouse to use SmartIcons — there's no way to select a SmartIcon from the keyboard. Actually, the time you save by using SmartIcons will easily justify the meager expense of a mouse (amortized over 3.5 years, assuming an annual salary of $35,000).

# Why SmartIcons?

Somewhere along the line, someone figured out that software users tend to use some commands more often than others. Because clicking an *icon* (a small graphic image) usually is faster than accessing the menu and dealing with a dialog box, software companies put together collections of icons to serve as shortcuts for the more commonly used commands. Lotus calls their collection of such icons *SmartIcons*.

# Smart Facts about SmartIcons

Before getting down to the main course, take a minute to digest the following appetizers:

- ✔ Remember, you must have a mouse attached to your computer to use SmartIcons.

- ✔ Normally, the SmartIcon palette appears directly below the edit line, but you can move it to the left, right, or bottom of your screen. Or you can have it floating around so that you can move it wherever you like. You can even hide it if you want.

- ✔ 1-2-3 for Windows actually has eight SmartIcon palettes, but it displays only one at a time.

- ✔ Sometimes 1-2-3 for Windows automatically changes its SmartIcon palette. For example, if you're working on a chart, the program automatically gives you a SmartIcon palette relating to charts.

- ✔ There are many additional SmartIcons available that don't appear in the predefined SmartIcon palettes.

- ✔ You can create custom SmartIcon palettes using the extra SmartIcons or using SmartIcons that appear on other palettes.

# But What Do They Do?

I'll be the first to admit that the purpose of each of these little icons isn't always obvious from looking at the picture. Fortunately, it's easy to get a written explanation. If you're using Release 4, just right-click a SmartIcon and a one-line description appears in the 1-2-3 for Windows title bar.

Learning about SmartIcons is even easier for Release 5 users. Just move the mouse pointer over a SmartIcon and wait about one second. A cartoon-like balloon then pops up and lets you in on its secret identity. The official term for this is *bubble help*.

# *So Many Palettes, So Little Time*

When you start 1-2-3 for Windows, you see the SmartIcon palette shown in
Figure 17-1. It is one of eight predefined SmartIcon palettes that you can use.
Table 17-1 lists the eight predefined SmartIcons and their uses.

**Figure 17-1:**
The Smart
Icon default
palette.

| Table 17-1 | The Eight SmartIcon Palettes and Their Uses |
|---|---|
| *Palette* | *Contents and Uses* |
| Default sheet | The standard palette, the one you see unless you choose another one |
| Editing | Handy for general worksheet editing, such as inserting or deleting rows and columns, copying and pasting, and so on |
| Formatting | Enables you to make stylistic changes to your worksheet |
| Goodies | Miscellaneous SmartIcons, many of which deal with rather advanced topics |
| Macro Building | Useful if you're into macros (if you don't plan on creating macros, you can forget this one even exists) |
| Printing | Includes handy SmartIcons that help you print your documents |
| Sheet Auditing | Helps you debug a complicated worksheet (hopefully, your worksheets won't get complicated enough to require these) |
| Working Together | Enables you to start running other Lotus products, which work only if you have the products installed |

Now that you know a little bit about the eight SmartIcon palettes, you need to
know how to get them to appear. Actually, there are two ways: by clicking a
SmartIcon (what else?) or by using the status bar.

## *Changing palettes with the special SmartIcon*

Each of the eight SmartIcon palettes supplied with 1-2-3 for Windows has a special
SmartIcon that appears in the last position. Figure 17-2 shows this SmartIcon.
You use this SmartIcon to change your palette to the next one in line.

**Figure 17-2:**
Clicking this
SmartIcon
displays the
next palette.

## Changing palettes with the status bar

You also can change SmartIcon palettes by clicking the icon on the status bar at
the bottom of the screen. When you do so, you get a popup list of the currently
defined SmartIcon palettes. Just click the one you want and it appears, as
shown in Figure 17-3. This method is faster than changing palettes with the
SmartIcon in the current palette, because you can jump directly to the palette
you want without cycling through them all.

**Figure 17-3:**
Selecting a
SmartIcon
palette by
clicking the
SmartIcon
icon on the
status bar.

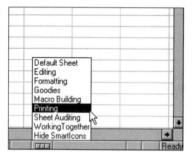

# Moving the Palette and Changing the Size of the Icons

Most the time, having the SmartIcons at the top of your screen works out fine.
However, some people (usually nonconformist communist hippy radicals)
prefer to keep them somewhere else. To change the location of the SmartIcon
palette, choose Tools⇨SmartIcons. You'll see the most interesting dialog box
1-2-3 for Windows has to offer (which appears in Figure 17-4).

To put the SmartIcon palette in a different position, select the Position drop-
down list and choose Left, Top, Bottom, Right, or Floating. If you select Floating,
the icon palette's position is up to you; you can move the palette around on-
screen and even change its proportions by dragging a border. Figure 17-5 shows
a floating palette.

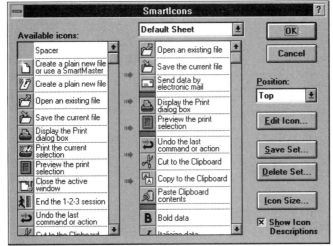

**Figure 17-4:**
The
SmartIcons
dialog box
enables you
to change
the
SmartIcons'
position and
size.

**Figure 17-5:**
Moving a
floating
SmartIcon
palette.

With the Icon Size button in the SmartIcons dialog box, you can change the size of the SmartIcons. Experiment to find which size you prefer.

# What Makes SmartIcons So Smart?

After all the votes are tallied, 1-2-3 for Windows has about 140 SmartIcons — some good, some bad, some mediocre. Many of these do not appear on any of the eight predefined SmartIcon palettes. Before you learn how to customize your palette, you need to become familiar with what some of these SmartIcons do.

I won't even try to describe all the SmartIcons that exist. If I did, it would take up several pages — and nobody would read it anyway. Throughout the book, I point out particularly useful SmartIcons. The others you probably will never need. And besides, if SmartIcons really turn you on, you'll enjoy discovering them on your own.

# Making your own palette

The final topic in this SmartIcon discussion may not appeal to everyone, but those who like to tinker with things may find it pretty interesting. I'm talking about creating a custom SmartIcon palette that includes only the icons that you like and use most. If this palette were a record album, you would call it *SmartIcons' Greatest Hits*.

In this example, you create a SmartIcon palette with a bunch of drawing icons (see Chapter 16 to learn about drawing on a worksheet). You can follow these instructions to create this palette, or — if you're really bold and daring — read through this section to get an idea of how to make your own. Then do it.

To construct a new palette, start with an existing palette, remove the icons you don't want, add the ones you *do* want, and then save the palette under a different name. The following list walks you through this very process:

1. **Choose the Tools⇨SmartIcons command.**

   You get the familiar dialog box shown in Figure 17-4. The icons on the left are the ones you choose from, and the icons on the right are those in the SmartIcon palette you're editing.

2. **Make sure Default Sheet is chosen in the drop-down list at the top.**

   In this example, you modify the Default Sheet palette. The icons in this palette appear in the next list.

3. **Remove the SmartIcons that you don't want.**

   For this example, remove all of the SmartIcons except the last one, called

*Select the next set of SmartIcons.* (Don't panic — you save this palette under a different name, so the Default Sheet palette is still available.) To remove icons from the list on the right, click them and drag them away — just drag them anywhere. Notice that some of the icons are called *Spacer*. Remove these also by dragging them away. The dialog box now looks like the following figure.

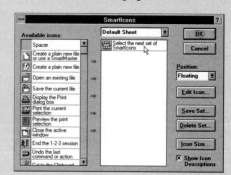

4. **Scroll through the Available icons list and select the SmartIcons to add to your custom palette.**

   You add an icon by dragging it from the list on the left to the list on the right. Just drag it to the position you want, and the other icons move out of the way. Start by dragging the Spacer icon from the left list to the position right above the Select the next set of SmartIcons icon in the right list.

   Next, scroll down the icon list on the left and find the Select several objects icon. Drag this one to the list on the right and put it directly below the Spacer you just added.

Do the same for the 17 icons on the left — all the way to and including the Display cells in default size icon. The dialog box should look like the following figure.

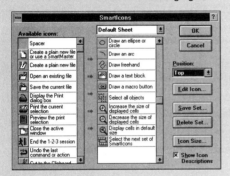

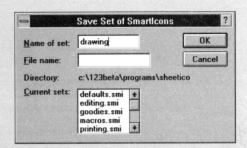

**5. Add some Spacers.**

This groups similar icons together. For example, you might want to put a Spacer before the Decrease the size of displayed cells icon to put all the sizing icons into a separate group.

**6. Select the Save Set button.**

1-2-3 for Windows displays the dialog box shown in the figure at the top of the next column.

**7. Type** Drawing **in the Name of set text box and click OK.**

The program saves this new icon palette in a file that you can call up whenever you want it.

**8. Choose OK to close the SmartIcons dialog box.**

Your new SmartIcon palette is displayed and ready for action. The following figure shows what it looks like with Spacers added.

When you customize a SmartIcon palette, it's a good idea to leave the "Select the next set of SmartIcons" icon in the last position. Doing so makes it easier to switch to other palettes (and conforms to the convention Lotus uses for its SmartIcon palettes).

Your custom palette

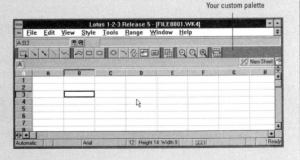

When 1-2-3 for Windows displays a SmartIcon palette, you can learn what a particular icon in that palette does by right-clicking it. A description of the SmartIcon appears on the title bar at the top of the screen.

Whatever you do, don't be afraid to use SmartIcons. The on-line description will give you a pretty good idea of what it does. If you're still not sure and it seems appropriate, just go for it. If it does something unexpected, you can always rely on the Edit⇨Undo command (Ctrl+Z) to reverse the effects. But make sure that you have Undo enabled. Use the Tools⇨User Setup command to ensure that the Undo check box is checked.

The Tools⇨SmartIcons command familiarizes you with SmartIcons. Choose this command and scroll through the Available icons list on the left side of the dialog box. This list provides the same one-line description for each icon that you see on the title bar when you right-click the icon.

# Shortcut Keys

SmartIcons are great time-savers, but there are other easy ways to save time — and you don't even have to move your hand from the keyboard to grab your mouse.

## Menu shortcuts

Many of the commands in the File and the Edit menus have shortcut keys assigned to them. When you select one of these menus, the shortcut keys are displayed next to their commands. Figure 17-6 shows the Edit menu. Eight of these commands have shortcuts; for example, Ctrl+V is the shortcut for the Edit⇨Paste command.

## Using the keyboard for menus

Even if a menu command doesn't have a shortcut listed, it's important to remember that you can still access all of the menu commands and navigate through dialog boxes using the keyboard. For example, Alt+FS is a shortcut for the File⇨Save command. In this case, press Alt and F at the same time (bringing up the File menu) and then immediately press S (to select the Save option). You don't have to wait for the File menu to drop down before pressing S.

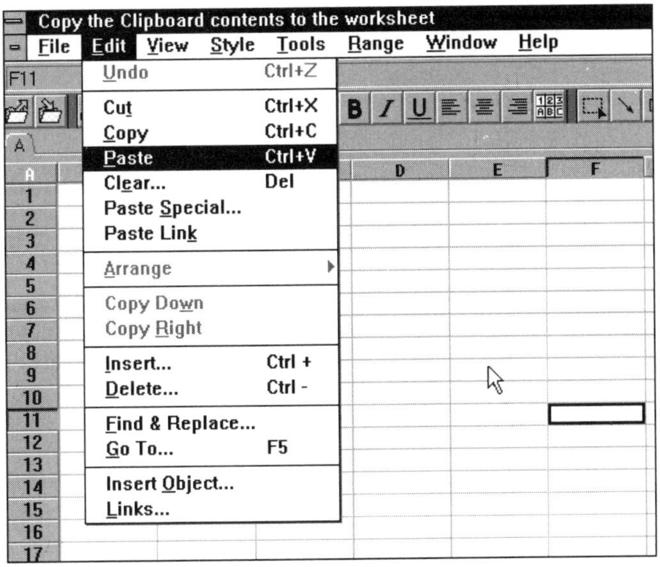

Figure 17-6:
The Edit
menu and
its shortcut
keys.

Learning the underlined letter, or *hot key,* for each menu command is the key to working faster in 1-2-3 for Windows. Notice that the hot key is not always the first letter of the command. If you learn the hot keys for the commands you use most often, you'll soon become a command whiz — and leave your mouse-toting colleagues in the dust. They'll wonder why you always leave the office on time.

## Function keys

Many shortcuts don't have menu equivalents and instead use the function keys on your keyboard. These keys are located along the top of your keyboard, on the left side, or in both locations. Table 17-2 lists these function keys and their uses.

| Table 17-2 | The Function Keys |
|---|---|
| **Key** | **What It Does** |
| F1 (HELP) | Displays on-line help that's usually relevant to what you're doing |
| F2 (EDIT) | Switches the program into Edit mode so that you can change the contents of the current cell |
| F3 (NAME) | Lists names of files, charts, ranges, collections, query tables, drawn objects, versions, @functions, macro key names, and macro commands |

*(continued)*

**Table 17-2** *(continued)*

| Key | What It Does |
| --- | --- |
| F4 | In Edit, Point, or Value mode, cycles the cell references in formulas from absolute to mixed to relative; in Ready mode, anchors the cell pointer so that you can select a range of cells |
| F5 (GOTO) | Moves the cell pointer to a cell, named range, worksheet, chart, drawn object, query table, version, or active file (equivalent to the Edit⇨Go To command) |
| F6 (PANE) | Moves the cell pointer between panes in split windows and between worksheets displayed in perspective view |
| F7 (QUERY) | Updates the records in a query table (equivalent to the Query⇨Refresh Now command) |
| F8 (TABLE) | Repeats the last Range⇨Analyze⇨What-if Table command |
| F9 (CALC) | In Ready mode, recalculates all formulas; in Edit or Value mode, converts a formula to its current value |
| F10 (MENU) | Activates the menu bar so that you can use the keyboard |

Some of the function keys do different things when you use the Alt key with them. Table 17-3 contains a list of the Alt+function key shortcuts.

| **Table 17-3** | **Alt+Function Key Shortcuts** |
| --- | --- |
| *Key Combination* | *What It Does* |
| Alt+F1 (COMPOSE) | Creates characters that you cannot enter directly from your keyboard |
| Alt+F2 (STEP) | Turns Step mode on or off |
| Alt+F3 (RUN) | Displays a list of the macros in the active files (equivalent to Tools ⇨ Macro⇨Run) |
| Alt+F6 (ZOOM PANE) | Enlarges the current horizontal, vertical, or perspective pane to the full size of the window or shrinks it to its original size |

## *Stylistic shortcuts*

Several shortcut keys exist for formatting your work stylistically (see Chapter 13). By getting into the habit of using them, you can save yourself a great deal of time — and get home at a reasonable hour. Table 17-4 lists these shortcuts.

| Table 17-4 | Stylistic Shortcuts with the Control Key |
|---|---|
| **Key Combination** | **What It Does** |
| Ctrl+B | Adds or removes boldface |
| Ctrl+E | Centers cell contents |
| Ctrl+I | Adds or removes italics |
| Ctrl+L | Left-aligns cell contents |
| Ctrl+N | Removes bold, italics, and underlining from the current selection |
| Ctrl+R | Right-aligns cell contents |
| Ctrl+U | Adds or removes underlining |

# Part IV
## Faking It

The 5th Wave    By Rich Tennant

"COMPATABILITY? NO PROBLEM. THIS BABY COMES IN OVER A DOZEN DESIGNER COLORS."

## In this part...

These three chapters address features that are considered advanced, such as databases and macros. Beginning users usually need not spend too much time mastering these topics, but I'll give you the basics so that you won't be left completely in the dark. This section also includes a chapter with a bunch of nifty (and even useful) formulas, all in language that you can understand.

# Chapter 18
# The Lowdown on Databases and Lists

*"It is a capital mistake to theorize before one has data."*

Sir Arthur Conan Doyle (1859–1930)

● ● ● ● ● ● ● ● ● ● ● ● ● ● ● ● ● ● ● ● ● ● ● ● ● ● ● ● ● ● ● ● ● ● ● ● ● ● ● ● ● ● ● ● ● ●

## In This Chapter

▶ Why 1-2-3 for Windows is good for keeping track of things

▶ What the difference between a simple list and a database means to a normal person like you

▶ How to keep track of information in lists and search for information in databases

● ● ● ● ● ● ● ● ● ● ● ● ● ● ● ● ● ● ● ● ● ● ● ● ● ● ● ● ● ● ● ● ● ● ● ● ● ● ● ● ● ● ● ● ● ●

Chances are, you also use a word processing program on your computer. And you've probably used your word processor to store lists of things. Compared to spreadsheets, typical word processing programs can best be classified as dumb. That is, most word processors don't enable you to use formulas to do calculations and require you to know about tab settings and other boring topics when working with tables and multicolumn lists.

Spreadsheets — including 1-2-3 for Windows — are great for dealing with lists, as you find out in this chapter. Keep reading to learn how to use 1-2-3 for Windows to create and manage these lists and keep track of items on them.

## Lists and Databases

Before going any further, check out these two definitions:

> ✔ A *list* is a collection of items, each of which is stored in a separate row in a worksheet. Each item may have more than one part (that is, use more than one column). The order of the items may or may not be important.

✔ A *database* is an organized collection of items. Each item is called a *record*, and each record has multiple parts called *fields*. Furthermore, each field has a designated *field name*.

Figure 18-1 shows a list developed in 1-2-3 for Windows. This particular list contains seven items. Each item has two parts (actually, one of the items includes a third part), and there's a blank line (row 8) in the middle of the list. Notice that the numeric formatting isn't the same for all items — typical of an informal list like this one. This worksheet also happens to use a formula that calculates the total.

| | BILLS.WK4 | | | | | |
|---|---|---|---|---|---|---|
| A | | | | | New Sheet | |
| | A | B | C | D | E | F |
| 1 | Bills to pay this month | | | | | |
| 2 | | | | | | |
| 3 | Mortgage | 755 | | | | |
| 4 | Telephone | ? | (bill hasn't come yet) | | | |
| 5 | Car payment | 352 | | | | |
| 6 | Cable TV | 24.95 | | | | |
| 7 | Visa card | 125 | | | | |
| 8 | | | | | | |
| 9 | Gas & electric bill | 27.55 | | | | |
| 10 | Carpet cleaning | 45.79 | | | | |
| 11 | | | | | | |
| 12 | | | | | | |
| 13 | Total damage –> | 1,330.29 | | | | |
| 14 | | | | | | |

**Figure 18-1:**
A simple
list stored
in 1-2-3 for
Windows.

Making a list in 1-2-3 for Windows is a snap. Just start putting stuff in, change the column widths if necessary, insert new rows if you need them, and do anything else you can think of to make the list do what you want it to do. Feel free to move things around — do whatever makes you happy. The early chapters in this book tell you how to do all of these things. The only rule for this type of list is that there are no rules.

Because lists are pretty easy to handle (and there are no rules), I'll drop this subject. The remainder of this chapter focuses exclusively on databases.

Figure 18-2 shows a database set up in 1-2-3 for Windows. This particular database tracks items by date purchased, value, and reason purchased (that is, for business or personal use). This database has 17 records and four fields. Notice that the first row contains labels that list the field names; this row is not counted as a record.

| | A | B | C | D | E |
|---|---|---|---|---|---|
| 1 | ITEM | PURCHASED | VALUE | USE | |
| 2 | 486/30 computer | 09/05/91 | 3,500 | Business | |
| 3 | 386/40 computer | 12/06/92 | 1,000 | Business | |
| 4 | Stereo system | 08/04/90 | 1,375 | Personal | |
| 5 | JV-80 keyboard | 06/02/92 | 1,800 | Personal | |
| 6 | Korg Wavestation/AD | 11/04/92 | 1,400 | Personal | |
| 7 | NEC Laser printer | 06/01/92 | 1,300 | Business | |
| 8 | Sony TV | 03/04/89 | 600 | Personal | |
| 9 | Office furniture | 02/04/91 | 1,800 | Business | |
| 10 | Roland Sound Canvas | 04/27/93 | 575 | Business | |
| 11 | Alesis D4 | 01/05/93 | 450 | Personal | |
| 12 | M120 mixer | 01/07/93 | 125 | Personal | |
| 13 | Household furniture | 04/06/89 | 3,000 | Personal | |
| 14 | Car | 01/16/92 | 22,450 | Business | |
| 15 | Toaster | 04/02/93 | 12 | Personal | |
| 16 | Video camera | 09/07/92 | 950 | Personal | |
| 17 | Nikon 35mm camera | 06/07/86 | 645 | Personal | |
| 18 | CD-ROM drive | 01/03/92 | 495 | Business | |

STUFF.WK4

**Figure 18-2:**
A database
stored in
1-2-3 for
Windows.

At this point, the difference between a list and a database may be rather fuzzy to you. To make a long story short, a database is basically a more *organized* list. In the example shown, every record is laid out identically, with the same number of fields and numeric formats. Because of this added degree of organization, a database makes it easier to locate the exact information you want. The trade-off, however, is that it takes a bit more work up front to set up a database, and the things you put into it have to conform to the fields that you define.

# Dancing with Databases

You can use a database to track and update customer information, account information, budget plans, sales figures, and myriad other important (and unimportant) data.

Because a database is more organized than a list, it allows you to do things that are more difficult (or impossible) with a simple list. For example, with a database you can:

✔ **Extract all records that meet some criteria and put them in another place.** This procedure is known as *querying* a database. In a customer database, you can easily find all of your customers who live in a certain state, those who have spent more than a specific amount of money with your company, and so on (assuming, of course, that your database actually has fields that store the information about which you're querying).

Querying a database enables you to make a *subset* of the database that contains only the records of immediate interest. When you extract data, you don't have to extract all the fields — just the ones you're interested in.

✔ **Delete all records that meet some criteria.** You can automatically trash records that you no longer need — and do it quickly.

✔ **Sort the records by any field.** You can sort any block of data in a spreadsheet — it doesn't have to be a database. But sorting databases is very common.

✔ **Aggregate data.** You can summarize information in a database. If you have customer records that include a field on purchase price for each product a customer buys, you can aggregate this database to show each customer's total purchases. 1-2-3 for Windows can do this for you automatically — no formulas required.

✔ **Cross-tabulate data.** You can create summary tables of your database. In a sales database, for example, you can create a crosstab table that shows the total amount of each product sold in each sales region. Again, you can do this without building any formulas.

# Creating a Database

If you decide that you want to do database things such as search for specific data — and your data is structured enough to qualify as a database — you need to be aware of a few rules. Learning the following rules pays off in the long run:

✔ Each field in the database must have a name, and no two names can be the same. Also, limit the field names to 15 characters and don't use spaces.

✔ Don't leave blank rows between the field names and the actual data.

✔ Don't leave blank rows in your database.

✔ Use the same type of data in each column. In other words, give some thought to what kind of data each field holds; don't mix labels and values in a single column.

✔ Give your database a name by using the Range⇨Name command. This step is optional, but it makes working with your database easier.

Entering your data is straightforward, because you use the data-entry methods you already know.

# Querying a Database

1-2-3 for Windows has a nifty way of working with databases. It's all based on dialog boxes and also uses some simple drag-and-drop techniques. The sample database shown in Figure 18-3 provides the examples in this section. This particular database has 154 records and six fields. The database keeps track of sales completed. For this example, assume that you're the sales manager (but don't let it go to your head!).

| | A | B | C | D | E | F | G |
|---|---|---|---|---|---|---|---|
| | Date | SalesRep | Product | UnitCost | Quantity | TotalCost | |
| 1 | Date | SalesRep | Product | UnitCost | Quantity | TotalCost | |
| 2 | 04-Jan-93 | Franks | A | 125 | 3 | 375 | |
| 3 | 05-Jan-93 | Peterson | B | 140 | 1 | 140 | |
| 4 | 07-Jan-93 | Sheldon | C | 175 | 1 | 175 | |
| 5 | 07-Jan-93 | Franks | D | 225 | 1 | 225 | |
| 6 | 09-Jan-93 | Sheldon | A | 125 | 2 | 250 | |
| 7 | 11-Jan-93 | Robinson | B | 140 | 2 | 280 | |
| 8 | 12-Jan-93 | Franks | C | 175 | 5 | 875 | |
| 9 | 12-Jan-93 | Sheldon | D | 225 | 2 | 450 | |
| 10 | 14-Jan-93 | Peterson | A | 125 | 3 | 375 | |
| 11 | 15-Jan-93 | Jenkins | B | 140 | 1 | 140 | |
| 12 | 16-Jan-93 | Franks | C | 175 | 1 | 175 | |
| 13 | 17-Jan-93 | Peterson | D | 225 | 1 | 225 | |
| 14 | 17-Jan-93 | Robinson | A | 125 | 5 | 625 | |
| 15 | 18-Jan-93 | Wilson | B | 140 | 3 | 420 | |
| 16 | 18-Jan-93 | Robinson | C | 175 | 4 | 700 | |
| 17 | 19-Jan-93 | Wilson | D | 225 | 5 | 1125 | |
| 18 | 21-Jan-93 | Sheldon | B | 140 | 6 | 840 | |

SALES-DB.WK4 — Data / Query — New Sheet

**Figure 18-3:**
The sample
database.

Don't feel like you have to enter 154 rows of data in order to follow along with this example. You can simply enter 10–15 rows. Doing so will be enough to give you a feel of how this example works. After you understand it, try it with some real live data.

The fields in the database are as follows:

- **Date:** the date the sale was made

- **SalesRep:** the last name of the salesperson (there are six sales reps in this database)

- **Product:** the name of the product

- **UnitCost:** the cost of the product sold (each of the four products has its own cost)

- **Quantity:** the number of products sold

- **TotalCost:** the total sale (this field uses a formula that multiplies the UnitCost field by the Quantity field)

This database is named *sales*. To name a database, select the entire database (including the field names) and choose the Range⇨Name command. Type the name in the Name box and click OK.

Notice that the first sheet is named *Data,* and the second sheet is named *Query.* When you query a database, you need to specify a place to put the query results. It can go anywhere, but using a separate sheet is a good idea.

As databases go, this is a pretty skimpy database. In real life, a database like this would probably have many more records. But for pedagogical purposes, I'll keep it simple.

Suppose your boss wants to see a list of all sales of product *D.* You walk back to your cubicle, fire up 1-2-3 for Windows, and load your database worksheet. You have all the information you need in it; now you need to isolate all the sales of product *D.* In other words, you need to query your database.

Here are the steps that produce the list your boss wants:

1. **Make sure that the entire database range is named *sales.***

   This way, when you query the database by name, the search is done on the whole database.

2. **Select the Tools⇨Database⇨New Query command.**

   1-2-3 for Windows displays the dialog box shown in Figure 18-4. Notice that the parts are numbered.

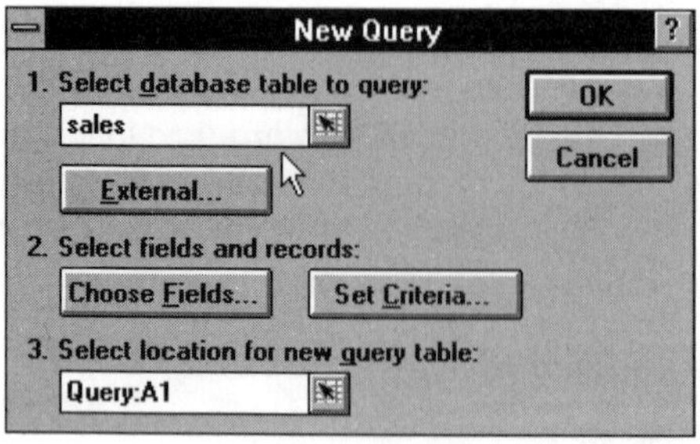

---

**Figure 18-4:**
The New Query dialog box.

> **New Query**    ?
>
> 1. Select database table to query:
>    sales
>    External...                         OK
>                                        Cancel
> 2. Select fields and records:
>    Choose Fields...    Set Criteria...
> 3. Select location for new query table:
>    Query:A1

---

3. **In part 1 of the dialog box, enter** sales, **the name of the database range you're querying.**

4. **Select the Set Criteria button in part 2.**

   1-2-3 for Windows displays the Set Criteria dialog box (see Figure 18-5), where you provide the details of the query.

**5. In part 3, type** Query:A1.

You put the results of the query starting in the upper left cell of the sheet named *query*.

**6. Specify the information you want in the drop-down listboxes.**

The criterion you want to isolate is pretty simple: you want all records that have a *D* in the product field. You do so using the drop-down listboxes labeled Field, Operator, and Value. When you activate one of these listboxes, you get a list of all options. You specify criteria by selecting Product from the Field listbox, = from the Operator listbox, and *D* from the Value listbox. As you do so, 1-2-3 for Windows lists the criteria in the Criteria box. Figure 18-5 shows you how this dialog box should look.

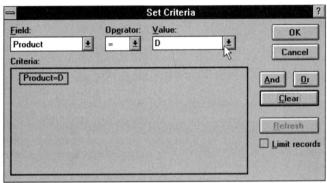

**Figure 18-5:**
Selecting all records that have a *D* in the product field.

**7. Choose OK to close the dialog box.**

1-2-3 for Windows returns to the previous dialog box, New Query.

**8. Choose OK to close the New Query dialog box.**

1-2-3 for Windows goes to work searching for the records you want and displays them beginning in cell A1 on the Query sheet. Figure 18-6 shows the result of this query.

| B | A | B | C | D | E | F | G |
|---|---|---|---|---|---|---|---|
| 1 | Date | SalesRep | Product | UnitCost | Quantity | TotalCost | |
| 2 | 07-Jan-93 | Franks | D | 225 | 1 | 225 | |
| 3 | 12-Jan-93 | Sheldon | D | 225 | 2 | 450 | |
| 4 | 17-Jan-93 | Peterson | D | 225 | 1 | 225 | |
| 5 | 19-Jan-93 | Wilson | D | 225 | 5 | 1125 | |
| 6 | 23-Jan-93 | Franks | D | 225 | 4 | 900 | |
| 7 | 26-Jan-93 | Sheldon | D | 225 | 1 | 225 | |
| 8 | 28-Jan-93 | Jenkins | D | 225 | 1 | 225 | |
| 9 | 31-Jan-93 | Wilson | D | 225 | 6 | 1350 | |
| 10 | 03-Feb-93 | Wilson | D | 225 | 2 | 450 | |
| 11 | 07-Feb-93 | Peterson | D | 225 | 2 | 450 | |
| 12 | 09-Feb-93 | Jenkins | D | 225 | 3 | 675 | |
| 13 | 15-Feb-93 | Sheldon | D | 225 | 6 | 1350 | |
| 14 | 16-Feb-93 | Jenkins | D | 225 | 2 | 450 | |
| 15 | 17-Feb-93 | Sheldon | D | 225 | 1 | 225 | |
| 16 | 20-Feb-93 | Jenkins | D | 225 | 3 | 675 | |
| 17 | 20-Feb-93 | Robinson | D | 225 | 3 | 675 | |
| 18 | 22-Feb-93 | Franks | D | 225 | 3 | 675 | |

SALES-DB.WK4 — Data / Query — New Sheet

**Figure 18-6:** The result of the query shows only the records that meet the criterion.

## Changing the query

The result of the query is a special kind of range, which has a box around it. To remind you of the fact that it's a special kind of range, the mouse pointer changes shape when you move it into this range (the pointer has a small square at the bottom). Notice that when the cell pointer is in this query output range, the program changes its Range menu to Query. When you select this menu, you get the commands shown in Figure 18-7.

The most useful command in this menu is Query➪Set Criteria. Use this to change your query by specifying new criteria. When you select this command, you get the Set Criteria dialog box, which displays the current criteria. If you change the criteria, the criteria output range is updated to show the results of the *new* query.

TIP

## Limiting query results

If you have an extremely large database, it might take the program a while to generate the results of a query. In such a case, you might want to limit the query results to a certain number of records while you're testing the query. You can do so by checking the Limit records check box in the Set Criteria dialog box. This option displays another control, in which you can enter the maximum number of records you want.

```
┌─ Set criteria to determine which records appear in a query table ─────── ▼ ◆
─  File  Edit  View  Style  Tools  Query  Window  Help                        ◆
Query1                    ▆@         Set Criteria...
                                     Choose Fields...⤡
                                     Sort...
Data Query                           Aggregate...                    New Sheet
                                     Show Field As...
     B       A        B       C                           F       G       H
  1       Date      SalesRep Product                     lCost
  2     07-Jan-93   Franks     D       Name...           25
  3     12-Jan-93   Sheldon    D                         50
  4     17-Jan-93   Peterson   D       Set Options...    25
  5     19-Jan-93   Wilson     D       Show SQL...       l25
  6     23-Jan-93   Franks     D                         00
  7     26-Jan-93   Sheldon    D       Set Database Table... 25
  8     28-Jan-93   Jenkins    D       Join...           25
  9     31-Jan-93   Wilson     D       Update Database Table  350
 10     03-Feb-93   Wilson     D       Refresh Now       50
 11     07-Feb-93   Peterson   D        225       2      450
 12     09-Feb-93   Jenkins    D        225       3      675
 13     15-Feb-93   Sheldon    D        225       6      1350
 14     16-Feb-93   Jenkins    D        225       2      450
 15     17-Feb-93   Sheldon    D        225       1      225
 16     20-Feb-93   Jenkins    D        225       3      675
 17     20-Feb-93   Robinson   D        225       3      675
 18     22-Feb-93   Franks     D        225       3      675
 19     23-Feb-93   Franks     D        225       4      900
 20     24-Feb-93   Peterson   D        225       1      225
Automatic          Arial MT        12  Height 14 Width 9              Menu
```

**Figure 18-7:**
The Query
menu is
available
only when
the cell
pointer lies
in a query
output
range.

# Summing query results

Sometimes you want to sum query results. For example, say your boss wants to know the total sales in March for each sales rep. Your database has a record for each sale, but in order to get totals by sales rep for a particular month, you have to do some sorting and create formulas to add them up, right? Wrong. There's actually an easier way. You can use the Query⇨Aggregate command *after* you do the query, as follows:

1. **Insert a new sheet after the sheet named** *Query* **and name the sheet** *Aggregate.*

   Use the New Sheet button to insert the sheet, and double-click the tab to give it a name.

2. **Select the Tools⇨Database⇨New Query command.**

3. **Specify** *sales* **as the database and** *Aggregate:A1* **as the location for the new query table.**

4. **Select the Choose Fields button in the New Query Dialog box.**

   To aggregate data, you must display only the fields to be used in the aggregation — in this case SalesRep and TotalCost. 1-2-3 for Windows displays another dialog box, shown in Figure 18-8.

**5. Clear all fields except SalesRep and TotalCost.**

Hold down the Ctrl key and click all fields *except* SalesRep and TotalCost. Doing so highlights the fields. Then Select Clear to get rid of all the fields except SalesRep and TotalCost. Close the dialog box by clicking OK, and you're back in the New Query dialog box.

**6. Specify your query criteria by selecting the Set Criteria button.**

In this case, the query needs to select all records with a date greater than or equal to March 1 *and* a date less than or equal to March 31.

**7. After you set the criteria, close the dialog box and then close the New Query dialog box.**

The program executes the query and shows only the two fields that you specified.

**8. At the location that holds your query results, click the TotalCost field name.**

This step selects this field for all of the records in the query results.

**9. Choose Query⇨Aggregate.**

The dialog box shown in Figure 18-9 appears.

**Figure 18-9:**
With the
Aggregate
dialog box,
you can
summarize
your query
results.

**10. Choose the Sum option and click OK.**

1-2-3 for Windows adds all the values in the TotalCost field for each separate entry in the SalesRep field.

The result of this aggregation is shown in Figure 18-10. Notice that the query results now show only six rows — one for each sales rep. Also notice that the program changed the name of the field to Total TotalCost (to remind you that it's aggregated).

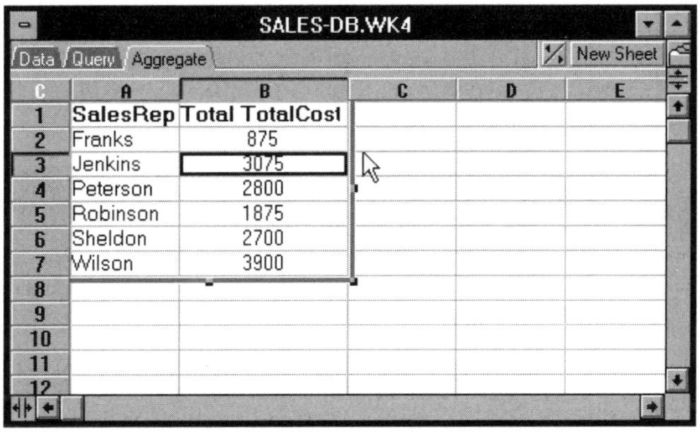

| | A | B | C | D | E |
|---|---|---|---|---|---|
| 1 | SalesRep | Total TotalCost | | | |
| 2 | Franks | 875 | | | |
| 3 | Jenkins | 3075 | | | |
| 4 | Peterson | 2800 | | | |
| 5 | Robinson | 1875 | | | |
| 6 | Sheldon | 2700 | | | |
| 7 | Wilson | 3900 | | | |
| 8 | | | | | |

SALES-DB.WK4

Data / Query / Aggregate

**Figure 18-10:** The aggregated data.

If you like, you can change this query by using the Query⇨Set Criteria command. For example, you might want to do another aggregation for April.

I've barely scratched the database surface in this chapter. There are many other things you can do with databases that the scope of this book does not warrant. This chapter is simply a tool to initiate your experience with databases and lists.

## Deleting records

You can delete records that you no longer need with the Tools⇨Database⇨Delete Records command. You get a dialog box that's similar to the New Query dialog box — except that you specify a query that describes the records you want to zap. After doing so, close the dialog box, and 1-2-3 for Windows wipes out all records that meet your criteria.

# Chapter 19
# Cool Formulas You Can Steal

*"Any sufficiently advanced technology is indistinguishable from magic."*

Arthur C. Clarke (b. 1917)

## In This Chapter

▶ Common formulas you can find many uses for

▶ Mathematical formulas that do slick things with numbers

▶ Formulas that manipulate your text

▶ Formulas that manipulate dates

I've found that people who use spreadsheets tend to want to do the same general sorts of tasks. Many of these procedures are built right into the spreadsheet in the form of menu commands or @functions. But many other popular spreadsheet actions require formulas.

I can't develop formulas for you (unless the price is right...). However, I *can* share with you some formulas that I find useful. Most of these formulas use @functions, so this chapter serves double-duty by also demonstrating some realistic uses of these functions. You might find one or two that are just what you need to get that report out on time.

In any case, feel free to do what you want with these formulas: study them diligently, ignore them completely, or anything in between.

## Read Me First

The formulas in this chapter use names for @function arguments, which means that you cannot simply enter the formulas into a worksheet and expect them to work. You have to make some minor changes to adapt the arguments to your own needs. When you incorporate these formulas into your worksheets, you must do one of the following:

✔ Substitute the appropriate cell or range reference for the range name I use. For example, the formula @SUM(*expenses*) uses a range named *expenses*. If you want to sum the values in A12..A36, substitute that range reference for *expenses*. Therefore, your adapted formula would be @SUM(A12..A36).

✔ Name cells or ranges on your worksheet to correspond to the range names used in the formulas. Following the previous example, you could simply use the Range⇨Name command to assign the name *expenses* to the range A12..A36.

✔ Use your own range names and make the appropriate changes in the formulas. If your worksheet has nothing to do with tracking expenses, define a name that applies.

# Common, Everyday Formulas

The formulas in this section are relatively simple (and perhaps even trivial). But they show up again and again in spreadsheets all over the world.

## Calculating a sum

To calculate the sum of a range named *expenses*, use the following formula:

```
@SUM(expenses)
```

The summation SmartIcon can write a formula like this for you automatically. Just move the cell pointer to the cell that you want the @SUM formula to be, and click the SmartIcon (it's the one that says 1+2=3). 1-2-3 for Windows inserts the formula in a jiff.

## Computing subtotals and grand totals

Some applications — budgets, for example — include subtotals as well as grand totals. Figure 19-1 shows an example that uses subtotals and a grand total at the bottom. Rather than use the @SUM function, you should know about the @SUBTOTAL and @GRANDTOTAL functions. The @SUBTOTAL function works just like the @SUM function. The @GRANDTOTAL function, however, adds only the cells that have an @SUBTOTAL function in them.

In the example shown, the @GRANDTOTAL function's argument is B1..B13, but the result includes only the three cells that have @SUBTOTAL functions in them.

| A | A | B | C | D |
|---|---|---|---|---|
| 1 | California | 345 | | |
| 2 | Oregon | 365 | | |
| 3 | Washington | 365 | | |
| 4 | **West Coast Subtotal** | **1075** | <— @SUBTOTAL(B1..B3) | |
| 5 | New York | 265 | | |
| 6 | New Jersey | 287 | | |
| 7 | Vermont | 226 | | |
| 8 | Massachusets | 456 | | |
| 9 | **East Coast Subtotal** | **1234** | <— @SUBTOTAL(B..B8) | |
| 10 | Kansas | 104 | | |
| 11 | Missouri | 98 | | |
| 12 | Illinois | 122 | | |
| 13 | **Midwest Subtotal** | **324** | <— @SUBTOTAL(B10..B12) | |
| 14 | **GRAND TOTAL** | **2633** | <— @GRANDTOTAL(B1..B13) | |

SUB-GRAN.WK4

**Figure 19-1:**
Dealing
with
subtotals
and grand
totals is
easy.

## Computing an average

To calculate the average (also known as the arithmetic mean) of a range named _expenses_, use the following formula:

```
@AVG(expenses)
```

If the range that you're averaging includes blank cells or labels, the @AVG function gives you the wrong answer because it treats these cells as zeros. Instead, use @PUREAVG, which ignores blanks and labels.

1-2-3 for Windows also provides the @MEDIAN function, which returns the median value of a range. If you rank all the values in the range, the median is the value that's in the middle of the ranked values (half of the values are greater than the median, and half are less than the median).

## Calculating a percentage change

If you want to calculate the percentage change between the value in a cell named _old_ and the value in a cell named _new_, use the following formula:

```
(new-old)/old
```

If _old_ is greater than _new_, the percentage change value is positive. Otherwise, the value is negative. You'll probably want to use the Style⇒Number Format command to format this cell to appear as a percentage.

If there's a chance that *old* will be equal to 0, use the following formula instead:

```
@IF(old=0,@NA,(new-old)/old)
```

This revised formula displays NA rather than ERR, which shows up if you attempt to divide by zero.

## Finding the minimum and maximum in a range

To find the largest number in a range named *scores*, use the following formula:

```
@MAX(scores)
```

To find the smallest number in a range named *scores*, use the following formula:

```
@MIN(scores)
```

1-2-3 for Windows considers labels to have a value of 0. Therefore, if the range argument for @MAX and @MIN has labels or blank cells, the function may not return what you want. You might want to use @PUREMAX and @PUREMIN, which ignore labels and empty cells in their argument range.

Another @function, @LARGE, tells you the nth largest number in a range. For example, to get the second highest value in the range *scores*, use `@LARGE(score,2)`. As you might expect, there's also an @SMALL function that returns the nth smallest number in a range.

## Calculating a loan payment

This example assumes that you have cells named *amount* (which is the loan amount), *term* (which is the length of the loan in months), and *rate* (which is the annual interest rate). The following formula returns the monthly payment amount:

```
@PMT(amount,rate/12,term)
```

Notice that this formula divides the annual interest rate (*rate*) by 12. This produces a monthly interest rate. If you are making payments every other month, divide *rate* by 6.

If you want to determine the amount of a loan payment that's applied to the principal, use the @PPAYMT function. To determine the amount that's applied to interest, use the @IPAYMNT function. These functions are demonstrated in Figure 19-2. Cell B5 contains the payment number (from 1 to 48 in this case). The amount allocated towards principal and interest varies with the payment number — more goes to interest earlier in the loan.

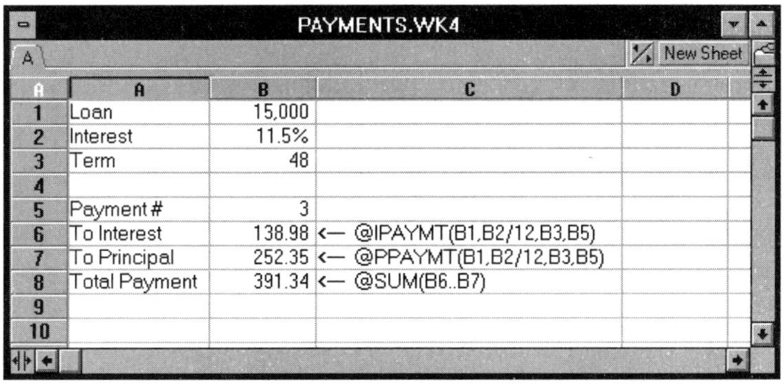

**Figure 19-2:**
@functions
calculate
the amount
of a loan
payment
that's
applied to
principal
and interest.

| | PAYMENTS.WK4 | | ▼ ▲ |
|---|---|---|---|
| A | | | ✂ New Sheet |
| | **A** | **B** | **C** | **D** |
| 1 | Loan | 15,000 | | |
| 2 | Interest | 11.5% | | |
| 3 | Term | 48 | | |
| 4 | | | | |
| 5 | Payment # | 3 | | |
| 6 | To Interest | 138.98 | ← @IPAYMT(B1,B2/12,B3,B5) | |
| 7 | To Principal | 252.35 | ← @PPAYMT(B1,B2/12,B3,B5) | |
| 8 | Total Payment | 391.34 | ← @SUM(B6..B7) | |
| 9 | | | | |
| 10 | | | | |

# Mathematical Formulas

These formulas have to do with mathematical operations: square roots, cube roots, random numbers, and so on.

## Finding a square root

The square root of a number is the number that, when multiplied by itself, gives you the original number. For example, 4 is the square root of 16, because $4 \times 4 = 16$. To calculate the square root of a cell named *value*, use the following function:

```
@SQRT(value)
```

## Finding a cube (or other) root

Besides square roots, there are other roots (like carrots and potatoes). The cube root of a number is the number that, when multiplied by itself twice, results in the original number. For example, 4 is the cube root of 64, because $4 \times 4 \times 4 = 64$. You can also calculate 4th roots, 5th roots, and so on. To get the cube root of a number in a cell named *value*, use the following formula:

```
+value^(1/3)
```

The fourth root is calculated as

```
+value^(1/4)
```

Calculate other roots in a similar manner by changing the bottom half of the fraction.

## Checking for even or odd values

To determine whether the value in a cell named *cointoss* is odd or even, use the following formula:

```
@MOD(cointoss,2)
```

This formula returns 1 if *cointoss* is odd and 0 if it's even.

For an even fancier formula that returns words rather than numbers, use this:

```
@IF(MOD(cointoss,2)=1,"ODD","EVEN")
```

The @MOD function, by the way, returns the remainder when the first argument is divided by the second argument. So in the first example, the value in *cointoss* is divided by 2, and the @MOD function returns the remainder of this division operation.

## Generating a random number

Spreadsheet users often use random numbers to simulate real events. For example, if you're trying to predict next year's sales, you might want to add some random numbers to this year's sales.

To get a random number between 0 and 1, use the following formula, which displays a new random number every time the worksheet is recalculated or every time you make a change to a cell:

```
@RAND
```

If you need a random integer (a whole number) that falls in a specific range, the formula gets a bit trickier. The following formula returns a random integer between two numbers stored in *low* and *high*. For example, if *low* contains 7 and *high* contains 12, the formula returns a random number between (and including) 7 and 12. The formula reads:

```
@INT(@RAND/(1/(high-low+1)))+low
```

## Rounding numbers

To round a number in a cell named *amount* to the nearest whole number, use the following formula:

```
@ROUND(amount,0)
```

To round the number to two decimal places, substitute a 2 for the 0 in the formula. In fact, you can round the number to any number of decimal places by changing the value of the second argument.

1-2-3 for Windows includes three other rounding @functions: @ROUNDUP, @ROUNDDOWN, and @ROUNDM. If your work involves rounding numbers, check out the 1-2-3 for Windows on-line help for a detailed explanation (and examples) of these @functions.

The value returned by the @ROUND function is the actual rounded value of its argument. If you merely want to change the number of decimal places displayed in a cell, you can change the numeric formatting with the Style⇨Number Format command. In other words, @ROUND affects not only how the value is displayed but also the value itself.

# Label Formulas

As you know, 1-2-3 for Windows can deal with text (or *labels*) as well as numbers. With these few formulas, you can manipulate labels.

## Adding labels

Joining two strings together is called *concatenation*. Assume the cell named *first* contains the label *Miles* and the cell named *last* contains *Davis*. The following formula concatenates these strings into a single name:

```
+first&" "&last
```

The ampersand (&) is the *concatenation operator*. Note that I concatenated a space character to separate the two names (otherwise the result would be *MilesDavis,* not *Miles Davis*). You can concatenate a label with a label but not a label with a value. However, you can get around this restriction, as shown in the following examples.

## Working with labels and values

If you want to concatenate a label with a value, you must first convert the value to a label. In this example, the cell named *word* holds the label *AMOUNT:*. The cell named *answer* holds the value 125. The formula following displays the label and the value in a single cell:

```
+word&" "&@STRING(answer,0)
```

@STRING converts a value to a label, and the second argument for the @STRING function gives the number of decimal places to be displayed (in this case, none).

The result of this formula is

```
AMOUNT: 125
```

Here's another example. Assume that you have a range of cells named *scores*. The following formula displays a label and the maximum value in *scores* in one cell:

```
+"Largest: "&@STRING(@MAX(scores),0)
```

If the largest value in scores were 95, this formula would display:

```
Largest: 95
```

The @STRING function converts the value returned by the @MAX function into a label. This label is then concatenated with the string "Largest:". Pretty neat, eh?

# Date Formulas

The date and time @functions depend on your computer's clock for their information. If you rely on any of these functions for serious work, make sure that the date and time are set properly in your computer.

## Finding out what day it is

If you would like a cell in your worksheet to display the current date, enter the following formula into any cell:

```
@TODAY
```

This formula returns a date serial number, so you need to use the Style➪Number Format command to format it as a date (you may also have to make the column wider so that the date shows up).

## Determining the day of the week

The following formula returns the current day of the week:

```
@CHOOSE(@WEEKDAY(@TODAY),"Mon","Tue","Wed","Thu","Fri",
"Sat","Sun")
```

You can replace @TODAY in the preceding formula with a reference to a cell that has a date serial number in it to get the day of the week for any date.

## Determining the last day of the month

In business situations, it's often necessary to know the last day of the month — the day that you have to produce the monthly reports. The following formula returns the last day of the current month:

```
@DATE(@YEAR(@TODAY),@MONTH(@TODAY)+1,1)-1
```

To figure out the last day of the month for any date serial number, substitute a reference to a cell that has a date for both occurrences of @TODAY.

# Miscellaneous Formulas

Here are a few more miscellaneous formulas for your computing pleasure.

## Looking up a corresponding value

Many spreadsheets need to look up a value in a table that is based on another value. Examples include parts lists and income tax tables: you need to look up the tax rate from a table, and the tax rate is based on a person's taxable income.

Figure 19-3 shows an example of a small lookup table. In this worksheet, the user can enter a part number into cell B3, which is named *partnum*. The formulas in cells B4 and B5 return the corresponding price and discount. The lookup table is in D2..F11 and has the name *partlist*. The values in the first column of any lookup table must be in ascending order (smallest to largest).

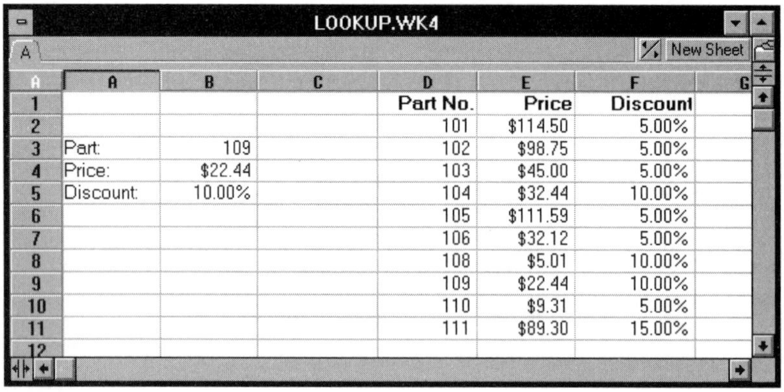

LOOKUP.WK4

| | A | B | C | D | E | F |
|---|---|---|---|---|---|---|
| 1 | | | | Part No. | Price | Discount |
| 2 | | | | 101 | $114.50 | 5.00% |
| 3 | Part: | 109 | | 102 | $98.75 | 5.00% |
| 4 | Price: | $22.44 | | 103 | $45.00 | 5.00% |
| 5 | Discount: | 10.00% | | 104 | $32.44 | 10.00% |
| 6 | | | | 105 | $111.59 | 5.00% |
| 7 | | | | 106 | $32.12 | 5.00% |
| 8 | | | | 108 | $5.01 | 10.00% |
| 9 | | | | 109 | $22.44 | 10.00% |
| 10 | | | | 110 | $9.31 | 5.00% |
| 11 | | | | 111 | $89.30 | 15.00% |
| 12 | | | | | | |

**Figure 19-3:** Looking up a value in a table.

The formula in cell B4, which displays the price, is

```
@VLOOKUP(partnum,partlist,1)
```

The formula in cell B5, which displays the discount, is

```
@VLOOKUP(partnum,partlist,2)
```

The @VLOOKUP function looks for the first argument (here, *partnum*) in the first column of the range specified by the second argument (here, *partlist*). It then returns the value in the column represented by the third argument (0 corresponds to the first column in the table, 1 to the second column, 2 to the third column, and so on). If the formula doesn't find an exact match, it simply uses the first row that's not greater than what it's looking for. In some cases this is OK, but in others it can be a problem.

## Looking up an exact corresponding value

The following formulas solve that problem. This time, the formula makes sure that the part number actually exists by using an @IF function. If the part number doesn't exist, the formula returns the string `Not found`.

The following formula substitutes for the formula in cell B4 in the preceding example:

```
@IF(partnum=@VLOOKUP(partnum,partlist,0),@VLOOKUP(partnum,
partlist,1),"Not found")
```

The following formula substitutes for the formula in cell B5 in the preceding example:

```
@IF(partnum=@VLOOKUP(partnum,partlist,0),@VLOOKUP(partnum,
partlist,2),"Not found")
```

There are many formulas and @ functions not discussed here. If this chapter ignites your desire for more function knowledge, use the on-line help or documentation to learn more.

# Chapter 20

## Just Enough about Macros to Survive

*"If you are sure you understand everything that is going on, you are hopelessly confused."*

Walter F. Mondale (b. 1928)

. . . . . . . . . . . . . . . . . . . . . . . . . . . . . . . . . . . . . . . . . . . . . . . . . . . . . . . . . . . . . . . . . . . .

### In This Chapter

▶ Introducing macros in 1-2-3 for Windows

▶ Creating simple macros — and why you may want to do so

▶ Learning some things about macros that you can safely ignore

▶ Using macros that other people create

. . . . . . . . . . . . . . . . . . . . . . . . . . . . . . . . . . . . . . . . . . . . . . . . . . . . . . . . . . . . . . . . . . . .

Somewhere along the line, you may have heard that computers are supposed to make your life easier and save time. When it comes to spreadsheets, the one feature most often cited as a time-saver is the *macro*. Leaning about macros is not essential to using 1-2-3 for Windows; in fact, most spreadsheet users don't know a macro from a mango. But you owe it to yourself to learn at least what macros can do so that you know what you're missing.

## A Macro by Any Other Name...

A *macro* is simply a shortcut for typing text, numbers, or even commands. The only hitch is that you have to create the macro before you use it.

Imagine that you have a worksheet set up and you need to enter the name of your company in several different places throughout the worksheet. You can type the company name each time you need it, or you can type the company name once and then use the Clipboard (with the Edit⇨Copy and Edit⇨Paste commands) to copy it to the other locations. Another way to save time is to create a macro to type the company name for you automatically upon command.

## Why the word *macro*?

Contrary to popular belief, *macro* does not stand for *Messy And Confusing Repeatable Operation.* Actually, I don't know why computer buffs use this term. Maybe so they can exclude all the normal people in the world from understanding their jargon, hoping someday to rule the world.

The dictionary tells me that *macro* means large and is the opposite of *micro.* My guess is that these things are called *macros* because you can perform a large operation by making a small effort. If anybody knows the real answer, please let me in on it.

If your company's name is Consolidated Biotechnical Research Resources of New Zealand, you can assign these letters to a key combination, such as Ctrl+C. Then whenever you press Ctrl+C, 1-2-3 for Windows spits out the name of the company instantly, and always spells it correctly, as a bonus — assuming, of course, that you spelled it correctly when you created the macro.

And — believe it or not — using macros gets even better. You also can create macros that execute a series of commands. Suppose that you like to apply specific formatting, such as bold, red text, and a border. You can assign all these commands to a key combination, such as Ctrl+F. Then pressing Ctrl+F executes these commands faster than you can say "holy macro."

## *Generals about Macros*

No, you aren't in the army, which should be a relief. But before you get too far into this chapter, you should know the following few ideas about macros in 1-2-3 for Windows:

- A macro plays back predefined keystrokes, and these keystrokes can even be the keys required to issue commands and work with dialog boxes.

- You can assign a macro to a key combination (such as Ctrl+Z) or attach it to an object on your worksheet (such as a button) to execute it.

- Playing back the predefined keystrokes is called *running the macro* or *executing the macro.* You run the macro by pressing the specific key combination that you assigned to the macro or by clicking the object that the macro is attached to.

- Store your macros in the worksheet in which you plan to use them. Actually, macros are labels — labels that have a special meaning to 1-2-3 for Windows.

✔ You must create the macro before you can use it, and you can create the macro manually or by recording your actions.

✔ You can use a macro as many times as you want; the macro always does exactly the same thing.

# Your First Macro (Don't Spoil It)

Ready to create your first macro? Although it's not as much fun as creating a symphonic masterpiece, it really isn't that difficult to do, and requires less time and effort. Follow the step-by-step directions in the next section.

## Creating the macro

First you create a macro that inserts your name into a cell and then moves the cell pointer to the cell directly below. Then you assign the macro to the Ctrl+N key combination. After you finish, you can go to any cell in the worksheet and press Ctrl+N to have 1-2-3 for Windows enter the text you specified and move the cell pointer down to the cell below. To create your first macro, follow these steps:

1. **Start with a blank worksheet.**

2. **Move the cell pointer to cell B1 and type your name in the cell, followed by a tilde (~).**

   The tilde character after your name represents the Enter key . When the program encounters a tilde, it's just like you pressed Enter (don't ask me where *that* came from).

   For example, if your name is Fred Flintstone, type **Fred Flintstone~.**

3. **Move the cell pointer to cell B2 and type {DOWN}.**

   The {DOWN} part of the macro is responsible for moving the cell pointer, because it is a macro command that represents the down-arrow key.

4. **Move the cell pointer to cell A1, and type '\n (a single quote, a backslash, and the letter *n*).**

   If you want to execute the macro by using a Ctrl+key combination, the first cell of a macro must have a name that starts with a backslash and has one additional character. This additional character is used with the Ctrl key to execute the macro. In this case, you're simply putting the name (\n) to the left of the first cell of the macro to make it easy to remember.

5. **With the cell pointer in cell A1, select the Range⇨Name command.**

6. **In the dialog box, select the Use Labels button (and make sure that the For cells listbox has To the right selected).**

7. **Click OK to close the dialog box.**

These last three steps assign the name \n to cell B1 (the name is stored in A1, but the cell being named is B1).

That's it. Your worksheet should look like Figure 20-1 (although the name in cell B1 should be different, if your name's not Fred Flintstone). This macro consists of two labels, one for column A and one for column B; and the macro also has a name, Ctrl+N.

| | A | B | C | D | E | F |
|---|---|---|---|---|---|---|
| 1 | \n | Fred Flintstone~ | | | | |
| 2 | | {DOWN} | | | | |
| 3 | | | | | | |
| 4 | | | | | | |
| 5 | | | | | | |
| 6 | | | | | | |
| 7 | | | | | | |
| 8 | | | | | | |
| 9 | | | | | | |
| 10 | | | | | | |

**Figure 20-1:** A simple macro that types Fred's name.

## Running the macro

You can now run the macro in one of two ways: you can use the macro's name (Ctrl+N, in this example) or you can use the Tools⇨Macro⇨Run command.

1-2-3 for Windows must be in Ready mode when you execute a macro.

### With the macro name

To run the macro by using the macro's name, do the following:

1. **Move the cell pointer to any blank cell in the worksheet.**

2. **Press Ctrl+N.**

The macro types your name and then moves the cell pointer down one cell. You can move all over the worksheet and press Ctrl+N as much as you want. Your name appears each time you execute this macro (this macro is great for egomaniacs).

# How a macro works

The simple two-cell macro I've been using as an example does two things: it types your name, and it moves the cell pointer down one cell. After you press Ctrl+N, 1-2-3 for Windows goes through the following thought process:

✔ Hmmm. This user just pressed Ctrl+N.

✔ Is there a macro named \n? If no, I'll just beep.

✔ Hey, there *is* a macro named \n. That means I'll have to execute the macro.

✔ I have to check out the first cell of the macro. The cell is full of a bunch of letters with a tilde at the end of them. I'll spit out the letters and then press Enter.

✔ There's another cell below, so I'll take a look at it.

✔ This cell has a command that tells me to move the cell pointer down. OK.

✔ Because there's nothing below this macro command, my job's over for now.

Remember that the tilde represents the Enter key and that {DOWN} is a macro command that represents the down-arrow key. 1-2-3 for Windows has quite a few macro commands, which are always enclosed in curly brackets. If this command is not in brackets, 1-2-3 for Windows simply types the letters *D, O, W,* and *N.* As you may expect, you can use other commands, such as {UP}, {LEFT}, and {RIGHT} to move the cell pointer around. Also remember to name a macro with a backslash and an additional character, if you want to run the macro with a Ctrl+key combination.

If the macro doesn't do what it's supposed to do, the source of the problem is probably in the name. Cell B1 must be named \n, which means Ctrl+N. Review steps 4-7 in the preceding procedure and try running the macro again.

### With the Tools⇨Macro⇨Run command

Although giving a macro a name does make the macro easier to work with, you do not have to name it. You can run a macro that doesn't have a name by following these steps:

1. **Use the Tools⇨Macro⇨Run menu command.**

   1-2-3 for Windows displays the Macro Run dialog box, shown in Figure 20-2.

2. **Enter the macro's starting cell address in the Macro name box (or point to the first cell of the macro) and click OK.**

   1-2-3 for Windows executes the macro commands. Alternatively, you can select the macro name from the All named ranges box.

**Figure 20-2:**
The Macro
Run dialog
box enables
you to run a
macro by
entering its
starting cell
address.

# Modifying the macro

You now get a chance to modify the macro so that is does even more. To add your address under your name in the macro, do the following:

1. **Move to cell B3 (the cell directly below the end of the existing macro) and type the first line of your address, followed by a tilde (~).**

   You're adding on to the existing macro to make it type an address.

2. **Move to cell B4 and type {DOWN}.**

   This makes the macro move to the cell below.

3. **Move to cell B5 and type the second line of your address, followed by a tilde (to represent pressing Enter).**

4. **Move to the cell below (B6) and type {UP 2}.**

   This macro command tells 1-2-3 for Windows to move the cell pointer up two times; therefore, after you execute the macro, the cell pointer returns to the spot where you started.

This modified macro types your name, moves down to the cell below, types the first line of your address, moves down one cell, types the next line of your address, and then moves up two cells (so that the cell pointer is where it was when the macro started).

Now move to a blank cell and press Ctrl+N. After 1-2-3 for Windows executes all the macro commands, the cell pointer returns to the place where it was when you executed the macro.

Notice that you don't have to rename this macro after you make the changes. The original name ( \n) still applies to the first cell of the macro.

## Some macro rules

With this minor bit of macro experience under your belt, you're ready for the following rules of the game:

- ✔ A macro consists of labels made up of text and special macro commands enclosed in curly braces.

- ✔ A macro is stored in one or more cells in a single column.

- ✔ You can edit the text that makes up a macro command just like you edit any other cell.

- ✔ 1-2-3 for Windows plays back the labels and executes the commands in order, starting at the top of the column and working down until it hits a blank cell.

- ✔ You can put any number of macro commands in one cell (but you make it easier on yourself if you use only one command per cell).

- ✔ You can enter macros directly into your worksheet, or you can use the macro recorder to record your keystrokes (see the next section).

# The Macro Recorder (Not Just Your Greatest Hits)

1-2-3 for Windows has a special built-in feature that's capable of storing your worksheet actions and creating a macro out of them. This feature works much like a tape recorder: you turn the recording mode on, do your thing, and then turn the recording mode off. The actions you perform are translated into macro commands and are displayed in a special window called the Transcript window. You can copy the commands from the Transcript window into your worksheet and turn them into a macro. Then you can execute the macro as many times as you want. Cool, eh?

Before I go through an example, here's a summary of the general steps you need to go through to record a macro:

1. **Figure out what you want the macro to do.**

   (Easier said than done: this step sounds funny, but it's more important than you think and saves you lots of steps further down the road, if you can decide from the beginning what you want the macro to do.)

2. **Turn on the macro recorder with the Tools⇨Macro⇨Record command.**

3. **Perform the action that you want recorded.**

4. Stop the macro recorder with the Tools⇨Macro⇨Stop Recording command.

5. Display the Transcript window with the Tools⇨Macro⇨Show Transcript command.

6. Select the macro commands in the Transcript window and copy them to the Clipboard with the Edit⇨Copy command.

7. Activate the worksheet in which you want to store the macro.

8. Move to the first cell that will hold the macro and copy the Clipboard contents there with the Edit⇨Paste command.

9. Give the macro a name (optional, but recommended).

# Recording a Macro (A Doo Wop Wop)

Now that you're vaguely familiar with the general steps for recording a macro, you should be ready and anxious to try out the procedure and actually record a macro. Ready or not, that's what this section does. At the risk of being bored to tears, you'll record the same name-and-address macro that you entered manually in the previous sections.

Start with a blank worksheet (not necessary, but it makes the process easier for me to describe) and then do the following steps:

1. Move the cell pointer to cell A1.

2. Select the Tools⇨Macro⇨Record command to turn on the macro recorder.

   From this point on, the program records all your actions.

3. Enter your name in cell A1 and press Enter.

4. Move down to cell A2, enter the first line of your address, and press Enter.

5. Move down to cell A3, enter the second line of your address, and press Enter.

6. Move the cell pointer back up to cell A1.

7. Select the Tools⇨Macro⇨Stop Recording command to turn off the macro recorder.

8. Select the Tools⇨Macro⇨Show Transcript command to display the Transcript window, shown in Figure 20-3.

   The Transcript window shows the macro commands that 1-2-3 for Windows writes as you record your actions.

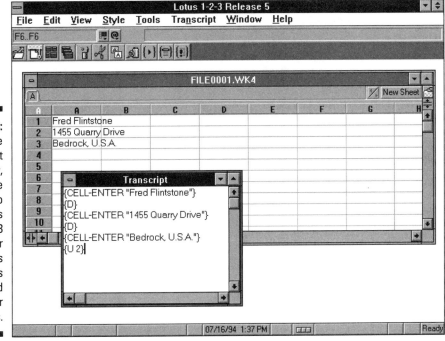

**Figure 20-3:** The Transcript window, with the macro commands that 1-2-3 for Windows writes as you record your actions.

9. **Activate the Transcript Window (by clicking it) and select all the text in it (by highlighting it).**

10. **Choose Edit⇨Copy (or press Ctrl+C) to copy the contents of the Transcript window to the Clipboard.**

11. **Activate your worksheet and move to cell E1, where you put the recorded macro.**

12. **Select the Edit⇨Paste command (or press Ctrl+V) to paste the Clipboard contents to the worksheet, beginning in cell E1.**

Your worksheet should now look like Figure 20-4.

13. **Move to cell E1 and select the Range⇨Name command.**

14. **Type \n for the name of the cell and choose OK.**

You have just assigned the name \n to cell E1 (which means you can execute it by pressing Ctrl+N).

Notice that you named cell E1 directly this time, and didn't place the cell name to the left. Either method is OK. In this case, you'll simply have to remember that the first cell of the macro is named \n.

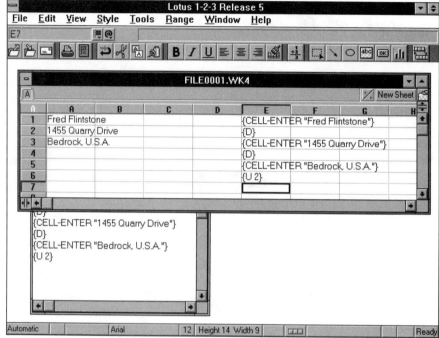

**Figure 20-4:**
Your
worksheet,
after
copying the
macro
commands
from the
Transcript
window.

Now the macro is in place, the first cell has a name, and you can try it out. Move to any cell and press Ctrl+N. If all goes well, the macro should play back your name and address and return the cell pointer to where it started out. If the macro doesn't work, recheck your work and try again.

You probably notice some resemblance between this recorded macro and the macro you entered manually in the original example. Why, you may ask, aren't the two macros identical? While you record a macro, 1-2-3 for Windows converts everything you type into a command. For example, the {CELL-ENTER "Fred Flintstone"} command places the name into a cell. The {D} command is simply a shorthand version of the {DOWN} command that you entered. (You could have used {D} when you entered the macro manually.)

Be careful when assigning Ctrl+key combinations to macro names. 1-2-3 for Windows has its own use for some of these Ctrl+key combinations. For example, Ctrl+R is a shortcut that makes the current selection right-aligned in the cell. If you name a macro \r, you can't use the normal Ctrl+R shortcut, because 1-2-3 for Windows executes your macro instead. Using any of these predefined shortcuts for a macro name cancels your ability to use the shortcut keys. Chapter 17 lists the 1-2-3 for Windows common Ctrl+key combinations that you should avoid using for your macros.

## More about the Transcript window

One or two of you may be curious about the Transcript window, a window that's somewhat similar to a worksheet window. After you activate the Transcript window, the Range command on the menu changes to Transcript and the SmartIcon palette changes to reflect the Transcript window.

If you record a macro and then copy it from the Transcript window into a worksheet, the commands remain in the Transcript window. If you start recording another macro, the Transcript window isn't cleared, so the new information follows the old information. If you like, you can clear the Transcript window contents before you record another macro. Just select the text and press Delete. An even easier way to clear out the Transcript window is to activate the window and then choose the Edit⇨Clear All command. This command is available only when the Transcript window is the active window.

Right-clicking with the mouse button is very handy in the Transcript window. After you right-click anywhere in the Transcript window, you get a list of commands, including a command to start and stop recording and a command to clear the entire window.

You also can edit text in the Transcript window, which works just as you would expect and is similar to a small word processor (except that you have no text formatting capabilities). You may, for example, want to make some minor changes to the commands in the Transcript window before you copy them into your worksheet.

# Getting More Advanced (Figaro, Figaro)

So far, the macros you've developed have been pretty wimpy — and not really all that useful. If you can't get enough of this stuff, this section tells you how to record a macro that actually does something constructive.

The macro that you create next changes the formatting of the selected cell. This macro (or one similar to it) may be useful for quickly formatting a bunch of headings in your worksheet.

To see what this macro can do, examine Figure 20-5. The macro converts the text in cell A2 in the worksheet so that it looks like the text in cell C2 — all with a single keystroke.

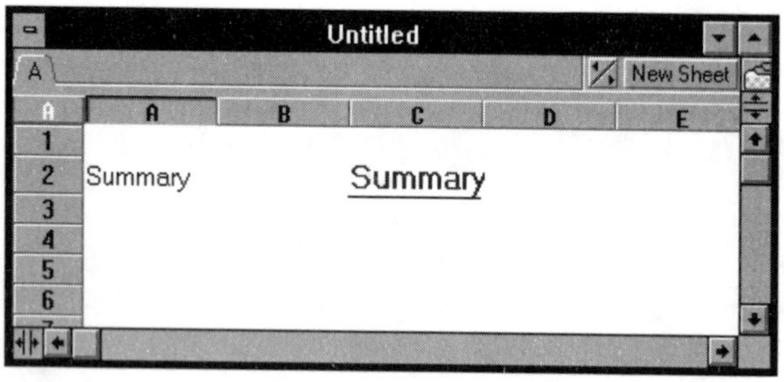

Figure 20-5:
Before
running the
macro (cell
A2), and
after running
the macro
(cell C2).

## Recording a formatting macro

Rather than typing in the macro commands manually, you can record the macro that does this formatting. In this case, recording is much easier than entering the macro commands manually. For simplicity, start with a blank worksheet. To record the macro that does the special formatting for your cells, do the following:

1. **Activate the Transcript window.**

   If the Transcript window is not displayed, choose the Tools⇨Macro⇨Show Transcript command.

2. **Choose Edit⇨Clear All to clear the current contents of the Transcript window.**

3. **Type** First Quarter **in cell B2 and keep the cell pointer in this cell and press Enter.**

   *First Quarter* is just a label to give you something to start with.

4. **Select the Tools⇨Macro⇨Record command to turn on the macro recorder.**

5. **Issue the Style⇨Font & Attributes command.**

   You get the standard dialog box.

6. **In the dialog box, set the text size to 14 points, click the Bold check box, choose dark blue for the color, and select OK.**

7. **Issue the Style⇨Lines & Color command.**

8. **In the resulting dialog box, check the Bottom option in the border section and choose OK.**

9. **Select Tools⇨Macro⇨Stop Recording.**

10. **Activate the Transcript window and examine the recorded commands.**

    Notice that there are two lines that read {SELECT B2}. You don't want these commands in the macro. If you leave them in, the macro always selects cell B2 for the formatting. So you must remove these lines and any blank lines that you have in the Transcript window.

11. **Select the lines that read {SELECT B2} and erase them with <u>E</u>dit⇨<u>C</u>ut.**

12. **Select all the remaining text in the Transcript window, as illustrated in Figure 20-6.**

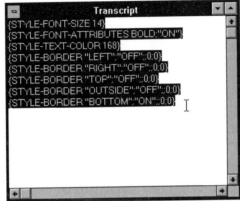

**Figure 20-6:**
Selecting
text in the
Transcript
window.

13. **Copy the selected commands to the Clipboard with <u>E</u>dit⇨<u>C</u>opy.**

14. **Activate your worksheet and move the cell pointer to E1.**

15. **Select <u>E</u>dit⇨<u>P</u>aste to paste the macro commands into the worksheet.**

16. **With the cell pointer in cell E1, choose the <u>R</u>ange⇨<u>N</u>ame command and type \f for the name of this macro.**

17. **Close the dialog box.**

The recorded macro is now stored in your worksheet, beginning in cell E1. Figure 20-7 shows what your worksheet should look like. The macro is named \f and can be executed by pressing Ctrl+F.

To try out the macro, type some text in one or more cells. Select all the text and press Ctrl+F. In a flash, the program executes the macro, and the font of the selected cells becomes 14 points, bold, and dark blue, with a border at the bottom. You've just performed four formatting commands with a single key combination. Depending on the length of your label, you may have to widen the cell so the bottom border underlines it completely.

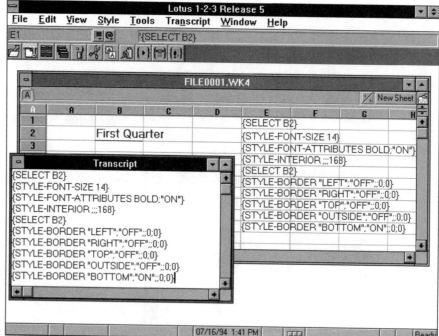

**Figure 20-7:**
A more complex macro that adds formatting.

## Why the macro looks strange

The macro you recorded in the preceding example looks pretty strange, don't you think? Some parts of the macro don't look anything like the keys you pressed when you recorded it. Rather, it has weird commands, such as {STYLE-FONT-ATTRIBUTES BOLD;"ON"} and {STYLE-TEXT-COLOR 168}.

As you record a macro, 1-2-3 for Windows interprets your actions and converts your keystrokes into special macro commands. Each of these commands has a very specific syntax. That's why it's usually much easier to *record* a macro than to enter it directly.

# *Using Other People's Macros*

You may, at some point in your career, receive a worksheet from someone who actually knows how to use macros (or you may even purchase a worksheet all set up to do something useful). This worksheet may have one or more macros on it, and you've been told that these macros make the spreadsheet do something useful. In fact, this scenario isn't all that unusual. Some people take great pride in developing macros that do useful things (and showing off their skills in the process).

If you're lucky, the worksheet has instructions that tell you what to do. For example, the worksheet may say, "To print this worksheet, press Ctrl+P" or "Press Ctrl+U to begin updating the monthly sales figures."

You don't have to know what the macro is doing in order to use it. Just press the appropriate key combination and sit back and relax while 1-2-3 for Windows follows the orders in the macro.

# Part V
## The Part of Tens

"WE FIGURE THE EQUIPMENT MUST HAVE SCARED HER AWAY. A FEW DAYS AFTER SETTING UP, LITTLE 'SNOWBALL' JUST DISAPPEARED."

## In this part...

For reasons that are historical as well as helpful, all the books in the Dummies series have chapters with lists in them. Because I'm a sucker for tradition, I went along with this tradition and prepared a few top-ten lists. These three chapters are good places to go if you've already learned 1-2-3 for Windows and you want to remind yourself of the shortcuts and special features.

# Chapter 21
# Ten Good Habits You Should Acquire

*"The second half of a man's life is made up of nothing but the habits he has acquired during the first half."*

Fyodor M. Dostoyevsky (1821–1881)
Russian novelist

● ● ● ● ● ● ● ● ● ● ● ● ● ● ● ● ● ● ● ● ● ● ● ● ● ● ● ● ● ● ● ● ● ● ● ● ● ● ● ● ● ● ● ● ● ● ● ●

*T*he opening quotation is actually relevant to using 1-2-3 for Windows. The habits that you form early on definitely stick with you over the years. All 1-2-3 for Windows users should try to develop the following ten habits as they learn to use the program:

1. **Use the SmartIcons and shortcut keys.** Many people completely ignore all the ease-of-use features that spreadsheet designers work so hard to include (and their ad agencies charge so much to promote). Using the menus and dialog boxes for routine things, like aligning the contents of a cell, is not only slower, but also introduces more chances for you to make mistakes.

2. **Don't save your worksheet files to a floppy disk.** Always use your hard disk as your primary file storage place, because file saves and retrieves are faster, and hard disks are less likely to go bad than floppy disks. However, you *should* use floppies to store backup copies of all your important files.

3. **Take advantage of multiple worksheet files.** If you have experience using a program (such as Lotus 1-2-3 Release 2 for DOS) that does not have 3-D capability, you may have a tendency to ignore the potential of extra sheets that are available in every 1-2-3 for Windows file. Using these extra sheets is a great way to organize your work and provides a quick way to jump to a particular part of your worksheet by simply clicking a tab.

4. **Use cell and range names whenever possible.** If you have some cells or ranges that are used a great deal in formulas, you should take a few minutes to give them names with the Range⇨Name command. By naming the frequently used cells or ranges, you can use their names in formulas (rather than obscure addresses) so that the formulas are easier to read

and understand. A side benefit is that you can use the range navigator icon in the edit line to quickly add a range name to a formula or to jump directly to a named cell or range. And on the off chance that you'll be writing macros, named cells and ranges make macro writing much easier (and safer).

5. **Don't forget that you can work with more than one program at a time.** When you're working away in your spreadsheet and need to do something else (like compose a memo in your word processor), you do not need to close down 1-2-3 for Windows. Just press Ctrl+Esc to access the Windows Task List, select Program Manager, and execute the program you need. 1-2-3 for Windows remains in the background.

6. **Take advantage of the on-line help in 1-2-3 for Windows.** Great as this book is, it doesn't tell you *everything* about 1-2-3 for Windows. If you get stuck, your first line of attack should be to press F1 and see what the on-line help has to say. You often can solve your problem by going no further than that.

7. **Don't be afraid to try new things.** As you know, dozens of weird commands lurk within the bowels of the 1-2-3 for Windows menu system and dialog boxes. Don't be afraid to try out these unfamiliar commands to see what happens. But to be on the safe side, have an unimportant worksheet open when you do so. And don't forget to use Edit⇨Undo if the command messes things up.

8. **Don't waste time printing drafts.** All too often, people print draft after draft of their worksheets, making only minor changes before each printing. A better approach is to use the Print Preview feature, which shows you exactly how your printed output will look. You even can zoom in to examine parts more closely.

9. **Don't go overboard with fancy formatting.** I know that it's very tempting to spend hours trying to get your worksheet to look perfect — it's actually kind of fun to experiment with fonts, type sizes, colors, borders, and the like. But the final product is probably not worth this much attention. Unless you have lots of time on your hands, focus on the content of your worksheet rather than on its appearance.

10. **Don't be afraid of macros.** After you get comfortable with using the basic features of 1-2-3 for Windows, you may want to explore the world of macros. Even a rudimentary knowledge of macros can save you a great deal of time when you're doing repetitive tasks.

# Chapter 22

# Top Ten Concepts Every 1-2-3 for Windows User Should Understand

*"Never trust the advice of a man in difficulties."*

Aesop (b. 6th century B.C.)

• • • • • • • • • • • • • • • • • • • • • • • • • • • • • • • • • • • • • • • • • • • • • • • • • •

*I*f you use 1-2-3 for Windows, you should live, breathe, and become the following information:

### 1. Many versions of 1-2-3 lurk out there.

When people talk about using 1-2-3, you have no reason to believe that they're referring to the same version that you use. Generally, the different versions of 1-2-3 are *very* different from each other. So someone who knows only how to use 1-2-3 Release 4 for Windows doesn't necessarily know how to use 1-2-3 Release 2 for DOS, 1-2-3 Release 3 for DOS, or even 1-2-3 Release 1 for Windows. However, Release 4 and 5 are similar enough that you should have no problem switching back and forth. Different 1-2-3 versions also use different file formats. So if someone asks you to send her a 1-2-3 file, make sure that you know which file format she wants.

Your choices are .WKS, .WK1, .WK3, and .WK4. 1-2-3 Release 4 and Release 5 for Windows uses .WK4 files, but you can save your work as a .WK1 or a .WK3 file by using the File⇨Save As command.

### 2. 1-2-3 for Windows is compatible with other Windows applications.

Windows programs are like Libras and Scorpios; they get along well. You should know that you can run more than one Windows program at a time, and switch among them whenever you need to. Furthermore, the Windows Clipboard is the language interpreter of the bunch. You easily can copy information between different programs by using the Windows Clipboard. When you use the Windows Clipboard, you can copy a range of cells from 1-2-3 for Windows and paste it into your Windows word processor. You also can use the Clipboard for copying and pasting graphics. The Clipboard is one of the most useful features in Windows, so don't ignore it!

### 3. 1-2-3 for Windows has other windows in its window.

Believe it or not, many users don't understand this Windows concept. Each program that you run, including 1-2-3 for Windows, has its own window, which you can resize, move, minimize, or maximize within the Windows environment. Within the 1-2-3 for Windows program window, each worksheet also has its own window, which can be resized, moved, minimized, or maximized. (There might be some potential for a window washing business out there...)

### 4. You can select ranges in myriad different ways.

For a small range that doesn't extend beyond the current screen, dragging the mouse over the range may be the fastest way to select it. But using the keyboard is usually more efficient. To select a range with the keyboard, press Shift and use the navigation keys. You also can combine this process with the End key, followed by an arrow key (this moves to the end of the range). And don't forget that you can select an entire row or column by clicking the row number or column letter in the worksheet frame. Finally, you can select noncontiguous ranges by holding down Ctrl while you make your selections.

### 5. You have many command options.

1-2-3 for Windows is a flexible program and usually offers several ways to execute one command. You can execute most operations by using the menu system, but it isn't always the most efficient way. Many menu commands have shortcut keys or SmartIcon equivalents. And the status bar at the bottom of the screen is the fastest way to change fonts, text sizes, and numeric formatting. But you should get used to right-clicking with your mouse to get to the shortcut menu. After you select a cell, range, or graphics object, you get a quick menu by right-clicking. Most the time, this menu has the command you need. And don't forget about drag and drop — for simple copy and move operations, this method can't be beat.

### 6. You can preselect a range to simplify data entry.

If you have to enter a bunch of numbers in a range, you soon get weary of using the arrow keys to move to the next cell. A better approach is first to select the range. Then you can use the Enter key to end each entry, and the cell pointer automatically moves to the next cell. Selecting the range is not only faster, but also saves wear and tear on your arrow keys. Theory has it that overusing your arrow keys causes the tips of the arrows to fall off.

### 7. 1-2-3 for Windows has more @functions than you ever need.

If you ever have a few spare minutes (like when you're put on hold during a telephone call), you may find it interesting to browse through the @function list. I guarantee you'll find something that you can use. The little @ icon on the edit line is one of the handiest tools in 1-2-3 for Windows. This icon can insert an @function into your formula — and it also tells you exactly what arguments it needs. And don't forget that you can click the **?** icon in the @Function List dialog box to get help on the selected @function.

### 8. The on-line help system is very comprehensive.

If you get stuck, your first course of action should be to press F1, the express route to the on-line help system. 1-2-3 for Windows' on-line help has a great deal of information and also has examples. And don't overlook the Help⇨Tutorial command — it's a good way to kill some time and maybe even learn something in the process.

### 9. Hard disks crash for no apparent reason.

With all the computers out there, you need to know that hard disks crash thousands of times a day. People turn on their computers, and DOS reports that it can't recognize the hard disks — in other words, everything stored on the hard disks is gone! Kaplooey! You can reinstall the software, but all the data files (including your 1-2-3 for Windows worksheets) are pushing up daisies. This, of course, will never happen to you, because either you are extremely lucky or you have taken the advice that I offer in several places throughout this book: *make a backup copy of your worksheet files on a floppy disk!*

### 10. The more you use 1-2-3 for Windows, the easier it gets.

I can understand how new users may be overwhelmed and intimidated by this program — it can do many things and has tons of commands. But just wait, you soon will be very comfortable with the commands that you use frequently. And as your comfort level increases, you'll find yourself wondering what some of those other commands can do. Before you even realize what's happening, you progress from being a beginning user to feeling very comfortable in the 1-2-3 environment. And you'll owe it all to this book...

# Chapter 23

# The Ten Commandments
# of 1-2-3 for Windows

*"I've been told that since the beginning of civilization, millions and millions of laws have not improved on the Ten Commandments one bit."*

Ronald W. Reagan (b. 1911)
40th President of the United States

ere, direct from a sellout engagement at beautiful Mount Sinai, are the Ten Commandments of 1-2-3 for Windows.

## I: Thou Shalt Always Maketh Backup Copies

Make backup copies, on a floppy disk, of every important file and store the disks in a safe place.

## II: Thou Shalt Check Thy Work Carefully

Check and double-check your work before making important decisions based on a 1-2-3 for Windows worksheet. It's all too easy to entereth an incorrect formula.

## III: Remember Thy Right Mouse Button

The right mouse button is invaluable — keep it holy.

# IV: Thou Shalt Not Take the Name of Bill Gates in Vain

Bill Gates, chairman and CEO of Microsoft Corporation, is a cult god to some. But if you are a true *Lotustian,* this commandment does not apply to you.

# V: Honor Thy SmartIcons and Shortcut Keys

Without these time-saving wonders, you would be a mere notebook page in the world of electronic spreadsheets.

# VI: Thou Shalt Not Copyeth the Program from Others

Get your own, licensed copy of 1-2-3 for Windows. You'll be privy to insiders information, a cool yellow box, and the gripping and poetic user's guide. And, you'll be able to sleep at night.

# VII: Save Thy File Beforeth Taking Drastic Measures

Remember that it takes only a few seconds to save your file, but hours and hours to re-create it if something were to go awry.

# VIII: Thou Shalt Enable Undo and Use It Daily

The Undo command can reverse the effects of about any action you take. To make sure that Undo is enabled, select the Tools⇨User Setup command. Make sure that the Undo option is checked; otherwise, Undo does not work.

# IX: Thou Shalt Consult Thy Local Guru with Matters of Importance

Don't be afraid to ask someone else — hopefully someone well versed in 1-2-3 for Windows. Chances are, if you have a problem, someone else has had that same problem.

# X: Thou Shalt Feareth Not to Experiment

Just remember Commandment VII. Save your work first!!

# Part VI
# Appendixes

# In this part...

**W**hat's a computer book without appendixes? Here, you'll find two of them: one covers installing 1-2-3 for Windows and one is a wonderful glossary full of weird and helpful terms you're likely to encounter in this book as well as when you are standing by the water cooler.

# Appendix A
# If You Gotta Install It Yourself

*"Many a time…from a bad beginning great friendships have sprung up."*

Terence (c. 186 – 159 B.C.)
Roman dramatist

● ● ● ● ● ● ● ● ● ● ● ● ● ● ● ● ● ● ● ● ● ● ● ● ● ● ● ● ● ● ● ● ● ● ● ● ● ● ● ● ● ● ●

*B*efore you can use 1-2-3 for Windows — or any software, for that matter —
you must install the software on your computer. When you install
software, you simply copy files from floppy disks to your hard disk in such a
way that the program works after you execute it. Most software (including 1-2-3
for Windows) includes a special Install program that automatically installs the
program for you.

If you're lucky, 1-2-3 for Windows is already installed on the computer that you
are using. (In most large companies, there are whole departments full of
computer wizards who specialize in these types of magical tasks.) If you are on
your own, you usually can find some sort of computer guru who is happy to
help you out (and at the same time demonstrate just how smart he or she is).

## For Do-It-Yourself Types

If you're sitting at your computer and holding a shrink-wrapped box that
contains 1-2-3 for Windows, you're probably going to have to install the sucker
yourself. If you've never installed a program before, don't be afraid to ask for
help from someone more experienced. However, installing 1-2-3 for Windows is
not a difficult process, if you can follow simple instructions and know how to
insert a floppy disk into a disk drive (skills that most 20th century people have).
If 1-2-3 for Windows is already installed, you can skip this appendix — unless
you thrive on redundancy redundancy redundancy.

## Preflight Checkout

If someone has assured you that your machine is ready for 1-2-3 for Windows to
be installed, you can skip this section. Otherwise, check out the following
details before you install 1-2-3 for Windows:

✔ **Make sure that Microsoft Windows is installed on your system.** 1-2-3 for Windows needs Microsoft Windows 3.0 or 3.1, a separate software program that is *not* included in your 1-2-3 for Windows package. You must purchase Microsoft Windows separately, and it must be installed on your computer before you attempt to install 1-2-3 for Windows.

To see whether Windows is installed on your system, type **WIN** at the DOS prompt. If you see a colorful Windows logo screen, you're in luck. If DOS spits back its Bad command or file name message, Windows is not installed (sorry 'bout that).

✔ **Make sure that you have the right equipment.** 1-2-3 for Windows requires a fairly fast computer. A system with an 80386 or 80486 processor is good. If your system uses an 80286 processor, you can still install 1-2-3 for Windows, but you'll have to be extremely patient. You also need at least four megabytes of random access memory (RAM). If your system is capable of running Microsoft Windows (and you have enough RAM), it can run 1-2-3 for Windows. Technically, 1-2-3 for Windows doesn't require a mouse, but I strongly suggest that you have one, especially if you want to use the SmartIcons.

✔ **Make sure that you have the correct disk drive to handle the 1-2-3 for Windows disks.** Some software packages include both 5 1/4- and 3 1/2-inch disks; other packages include only one size or the other. Make sure that you have a disk drive that can handle the disks in your 1-2-3 for Windows box. If not, call Lotus at (800) 343-5414 (U.S. only), and Lotus will send you the correct disks. Or you can get someone with both size floppy drives to copy the disks to the format that your system uses.

✔ **Make sure that you have enough room on your hard disk to hold the program and its files.** To install the complete 1-2-3 for Windows program, you need about 13 megabytes of free disk space (or 13,000 kilobytes).

If you don't have enough free disk space, the Install program warns you of this fact. If you encounter this warning, you need to delete some unnecessary files before you can install 1-2-3 for Windows. Or you can choose not to install some of the components of the program. But unless you have good reasons to do otherwise, I recommend that you free up some disk space and install the complete package.

If you don't know what you're doing, I strongly suggest that you seek assistance before deleting files. Otherwise, you may delete files that your system needs to work properly.

# Installing 1-2-3 for Windows

To install 1-2-3 for Windows, follow these steps:

1. **Turn on your computer.**

2. **If your computer does not start Microsoft Windows automatically, type WIN at the DOS prompt.**

   The Windows Program Manager screen appears. If your system is set up to run some other third-party Windows menu program instead of the Program Manager, you should consult that program's documentation to determine how to execute the Install program from a floppy disk.

3. **Tear the shrink wrap off the 1-2-3 for Windows box and open the box.**

   (The packaging is terrible, but all Lotus products are like this.) Dig around until you find the disks. Tear the shrink wrap off the disks (software companies just love shrink wrap) and find the disk labeled *Disk 1 Install*.

4. **Insert Disk 1 in your disk drive.**

5. **From the Windows Program Manager menu, select the File command with your mouse by clicking File.**

   The drop-down menu in Figure A-1 appears.

6. **Select the Run command.**

   The dialog box in Figure A-2 appears.

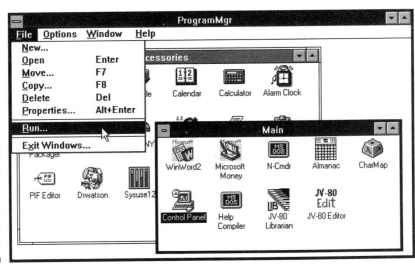

**Figure A-1:**
The File command in the Program Manager screen.

**Figure A-2:**
The Run
dialog box,
where you
type install.

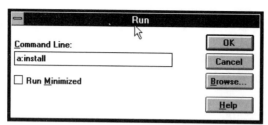

7. **Type** a:install **if you're installing the program from drive A.**

   Type **b:install** if you're using drive B.

8. **Press Enter (or click the OK button).**

9. **Follow the instructions on-screen.**

   You are asked whether you want to install the complete program or do a custom installation. I suggest that you install the complete program (unless you're really short on hard disk space).

You may be asked some questions during installation. I strongly suggest that you simply accept the default options. This is the safest approach.

# How much disk space is left?

To see how much disk space you have, you can run the Windows File Manager program. You can find its icon, which looks like the icon in the accompanying figure, in one of your Windows Program Manager program groups. Just double-click this icon to get to the Windows File Manager program.

File Manager

In File Manager, click the icon that corresponds to the drive that you'll be using to do the installation (usually drive C:). The status line shows you how much disk space is remaining on that drive. The number that appears on the status line at the bottom of the File Manager window tells you how much disk space is left in the drive you have selected. Drive C in the File Manager figure has 38,312K (kilobytes) available. One kilobyte is 1,000 bytes.

Status line

If you find the installation instructions confusing, refer to the 1-2-3 for Windows manual. It tells you everything that you need to know (and more). Or you can recruit your favorite computer guru, who will happily install the program for you.

After installation is complete, you return to the Program Manager screen. If you accept the defaults during installation, 1-2-3 for Windows is installed in the *Lotus Applications* program group. Chapter 2 explains how to start 1-2-3 for Windows, but I suggest that you begin with Chapter 1 for some background information.

# Appendix B
# Glossary

*"I hate definitions."*

Benjamin Disraeli (1804 – 1881)
Former Prime Minister of England
From *Vivian Grey* [1826], bk. II, ch. 6

• • • • • • • • • • • • • • • • • • • • • • • • • • • • • • • • • • • • • • • • • • • • • • •

This glossary contains terms that you may encounter while using 1-2-3 for Windows, reading this book, or listening to people talk about computers. Although it does not substitute for a real computer dictionary (try the *Illustrated Computer Dictionary For Dummies*), you may find that it contains enough terms so you can hold your own at the water cooler.

## A

### @function
A special process (preceded by an "at" sign) that performs some calculation for you in a formula. 1-2-3 for Windows has hundreds of @functions, some that are very useful to real people, and others that are designed for scientists and mathematicians. Most @functions use arguments. (See also *formula.*)

### absolute cell reference
A cell reference in a formula that always refers to a specific cell (as opposed to a *relative cell reference*). After the formula is copied to another cell, it still refers to the original cell. Use dollar signs to specify an absolute cell reference (for example, $A$1). (See also *relative cell reference.*)

### active cell
The cell in a worksheet that's ready to receive input from you. The contents of the active cell appear in the edit line. (See also *cell, edit line,* and *worksheet.*)

### active worksheet
The worksheet file that you're currently working on. You can have several worksheet files in memory, but only one of them can be the active worksheet file. The active worksheet's title bar is a different color than the title bar in the other windows. (See also *worksheet.*)

### address
The way you refer to a cell. Every cell has its own address (some are on the wrong side of the tracks). An address consists of a sheet letter, a colon, a column letter, and a row number (the sheet letter is optional — if you omit it, also omit the colon). Here are some examples of addresses: A:C4, C:Z12, A1, and K9 — also known as the dog cell. (See also *cell reference.*)

### arguments
The information you provide that gives the details for a particular @function or macro command. For an @function, the arguments are in parentheses, separated by commas. For a macro command, the arguments follow the macro command name, separated by commas. (See also *macro.*)

## ASCII file
See *text file*.

## auditing
The process of checking your worksheet for errors. The Tools⇨Audit command provides some assistance with this process. Believe me, this is the best audit you'll ever have.

# B

## backsolving
Also known as *goal seeking*. This is the process of letting 1-2-3 for Windows determine the value of a cell that gives you a desired result in a cell that has a formula.

## backup
An extra copy of a file, which is usually stored on some other disk. It's a good idea to make a backup copy of every important file and to keep the backup copy on a floppy disk. That way, if you turn on your computer and discover that your hard disk died during the night, it won't ruin your whole day (just your morning).

## borders
The different type of line you can put around a cell or range. You have a good choice of border types, and you even can specify different colors and thicknesses. (See also *range*.)

## Borland International
This software company makes Quattro Pro, Quattro Pro for Windows, and several programming languages and database products. One of the industry's favorite success stories, Borland started with virtually nothing but is now one of the top international software companies.

## bubble help
The term for the balloon-like text that appears when you hold the mouse pointer over a SmartIcon for about one second. This tells you what the SmartIcon is good for. Release 4 users must be content to right-click a SmartIcon to learn its reason for existence.

## bug
To bother, or pester. This is what you do to the office guru when you need his or her help. This term also refers to a software problem that causes strange things to happen, or can crash your system.

## button
A rectangular box, usually found in a dialog box, that causes something to happen after you click it with your mouse. You also can put a button directly on a worksheet and attach a macro to it.

## byte
The amount of memory or disk space needed to store one character, such as a letter or number. (See also *memory*.)

# C

## callipygian
Having nicely proportioned buttocks.

## CD-ROM
CD-ROM (an acronym for Compact Disc Read-Only Memory) is rapidly gaining popularity as a method to store information. This technology requires a special drive, and it uses CDs that look exactly like audio CDs. These discs can hold massive amounts of information — the equivalent of about 300,000 typewritten pages (three stories tall). Unlike hard and floppy disks, however,

you cannot write information to CDs. Once you buy one, you cannot change anything on it. Also, CD-ROM is _much_ slower than normal disks.

### cell
The basic building block of life. Also, the intersection of a row and a column in a worksheet. A cell can hold a value, a label, a formula, a prisoner, or nothing at all. (See also _formula_ and _label._)

### cell pointer
A heavy outline that lets you know which cell in the worksheet you selected. You can move the cell pointer by pressing the cursor movement keys or by clicking another cell with your mouse.

### cell reference
Identifies a cell by giving its column letter and row number. For example, C5 refers to the cell at the intersection of column C and row 5. If you refer to a cell on a different sheet, you need to tack on a sheet letter before the cell reference. For example, B:C5 refers to the cell at the intersection of column C and row 5 on the second sheet (B). You can have relative cell references (most common) or absolute cell references. (See also _absolute cell reference_ and _relative cell reference._)

### central processing unit
Your computer's _central processing unit_ (CPU) is located on the motherboard. The CPU is your computer's brain and determines how fast and powerful your computer is. Your CPU is probably made by Intel and labeled 80386 or 80486. (See also _motherboard._)

### cereal port
The wharf where Cheerios and Cap'n Crunch are unloaded. (See also _serial port._)

### chart
A graphic representation of a range of values in a worksheet. Charts (or graphs) are stored on the draw layer of a worksheet. 1-2-3 for Windows has many different chart types — probably more than you'll ever need.

### check box
In a dialog box, an option that can be turned either on or off by clicking the mouse (not the same as a radio or option button). You can activate more than one check box at a time.

### Cheetos
Bits of a puffed-up orange processed cheese-like food that are effective bribes for getting computer gurus to help you do things on your computer. If Cheetos don't work, splurge for a large pepperoni pizza (extra cheese).

### circular reference
An error condition in which the result of a formula depends on the formula itself (either directly or indirectly). For example, if you put @SUM(A1..A10) in cell A10, the formula refers to its own cell — a circular reference. If your worksheet has a formula with a circular reference, you see CIRC displayed in the status bar. (See also _formula._)

### click
To press and release the left mouse button. (See also _right-click._)

### clip art
An image stored in a file that can be used by various software (including 1-2-3 for Windows). There are thousands and thousands of clip art files available, which you can use freely in your work.

### Clipboard

An area of memory managed by Windows that stores information (usually to be pasted somewhere else). You can put information on the Clipboard with the Edit⇨Copy command or the Edit⇨Paste command.

### collection

A group of noncontiguous cells, ranges, stamps, or baseball cards. You can select a collection by holding down the Ctrl key while you select the cells or ranges that you want. (See also *range.*)

### column

A vertical group of 8,192 cells in a worksheet. Columns are identified by letters. (See also *row.*)

### command

What your wish is to me. Also, an order that you give to 1-2-3 for Windows by using the menu system, a SmartIcon, or a shortcut key. (See also *SmartIcon.*)

### crash

The term for what happens when your computer stops working for no apparent reason. If you're running Windows, you'll get a message that tells you there's been a serious error, and asks you if you want to continue or ignore it. Ignoring it never does any good, so you may as well kiss your work good-bye. This is a good reason to save your work often. Usually, a system crash is the result of a software bug. (See also *bug.*)

### cursor movement keys

The keys on your keyboard that cause the cell pointer to move, such as the arrow keys and the Home, End, PgUp, and PgDn keys.

# D

### database

An organized list made up of records (rows) and fields within records (columns). You can work with a database by performing a query or by sorting. (See also *list.*)

### default

Settings that come automatically with a computer program, designed to include the most popular choices that people make. If you don't specify some options, your work looks the way it does because of its default settings. (For example, the default type size may be 12 points.) When something goes wrong, you can always say, "It's not my fault. It's default of the software."

### dialog box

A box that pops up after you have chosen a command and lets you make even more choices. After you make the choices, you close the dialog box by clicking the OK button. If you change your mind or if you want to undo any change you make in the dialog box, simply click the Cancel button.

### disks

Every computer has at least one disk drive. Most computers have at least two, and many computers have three. There are two types of disks: *hard disks* and *floppy disks.* Both types store information as a series of magnetic impulses. (See also *floppy disk* and *hard disk.*)

### double-click

To click the left mouse button twice in rapid succession.

### Dove soap
See *mouse.*

### drag-and-drop
To use the mouse to grab an item, move it, and drop it somewhere else. You can use drag-and-drop to move a cell, a range, or a graphic object.

### draw layer
The invisible layer on top of every 1-2-3 for Windows worksheet that holds charts and drawn objects.

### drawing tools
SmartIcons that let you draw or manipulate graphic objects on the draw layer. (See also *draw layer.*)

### drop-down listbox
In a dialog box, a listbox that normally shows only one option but has an arrow next to it, indicating that there are more options available. If you click the arrow, the listbox drops down to show more options.

### DumbIcon
A SmartIcon that doesn't do what you thought it would do.

# E

### edit line
The line at the top of the 1-2-3 for Windows screen that shows the address of the active cell. The contents of the active cell also appear in the edit line. (See also *active cell.*)

### endless loop
See *infinite loop.*

### Enya
A female singer/musician from Ireland. Practically everybody likes her music, and it sounds particularly good when you're writing computer books.

### expansion cards
Your computer probably has several expansion cards. These cards stick out of the back of your computer and often have jacks into which you plug wires and cords. Some expansion cards are necessary for the computer to operate (for example, video cards), and some give it added power (such as sound cards). You probably have at least one expansion card that supplies your system with serial and parallel ports to connect a modem, printer, or some other device. (See also *modem* and *port.*)

### extension
The part of a file's name that follows the period. For a file named BUDGET.WK4, .WK4 is the extension. Usually, a filename's extension tells you what type of file it is (files created by 1-2-3 for Windows have a .WK4 extension).

# F

### field
In a database, this is a column that holds a particular part of a record. In the country, this is a bunch of dirt with crops coming out of it. (See also *record.*)

### file
An entity stored on a disk. A 1-2-3 for Windows worksheet, for example, is stored in a file that has a .WK4 extension on the filename. This is used also to help prisoners escape from a cell.

### floppy disk

*Floppy disks* are removable disks (used for memory storage) and come in two sizes: 3½-inch and 5¼-inch. Contrary to popular belief, 3½-inch disks are not floppy; they have a sturdy, plastic case. The smaller floppies can store either 740K (double density) or 1.44MB (high density), and the larger ones store either 360K (double density) or 1.2MB (high density). Your primary floppy disk drive is known as drive A. If you have another floppy drive, it's called drive B.

### font

The combination of a typeface and a type size.

### formatting

The process of changing the way your information looks. You can have two general types of formatting: numeric formatting and stylistic formatting. (See also *numeric formatting* and *stylistic formatting*.)

### formula

Information that you put into a cell that performs a calculation. A formula can use the results of other cells in its calculation, and it also can use @functions.

### frozen titles

The process of keeping certain top rows or left columns always displayed, no matter where the cell pointer is. You can freeze titles by using the View⇨Freeze Titles command.

### frozen tykes

The neighbor's cute little children, after spending four hours sledding outside in Michigan in February.

### function

See *@function*.

# G

### graph

See *chart*.

### graphic object

Something that you draw on the draw layer of a worksheet. You can move and resize these graphic objects. (See also *draw layer*.)

### group mode

Setting things up so that when you format one sheet in a worksheet, all other sheets in the file are formatted at the same time. You turn group mode on and off using the Style⇨Worksheet Defaults command.

### guru

Someone who appears to know everything there is to know about computers and software. (See also *Cheetos*.)

# H

### handles

The little square objects at the corners and on the sides of graphic objects that you can drag with a mouse to change the size of the graphic object. Also, the names truck drivers give to themselves when they talk on CB radios.

## *hard disk*

A *hard disk* is fixed inside your computer, and normally you can't remove it — although there is such a thing as a removable hard disk. Hard disks store a large amount of information, and they transfer the information quickly. Hard disks come in a variety of sizes, from 40MB up to a gigabyte or more. Your hard disk is known usually as drive C. You can have more than one hard disk in a PC, and a single hard disk can be partitioned so that it appears as more than one disk.

# *I*

## *IBM*

If you've never heard of IBM, you probably just arrived from the planet Zordox. IBM has always been known as *the* computer company. It started out by making big, expensive mainframes and then developed the IBM PC. Other companies soon copied its PC, and many people think the clones are better than the original. In practically every case, clones are much cheaper than real IBMs. IBM recently posted an $8 billion (yes, *billion*) loss and is in the process of big layoffs. And most people still think IBM PCs are way over-priced, except for the ValuePoint line.

## *infinite loop*

See *endless loop.*

## *insertion point*

The position where new text is inserted when you're editing the contents of a cell. You can tell the insertion point, because the cursor looks like a vertical bar.

## *installation*

The process of copying the files needed by 1-2-3 for Windows from floppy disks to your hard disk. (See Appendix A.)

# *J*

## *John Walkenbach*

The author of this book. (See also *guru.*)

# *K*

## *keyboard*

You give information to your software through the keyboard. There are a number of different keyboard layouts available, and most people don't really give much thought to which one they choose. Keyboards feel different; some people prefer clicky keys, while others like a more mushy feel. Pianos also have keyboards, but most of them don't have a Ctrl key.

## *kilobytes*

A kilobyte is 1000 bytes and is normally abbreviated as KB or K. Used as a measure of storage capacity of disks and memory. 1K of memory stores about 1,024 characters. (See also *memory.*)

# *L*

## *label*

A bunch of letters (and even numbers) that you put into a cell, basically to provide information about your worksheet or other cells.

A label is not a value and it's not a formula, but it's handy to have in your worksheet for clarity.

### laptop computers

Laptop computers (also called *notebooks*) come with all different types of processors. Their diminutive size sets them apart from standard desktop computers and makes them convenient for people who travel a great deal. Notebooks usually run on batteries, and people on planes like to show them off. Although notebooks have become very powerful over the years, they're much more expensive than equally powerful desktop models.

### law suit

A common activity among the lawyers at software companies. This gives the lawyers justification for their six-figure salaries.

### list

A collection of items, each of which is stored in a separate row. Each item may have more than one part (that is, use more than one column). The order of the items may or may not be important. (See also *database.*)

### listbox

A list you find in a dialog box that displays a group of options from which you can choose.

### Lotus Development Corporation

Lotus created the original 1-2-3 about a decade ago. Although 1-2-3 wasn't the first spreadsheet for PCs, it was great in its time and became one of the most successful software products ever. The original version of 1-2-3 for Windows is no longer anything to write home about, but Release 4 and Release 5 of this product are great (as you should know by now).

# M

### macro

A series of special commands that 1-2-3 for Windows can process automatically upon command. You can write macro commands directly or you can record them while you make them with the Macro Recorder that comes with 1-2-3 for Windows.

### map

A representation of a geographic area. 1-2-3 for Windows Release 5 can generate maps using labels and numbers stored in your worksheet.

### math coprocessor

Some computers (notably 80286s and 80386s) have a chip on their motherboard known as a math coprocessor. This chip speeds up mathematical operations a great deal and can make spreadsheets like 1-2-3 for Windows recalculate results faster than lightning (reducing your coffee break time considerably). If your computer is an 80486, a math coprocessor is built into the CPU. If you find yourself waiting for large spread-sheets to recalculate, you might consider popping one of these puppies into your PC. (See also *motherboard.*)

### Maximize button

The up-arrow button on the title bar of a window that makes the window as large as it can be after you click it with your mouse. If the window is already maximized, this button is replaced with a different button (a Restore button), which returns the window to its previous size. (See also *Minimize button* and *Restore button.*)

## memory

Every computer has memory, which usually ranges from 640K to 8 or more megabytes. 640K of memory is roughly equivalent to 640,000 characters. Eight megabytes works out to about 8 million characters. The more memory your computer has, the better off you are.

The three types of memory are

- **Conventional memory.** Normal memory, also known as the lower 640K.

- **Extended memory.** Memory above 640K, used by Windows and some non-Windows programs.

- **Expanded memory.** Special memory above 640K used by some non-Windows programs, such as 1-2-3 for DOS.

---

## Ks, megs, and Gbytes

You can't be around computers for long without learning new measurement units. Computer memory and disk storage come in different capacities. Here's the lowdown:

| Unit | What It Means |
|---|---|
| Bit | The smallest unit of computer measurement. A bit is either on (1) or off (0) |
| Byte | Eight bits |
| Kilobyte | 1000 bytes (abbreviated as K) |
| Megabyte | A million bytes, or 1000K (abbreviated as MB) |
| Gigabyte | A billion bytes, or 1000MB (abbreviated as Gbyte or GB) |

---

## menu bar

The group of words at the top of the 1-2-3 for Windows screen (File, Edit, and so on). After you select one of these words, the menu drops down to display commands.

## Microsoft

The mother of all software companies. It makes MS-DOS, Windows, Excel, Word for Windows, and many other popular software programs. Some people think Microsoft has an unfair advantage because it created DOS and Windows — which everyone has to use to develop new software. As you might expect, Microsoft is sued frequently. The company's CEO, Bill Gates, is the richest man in the United States.

## Minimize button

The down-arrow button on the title bar of a window that turns the window into an icon after you click it with your mouse. (See also *Maximize button.*)

## mode indicator

The word at the right corner of the status bar that tells you what mode 1-2-3 for Windows is currently in. (See also *status bar.*)

## modem

The device used to communicate directly with other computers. A modem connects your PC (via a serial port) to a normal phone line and (if you're lucky) makes a connection with another computer that has a modem. If you want to call computer bulletin board systems, connect to on-line services such as CompuServe or Prodigy, or send and receive faxes, you need a modem. (See also *serial port.*)

### monitor
The hardware device that displays information that your software wants you to see. There are many types and sizes of monitors, and they vary in resolution. Your monitor works in conjunction with your video card, and the combination determines how the information looks on-screen. Today, the standard monitor is VGA (640 pixels wide x 480 pixels high), although SuperVGA (800 x 600) is quite common also. (See also *resolution*.)

### motherboard
A printed circuit board with a bunch of electronic-looking gizmos sticking out that sits at the bottom of the inside of your computer. It contains all the circuitry that makes a computer a computer. The motherboard also contains chips that hold your computer's memory and a number of slots. Some of these slots should hold expansion cards, and some should be empty. (See also *central processing unit, expansion cards*.)

### mouse
The device connected to your computer that looks like a bar of Dove soap.

### mouse pointer
A representation of the mouse on-screen. Normally, the mouse pointer is an arrow, but it often changes shape to let you know that you can do certain things.

### multisheet worksheet
A 1-2-3 for Windows file that has more than one sheet in it. You insert new sheets by clicking the New Sheet button.

### named range
A range of cells (or even a single cell) that has been given a meaningful name. Naming cells and ranges makes using them easier in formulas and makes the formulas more readable. Use the Range⇨Name command to name the cell or range.

### numeric formatting
The process of changing the way a number looks when it's displayed in a cell (for example, displaying a number with a percent sign). Changing the numeric formatting does not affect the value in any way — it just affects its appearance.

### option button
In a dialog box, a group of buttons from which only one can be selected at any time (also known as a radio button).

### pain
That unpleasant sensation you experienced when Howard, your clumsy coworker, dropped the laser printer on your foot. Frequently accompanied by screams of horror and profanities.

### pane
One of two parts of a worksheet window that has been split with the View⇨Split command. Splitting a screen into panes lets you see and work with two different parts of a worksheet without having to do a great deal of scrolling around. (See also *window.*)

### parallel port
A part of your computer that sends and receives information in several different (parallel) streams. This process allows for faster communication. Printers usually use parallel ports. (See also *ports* and *serial port.*)

### paste
To copy an item that has been stored on the Windows Clipboard into a worksheet or chart. You can paste a cell, a range, a chart, or a graphic object (but it must be copied to the Clipboard first). (See also *Clipboard.*)

### pointing
The process of selecting a range by using either the keyboard or the mouse. When you need to indicate a cell or range address, you either can enter it directly or point to it by selecting cells with your mouse or highlighting cells using the keyboard.

### ports
The means by which computers communicate with external devices (such as printers, modems, and mice). There are two types of ports: serial ports and parallel ports. (See also *parallel port* and *serial port.*)

### preview
To see on-screen how your worksheet will look after it's printed. Use the File⇨Print Preview command to do this. Also, what movie theaters force you to sit through so you'll buy more popcorn.

### printer
That device that spits out paper with black stuff on it.

### Program Manager
The Windows program that organizes your other programs — it's the one with all the cute icons. Normally, Program Manager appears when you start Microsoft Windows.

### query
The process of locating specific records in a database. You can specify the exact criteria that you want. (See also *database* and *record.*)

### quick menu
The menu that appears when you right-click the mouse after an item is selected. Most of the time, you find the command that you need here.

### radio button
See *option button.*

### random access memory (RAM)
A type of memory that can be written to and read from; commonly referring to the internal memory of your computer. The random means that any one location can be read at any time; it's not necessary to read all of the memory to find one location. (See also *memory.*)

### range

Where the deer and the antelope play. Also two or more contiguous cells. (See also *cell* and *collection.*)

### recalculation

The process of evaluating all of the formulas in a worksheet. Normally, this is all done automatically. If your worksheet is in manual recalc mode, however, you have to specify when to recalculate (by pressing F9).

### record

One unit (row) of a database that's comprised of fields (columns). It is also an obsolete (albeit nostalgic) method of storing music. (See also *database* and *field.*)

### relative cell preference

The decision you must make on visiting day at San Quentin. Should you go see Uncle Ned or Cousin Chuck?

### relative cell reference

A normal cell reference in a formula. If the formula is copied to another cell, the cell references adjust automatically to refer to cells in their new surroundings. (See also *absolute cell reference* and *cell.*)

### resolution

What you make on New Year's eve and forget about by January 3rd. This term also refers to the number of pixels a monitor has. The more pixels, the higher the resolution, and the higher the resolution, the better the picture.

### Restore button

On a maximized window, the dual-arrow button on the title bar that returns the window to its previous size. (See also *Maximize button.*)

### right-click

To press and release the right mouse button. In 1-2-3 for Windows, right-clicking displays a quick menu that's relevant to whatever you have selected at the time. Some people refer to this as squeezing the mouse's right ear.

### row

A horizontal group of 256 cells. Rows are identified by numbers. (See also *column.*)

# S

### scroll bar

Not your neighborhood pub, but one of two bars (either the *vertical* or *horizontal scroll bar*) on the worksheet window that enables you to scroll through the worksheet quickly by using the mouse.

### selection

The cell, range, collection, chart, or graphic object that is affected by the command you choose.

### serial port

A computer device that sends and receives information in a single stream of bits. These ports are sometimes known as COM ports. Modems, mice, and some printers use serial ports. (See also *ports* and *parallel port.*)

### sheet

One of 256 possible sheets in a multisheet worksheet. You add a new sheet to a worksheet with the Edit⇨Insert command, or by clicking the New Sheet button. (See also *multisheet worksheet.*)

### shortcut key
A Ctrl+key combination (such as Ctrl+C) that is a shortcut for a command.

### SmartIcon
One of the buttons (or elements) on a SmartIcon palette that is usually a quicker way of issuing a menu command when clicked.

### SmartIcon palette
A collection of SmartIcons on a toolbar of sorts. There are eight of these included with 1-2-3 for Windows.

### SmartMasters
Ready-made worksheet templates are provided with 1-2-3 for Windows Release 5. These templates are available for common spreadsheet tasks and can save you lots of time and effort — and they don't contain any mistakes!

### sorting
The process of rearranging the rows of a range by using one or more columns in the range as the sort key. Use the Range⇨Sort command.

### sound cards
A device that is inserted into a slot on your motherboard, and is capable of generating much better sound than the normal tinny speaker. (See also *motherboard.*)

### spreadsheet
The generic word for a worksheet file or for such a program as 1-2-3 for Windows.

### status bar
The line at the bottom of the 1-2-3 for Windows screen that shows the status of several items in the program or on-screen. You also can use the status bar to quickly change the font, type size, numeric format, or number of decimal places displayed.

### stylistic formatting
The process of changing the appearance of cells and ranges, which involves changing colors, modifying type sizes and fonts, and adding borders.

# T

### tab
What you hope your friend picks up when you go out to dinner. In a multisheet worksheet, it's the item that displays the sheet letter (or the name you gave to the sheet by double-clicking it). To activate another sheet, click its tab.

### text box
In a dialog box, a small box in which you type letters or words.

### text file
A generic computer file that holds information, but no special formatting commands. Most programs (including 1-2-3 for Windows) can read and write text files.

### title bar
The colored bar at the top of every window. You can move a nonmaximized window by dragging its title bar with the mouse.

# U

### undo
To reverse the effects of the last command. Use the Edit⇨Undo command (or Ctrl+Z).

# V

### value
A number entered into a cell.

### Version Manager
A feature that enables you to keep track of different scenarios in a worksheet. Access this feature with the Range⇨Version command.

# W

### window
Where a worksheet is displayed or held. 1-2-3 for Windows is also a window — a window that holds other windows. (See also *Windows*.)

### Windows
The software product made by Microsoft which runs *over* DOS. This product is required to run 1-2-3 for Windows.

### WITTGOOHOT
An acronym for "Whatever It Takes To Get Out Of Here On Time." People often use this term when it's getting close to quitting time.

### worksheet
Where your cells are stored. A worksheet appears in a window and is stored in a file.

### worksheet file
See *worksheet*.

### WYSIWYG
An acronym for "What You See Is What You Get." This acronym refers to the fact that the formatting you perform on-screen also applies to what is printed.

# X

### x-ray
The only word I could think of that starts with an *x*.

# Z

### zoom
The process of changing the size of the information displayed in a worksheet. You can zoom in (with View⇨Zoom In) to enlarge the on-screen display or zoom out (with View⇨Zoom Out) to minimize the on-screen display.

# Index

# Notes

# Notes

# Notes

# Notes

# Notes

# Notes

# Notes

# Notes

# Notes

# Notes

# Notes

# Notes

# The Fun & Easy Way™ to learn about computers and more!

## Here's a complete listing of IDG Books' ...For Dummies® titles

| Title | Author | ISBN | Price |
|---|---|---|---|
| **DATABASE** | | | |
| Access 2 For Dummies® | by Scott Palmer | ISBN: 1-56884-090-X | $19.95 USA/$26.95 Canada |
| Access Programming For Dummies® | by Rob Krumm | ISBN: 1-56884-091-8 | $19.95 USA/$26.95 Canada |
| Approach 3 For Windows® For Dummies® | by Doug Lowe | ISBN: 1-56884-233-3 | $19.99 USA/$26.99 Canada |
| dBASE For DOS For Dummies® | by Scott Palmer & Michael Stabler | ISBN: 1-56884-188-4 | $19.95 USA/$26.95 Canada |
| dBASE For Windows® For Dummies® | by Scott Palmer | ISBN: 1-56884-179-5 | $19.95 USA/$26.95 Canada |
| dBASE 5 For Windows® Programming For Dummies® | by Ted Coombs & Jason Coombs | ISBN: 1-56884-215-5 | $19.99 USA/$26.99 Canada |
| FoxPro 2.6 For Windows® For Dummies® | by John Kaufeld | ISBN: 1-56884-187-6 | $19.95 USA/$26.95 Canada |
| Paradox 5 For Windows® For Dummies® | by John Kaufeld | ISBN: 1-56884-185-X | $19.95 USA/$26.95 Canada |
| **DESKTOP PUBLISHING/ILLUSTRATION/GRAPHICS** | | | |
| CorelDRAW! 5 For Dummies® | by Deke McClelland | ISBN: 1-56884-157-4 | $19.95 USA/$26.95 Canada |
| CorelDRAW! For Dummies® | by Deke McClelland | ISBN: 1-56884-042-X | $19.95 USA/$26.95 Canada |
| Desktop Publishing & Design For Dummies® | by Roger C. Parker | ISBN: 1-56884-234-1 | $19.99 USA/$26.99 Canada |
| Harvard Graphics 2 For Windows® For Dummies® | by Roger C. Parker | ISBN: 1-56884-092-6 | $19.95 USA/$26.95 Canada |
| PageMaker 5 For Macs® For Dummies® | by Galen Gruman & Deke McClelland | ISBN: 1-56884-178-7 | $19.95 USA/$26.95 Canada |
| PageMaker 5 For Windows® For Dummies® | by Deke McClelland & Galen Gruman | ISBN: 1-56884-160-4 | $19.95 USA/$26.95 Canada |
| Photoshop 3 For Macs® For Dummies® | by Deke McClelland | ISBN: 1-56884-208-2 | $19.99 USA/$26.99 Canada |
| QuarkXPress 3.3 For Dummies® | by Galen Gruman & Barbara Assadi | ISBN: 1-56884-217-1 | $19.99 USA/$26.99 Canada |
| **FINANCE/PERSONAL FINANCE/TEST TAKING REFERENCE** | | | |
| Everyday Math For Dummies™ | by Charles Seiter | ISBN: 1-56884-248-1 | $14.99 USA/$22.99 Canada |
| Personal Finance For Dummies™ For Canadians | by Eric Tyson & Tony Martin | ISBN: 1-56884-378-X | $18.99 USA/$24.99 Canada |
| QuickBooks 3 For Dummies® | by Stephen L. Nelson | ISBN: 1-56884-227-9 | $19.99 USA/$26.99 Canada |
| Quicken 8 For DOS For Dummies® 2nd Edition | by Stephen L. Nelson | ISBN: 1-56884-210-4 | $19.95 USA/$26.95 Canada |
| Quicken 5 For Macs® For Dummies® | by Stephen L. Nelson | ISBN: 1-56884-211-2 | $19.95 USA/$26.95 Canada |
| Quicken 4 For Windows® For Dummies® 2nd Edition | by Stephen L. Nelson | ISBN: 1-56884-209-0 | $19.95 USA/$26.95 Canada |
| Taxes For Dummies™ 1995 Edition | by Eric Tyson & David J. Silverman | ISBN: 1-56884-220-1 | $14.99 USA/$20.99 Canada |
| The GMAT® For Dummies™ | by Suzee Vlk, Series Editor | ISBN: 1-56884-376-3 | $14.99 USA/$20.99 Canada |
| The GRE® For Dummies™ | by Suzee Vlk, Series Editor | ISBN: 1-56884-375-5 | $14.99 USA/$20.99 Canada |
| Time Management For Dummies™ | by Jeffrey J. Mayer | ISBN: 1-56884-360-7 | $16.99 USA/$22.99 Canada |
| TurboTax For Windows® For Dummies® | by Gail A. Helsel, CPA | ISBN: 1-56884-228-7 | $19.99 USA/$26.99 Canada |
| **GROUPWARE/INTEGRATED** | | | |
| ClarisWorks For Macs® For Dummies® | by Frank Higgins | ISBN: 1-56884-363-1 | $19.99 USA/$26.99 Canada |
| Lotus Notes For Dummies® | by Pat Freeland & Stephen Londergan | ISBN: 1-56884-212-0 | $19.95 USA/$26.95 Canada |
| Microsoft® Office 4 For Windows® For Dummies® | by Roger C. Parker | ISBN: 1-56884-183-3 | $19.95 USA/$26.95 Canada |
| Microsoft® Works 3 For Windows® For Dummies® | by David C. Kay | ISBN: 1-56884-214-7 | $19.99 USA/$26.99 Canada |
| SmartSuite 3 For Dummies® | by Jan Weingarten & John Weingarten | ISBN: 1-56884-367-4 | $19.99 USA/$26.99 Canada |
| **INTERNET/COMMUNICATIONS/NETWORKING** | | | |
| America Online® For Dummies® 2nd Edition | by John Kaufeld | ISBN: 1-56884-933-8 | $19.99 USA/$26.99 Canada |
| CompuServe For Dummies® 2nd Edition | by Wallace Wang | ISBN: 1-56884-937-0 | $19.99 USA/$26.99 Canada |
| Modems For Dummies® 2nd Edition | by Tina Rathbone | ISBN: 1-56884-223-6 | $19.99 USA/$26.99 Canada |
| MORE Internet For Dummies® | by John R. Levine & Margaret Levine Young | ISBN: 1-56884-164-7 | $19.95 USA/$26.95 Canada |
| MORE Modems & On-line Services For Dummies® | by Tina Rathbone | ISBN: 1-56884-365-8 | $19.99 USA/$26.99 Canada |
| Mosaic For Dummies® Windows Edition | by David Angell & Brent Heslop | ISBN: 1-56884-242-2 | $19.99 USA/$26.99 Canada |
| NetWare For Dummies® 2nd Edition | by Ed Tittel, Deni Connor & Earl Follis | ISBN: 1-56884-369-0 | $19.99 USA/$26.99 Canada |
| Networking For Dummies® | by Doug Lowe | ISBN: 1-56884-079-9 | $19.95 USA/$26.95 Canada |
| PROCOMM PLUS 2 For Windows® For Dummies® | by Wallace Wang | ISBN: 1-56884-219-8 | $19.99 USA/$26.99 Canada |
| TCP/IP For Dummies® | by Marshall Wilensky & Candace Leiden | ISBN: 1-56884-241-4 | $19.99 USA/$26.99 Canada |

For scholastic requests & educational orders please call Educational Sales at 1. 800. 434. 2086

**FOR MORE INFO OR TO ORDER, PLEASE CALL ▶ 800. 762. 2974**

For volume discounts & special orders please call Tony Real, Special Sales, at 415. 655. 3048

| | | | |
|---|---|---|---|
| The Internet For Macs® For Dummies® 2nd Edition | by Charles Seiter | ISBN: 1-56884-371-2 | $19.99 USA/$26.99 Canada |
| The Internet For Macs® For Dummies® Starter Kit | by Charles Seiter | ISBN: 1-56884-244-9 | $29.99 USA/$39.99 Canada |
| The Internet For Macs® For Dummies® Starter Kit Bestseller Edition | by Charles Seiter | ISBN: 1-56884-245-7 | $39.99 USA/$54.99 Canada |
| The Internet For Windows® For Dummies® Starter Kit | by John R. Levine & Margaret Levine Young | ISBN: 1-56884-237-6 | $34.99 USA/$44.99 Canada |
| The Internet For Windows® For Dummies® Starter Kit, Bestseller Edition | by John R. Levine & Margaret Levine Young | ISBN: 1-56884-246-5 | $39.99 USA/$54.99 Canada |

## MACINTOSH
| | | | |
|---|---|---|---|
| Mac® Programming For Dummies® | by Dan Parks Sydow | ISBN: 1-56884-173-6 | $19.95 USA/$26.95 Canada |
| Macintosh® System 7.5 For Dummies® | by Bob LeVitus | ISBN: 1-56884-197-3 | $19.95 USA/$26.95 Canada |
| MORE Macs® For Dummies® | by David Pogue | ISBN: 1-56884-087-X | $19.95 USA/$26.95 Canada |
| PageMaker 5 For Macs® For Dummies® | by Galen Gruman & Deke McClelland | ISBN: 1-56884-178-7 | $19.95 USA/$26.95 Canada |
| QuarkXPress 3.3 For Dummies® | by Galen Gruman & Barbara Assadi | ISBN: 1-56884-217-1 | $19.99 USA/$26.99 Canada |
| Upgrading and Fixing Macs® For Dummies® | by Kearney Rietmann & Frank Higgins | ISBN: 1-56884-189-2 | $19.95 USA/$26.95 Canada |

## MULTIMEDIA
| | | | |
|---|---|---|---|
| Multimedia & CD-ROMs For Dummies® 2nd Edition | by Andy Rathbone | ISBN: 1-56884-907-9 | $19.99 USA/$26.99 Canada |
| Multimedia & CD-ROMs For Dummies® Interactive Multimedia Value Pack, 2nd Edition | by Andy Rathbone | ISBN: 1-56884-909-5 | $29.99 USA/$39.99 Canada |

## OPERATING SYSTEMS:
### DOS
| | | | |
|---|---|---|---|
| MORE DOS For Dummies® | by Dan Gookin | ISBN: 1-56884-046-2 | $19.95 USA/$26.95 Canada |
| OS/2® Warp For Dummies® 2nd Edition | by Andy Rathbone | ISBN: 1-56884-205-8 | $19.99 USA/$26.99 Canada |

### UNIX
| | | | |
|---|---|---|---|
| MORE UNIX® For Dummies® | by John R. Levine & Margaret Levine Young | ISBN: 1-56884-361-5 | $19.99 USA/$26.99 Canada |
| UNIX® For Dummies® | by John R. Levine & Margaret Levine Young | ISBN: 1-878058-58-4 | $19.95 USA/$26.95 Canada |

### WINDOWS
| | | | |
|---|---|---|---|
| MORE Windows® For Dummies® 2nd Edition | by Andy Rathbone | ISBN: 1-56884-048-9 | $19.95 USA/$26.95 Canada |
| Windows® 95 For Dummies® | by Andy Rathbone | ISBN: 1-56884-240-6 | $19.99 USA/$26.99 Canada |

## PCS/HARDWARE
| | | | |
|---|---|---|---|
| Illustrated Computer Dictionary For Dummies® 2nd Edition | by Dan Gookin & Wallace Wang | ISBN: 1-56884-218-X | $12.95 USA/$16.95 Canada |
| Upgrading and Fixing PCs For Dummies® 2nd Edition | by Andy Rathbone | ISBN: 1-56884-903-6 | $19.99 USA/$26.99 Canada |

## PRESENTATION/AUTOCAD
| | | | |
|---|---|---|---|
| AutoCAD For Dummies® | by Bud Smith | ISBN: 1-56884-191-4 | $19.95 USA/$26.95 Canada |
| PowerPoint 4 For Windows® For Dummies® | by Doug Lowe | ISBN: 1-56884-161-2 | $16.99 USA/$22.99 Canada |

## PROGRAMMING
| | | | |
|---|---|---|---|
| Borland C++ For Dummies® | by Michael Hyman | ISBN: 1-56884-162-0 | $19.95 USA/$26.95 Canada |
| C For Dummies® Volume 1 | by Dan Gookin | ISBN: 1-878058-78-9 | $19.95 USA/$26.95 Canada |
| C++ For Dummies® | by Stephen R. Davis | ISBN: 1-56884-163-9 | $19.95 USA/$26.95 Canada |
| Delphi Programming For Dummies® | by Neil Rubenking | ISBN: 1-56884-200-7 | $19.99 USA/$26.99 Canada |
| Mac® Programming For Dummies® | by Dan Parks Sydow | ISBN: 1-56884-173-6 | $19.95 USA/$26.95 Canada |
| PowerBuilder 4 Programming For Dummies® | by Ted Coombs & Jason Coombs | ISBN: 1-56884-325-9 | $19.99 USA/$26.99 Canada |
| QBasic Programming For Dummies® | by Douglas Hergert | ISBN: 1-56884-093-4 | $19.95 USA/$26.95 Canada |
| Visual Basic 3 For Dummies® | by Wallace Wang | ISBN: 1-56884-076-4 | $19.95 USA/$26.95 Canada |
| Visual Basic "X" For Dummies® | by Wallace Wang | ISBN: 1-56884-230-9 | $19.99 USA/$26.99 Canada |
| Visual C++ 2 For Dummies® | by Michael Hyman & Bob Arnson | ISBN: 1-56884-328-3 | $19.99 USA/$26.99 Canada |
| Windows® 95 Programming For Dummies® | by S. Randy Davis | ISBN: 1-56884-327-5 | $19.99 USA/$26.99 Canada |

## SPREADSHEET
| | | | |
|---|---|---|---|
| 1-2-3 For Dummies® | by Greg Harvey | ISBN: 1-878058-60-6 | $16.95 USA/$22.95 Canada |
| 1-2-3 For Windows® 5 For Dummies® 2nd Edition | by John Walkenbach | ISBN: 1-56884-216-3 | $16.95 USA/$22.95 Canada |
| Excel 5 For Macs® For Dummies® | by Greg Harvey | ISBN: 1-56884-186-8 | $19.95 USA/$26.95 Canada |
| Excel For Dummies® 2nd Edition | by Greg Harvey | ISBN: 1-56884-050-0 | $16.95 USA/$22.95 Canada |
| MORE 1-2-3 For DOS For Dummies® | by John Weingarten | ISBN: 1-56884-224-4 | $19.99 USA/$26.99 Canada |
| MORE Excel 5 For Windows® For Dummies® | by Greg Harvey | ISBN: 1-56884-207-4 | $19.95 USA/$26.95 Canada |
| Quattro Pro 6 For Windows® For Dummies® | by John Walkenbach | ISBN: 1-56884-174-4 | $19.95 USA/$26.95 Canada |
| Quattro Pro For DOS For Dummies® | by John Walkenbach | ISBN: 1-56884-023-3 | $16.95 USA/$22.95 Canada |

## UTILITIES
| | | | |
|---|---|---|---|
| Norton Utilities 8 For Dummies® | by Beth Slick | ISBN: 1-56884-166-3 | $19.95 USA/$26.95 Canada |

## VCRs/CAMCORDERS
| | | | |
|---|---|---|---|
| VCRs & Camcorders For Dummies™ | by Gordon McComb & Andy Rathbone | ISBN: 1-56884-229-5 | $14.99 USA/$20.99 Canada |

## WORD PROCESSING
| | | | |
|---|---|---|---|
| Ami Pro For Dummies® | by Jim Meade | ISBN: 1-56884-049-7 | $19.95 USA/$26.95 Canada |
| MORE Word For Windows® 6 For Dummies® | by Doug Lowe | ISBN: 1-56884-165-5 | $19.95 USA/$26.95 Canada |
| MORE WordPerfect® 6 For Windows® For Dummies® | by Margaret Levine Young & David C. Kay | ISBN: 1-56884-206-6 | $19.95 USA/$26.95 Canada |
| MORE WordPerfect® 6 For DOS For Dummies® | by Wallace Wang, edited by Dan Gookin | ISBN: 1-56884-047-0 | $19.95 USA/$26.95 Canada |
| Word 6 For Macs® For Dummies® | by Dan Gookin | ISBN: 1-56884-190-6 | $19.95 USA/$26.95 Canada |
| Word For Windows® 6 For Dummies® | by Dan Gookin | ISBN: 1-56884-075-6 | $16.95 USA/$22.95 Canada |
| Word For Windows® For Dummies® | by Dan Gookin & Ray Werner | ISBN: 1-878058-86-X | $16.95 USA/$22.95 Canada |
| WordPerfect® 6 For DOS For Dummies® | by Dan Gookin | ISBN: 1-878058-77-0 | $16.95 USA/$22.95 Canada |
| WordPerfect® 6.1 For Windows® For Dummies® 2nd Edition | by Margaret Levine Young & David Kay | ISBN: 1-56884-243-0 | $16.95 USA/$22.95 Canada |
| WordPerfect® For Dummies® | by Dan Gookin | ISBN: 1-878058-52-5 | $16.95 USA/$22.95 Canada |

## Fun, Fast, & Cheap!™

**NEW!**

**The Internet For Macs® For Dummies® Quick Reference**
*by Charles Seiter*

ISBN:1-56884-967-2
$9.99 USA/$12.99 Canada

**NEW!**

**Windows® 95 For Dummies® Quick Reference**
*by Greg Harvey*

ISBN: 1-56884-964-8
$9.99 USA/$12.99 Canada

**SUPER STAR**

**Photoshop 3 For Macs® For Dummies® Quick Reference**
*by Deke McClelland*

ISBN: 1-56884-968-0
$9.99 USA/$12.99 Canada

**SUPER STAR**

**WordPerfect® For DOS For Dummies® Quick Reference**
*by Greg Harvey*

ISBN: 1-56884-009-8
$8.95 USA/$12.95 Canada

| Title | Author | ISBN | Price |
|---|---|---|---|
| **DATABASE** | | | |
| Access 2 For Dummies® Quick Reference | by Stuart J. Stuple | ISBN: 1-56884-167-1 | $8.95 USA/$11.95 Canada |
| dBASE 5 For DOS For Dummies® Quick Reference | by Barrie Sosinsky | ISBN: 1-56884-954-0 | $9.99 USA/$12.99 Canada |
| dBASE 5 For Windows® For Dummies® Quick Reference | by Stuart J. Stuple | ISBN: 1-56884-953-2 | $9.99 USA/$12.99 Canada |
| Paradox 5 For Windows® For Dummies® Quick Reference | by Scott Palmer | ISBN: 1-56884-960-5 | $9.99 USA/$12.99 Canada |
| **DESKTOP PUBLISHING/ILLUSTRATION/GRAPHICS** | | | |
| CorelDRAW! 5 For Dummies® Quick Reference | by Raymond E. Werner | ISBN: 1-56884-952-4 | $9.99 USA/$12.99 Canada |
| Harvard Graphics For Windows® For Dummies® Quick Reference | by Raymond E. Werner | ISBN: 1-56884-962-1 | $9.99 USA/$12.99 Canada |
| Photoshop 3 For Macs® For Dummies® Quick Reference | by Deke McClelland | ISBN: 1-56884-968-0 | $9.99 USA/$12.99 Canada |
| **FINANCE/PERSONAL FINANCE** | | | |
| Quicken 4 For Windows® For Dummies® Quick Reference | by Stephen L. Nelson | ISBN: 1-56884-950-8 | $9.95 USA/$12.95 Canada |
| **GROUPWARE/INTEGRATED** | | | |
| Microsoft® Office 4 For Windows® For Dummies® Quick Reference | by Doug Lowe | ISBN: 1-56884-958-3 | $9.99 USA/$12.99 Canada |
| Microsoft® Works 3 For Windows® For Dummies® Quick Reference | by Michael Partington | ISBN: 1-56884-959-1 | $9.99 USA/$12.99 Canada |
| **INTERNET/COMMUNICATIONS/NETWORKING** | | | |
| The Internet For Dummies® Quick Reference | by John R. Levine & Margaret Levine Young | ISBN: 1-56884-168-X | $8.95 USA/$11.95 Canada |
| **MACINTOSH** | | | |
| Macintosh® System 7.5 For Dummies® Quick Reference | by Stuart J. Stuple | ISBN: 1-56884-956-7 | $9.99 USA/$12.99 Canada |
| **OPERATING SYSTEMS:** | | | |
| **DOS** | | | |
| DOS For Dummies® Quick Reference | by Greg Harvey | ISBN: 1-56884-007-1 | $8.95 USA/$11.95 Canada |
| **UNIX** | | | |
| UNIX® For Dummies® Quick Reference | by John R. Levine & Margaret Levine Young | ISBN: 1-56884-094-2 | $8.95 USA/$11.95 Canada |
| **WINDOWS** | | | |
| Windows® 3.1 For Dummies® Quick Reference, 2nd Edition | by Greg Harvey | ISBN: 1-56884-951-6 | $8.95 USA/$11.95 Canada |
| **PCs/HARDWARE** | | | |
| Memory Management For Dummies® Quick Reference | by Doug Lowe | ISBN: 1-56884-362-3 | $9.99 USA/$12.99 Canada |
| **PRESENTATION/AUTOCAD** | | | |
| AutoCAD For Dummies® Quick Reference | by Ellen Finkelstein | ISBN: 1-56884-198-1 | $9.99 USA/$12.95 Canada |
| **SPREADSHEET** | | | |
| 1-2-3 For Dummies® Quick Reference | by John Walkenbach | ISBN: 1-56884-027-6 | $8.95 USA/$11.95 Canada |
| 1-2-3 For Windows® 5 For Dummies® Quick Reference | by John Walkenbach | ISBN: 1-56884-957-5 | $9.95 USA/$12.95 Canada |
| Excel For Windows® For Dummies® Quick Reference, 2nd Edition | by John Walkenbach | ISBN: 1-56884-096-9 | $8.95 USA/$11.95 Canada |
| Quattro Pro 6 For Windows® For Dummies® Quick Reference | by Stuart J. Stuple | ISBN: 1-56884-172-8 | $9.95 USA/$12.95 Canada |
| **WORD PROCESSING** | | | |
| Word For Windows® 6 For Dummies® Quick Reference | by George Lynch | ISBN: 1-56884-095-0 | $8.95 USA/$11.95 Canada |
| Word For Windows® For Dummies® Quick Reference | by George Lynch | ISBN: 1-56884-029-2 | $8.95 USA/$11.95 Canada |
| WordPerfect® 6.1 For Windows® For Dummies® Quick Reference, 2nd Edition | by Greg Harvey | ISBN: 1-56884-966-4 | $9.99 USA/$12.99/Canada |

For scholastic requests & educational orders please call Educational Sales at 1. 800. 434. 2086

**FOR MORE INFO OR TO ORDER, PLEASE CALL ▶ 800- 762- 2974**

For volume discounts & special orders please call Tony Real, Special Sales, at 415. 655. 3048

# ORDER FORM

IDG
BOOKS
WORLDWIDE

*Order Center:* **(800) 762-2974** *(8 a.m.–6 p.m., EST, weekdays)*

| Quantity | ISBN | Title | Price | Total |
|----------|------|-------|-------|-------|
|  |  |  |  |  |
|  |  |  |  |  |
|  |  |  |  |  |
|  |  |  |  |  |
|  |  |  |  |  |
|  |  |  |  |  |
|  |  |  |  |  |
|  |  |  |  |  |
|  |  |  |  |  |
|  |  |  |  |  |
|  |  |  |  |  |
|  |  |  |  |  |
|  |  |  |  |  |
|  |  |  |  |  |
|  |  |  |  |  |
|  |  |  |  |  |
|  |  |  |  |  |
|  |  |  |  |  |

## *Shipping & Handling Charges*

|  | Description | First book | Each additional book | Total |
|--|-------------|------------|----------------------|-------|
| *Domestic* | Normal | $4.50 | $1.50 | $ |
|  | Two Day Air | $8.50 | $2.50 | $ |
|  | Overnight | $18.00 | $3.00 | $ |
| *International* | Surface | $8.00 | $8.00 | $ |
|  | Airmail | $16.00 | $16.00 | $ |
|  | DHL Air | $17.00 | $17.00 | $ |

*For large quantities call for shipping & handling charges.
**Prices are subject to change without notice.

**Ship to:**

Name _____

Company _____

Address _____

City/State/Zip _____

Daytime Phone _____

**Payment:** ☐ Check to IDG Books Worldwide (US Funds Only)

☐ VISA ☐ MasterCard ☐ American Express

Card # _____ Expires _____

Signature _____

**Subtotal** _____

CA residents add
applicable sales tax _____

IN, MA, and MD
residents add
5% sales tax _____

IL residents add
6.25% sales tax _____

RI residents add
7% sales tax _____

TX residents add
8.25% sales tax _____

**Shipping** _____

**Total** _____

*Please send this order form to:*
**IDG Books Worldwide, Inc.
7260 Shadeland Station, Suite 100
Indianapolis, IN 46256**

*Allow up to 3 weeks for delivery.
Thank you!*